Across Wide Fields

Teacher's Edition
Part I

Level 4

ODYSSEY An HBJ Literature Program
Second Edition

Sam Leaton Sebesta, General Consultant
Sandra McCandless Simons, Content Area Consultant

HBJ **Harcourt Brace Jovanovich, Publishers**
Orlando   San Diego   Chicago   Dallas

ISBN 0–15–333346–4

Acknowledgments

For permission to reprint copyrighted material, grateful
acknowledgment is made to the following sources:

Curtis Brown, Ltd.: "Old Joe Clarke" by Ruth Crawford Seeger from
  American Folk Songs for Children. Copyright 1948 by Ruth
  Crawford Seeger; renewed © 1976 by Michael Seeger.
E. P. Dutton: "Public Library" from *Street Poems* by Robert Froman.
  Copyright © 1971 by Robert Froman
Harper & Row, Publishers, Inc.: Specified excerpt from p. 27 in *The
  Odyssey of Homer,* translated by Richmond Lattimore. Copyright
  © 1965, 1967 by Richmond Lattimore. From *A Tree Grows in
  Brooklyn* by Betty Smith. Copyright 1943 by Betty Smith.
Macmillan Publishing Co., Inc.: From "The Moon's the North
  Wind's Cooky" in *Collected Poems* by Vachel Lindsay. Copyright
  1914 by Macmillan Publishing Co., Inc.; renewed 1942 by
  Elizabeth C. Lindsay.
Macmillan Publishing Company: Adapted from *The House of Dies
  Drear* by Virginia Hamilton. Copyright © 1968 by Virginia
  Hamilton. From an adaptation of "The Elves and the Shoemaker"
  in *Grimm Brothers Household Stories,* translated from the
  German by Lucy Crane, New York: Macmillan Publishing
  Company, 1927.
Eve Merriam: From "Thumbprint" in *It Doesn't Always Have to
  Rhyme* by Eve Merriam. Copyright © 1964 by Eve Merriam. From
  "Benjamin Franklin" in *Independent Voices* by Eve Merriam.
  Copyright © 1968 by Eve Merriam.
Clarkson N. Potter, Inc. a division of Crown Publishers, Inc.: From
  "The Walrus and the Carpenter" in *The Annotated Alice* by Lewis
  Carroll. Introduction and notes by Martin Gardner. Copyright
  © 1960 by Martin Gardner.
United Educators, Inc.: From "East O' the Sun and West O' the
  Moon" in *The Magic Garden of My Book House* (Vol. 7) in *My
  Book House,* edited by Olive Beaupre Miller. © The United
  Educators, Inc!
Frederick Warne & Co., Inc.: From "The Jumblies" by Edward Lear.

A Teacher's Edition, Parts I and II, when used with
the pupil's textbook, provides a complete program.

A Teacher's Edition, Parts I and II, is not automatically
included with each shipment of a classroom set of
textbooks. However, a Teacher's Edition will be
forwarded when requested by a teacher, an admini-
strator, or a representative of Harcourt Brace
Jovanovich, Inc.

Part II of the Teacher's Edition is available for Levels
1-6 of ODYSSEY: AN HBJ LITERATURE PROGRAM,
Second Edition. For information, please contact your
sales representative.

General Consultant

Sam Leaton Sebesta is on the faculty of the University of Washington in Seattle, where he teaches reading and children's literature. A former elementary grade teacher, Dr. Sebesta has written numerous books and articles in the field of reading, and has earned national recognition for his speeches and workshops on teaching literature. He has been a regional coordinator for Children's Choices, a joint project of the Children's Book Council and the International Reading Association; from 1983 through 1986 he authored the "Literature for Children" book-review column in *The Reading Teacher*. He received his doctorate from Stanford University.

Consultants

Elaine M. Aoki
Administrative Program
Developer—Reading
Seattle Public Schools
Seattle, Washington

Willard E. Bill
Supervisor of Indian Education
Office of the Superintendent of
    Public Instruction
Olympia, Washington

Sonya Blackman
Lecturer in children's literature
College of Marin and Sonoma
    State University
California

Sylvia Engdahl
Science fiction author and
    anthologist
Portland, Oregon

Myra Cohn Livingston
Poet, anthologist, and teacher
Beverly Hills, California

Daphne P. Muse
Children's literature author/
    consultant
Oakland, California

Sandra McCandless Simons
Specialist in reading in the
    content area
Eugene, Oregon

Margaret D. Simpson
Specialist in children's books
San Francisco, California

Barre Toelken
Professor of English and Director
    of Folklore and Ethnic Studies
    Program
University of Oregon
Eugene, Oregon

Consulting Educators

Katherine J. Adams
Assistant Director
Barker Texas History Center
University of Texas at Austin
Austin, Texas

William Anderson
Department of English
California State University
    at Northridge
Northridge, California

Gwen Batey
Teacher
Abbott Middle School
San Mateo, California

Dorothy W. Blake
Coordinator of Planning for
    Media Resources and
    Utilization
Division of Instructional
    Planning and Development
Atlanta Public Schools
Atlanta, Georgia

Joan Cheifetz
Principal
Language Arts Consultant
Oakland Unified School District
Oakland, California

Ann Cheleen
Teacher
H. O. Sonnesyn Elementary
    School
New Hope, Minnesota

Ann Cotton
Social Studies Instructional
    Specialist
Fort Worth Public Schools
Fort Worth, Texas

Harold Fenderson
Principal
Eugene J. Butler
Seventh Grade Center
Jacksonville, Florida

Barbara Friedberg
Teacher
Martin Luther King, Jr.,
    Laboratory School
Evanston, Illinois

Hildagarde Gray
Librarian
St. John the Baptist School
Pittsburgh, Pennsylvania

Stephanie Abraham Hirsh
Consultant, Staff Development
    and Free Enterprise Education
Richardson Independent School
    District
Richardson, Texas

Franklin Koontz
Director of Instruction
Bellevue School District
Bellevue, Washington

Joanne Lincoln
Librarian, Professional Library
Atlanta Public Schools
Atlanta, Georgia

Richard McBreen
Teacher
Bayside Middle School
San Mateo, California

Evelyn Myton-Plantillas
Resource Specialist
San Jose Unified School District
San Jose, California

E. Renee Nathan
Director of Curriculum, K–12
Palos Verdes Peninsula Unified
    School District
Palos Verdes Estates, California

Ben Nelms
Department of English and
    College of Education
University of Missouri
Columbia, Missouri

Elizabeth Nelms
Teacher
Hickman High School
Columbia, Missouri

Soledad P. Newman
Department of English
Miami University
Oxford, Ohio

Barbara K. Rand
Teacher
Laveen Junior High
Laveen, Arizona

Doris Shriber
Former Teacher
San Mateo, California

Barbara M. Shulgold
Teacher
Vallemar Structured School
Pacifica, California

Clarice Stafford
Associate Superintendent for
    Instruction and Planning
Wayne-Westland Schools
Wayne, Michigan

Ann Terry
School of Education
University of Houston–
    Clear Lake
Houston, Texas

Kelley Tucker
Teacher
Sun Valley Elementary School
San Rafael, California

Lois Wendt
Teacher
Neill Elementary School
Crystal, Minnesota

CONTENTS

Teaching Plans

Unit 1, Problems and Puzzles

Unit 2, When the Moon Shines

Unit 3, Across the Land and Sea

The adventure continues...

ODYSSEY

An HBJ Literature Program
Second Edition Levels 1–6

The Second Edition of ODYSSEY continues the adventurous journey into the imaginative world of literature. Take your students on a magical tour through drama, adventure, mystery, humor, and fantasy. Let them experience the excitement as they begin a personal ODYSSEY through fine literature.

In ODYSSEY you'll find

Outstanding literature

ODYSSEY is a collection of the very best in classic and contemporary children's literature. The high-interest selections represent a variety of cultures and historical periods, helping students develop a rich experiential background.

Award-winning authors

Your students will delight in the stories and poems of Scott O'Dell, Isaac Bashevis Singer, Beverly Cleary, Virginia Hamilton, Ernesto Galarza, Karla Kuskin, and David McCord — among others.

A variety of genres

ODYSSEY offers a rich variety of literature. Your students will experience the excitement, the beauty, the wonder of poems, short stories, novels, folk tales, plays, and songs from throughout the world.

Thematic structure

ODYSSEY presents literature in a thematic structure focusing on such universal themes as self-awareness and identity, family and friendship, adventure and suspense, and challenges and solutions to problems. Carefully chosen selections will appeal to all your students.

Brilliant illustrations

Every selection is illustrated with beautiful, instructive art to enhance the content. The work of fine illustrators such as Maurice Sendak, Edward Gorey, Ed Young, Fernando Krahn, or Arnold Lobel may be seen throughout the program.

Selections that inspire a love of reading

Stimulating selections involve all your students and keep them involved — leading them to a lifetime of reading enjoyment.

Selections for students of varying abilities

Easy, average, and challenging selections are included in every book to ensure that *all* your students will enjoy reading ODYSSEY. Interesting selections motivate students to become independent readers.

Solid skills support

ODYSSEY supports basal reading and language arts instruction by emphasizing reading and writing skills including word attack, vocabulary development, critical thinking, and creative writing.

Content that reaches across the curriculum

Connections help students see relationships between fact and fiction, literature and the content areas, thus making their reading experience more meaningful. Each fact-based **Connections** links literary themes or content to many areas of the curriculum — social studies, language arts, science and health.

Spark imagination with ODYSSEY!

From Level 2

The Elves and the Shoemaker

Adapted from the German folk tale collected by
the Brothers Grimm

Pictures by Gene Sharp

Once there lived a fine shoemaker who
became very poor. At last, he had only
enough leather to make one pair of shoes.

As he cut th...
looked sadly at ...

"Dear wife,"...
make these shoe...

He laid the ...
table. Then he ...

274

Many original works are
presented in their entirety.

All excerpts are carefully chosen,
with the original work clearly
identified and acknowledged.

From Level 4

Wol to the Rescue

From the story *Owls in the Family* by Farley Mowat
Illustrated by Jenny Rutherford

*Wol, who was f...
an owl who doesn't...
walking to flying, e...
bicycle, and loves p...
smaller owl, was re...
menting him, and ...
Both are very tame...*

376

Stories, plays, folk tales,
poems, songs, myths, and
legends — every major
form of literature is
represented.

From Level 1, Preprimer

The Little Red Hen and the Grain of Wheat

A play based on an English folk tale retold by
Veronica S. Hutchinson

Pictures by Dan Siculan

Characters

Storyteller/Teacher

Little Red Hen

Duck

Cat

Dog

Teacher: One day the Little Red Hen was
scratching in the farmyard when she
found a grain of wheat. "Who will
plant the wheat?" she asked. The
duck and the cat and the dog
answered,

32

The Second Edition of ODYSSEY
contains even more quality literature for your students to explore.

Outstanding illustrations accompany each selection to spark students' curiosity and enrich their reading experiences.

Five Little Pumpkins
A rhyme

60

Pictures by Christa Kieffer

61

The variety of genres represented in ODYSSEY allows students to appreciate literature in all its forms.

A HERO'S PROMISE
A Greek legend retold by Ian Serraillier

Illustrated by Kinuko Craft

Stories about Theseus,[1] one of the greatest heroes of ancient Greece, have been told for centuries. The story of his struggle with the Minotaur[2] is but one of many tales about Theseus' strength and bravery.

1. Theseus (THEE-see-uhs).
2. Minotaur (MIN-uh-tawr).

138

Sample pages are reduced. Actual sizes are 7½" x 9".

Start a lifetime of reading enjoyment with ODYSSEY!

From Level 5

From
The House of Dies Drear
A novel by Virginia Hamilton
Illustrated by Jack White

Thomas Small and his family are on their way to a new home in Huntington, Ohio. Thomas's father is going to teach at a small college there. Thomas is so excited that he finds it almost as hard to keep still as his little twin brothers do. It is not his father's job, or the thoughts of a new town or a new school, that Thomas is excited about. Thomas is excited about the family's new house.

The house is not just any house. It is a house with a history. More than a hundred years ago, the house was a station on the Underground Railroad. The owner of the house, Dies Drear, had been one of the many "conductors" who had hidden run-away slaves and helped them escape to freedom.

Thomas finally falls asleep and misses crossing the Ohio River and coming into Huntington. When he wakes, the first thing Thomas sees is the house of Dies Drear.

316

Thomas lurched awake a long time after. The car went slowly; there was hardly any rain now. His mother spoke excitedly, and Thomas had to shake his head rapidly in order to understand what she was saying.

"Oh dear!" Mrs. Small said. "Why it's huge!"

Mr. Small broke in eagerly, turning around to face Thomas. "You've waited a long time," he said. "Take a good look, son. There's our new house!"

Thomas looked carefully out of his window. He opened the car door for a few seconds to see better, but found the moist air too warm and soft. The feel of it was not nice at all, and he quickly closed the door. He could see well enough out of the window, and what he saw made everything inside him grow quiet for the first time in weeks. It was more than he could have dreamed.

The house of Dies Drear loomed out of mist and murky sky, not only gray and formless, but huge and unnatural. It seemed to crouch on the side of a hill high above the highway. And it had a dark, isolated look about it that set it at odds with all that was living.

317

A Bear Went Over the Mountain

An American folk rhyme

A bear went over the mountain,
A bear went over the mountain,
A bear went over the mountain
To see what he could see.

The other side of the mountain,
The other side of the mountain,
The other side of the mountain
Was all that he could see!

56

The beautiful illustration program helps students to visualize story settings, characters, and events, making reading a more rewarding experience.

At Levels 1 and 2, picture stories help young children develop oral vocabulary and visual literacy (not shown).

From Level 1, Reader

ODYSSEY contains the classics of children's literature — *The Walrus and the Carpenter, The Chronicles of Narnia, Charlotte's Web* — and also helps students develop contemporary favorites — *Frog and Toad Together, Island of the Blue Dolphins, Dragonwings.*

The Walrus and the Carpenter

A poem by Lewis Carroll

Illustrations by Robert Van Nutt

based on the drawings of Sir John Tenniel

The sun was shining on the sea,
    Shining with all his might:
He did his very best to make
    The billows smooth and bright—
And this was odd, because it was
    The middle of the night.

The moon was shining sulkily,
    Because she thought the sun
Had got no business to be there
    After the day was done—
"It's very rude of him," she said,
    "To come and spoil the fun!"

The sea was wet as wet could be,
    The sands were dry as dry.
You could not see a cloud, because
    No cloud was in the sky:
No birds were flying overhead—
    There were no birds to fly.

42

The Walrus and the Carpenter
    Were walking close at hand:
They wept like anything to see
    Such quantities of sand:
"If this were only cleared away,"
    They said, "it would be grand!"

"If seven maids with seven mops
    Swept it for half a year,
Do you suppose," the Walrus said,
    "That they could get it clear?"
"I doubt it," said the Carpenter,
    And shed a bitter tear.

nd walk with us!"
beseech.
pleasant talk,
beach:
more than four,
to each."

43

All Things Are Connected

From a letter by Chief Sealth

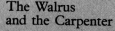

In 1855 Chief Sealth[1] of the Duwamish tribe of the State of Washington sent a letter to President Franklin Pierce. The letter was in response to an offer by the government to buy the tribe's land. Here is part of that letter.

1. Sealth (SELTH).

396

Students learn about American history through fascinating selections depicting America's story.

Sample pages are reduced. Actual sizes are 7½" x 9".

Connections reach across the curriculum

From Level 3

Connections relate literature to other areas of the curriculum.

From Level 3

Connections develop critical thinking skills by helping students relate ideas and synthesize information.

CONNECTIONS

From Sea to Shining Sea

The new land of the United States seemed a land of promise to many people. People came from many places, across great oceans, north from Mexico, and south from Canada, to settle in the new country. Still other people moved from one part of the United States to another. This is the land these people traveled in their search for land or riches or a new home.

162

Questions (not shown) at the end of each **Connections** assess students' understanding of the selection.

Activities (not shown) provide for a variety of experiences — researching, writing, and making and using maps, charts, and diagrams.

Crossing the Creek

From the story *Little House on the Prairie*
by Laura Ingalls Wilder
Illustrated by Michel Allaire

142

Sample pages are reduced. Actual sizes are 7½" x 9".

Skill-building features structured for success

Learn About Literature helps students examine various literary elements including plot, characterization, setting, and theme.

From Level 1, Reader

Learn About
Stories

Story Sounds

Some words in stories tell how things sound.

When the Wind blows, the sound is "you-ou-ou."

When the Gunniwolf runs, the sound is "hunker-cha, hunker-cha."

When the Billy Goats Gruff walk over the bridge, the sound is "trip, trap, trip, trap."

186

Pictures by Ed Taber

Get ready to read a story about us.

These things are in the story.
Make up words to tell how each thing sounds.

Say your sounds for these things as you read the story on the next page.

187

Students learn to use literary devices such as figurative language, repetition, and rhythm and become aware of illustration styles, uses of the library, and more.

Questions

1. In this story, who got into deep, serious trouble? What was that trouble?

2. What three things did Miss Pickerell do to make the trouble seem less serious?

3. What was Miss Pickerell's greatest discovery? Why was the discovery important?

4. Complete these sentences by using three of these words from the story: **ladle, chamber, hearth, shoring.**
   a. Boards to keep dirt from caving in are called _____.
   b. A closed-up room is a _____.
   c. The floor of a fireplace is a _____.

Activity   Write a News Report

Sam Scoop, news reporter, wrote three headlines about Miss Pickerell's adventure. Readers said that Sam's headlines were puzzling and untrue. Fix the headlines. Make them truthful and important. Then write the first paragraph to put under one of the headlines. Include the following parts in your paragraph:
1. WHO was there;   4. WHERE it happened
2. WHAT happened;   5. HOW or WHY it
3. WHEN it happened;   happened.

Questions and Activity pages at the end of most selections help develop critical thinking and creative writing skills.

The questioning strategies help students learn to analyze, appreciate, and respond to literature.

Questions

1. Why didn't Susan want to be Crystal's friend?

2. What two things changed Susan's mind about being Crystal's friend?

3. When the teacher ''looks down his nose'' at Crystal and Susan, he is
   a. having amnesia
   b. looking down a telescope
   c. feeling cross

4. Do you think that Susan and Crystal should sit together at school? Why or why not?

5. Why did Susan say, ''I wish there was school tomorrow''?

6. What do you think happened to Susan and Crystal the next year?

Activity   Write Ways to Welcome Someone

A new person has come to your class. Write three things you might do to make that person feel welcome.

311

Sample pages are reduced. Actual sizes are 7½″ x 9″.

Special features to interest and instruct

From Level 1, Reader

About ARNOLD LOBEL

(To be read by the teacher)

Ever since he was seven years old, Arnold Lobel has been telling stories. First he made up stories for his friends at school, then for his own children when they were small. Now Arnold Lobel is an author and illustrator of books. Many children enjoy his stories and drawings.

Arnold Lobel says, "When I write my stories, I always sit in the same chair. I do my writing in the late afternoon. That is a good time to think about frogs and toads and mice and crickets."

More Books by Arnold Lobel

Mouse Tales
Frog and Toad Together
Days with Frog and Toad
Owl at Home
Fables

20

About the Author features (beginning in Reader 1) provide insight into authors' lives and work, enhance reading experiences, and motivate students to read more of their favorite author's works.

From Level 5

About VIRGINIA HAMILTON

Virginia Hamilton was born in Yellow Springs, Ohio, where her grandfather and his mother had settled after traveling the Underground Railroad to freedom. She grew up in a large family that owned a small farm. As a child, Virginia Hamilton freely explored the farm land owned by her family and nearby relatives and kept notebooks in which she often wrote down her thoughts. Because she came from a family of storytellers, she also listened—and learned. Virginia Hamilton says that her brother Billy's stories of his life's dreams "taught me to dream large and lucky—which is something all young people should learn to do."

Virginia Hamilton left Yellow Springs to attend college at Ohio State, where she studied writing. After college she went to New York to work. She submitted many stories to magazines, but none were published. Then an old college friend urged her to rewrite a story she had written at Ohio State. That story, *Zeely,* became her first published book, followed by *The House of Dies Drear* and many others. Though her childhood is long past, Virginia Hamilton keeps the memory of it "very much alive. And it is from such memories . . . that the best of my writing comes."

More Books by Virginia Hamilton

Zeely
The Time-Ago Tales of Jahdu
Arilla Sun Down

333

Sample pages are reduced. Actual sizes are 7½" x 9".

Bookshelf encourages independent reading by providing an annotated list of related reading selections that students may read on their own for enjoyment and for further study of each unit theme. This feature appears at the end of each unit in Levels 2–6.

From Level 5

BOOKSHELF

Fledgling by Jane Langston. Harper & Row, 1980. Georgie, the youngest child in her family, wants to learn how to fly. Despite her family's feelings, she fulfills her wish with the help of an unusual goose.

The Dollhouse Caper by Jean S. O'Connell. T. Y. Crowell, 1975. The Dollhouse Family is worried about being thrown away by three boys in the Human Family. They hope to be saved by warning the boys of a burglary that is about to happen.

The Mightiest of Mortals: Heracles by Doris Gates. Viking Press, 1975. Heracles, the half-god, half-human son of Zeus, perform twelve labors in order to

Adventures with the Giants by Cath Little, Brown, 1950. These stories of the Norse gods include Thor's the giants.

The Piemakers by Helen Cresswell. The Roller family of Danby Dale in been piemakers for generations. Y have the Rollers made such an er pie—a pie to feed two thousand p the King.

At Levels 3–6, a **Glossary** provides definitions of important words for independent vocabulary study (not shown).

At Levels 4–6, explanations and examples of **Literary Terms** help develop students' literary vocabulary and appreciation.

From Level 5

LITERARY TERMS

BIOGRAPHY *A history of a person's life written by another person.* A successful biography combines facts with an interesting story. Facts make a biography seem truthful and real. The facts about a person in a biography must be accurate. Historical details must be *authentic*, or genuine. Famous people are often the subjects of biographies. For example, Patrick Henry is the subject of Jean Fritz's biography *Where Was Patrick Henry on the 29th of May?*

CHARACTERS *The people (or animals) in a story, poem, or play.* Sometimes authors are concerned mainly with bringing their story characters to life. How the characters think, feel, act, and change are more important than the story's main action or plot. For example, in "Something for Davy," author Barbara Cohen gives us much information about Sam Greene. We learn what he thinks and feels, and how he acts. The story is *about Sam*, not just about a baseball game. Other stories, such as "Emergency in Space," by Robert A. Heinlein, are built around the plot.

CHARACTERIZATION *The ways in which writers present and develop characters to make the characters seem real.* Here are several ways in which writers develop their characters:

1. *By describing how the character looks:* "He had a strange, but pleasant face with a short pointed beard and curly hair. . . ."

2. *By showing the character's words and actions and letting the character speak:* "'Ohhhhh,' I said, touching my lips to his warm head. 'You are a beautiful baby brother.'"

3. *By telling the character's thoughts and feelings:* "How could I yell and tell everyone what a fool I was to be

546

From Level 1, Preprimer

Sounds and Letters

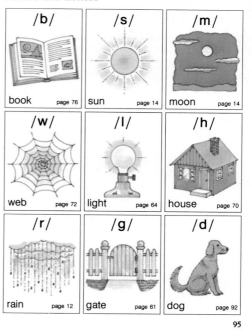

/b/	/s/	/m/
book page 76	sun page 14	moon page 14
/w/	/l/	/h/
web page 72	light page 64	house page 70
/r/	/g/	/d/
rain page 12	gate page 61	dog page 92

95

In Levels 1–3, **Sounds and Letters** is a picture dictionary to help young readers identify pictures, sounds, and words. At Levels 4–6, **Words and Word Parts** (not shown) contains words and activities for word study.

Useful Teacher's Editions

Designed for flexible use, a comprehensive, two-part *Teacher's Edition* is available for each level of ODYSSEY.

Features of *Part I* (Annotated Edition with Teacher's Manual)

- Easy-to-use, three-step teaching plans
- Complete listing of resources for each lesson
- Numerous **prereading** questions and activities to set the stage for reading
- Helpful **reading** strategies to guide the students in reading the selection
- **Postreading** questions and activities that meet a wide range of student needs
- Numerous opportunities to develop **critical thinking** and **creative writing** skills
- Helpful annotations on many student's pages, with answers to all questions posed in the student's book
- Helpful professional articles with teaching strategies for using literature in the classroom
- The **Resource Center,** with additional background information and resources

Features of *Part II*

- Home letters in English and Spanish
- Copying masters for **Enrichment** and **Evaluation** with suggested lesson plans

Teacher's Edition, Part I
designed for flexible use...

The theme of each unit is clearly stated.

Unit Materials list Home Letter, Evaluation, and Enrichment copying masters.

UNIT OVERVIEW
6 I'm Growing
pages 173–218

Theme: The awareness of physical growth and change.

Selections
Okay Everybody! (poem)
Message from a Caterpillar (poem)
CONNECTIONS: Penguins
LEARN ABOUT STORIES: Story Sounds
Umbrella (story)
About TARO YASHIMA
He Bear, She Bear (story)

Unit Materials

Home Letter* Home Letter 6 may be sent home at the beginning or the end of the unit.

Copying Master for Evaluation*
Copying master 28.

Copying Masters for Enrichment* (Optional) Copying masters 27, 29, 30, and 31.

Introducing the Unit

To introduce the children to the unit, have them read the unit title, look at the picture, and discuss the idea that people and other living things grow. To begin the discussion, *ask:* ☐ *What is happening in the picture?* (Possible responses: The girl is riding a bicycle; she is giving her dog a ride.) ☐ *Why isn't the girl riding the tricycle?* (Possible response: She is too big.) ☐ *What do you think the girl will be riding or driving*

*Note that the copying masters indicated here are from the *Teacher's Edition, Part II.*

in ten more years? (Possible responses: a car, a ten speed bicycle) ☐ *In a few more years, the girl's legs will grow long enough for her to be able to ride a ten speed bike. In what other ways will we be able to tell that the girl is growing up?* (Possible responses: She will be taller and stronger; she will have learned more; she may be more responsible; she may be able to take care of herself.) ☐ *How are you growing?* (Possible responses: getting taller, stronger, heavier; learning skills such as reading and writing)

Tell the children that in this unit they will be reading poems and stories about how some other children, penguins, and caterpillars grow and change.

Unit Projects and Activities

Learning About Animals **(Easy)** Have the children **brainstorm** names for animal babies. (Possible responses: chicks, calves, ponies, puppies, kittens) List all responses on the chalkboard. Then write the names for these animal babies when they are grown. (Possible responses: hens, cows, horses, dogs, cats) Have the children choose an animal from the list and draw it as a baby and as an adult.

Growing Plants **(Average)** Have children bring in the top of a carrot from home. Give them cups labeled with their names. Have the children put a crumpled paper towel in the bottom of their cup. Partially fill the cup with water. Then have the children place their carrot top on the paper

T155

From Level 1, Reader

Introducing the Unit offers suggestions for preparing students for the unit theme.

Unit Projects and Activities, ranging in difficulty from easy to challenging, provide suggestions for a variety of student needs and abilities.

Sample pages are reduced. Actual sizes are 7½″ x 9″.

with a logical lesson plan...

STEP 1: PREREADING

This section offers a variety of suggestions to prepare students for reading the selection.

STEP 2: READING

Helpful suggestions set a purpose for reading and provide a guide for developing reading strategies that are appropriate to the selection and to students' needs.

---

ments of other animals. Have them take turns imitating their animals while the others guess what the movement is and the kind of animal that makes that particular movement. (Possible responses: a fish swimming, a snake slithering, a horse galloping, a bear lumbering, a lion or tiger stalking or leaping)

Asking a Question (Challenging) Review the question–answer pattern in the rhyme. Tell the children to think of an animal they would like to ask a question of and a question they want to ask. Children can brainstorm their ideas as a class or in small groups. Children who are having difficulty getting started might name favorite animals and their traits. Then they could think of a "how" or "why" question about that trait and finally suggest an answer to the question. The answers can be real or make–believe. Final versions of the questions and answers may be presented to the class.

Related Reading

The following children's books can be used to extend the lesson.

Who's in Rabbit's House? by Verna Aardema. Dial Press, 1977. A fascinating African folk tale. This book has won several awards. (Average)

Henry and the Red Stripes by Eileen Christelow. Clarion Books, 1982. Henry, a young rabbit, learns the hard way why rabbits do not have red stripes. (Average)

The Little Rabbit by Judy Dunn. Random House, 1980. Full–color photographs show the world of a rabbit family. (Easy)

Alex Remembers by Helen V. Griffith. Greenwillow Books, 1983. When Robbie lets his restless pets outside, he's left staring at the full, orange moon, and strange sounds seem to happen. (Average)

Run, Rabbit, Run by Rodney Peppe. Delacorte, 1982. Children help a rabbit to escape and stay one step ahead of danger. (Challenging)

Magic and the Night River by Eve Bunting. Harper & Row, 1978. Full–page drawings give a fine Japanese background to a story of a young Japanese boy who loves his grandfather. (Easy)

The Moon Seems to Change by Franklin Branley. T. V. Crowell, 1960. Bold two–color pictures show the moon from crescent to full. (Easy)

On the Moon by Jenny Vaughan. Franklin Watts, 1983. A simple look at the moon and what the astronauts found when they got there. Good illustrations. (Average)

A House Is a House for Me

pages 70–79

Objectives

Literature
● Enjoying and appreciating sound devices or rhyme, repetition, and alliteration.

Comprehension
● Expressing the main idea of a poem.

● **Recalling facts.**

Vocabulary/Decoding
● Acquiring a basic reading vocabulary.

● Using initial consonant *h*.

Content Area (Science)
● Classifying subjects from the environment by comparing similarities and differences.

● **Matching animals with their homes.**

T116

Materials

For Evaluation

COMPREHENSION/SCIENCE copying master 15, "Find a Home"

For Enrichment (Optional)

VOCABULARY copying master 16, "Find the Matching Words"

SOCIAL STUDIES copying master 17, "Find the Homes"

Awards

A House Is a House for Me was a Children's Choice and a recipient of an American Book Award in 1978.

1 PREREADING

Key Vocabulary Words

hive: a box or other container for bees to live in. (page 70)
mole: a small burrowing animal with dark velvety fur and very small eyes. (page 71)
web: the network of fine strands made by a spider. (page 72)
stall: a stable or cow barn; a compartment for one animal. (page 78)
earth: the planet on which we live; the world in which we live. (page 79)

Introducing the Vocabulary

Write the key vocabulary words on the chalkboard and pronounce each word for the children. Frame each word and ask the children to pronounce it. Have the children try to use each word in a sentence. When necessary, use the definitions above to explain each word. Point out to

the children that the word *earth* can mean soil as opposed to rock, ground as opposed to bodies of water, or the whole planet on which we live.

Introducing the Poem

Relating to Students' Experiences *Ask:*
□ *What do you think of when you hear the word* house? (Possible responses: a building with many different rooms where people live) Name the different kinds of houses you know or have heard about. (Possible responses: apartment buildings, farmhouses, igloos, tents)

Previewing and Predicting Tell the children that you will read a poem called "A House Is a House for Me." *Ask:* □ *What do you think the poem will be about?* (Possible responses: a house for me, a house for a child)

2 READING

Setting a Purpose for Reading

Explain to the children that a poet uses words in a special way to help people think about things differently from the way they usually think about them. Tell the children that the words in the poem may help them change their minds about what makes something a house. Suggest that as they listen to the poem, they should let their imaginations roam freely.

Planning a Reading Strategy

Read through the poem once for pure enjoyment. As you read, ask the children to close their eyes and picture each of the houses named in the poem. Then read the poem a second time. Have them open

T117

From Level 1, Preprimer

Lesson **Objectives** are clearly identified and labeled. Boldfaced type indicates which objective will be evaluated.

Strategies for previewing and predicting, as well as techniques for relating to students' experiences, help prepare students for reading.

Important vocabulary words are listed and defined, with suggestions for developing vocabulary.

STEP 3: POSTREADING

Enjoyable and thought-provoking questions and activities help students to review each selection.

For major selections, references are provided to **Enrichment** and **Evaluation** copying masters.

---

their books and examine the illustrations to compare the way each picture looks to how they imagined it should look.

Write an exclamation mark on the chalkboard. Ask the children to find the exclamation marks in the poem. *Ask:* □ *What do you think this symbol means?* (Possible responses: that the sentence is exciting, that you should read the sentence with excitement in your voice) Write *This is my house* on the chalkboard. Read the sentence with a period and then with an exclamation mark. Point out that an exclamation mark means that the sentence should be read with enthusiasm. Read the poem again, and ask the children to join you in reciting the lines that say "and a house is a house for me!"

You may want the class to read the poem chorally. Ask volunteers to repeat the first three lines of each verse. The whole class can join in for the final line of each verse. (Children who especially like the poem may want to memorize all or part of it and present it to the class or to other classes in the school.)

Read aloud the poem again and ask the children to listen for words that rhyme. Help them by stressing the first word in each rhyming pair and pausing before the second word. Begin with the rhyming pairs formed by the last word in the second and fourth lines of each verse. (bee/me, tree/me, stall/all) Lead the children to discover the rhyming words in the third line of each verse. (house/mouse, snug/bug/rug, known/own)

Explain to the children that one of the ways poets make words more interesting is by choosing words for their poems that begin with the same sound.

Read the poem and emphasize the initial consonant "h" throughout. *Ask:*

□ *What sound did you hear at the beginning of many of the words?* (The "h" sound is at the beginning of the words *hill, hive, hole, home,* and *house.*) You might want to have the children clap each time they hear an "h" word as you read the poem again.

3 POSTREADING

Reviewing the Poem

The following questions may be used to review the poem.

Have the children call out the names of the houses that were mentioned in the poem as you list them on the chalkboard. Next to each house, have the children name the animal or thing that lives in that house. (hill/ant, hive/bee, hole/mole or mouse, house/me, web/spider, bird/nest, bug/rug, glove/hand, stocking/knee, shoe or boot/foot, book/story, rose/smell, head/secret, flower/garden, donkey/stall, earth/all)

Discussing the Poem

You may wish to use the following questions to discuss the poem further.

Ask: □ *How would you describe a house now that you have heard the poem?* (Possible responses: anything that can be used as a place to live; a place where all animals or things feel "at home")

Focus on the last two lines of the poem and ask the children to put these messages in their own words. *Ask:* □ *What is the poet telling us in this poem?* (Possible responses: Everything has its own house; we all have and share the earth as a house.)

Evaluating the Poem

To evaluate the children's comprehension of the poem, use **EVALUATION** copying master 15. **Objectives: Recalling facts; matching animals with their homes.**

Extending the Poem

Designing a House for Me (Average) Talk about the tree house and cardboard houses that are pictured in "A House Is a House for Me." Have the children draw a house or use materials of their choosing to make a house. Tell them to include any animals or people with whom they would like to share their houses.

Making Up Metaphors (Challenging) Explain that in *A House Is a House for Me* the poet calls certain things houses that are not usually thought of as houses. For example: a book is a house for a story, a rose is a house for a smell. *Ask:* □ *What other unlikely houses can you think of?* (Encourage the children to think of places or objects that become houses when a person, animal, or thing uses them as a house.) As the children name metaphors for other houses and their inhabitants, list the metaphors on the chalkboard.

If the children have difficulty getting started, name possible houses and ask who could live there. (an oven—muffins, cake; a balloon—air; a drinking straw—juice, milk; a piano—music or notes) Children who show a special interest in this activity may continue to make up related metaphors individually or with a partner. They may use the format "A _____ is a house for a _____" to record their ideas and draw accompanying illustrations.

Optional Copying Masters for Enrichment

The following copying masters may be assigned as classroom work or as home activities to be completed with parents' help.

VOCABULARY copying master 16. **Objective:** Acquiring a basic reading vocabulary.

SOCIAL STUDIES copying master 17. **Objective:** Recognizing different types of shelters.

Related Reading

The following children's books can be used to extend the lesson.

Tony's Hard Work Day by Alan Arkin. Harper & Row, 1972. A small boy, who has been told he is too little to help his family as they fix up an old house, goes off and builds himself a complete log cabin. Delightfully tongue–in–cheek. (Challenging)

Animals Live Here by Muriel Batherman. Greenwillow Books, 1979. A look at animals that have been grouped by the way they live. (Challenging)

The Little House by Virginia Lee Burton. Houghton Mifflin, 1942. The little house starts life far out in the country, but slowly the city grows up around it. A classic. (Average)

Benedict Finds a Home by Chris L. Demarest Lothrop, Lee & Shepard, 1982. The bird, Benedict, is tired of living in a crowded nest and sharing toys, so he decides to look for a new home, but he soon finds each animal has its own special home. (Average)

T118

T119

Discussion questions help students to understand and appreciate literature as well as sharpen their abilities to think clearly and critically.

Related Reading lists additional books to extend the lesson and provide further reading opportunities for children of different reading abilities.

Creative activities for students' individual differences are suggested in extending activities. Particular emphasis is given to writing activities in many lessons.

Sample pages are reduced. Actual sizes are 7½" x 9".

and useful teaching notes

Ambassador to France,
                        peace treaty-maker,
                                        supervisor,
                                                organizer,
mover and shaker!
                        With only a kite
                                (and courage)
                                        and a key,
                        Ben proved that lightning is electricity.

A daydreamer schemer,
an on-the-go-getter,
there was always a *Ben* way
to do something better!

A planner,
a spanner,
a tinker-er,
a thinker-er,
a champion non-stopper idea hopper!

> *The* Franklin stove
> (line 5 from the foot of
> the page) was invent-
> ed by Ben Franklin.
> Made of cast iron, it
> was shaped like a
> fireplace.

        Put on your Franklin specs[1] and
        gather around the Franklin stove;
        read aloud *Poor Richard's Almanac*[2] —
        it's still a treasure trove.

                Early to bed and early to rise
                made Ben Franklin wealthy and wise.

1. **Franklin specs:** refers to the eyeglasses, or spectacles, Benjamin Franklin invented.
2. *Poor Richard's Almanac:* an almanac, or yearly calendar, written, printed, and published from 1733 to 1758 by Benjamin Franklin. Franklin's almanac provided weather and astronomical information, and included such proverbs, or wise sayings, as "Early to bed, early to rise/ Makes a man healthy, wealthy, and wise."

28

When Ben became rich,
he still hated waste:
solid silver <u>porringers</u>
were not to his taste;

> *Porringers*
> /pôr'·in·jərz/ are
> small, shallow bowls
> used for porridge or
> soup.

a wooden bowl
would serve quite as well
(so long as it was full)
and the suit he liked the best
was his plain brown wool.

With owlish eyes
and forehead high,
the sound that he hooted
was always
                        WHY.

        Why not invent
        a new rocking chair
        with a fan
        that in summer
        can cool off the air?

        And why not a pick
        to reach a high shelf?
        A mechanical long arm—
        he could use one himself!

Ben, Ben, curious Ben,
Ben with a powerful
quirk
for work.

29

**Clear annotations provide pronunciations
and definitions of words and clarify and highlight portions of the text.**

Questions

1. What was the first sign that something was wrong on the dark, rocky path?

2. "On the edge of a match's dim glow, evil shrank against stone and coiled in a way that was as fluid as smoke." (page 190) Why did the author write that sentence description instead of writing, "It was a rattlesnake"?

3. Tell three things that Bill did to get the group through the pathway. What else could he have done?

4. Could Greg and Beebe have made the trip successfully without Bill? Why or why not?

5. At the end of the story, the boys "did not talk about what had happened." Why not?

6. If someone were to ask the boys to prove that their adventure really happened, what proof could they give?

Activity   **Describe a Setting**

In "Fear in the Dark," the setting is conveyed not just by what the characters *see,* but also by what they *smell* and *hear.* The author has made the setting more vivid by using descriptive words: "twisting, tortuous route"; *odd, musky* odor"; "*dry, rasping* sounds."

Find a magazine photograph of a place that would make a good setting for an adventure or a suspense story. Try to see, hear, and feel your way into the setting. Then write at least three descriptive phrases that could be used in a story with that setting.

1. Literal / Sequence the musky odor and dry rasping sounds
2. Interpretive / Judgment The sentence creates suspense.
3. Literal / Details and **Critical / Application** Possible answer: He called for light so that they could see what was making the noise; he explained the habits of rattlesnakes; he killed snakes along the path. He could have built a fire, created a disturbance to try to make the snakes go away, or made a shelter for protection from the snakes.
4. Critical / Evaluation Yes, they would have been frightened, but they would have gotten through it. No, they were too panicked and inexperienced. (pages 185, 190, 197)
5. Interpretive / Conclusion Possible answer: The experience was overwheming; once it was over, it seemed impossible that it had happened.
6. Literal / Details The picture Greg took. (page 192) Bill's torn shirt with venom on it. (page 197)

199

Annotations clearly identify the levels of thinking skills to be used in answering the questions.

Annotations provide answers to all student-book questions and offer helpful page references for checking responses.

Sample pages are reduced. Actual sizes are 7¹/₂″ x 9″.

Teacher's Edition, Part II
a wealth of teaching resources

Find the Meaning

Name _____

EVALUATION
Vocabulary/
Comprehension **16**

A. The words in the Word Key come from "The Great Minu." Read each meaning. Choose the word from the Word Key that best fits each meaning. Write it on the line.

Word Key   outskirts   trudged   procession   inquired   cargo

1. freight carried by ship or airplane _____

2. walked wearily or with great effort _____

3. outer edges of a city _____

4. asked; questioned _____

5. line of people moving in an orderly formal manner _____

B. Now use the "key" words to finish the sentences.

1. The farmer _____ a long way, to the city.

2. The farmer saw cows at the _____ of the city.

3. As the farmer walked through Accra, he _____ about who owned the cows, the buildings, and all of the goods.

4. At the harbor, the farmer saw workers loading a _____ of cocoa, bananas, and mahogany on the ships.

5. Back in the city, the farmer passed a long _____ of men and women who were going to a funeral.

C. The key to this story is the meaning of one word.

1. What is that word? _____

2. The farmer thought the word meant _____

3. But you know the word really means "_____"

Objectives: Parts A and B, using definitions and context clues to identify words; **Part C,** recalling details and making inferences.

ODYSSEY, *Across Wide Fields*, Level 4 "The Great Minu," pages 82-91

Evaluation copying masters for each major selection assess vocabulary, comprehension, and literary appreciation skills.

From Level 4

From Level 4

A **Suggested Lesson Plan** on the back of each copying master includes introductory activities, a reduced version of the copying master with answers, a separate answer key, and follow-up activities that extend the activity on the master and provide for individual differences.

Suggested Lesson Plan

EVALUATION
Vocabulary/Comprehension **16A**

Introducing the Copying Master

To prepare the students for the copying master, read the directions with them. Have them pronounce the words in the Word Key aloud. Be sure that students understand that they are to use the same words for parts A and B.

Copying Master Followup

Listing Synonyms **(Average)** Write the words *trudged* and *inquired* on the chalkboard. Have the students brainstorm to supply as many synonyms as they can for each word. List the synonyms on the chalkboard under each key word.

Answer Key

A.
1. cargo
2. trudged
3. outskirts
4. inquired
5. procession

B.
1. trudged
2. outskirts
3. inquired
4. cargo
5. procession

C.
1. minu
2. a person's name
3. I don't understand

ODYSSEY, *Across Wide Fields*, Level 4

Enrichment copying masters for each major selection include a range of activities to develop skills such as word attack, sequencing, problem solving, map reading, and writing. (**Suggested lesson plan** not shown.)

ENRICHMENT
Literature/
Comprehension
21

Name _____

Tell the Story Order

Draw the animals in the story order. Make a pull-through viewer. Then tell the story.

B   A

First

Next

Then

Last

ran after

Directions: Read the above directions with the children. The children will draw the animals on strip A in the order they appear in the story. Then they will cut out strips A and B. Have them pull strip A through viewer B, retelling the sequence of the story.
Objectives: Recall ... in a story; drawing ...
ODYSSEY, *Hello and Good-bye*, Level Primer **"The Gingerbread Man,"** pages 114–135

ODYSSEY
Home Letter
2

Dear _____,

Your child has been reading Unit 1 of *Where the Clouds Go* in ODYSSEY *An HBJ Literature Program.* The theme of this first unit is "Let's Go Together." This theme is carried through in the literature, which focuses on poems and stories about relationships among family and friends.

The following children's books also relate to the theme of this unit. You may want to help your child find these books in your local library.

I'll Be the Horse If You'll Play with Me by Martha Alexander. New York: Dial Press, 1975.
A young girl never seems to get her turn to ride when she plays with her older brother. When she plays with her younger brother, however, she no longer has to be the horse—he is.

Mr. Rabbit and the Lovely Present by Charlotte Zolotow. New York: Harper & Row, 1962.
Mr. Rabbit helps a little girl find a present for her mother's birthday.

Evan's Corner by Elizabeth Starr Hill. New York: Holt, Rinehart & Winston, 1967.
Since Evan has a large family, he longs for privacy and a place of his own.

Mr. Gumpy's Outing by John Burningham. New York: Holt, Rinehart & Winston, 1970.
One sunny day, Mr. Gumpy invites his friends for a ride in his small boat, where the overcrowding results in a funny, and finally happy, conclusion.

You may wish to read these books aloud to your child. Many of these books have detailed illustrations that your child will enjoy discussing.

Sincerely,

ODYSSEY, *Where the Clouds Go*, Level 1

Home Letter copying masters in English and Spanish (not shown) are provided for each unit, complete with annotated lists of children's books.

Sample pages are reduced. Actual sizes are 8¼" x 10⅞".

Introduction to ODYSSEY

Tell me, Muse, of the man of many ways, who was driven
far journeys, after he had sacked Troy's sacred citadel.
Many were they whose cities he saw, whose minds he learned of,
many the pains he suffered in his spirit on the wide sea,
struggling for his own life and the homecoming of his companions.
. . . .
. . . Goddess, daughter of Zeus, speak, and begin our story.

The Odyssey of Homer

THE "MAN OF MANY WAYS" was Odysseus—king of Ithaca in ancient Greece, hero in the war against Troy, husband of Penelope, father of Telemachus, and, in all his endeavors, a man of unusual cunning and courage. Homer's great epic poem the *Odyssey* recounts Odysseus' long wandering journey home from the Trojan War. Three thousand years later, the *Odyssey* remains one of the enduring works of literature, and Odysseus, one of the enduring heros.

When we hear the word *odyssey* today, however, we think of more than the epic journey of Odysseus. For as time has passed, *odyssey* has taken on other meanings: a long wandering, a series of adventurous journeys marked by many changes of fortune, an intellectual or spiritual quest. In its broadest sense, we could say that *odyssey* describes the lifelong journey that all people undertake from birth.

It is that continuing human odyssey and our continuing wonder about it that are at the center of all literature. Though it is history that records our deeds, it is literature that seeks to express our thoughts, feelings, dreams, and wonderings about the world. Since its origins in the chants and tales of unknown storytellers, literature has recorded events vividly, recalled our shared experience, and taught us about ourselves. In doing so, it has come to us in diverse forms—both oral and written—and in divergent voices, the sum of which is our literary heritage, drawn from the past and growing into the future.

Children's literature is one part of our literary heritage that has grown tremendously in this century. With more than forty thousand children's books—in more than six thousand subject categories—in print, the range of genres and content available to young people today is far greater than ever before.

This abundance of literature, however, may lead us to wonder which books, of so many, children should read: Which books meet children's interests better than others do; which books best suit children's development at one stage or another; which selections offer the most pleasure, the best content, the most compelling themes; and which books pass on the important parts of our literary heritage—the classic and traditional stories, poems, and rhymes that we turn to again and again to reaffirm our common experience.

Perhaps there will never be total agreement about the literature that should comprise each child's basic literary education. But there *is* agreement that children should explore a variety of literature in order to build a foundation for a lifetime of reading pleasure.

One purpose of an elementary literature program is to provide children with such a basic foundation of literature. A literature program provides a structure within which children are guided not only in reading a variety of selections but also in thinking about, discussing, and responding to them.

But a literature program does even more than that. A literature program helps children make connections: to notice how one selection and another are linked by an underlying theme; to trace how the structure of one work is like the structure of another; to find out that people of different times and places share common feelings, experiences, and ideas; and to discover how language makes all these connections clear.

By helping children make these connections, we give them a basis for making other connections in their reading, their thinking, and their writing. For reading, thinking, and writing are bound together in a mutually enriching process.

Purposes of ODYSSEY

ODYSSEY is a carefully planned program designed to provide children with a basic literary education. The program's selections and instructional material are all aimed toward its main objective: to provide a solid foundation of literary experiences on which students may build a lifetime of reading pleasure. To reach this objective, ODYSSEY has the following goals:

- To offer students a wide variety of pleasurable, independent reading of the highest literary quality

- To demonstrate the value of literature and to foster interest in reading

- To increase understanding of literature's relationship to human experience

- To develop insights into personal thoughts, feelings, and experiences

- To promote recognition of the individual's role in the community and in society

- To develop an awareness of other people and cultures and their contributions to American life and culture as well as to world civilization

- To gain an appreciation for the literary heritage that is a legacy from one generation to another

- To develop an awareness of the meanings and nuances of words

- To show the power and possibilities of language as a tool for self-expression and to develop an awareness of the persuasive power of words

- To develop an understanding of literary forms, techniques, and styles

- To demonstrate the unique artistry of individual authors and illustrators

- To encourage thoughtful and critical responses to literature and to develop respect for the responses of others

- To develop the skills of reading comprehension, writing, and the other language arts, as well as logical thinking skills

- To develop an awareness of the relationship between literature and other subject areas

Criteria for Selections

In choosing selections for ODYSSEY, the program's developers consulted children's literature specialists, teachers, librarians—and children and young people themselves. After potential selections were identified, program consultants (see page Tiii) evaluated each selection using the following criteria:

Interest Level   Is the selection likely to interest children at this age level?

Reading Level   Will most of the children at this level be able to read the selection independently?

Quality   Does the selection have high literary quality?

Experience   Is the selection worthwhile, either because it brings pure enjoyment to young readers or because it fosters their personal growth?

Portrayal of Ethnic, Minority, and Special Groups   Does the selection portray all groups fairly?

Further considerations were the selections' relevance to thematic strands and their balance in such areas as content, literary type, multicultural representation, and authorship. The final choices were made after extensive classroom testing.

Organization of ODYSSEY

The literature in ODYSSEY is organized thematically around the following strands. Beginning with Reader One, the strands form the basis of thematic units in each textbook. The Heritage strand is added only at the upper levels of the program.

STRANDS IN ODYSSEY

GROWING AND CHANGING	Roles, relationships, and personal growth
ADVENTURE AND SUSPENSE	Real and imaginary adventures
HUMOR	The humorous side of life
FANTASY	Realms of the imagination
EARTH, SEA, AND SPACE	Humans and the natural world
QUEST AND HEROISM	The many aspects of courage
HERITAGE	Historic legacies from the past

The thematic strands in the program appear in the chart beginning on page T17.

Readability in ODYSSEY

In ODYSSEY, prose selections below grade level are usually labeled *Easy,* selections at grade level are labeled *Average,* and selections above grade level are labeled *Challenging.* The selections were evaluated on the basis of their syntactic and conceptual difficulty as well as by the appropriate readability formula.

Level One   Because most first-grade children are not independent readers, the selections in the three textbooks at Level One are intended for teacher-directed reading and for shared reading experiences. For example, the teacher might begin by reading aloud a selection such as a poem with a refrain or a story with repetition or predictable "next sentences." The teacher can then invite the class to "take the next part" or to read aloud in unison. Simple plays—usually presented in the Readers Theatre format—provide still more opportunities for shared reading experiences. To promote oral language development, the Level One readers include content-rich pictures and wordless picture stories so that children may tell or write the story they "read" in the illustrations. Some easy stories, which are labeled as such in this Teacher's Edition, can be read independently by able readers.

Levels Two Through Six   Throughout these levels, selections of different lengths, content, and complexity have been included for students with different interests and reading abilities. Teacher review and student testing helped determine that these selections were both interesting and accessible to students at particular grade levels. In addition, text format and organization, page format, and the use of illustration and color not only provide motivation for young readers but also support their reading efforts. Where appropriate, definitions, pronunciations, and explanations of difficult words or foreign terms and expressions are provided on the student-book pages. At Level 6, in particular, this explanatory text often takes the form of footnotes.

Evaluation in the Program

In evaluating the program's success in the classroom, the central question should be whether the selections have enhanced the students' enjoyment of literature. This is an affective outcome that no written test can assess, but teachers can assess progress informally, asking students for their opinions about the literature; listening to their spontaneous comments, especially their expressions of interest in reading and literature; and observing whether they seek out further literary experiences. Brief anecdotal records of the students' responses will provide valid and direct evidence that the program's goal is being met.

In addition to enhancing the students' enjoyment of literature, the ODYSSEY program supports students' abilities to think about and respond to what they have read. The program provides three ways to assess students' growth in these skills: through the questions and activities in each *Pupil's Edition,* through the review and discussion questions in each *Teacher's Edition,* and through the Evaluation copying masters in each *Teacher's Edition, Part II.*

The questions and activities in the Pupil's and Teacher's Editions can be used to evaluate the students' knowledge of literary elements and techniques, and their growth in literary appreciation, reading comprehension, and both oral and written composition. Questions at the literal level will yield brief yet adequate information on students' abilities in literal comprehension. Questions at the interpretive level can provide information about students' abilities to make inferences, to express opinions based on their reading, and to substantiate both kinds of responses. Questions that require critical thinking skills can assess students' abilities to

read "beyond the lines," that is, to integrate what they have read with their own experience or to apply it in a different context. Even though their answers to critical-level questions are subjective and thus will vary greatly, the students' responses can be evaluated in terms of their fluency, flexibility, elaboration, originality, and logic.

The discussion sections in the teaching lessons of each Teacher's Edition include a number of questions that can be used to assess students' abilities to use thinking skills.

The Evaluation copying masters provided for each major prose (literature) selection can be used to evaluate literature appreciation skills such as elements of characterization and plot development, comprehension skills such as identifying a sequence of events and recalling details, and vocabulary skills such as using context clues and employing phonetic analysis and word attack to decode words.

Literature for a Lifetime

A literature program for children requires faith in the lasting effects of teaching and learning. Such faith seems warranted. Most adults who like to read literature can describe one or a hundred rewarding contacts with books in childhood and adolescence. Many such readers might identify with Francie, the child in Betty Smith's novel *A Tree Grows in Brooklyn,* who realizes suddenly the benefits of having learned to read:

From that time on, the world was hers for the reading. She would never be lonely again, never miss the lack of intimate friends. Books became her friends and there was one for every mood. There was poetry for quiet companionship. There was adventure when she tired of quiet hours. There would be love stories when she came into adolescence, and when she wanted to feel a closeness to someone she could read a biography. On that day when she first knew she could read, she made a vow to read one book a day as long as she lived.

Thematic Strands in ODYSSEY

Level	GROWING AND CHANGING	ADVENTURE AND SUSPENSE	HUMOR
1	**Let's Go Together** The positive aspects of relationships with friends and family	**Far, Far Away** The call of adventure	**What a Surprise!** Humorous experiences with an element of surprise
2	**We Could Be Friends** The many aspects of friendship	**Something Is There** Mysterious happenings all around	**Tell Me Something Very Silly** The humor of comical characters and improbable events
3	**Helping Hands** Relationships based on mutual help and support	**You Can't Catch Me** Clever and resourceful escapes from danger	**One of a Kind** Unique characters and their humorous predicaments
4	**When Paths Cross** The relationship between contrasting points of view and personal growth	**Across the Land and Sea** The excitement of journeys to new lands	**What a Character!** The actions of remarkable characters in humorous situations
5	**Never Give Up** The role of perseverance in personal growth	**Facing the Unknown** Suspenseful encounters in a variety of settings	**It Must Be a Trick** Tricksters and trickery of many kinds
6	**Dream Keepers** Achievements based on individual dreams and abilities	**Expect the Unexpected** Unexpected encounters and surprise endings	**Funny Side Up** Mix-ups, mishaps, and misunderstandings

*Refers only to Level 1 Reader. Strands are not grouped by units in Preprimer and Primer.

FANTASY	EARTH, SEA, AND SPACE	QUEST AND HEROISM	HERITAGE
Tell Me a Story Adventures of fantasy characters	**I Wonder** The wonders of the natural world	**I'm Growing** Awareness that people and other living things grow and seek independence	
Long, Long Ago Magical beings, places, and things in a world of fantasy	**Animals All Around** Animals and their natural environments	**I Can Do It!** The courage to act independently and assume new roles	
Would You Believe It! Tall tales and amazing events	**There Is a Season . . .** Cycles of life and the seasons	**Tell Me the Name** The search for personal identity and history	
When the Moon Shines Illusions and transformations	**To Live with Animals** Relationships between animals and humans	**Problems and Puzzles** Challenges to be met and problems to be solved	**Tales of Texas** Texas, past and present
Truly Amazing Talents Characters with amazing or unusual talents	**To Live with Nature** Animals and the forces of nature and their effects on human survival and the quality of life	**From America's Past** Heroic characters and events from American history in the 18th and 19th centuries	**America Grows Up** Heroic characters and events from American history in the 19th and 20th centuries
Time Travelers Explorations of the many aspects of time	**A Tree of Ice, A Rain of Stars** Nature as a source of inspiration and beliefs	**Tests of Courage** The many forms of courage in myth, legend, and contemporary life	**Across Time, Around the World** Contributions of various cultures to world civilization

Skills Index for Level Four

This Skills Index will help you to locate the pages on which each listed skill is presented in a level of ODYSSEY: AN HBJ LITERATURE PROGRAM, Second Edition. Boldfaced page references indicate that the skill is presented in the pupil's textbook. Other references are to teaching suggestions and activities in this Teacher's Edition or to the Copying Masters in the Teacher's Edition, Part II.

The numbers preceding the items in the index correspond to the HBJ Skills Code. This code may be used to correlate skills in ODYSSEY with other language arts and reading programs published after 1980 by Harcourt Brace Jovanovich. Teachers who wish to cross-reference these programs may do so by referring to these same numbers that appear in other programs. The index can also serve as a basis for correlating ODYSSEY with the management system or curriculum guide used in your school.

Skills Code Number	SKILL	PAGES
	PHONICS: DECODING AND ENCODING	
2.1	**To Recognize Sound-Letter Relationships: Consonants**	T88, T100, T111, T124
2.1.3	Recognize silent letters	T142, CM36–36A
2.2	**To Recognize Sound-Letter Relationships: Vowels**	CM69–69A, CM75–75A, CM76A
2.6	**To Identify Syllables (Number of Vowel Sounds Heard)**	T100, CM26–26A
2.8	**To Recognize Rhyming Words**	**27, 124, 170, 172–175, 300–301,** T91–92, T120–121, T132–133, T172–174, CM30–30A, CM69A
	COMPREHENSION	
3.0	**To Identify and Use Context Clues**	
3.0.1	Word identification	**103, 215, 284, 433,** T84–85, T107–T110, T164–165, T170, CM16–16A, CM53–53A, CM60–60A, CM69–69A, CM76–76A, CM78–78A
3.0.2	Word meaning	**23, 373, 411,** T186–190, T204–209, CM44–44A, CM57–57A

LITERATURE APPRECIATION

ODYSSEY Correlates with Other Content Areas

This correlation chart will help you to locate pages on which content area material is presented in Level 4 of ODYSSEY: AN HBJ LITERATURE PROGRAM, Second Edition. Boldfaced page references indicate that the content area material is presented in the pupil's textbook. Other references are to teaching suggestions and activities in this Teacher's Edition (T) or to the Copying Masters (CM) in the Teacher's Edition, Part II.

Mathematics

Use decimals (place value)	CM50–50A
Use fractions (models)	CM32–32A
Recognize equivalent fractions (using models)	CM32–32A
Read and write whole numbers and decimals (money)	**34–49,** CM11–11A, CM50–50A
Add and subtract whole numbers	CM9–9A
Use charts and graphs	CM8–8A, CM17–17A, CM20–20A, CM47–47A, CM49–49A, CM61–61A, CM75–75A, CM82–82A
Collect data and use to construct graphs	T147, T223, CM8A, CM42A, CM82A
Interpret pictographs and use information to solve story problems	CM8–8A

Health

Identify practices that promote self-concept	**230–245, 270–284, 392–411,** T143–146, T163–165, T196–197
Relate fluoridation and snacking habits to dental health	CM3–3A
Recognize the health of the family is dependent upon the contributions of each of its members	**50–71, 142–160, 230–245, 356–373,** T99–102, T126–129, T154–157, T186–189
Recognize hazards of the environment, and acquire knowledge and skills needed to avoid injury and to prevent accident	**50–71, 142–160,** T99–102, T126–129
Identifying terms	CM57–57A

Science

Observe phenomena and apply knowledge of facts and concepts	T106, T194, CM61–61A
Observe that all living organisms depend on plants (food chains, food webs)	CM64–64A
Describe changes in objects over a period of time (position, rate of speed)	**330–351,** T179–182
Describe the changes that occur in weather and their effects	**50–71, 72–77, 434–443,** T102–104
Describe how plants and animals protect themselves	**384–391, 392–411,** T185, T188, T192, T193–195, T195–198

Social Studies

Accept the responsibilities of membership in various groups	**72–75, 422–433, 454–463, 464–475,** T204–207, T217–220
Support individuals' rights to have differing opinions	**206–215, 246–249,** T146–148, T157–158
Explain the importance of economic interdependence within and among regions of Texas	**464–475, 490–497,** T225–226

Understand Texas' economic relationships to other states and to the world	**464–475, 490–497**
Identify examples of the factors of production (land, labor, capital, enterprise)	**34–49, 136–141, 464–475, 490–497,** T86, T96–99, T217–220, T225–226, CM11–11A, CM12–12A, CM17–17A, CM50–50A
Identify major economic resources of regions of Texas	**478–488, 490–497,** T221–224, T225–226
Describe the influence of geography on the history of Texas	**444–445, 490–497**
Know basic facts about the founding of Texas as a republic and a state	**420–421, 444–445, 448–450, 451–453, 454–463,** T213–214, CM79–79A
Identify significant individuals and their contributions to Texas history	**444–445, 448–450, 451–453, 454–463,** T209–210, T211–212, T213–214, T215–217, CM79–79A
Describe how the various geographical regions of Texas, the United States, and the world are similar and different	**72–77, 162–169,** T129–131
Recognizing a major event in United States history	**136–141,** T124–126
Understand how people adapt to their physical environment	**50–71, 72–77, 142–160, 162–169, 420–421, 464–475,** T99–102, T102–104, T126–129, T131, T202–204, T217–220, CM14–14A
Know how landforms and climate interact	**72–77, 162–169**
Describe landforms and climates of various regions	**72–77,434–443,** T207–209
Locate major geographical features of Texas on maps and globes	**434–443, 490–497,** T208, T226
Describe how traditions, customs, folkways, and religious beliefs differ among individuals and groups	**126–132, 250–266, 288–295, 420–421,** T99–102, T116–119, T121–122, T158–161, T204–207
Describe the influence of other cultures on Texas	**444–445, 446–447,** T209–210, T210–211
Interpret visuals (pictures, charts, graphs, tables)	**420–421, 434–443, 444–445, 490–497,** CM8–8A, CM11–11A, CM17–17A, CM20–20A, CM26–26A, CM47–47A, CM61–61A
Interpret maps, keys, symbols	**77, 136, 162–169, 420–421, 434–443, 444–445, 490–497,** T129–131, T132, T185, T202–204, T225–226, CM15–15A, CM18–18A, CM28–28A, CM46–46A, CM66–66A
Construct maps, charts	**71, 475,** T101, T143, T185, T194, T201, T209, CM46–46A

Fine Arts

Express individual ideas, thoughts, and feelings in simple artistic media	**49, 77, 245,** T84, T95, T115, T119, T122, T137, T158, T176, T212, T219, CM30A
Sing songs including total group singing of action, seasonal, patriotic, and popular songs and rounds	**137–141, 352, 476–477,** T124–126, T125, T131, T183–184, T221
Sing and identify simple music forms	CM26–26A
Develop body awareness and spatial perception using rhythmic and imitative movement, sensory awareness, and pantomime	T160, T165, T188
Perform a play or a scene from a play	**302–323,** T109, T134, T143, T171, T179
Create original dialogue	T134, T143, T177, T179, T193
Recall sensory and emotional experience	**92–102, 206–215, 230–245**

Teaching Literature in the Classroom

Sam Leaton Sebesta

I hear, and I forget.
I see, and I remember.
I do, and I understand.

Chinese proverb

MANY CHILDREN come to school with a developing interest in literature. In their preschool years, they have become acquainted with literature in one form or another. They have responded, for instance, to the rhythms, rhymes, and repetitions of verses and songs. They have experienced the pleasure of looking at and listening to stories in books. They have followed the chain of events around a central idea or theme that forms a story.

Children's school experience with literature, then, is an extension of this developing interest from early childhood; thus the goals of a school literature program should be to increase enjoyment and understanding—to broaden and deepen literature experience. These goals are served in two ways: first, by presenting excellent literary selections with increasing variety and complexity; and second, by encouraging and guiding response.

Ideally, response begins before a selection is read. It includes a discussion or activity to help children connect the world to be met in literature with their own experience. The reading itself invites immediate response, as do questions to elicit discussion after reading. However, children's literary experience should not end there. It should go on to include focused activities that may make each selection special in each reader's life. The result should be self-generating: readers of literature build anticipation and skill for their next literary encounter, and they increase their desire to read literature independently for their own enjoyment.

Perhaps it goes without saying that the teacher is the key to activate experience with literature. Teachers who, themselves, love literature are priceless models of response. They inspire interest and a search for meaning in the encounter with each new story, poem, play, or work of nonfiction. They increase enjoyment and understanding through thoughtful questioning and purposeful activities—oral and written composition, interpretive reading and dramatization, music and the visual arts, and extensions of literary experience related to the other content areas. Such teachers know that literature is a legacy to be given to children with love and enthusiasm. We hope that the techniques described in the following pages, along with suggestions included throughout the lessons in this Teacher's Edition, will serve them well.

The Reading Experience

PREPARING FOR READING

The preparation for reading literature can be as important as the reading experience itself. You may prepare students for reading a selection in three ways: by providing *motivation,* by building *schema*—knowledge central to understanding the selection, and by presenting *new terms* (vocabulary). Motivation can begin with a question or an activity to show students that the selection to be read has some connection to their lives, or to their interests. For example, you might say, "Look at the picture on page 7. Have you ever known a character who did something like that? Show us by speech and action what that character might do next."

When students are motivated, you can then build schema by telling and showing information that will place students in the appropriate context, or set the scene for what they are to read.[1] For example, you might sketch a map to show the relative locations of the village and the cliff that comprise the setting of the story "The Megrimum" (ODYSSEY, Level 5) and elicit examples of fears that might grip the villagers living at the base of a monster's home.

New vocabulary and concepts—those that are most important for comprehending and enjoying the selection—should also be presented as part of the preparation for reading. Present these words actively by asking students to give or elaborate upon definitions, to relate new terms to familiar related terms, and when possible to demonstrate new concepts with a quick sketch or action. The ODYSSEY Teacher's Editions offer suggestions for all these ways to bring students to their reading with "warmed-up motors" and the confidence and knowledge they will need both to enjoy and interact with the literary work.

SILENT AND ORAL READING

For beginning readers, the first reading of a poem or a story is usually a shared experience, with the teacher reading aloud and the students joining in on a refrain or a predictable passage. Beyond this stage, students can usually be expected to read selections independently.

Most reading specialists recommend that first readings always be silent, independent readings. They point out that silent reading permits each student to read at his or her own pace. It also encourages reflection and allows both time for response and time to go back and *reread* a passage before going on. Initial silent reading helps students enjoy and interpret a selection further during a later oral reading.

Yet this recommendation for silent reading first has exceptions. Most poems should be read aloud initially. Anecdotes and funny stories beg for sharing and may lose their appeal if assigned to be read silently. When the content, language, or theme of a selection is complex, guided oral reading helps students share the literary experience from the start.

At no time, however, should oral reading be considered a mere exercise in "getting all the words right." Rather, it is a means to guiding understanding. Most

---

1. David Rumelhart, "Schemata: The Building Blocks of Cognition," in *Theoretical Issues in Reading Comprehension,* ed. R. Spiro, B. Bruce, and W. Brewer (Hillsdale, N.J.: Erlbaum, 1980), 33–58.

often, this guidance is better done by (1) preparing students to read silently, (2) encouraging silent reading according to each student's rate and reading strategies, and (3) later having students reread all or part of a selection for a purpose—to support a point, to share an enthusiasm, or to enliven a work through oral interpretation.

POSTREADING DISCUSSION

Once a selection is read, discussion can enhance the literary experience. The main purpose of such discussion is to allow students to speak, to express their responses to the literature they are reading, and to listen to the varied responses of their classmates. Discussions can thus provide opportunities for students not only to express their own opinions but also to learn from the opinions of others. In addition, discussion can be an informal way for you to assess students' enjoyment, involvement, and understanding of what they have read. Asking a general opening question and inviting students to ask questions are good ways to begin a discussion that leads to more structured questions and activities.

General Discussion Strategies Opening discussion should be nonthreatening. It should invite immediate, pertinent response. It should, if possible, set the stage for more focused questions and activities to follow. Here are four effective ways to begin a discussion. (Consult each selection in this Teacher's Edition for specific suggestions.)

1. Offer students the opportunity to retell all or part of the selection, encouraging them to add to, or elaborate upon, incidents that especially interest them. Sometimes it is a good idea to pair students for this retelling; each member of the pair tells the other a part of the selection. At other times, you may need to guide the retelling as a whole-group endeavor, using guiding questions to help students summarize, elaborate, or discover implied motives or connections between events.[2]

2. Ask what the students discovered as a result of their reading. Sometimes this may be a focusing question, based on a preparation question posed before the reading. Sometimes the question can be a more general opener ("Tell me about the story") that invites students to share their responses, fresh from reading, without imposing a structure.

3. Refer to the question-and-activity page in the pupil's textbook, which is included after most of the longer prose selections. Students who have prepared responses to items on the page will have something to contribute at once, and discussion will get off to a good start.

4. Ask each student to find one passage in the story that is exciting to read aloud—a segment that might entice a listener to read the entire story. Subsequent discussion can begin with a request for justification: "Why did you choose that part?"

Early in the discussion, invite student questions: "What did you wonder about as you read the story? Did a question come to your mind as you read this poem?" Such a procedure encourages self-generated questioning as one reads, a basic strategy that good readers use constantly.

---

2. John D. McNeil, *Reading Comprehension: New Directions for Classroom Practice* (Glenview, Ill.: Scott, Foresman, 1984), Chapter 1.

The end of a discussion should come when, in your judgment, the discussion has served its purpose. Most discussions should conclude with a reading assignment or extending activities.

Specific Question Strategies in the Program   In ODYSSEY, a variety of questions in both the Pupil's and Teacher's Editions help teachers focus and extend discussions about literature, and also help provide well-rounded, unified lessons. Some of the questions are derived from the teaching objectives for each selection. Other questions review objectives from earlier readings or seek to broaden the lesson. In each case, questions pertain to the central meaning and significance of the work, their chief purpose being to enhance students' enjoyment and understanding and to allow them to use their listening, speaking, thinking, and writing skills when responding.

The following are the three broad categories of questions used in the ODYSSEY program, with emphasis placed on questions that involve the higher orders of thinking skills.

1. Literal questions ask students to recall specific information presented in a story, poem, or nonfiction selection. Good literal questions do not ask for random facts. Instead, they help readers focus on what is important in the selection: main events and their sequence, main ideas and details that support them, characters' motives or traits explicitly stated in the text.

Though they are sometimes considered "low-level" thinking, answers to literal questions can help students remember, organize, and assemble a "data bank" of information. The data bank can then be accessed to help students respond to higher-level questions, to write longer responses to literature, to dramatize, or to do other related activities. With some students, the literal level needs little reinforcement. With others, it is a necessary, though insufficient, part of the literature lesson.

2. Interpretive questions ask students to respond to literature by using their own experience and reasoning. Interpretive questions are designed to help students develop thinking skills beyond the recall level. For example, the author of a poem about a winter day may present three explicit details; an interpretive question may then ask the reader to add three more details to be expected of a winter day. The author of a biography may discuss several important times in the subject's life; an interpretive question may then ask the reader to predict what happened between these events, based on the evidence given in the selection but also going beyond this evidence. After reading a fiction selection, students may be asked to interpret the "world" described there and to compare or contrast it to their own world. Some interpretive questions ask the students to use the "data bank" of specifics drawn from literature to think more broadly—to classify, deduce, and generalize.

Avid readers apply interpretive thinking skills almost automatically as they read literature. Other readers do not. In either case, interpretive questions can focus interpretion, strengthening interaction between the selection and the reader's experience. Such questions often prepare the way for interpretive activities involving the visual arts, dramatization, oral and written composition, and related reading. Interpretive questions should also enhance the reading and rereading of the selection itself. Much of the enjoyment of reading literature comes from well-focused interpretation.

3. Critical questions ask students to *do something* with the selection: to evaluate it as a work of literature, to apply it to a new situation, to solve a problem based on an understanding of the selection, to investigate a new area connected to the work. A fantasy, for instance, may present a world in which the law of gravity is changed. Students may evaluate the fantasy: How consistently is this change presented in the fantasy? How would our world be different if the change occurred here? How desirable or undesirable would the change be? A biography, for instance, may tell how a famous person developed a skill despite difficult circumstances. Students may then be asked to devise another plan: What other ways might the person have used to develop a skill?

In a sense, literature provides children with "free experience." The children experience not only how certain story characters perceive their problems or goals but also how these characters use thinking skills to try to solve those problems or attain those goals. Critical questions are designed to help students analyze this goal seeking and problem solving; to investigate, evaluate, and often appreciate such endeavors; and finally, to weigh the pros and cons of applying the resulting information to their own thoughts and actions. Critical questions elicit and guide judgment about a literary work itself and about its application.

As explained in this Teacher's Edition, each question in the ODYSSEY Pupil's Editions has a label identifying the category and subcategory of reading and thinking skills that students will use when responding. For example, a series of three questions might be labeled Literal/Sequence, Interpretive/Prediction, and Critical/Appreciation. The labels for these categories and subcategories appear in blue with the students' text questions to which they refer.

Using Questions to Teach The question types described in the preceding section are used in ODYSSEY mainly for teaching purposes, not for testing. Most questions can start a series of responses, and one question may lead to another without interrupting the main topic of discussion. The resulting pattern of discussion may not be question–answer, question–answer, as it is likely to be in testing. Instead, the pattern for the discussion of a story may be the following: a question asking for clarification of a word or phrase leads to a question involving recall of the story events, which in turn leads to a question asking for an interpretation of a character's reaction to those events.

Try applying some of the following strategies during your classroom discussions:

1. Probing A probe can be a request for additional information to clarify or elaborate on a response, or it can be a request for other answers. Such probing questions as "Do you have any other ideas?" or "Can you tell us more about that idea?" can develop a discussion without fragmenting it. Listen to a student's response and decide whether a probe is needed.

2. Requesting verification Ask students to return to the text in order to verify a point. Students may be asked to substantiate opinions as well as locate bases for statements of fact. At other times students may be called upon to use other sources, including their own experience, to verify a statement.

3. Providing wait time The *wait time,* or *think time,* principle simply means that a time of silence comes between a teacher's question and a student's response.[3] Research shows that classes us-

---

3. Linda B. Gambrell, "Think-Time: Implications for Reading Instruction," *The Reading Teacher,* 34 (November 1980): 143–146.

ing wait time have better discussions. Responses are longer, and students show higher-level thinking than when the wait-time principle is ignored.

To apply this strategy, you might begin by saying, "Now I'm going to ask you a very thought-provoking question. Take time to think about it before you tell us what you think." Ask the question, and then allow several seconds to elapse before calling for a response. *After* hearing a response, wait several seconds before commenting or asking for other responses.

4. Modeling Recent research in reading comprehension supports a teaching strategy called *teacher modeling,* which means that the teacher shows the class his or her own thought processes for working out the answer to a challenging question.[4] For example, you may ask an interpretive question about a scene from the story "Charlotte's Web" (Level 4): "What can Wilbur do the next time he gets bored?" Then you say, "This time, I'll begin the answering." Step-by-step, you talk through the thought process you use in responding to the question. That process might include (1) looking back through the selection to pinpoint some literal information ("Last time, Wilbur tried to escape from his pen when he got bored, but that didn't work for long. He'd better try something else."), (2) considering options ("Let's see. What do pigs do if they're bored? What do I know about that? Wilbur is a special pig—but he's still a pig. I couldn't have him read a book or play baseball."), and (3) coming to a conclusion ("Perhaps he could start a club. I'll explore that possibility.")

By describing your thought processes in this way, you have modeled the three steps in answering an interpretive question: (1) searching the literal-level "data bank" as a basis for the response; (2) considering alternative responses, rejecting some; and (3) deciding on what appears to be a good answer, then examining it long enough to explore its value.

After you have modeled your response, discuss the modeling with the students. Then pose another, higher-level question and lead the students through the procedure, returning to the modeling when necessary. On a subsequent question, you should observe whether the students use the procedure independently. Finally, you can evaluate: Has modeling improved the students' abilities to think and respond?

EVALUATING READING EXPERIENCES

To evaluate whether your literature discussions, along with prereading preparation and silent, independent reading, are of benefit to the students, observe the students in the following ways:

1. Notice whether students seem to seek new reading experiences and whether literature lessons are eagerly anticipated. If these reactions occur, the students are attaining the goals of the reading experience, including pleasure, insight into human behavior, and appreciation for language and style.

2. Consider students' responses during discussions. Do they enter discussions enthusiastically? Do all contribute? Is there a give-and-take during the discussions that seems to produce a deepened understanding of the selection? (The importance of building enthusiasm should not be underestimated. Each new reading experience enjoyed by a child

---

4. P. David Pearson, "A Context for Instructional Research on Reading Comprehension," in *Promoting Reading Comprehension,* ed. by James Flood (Newark, Del.: International Reading Association, 1984), 1–15.

makes it less likely that he or she will become a nonreader.)

3. Consider students' answers to the questions themselves, in order to identify students' level of reading comprehension. The literal-level items (recalling details and sequence, for example) are usually easy to evaluate since they call for *convergent thinking.* This means that students will come to an agreement on a "right answer." Though suggested "right answers" are provided in this Teacher's Edition, students' answers may vary and still be "right."

Above-literal items (interpretive and critical) seek to develop *divergent thinking.* This means that students' answers will be different from one another since they are based on individual opinion and experience. Although examples of responses presented in the Teacher's Editions are labeled "Possible response(s)," no one can predict the range of responses that can arise from divergent thinking. The following criteria can be used, however, in evaluating such responses:

- **Fluency** Do students contribute easily to the discussion? Are they able to produce many responses?
- **Flexibility** Are responses varied so that several *different* ideas are contributed?
- **Originality** Are some students' responses creative as well as appropriate to the question; that is, do some students demonstrate a unique ability to discern and to solve the problems posed by the question?
- **Elaboration** When probed, can students expand their responses by adding details?

4. Observe the students' responses to the reading through activities such as oral or written composition, dra- **matization, or creative expression in the arts.** If the reading experience and discussion are indeed promoting students' responses to literature, activities will help reveal and develop such responses.

5. Review the students' responses to the Evaluation copying masters provided for most prose (literature) selections. Students' abilities to recognize elements of literature, recall and infer information, and identify words and word meanings can be assessed by using these literature, comprehension, and vocabulary masters.

Additional Readings

Dillion, J. T. "Research on Questioning and Discussion." *Educational Leadership* 42 (November 1984): 50–56. Emphasis is placed upon procedures that obtain results according to research on devising questions and eliciting response.

Norton, Donna E. *Through the Eyes of a Child.* Columbus, Ohio: Charles E. Merrill, 1983. This book offers excellent, specific help in devising questions for realistic fiction; see pages 420–423. The entire book stresses interaction-with-literature techniques.

Sebesta, Sam Leaton, and William J. Iverson. *Literature for Thursday's Child.* Chicago: Science Research Associates, 1975. Part III contains a plan for integrating questions and activities of different types and levels.

Torrance, E. Paul, and R. E. Myers. *Creative Learning and Teaching.* New York: Dodd, Mead, 1970. Chapters 7 through 10 contain suggestions for asking good divergent-thinking questions, with factors to consider in evaluating responses.

Oral and Written Composition

FROM DISCUSSION TO COMPOSITION

Where does discussion end and composition begin? It is sometimes hard to tell. As discussion evolves from literal to interpretive to critical-creative levels, students' responses are likely to become longer and more complex, as these three sets of questions imply:

1. "What would happen if that problem occurred here instead of in the story?"
2. "Imagine that you are the cow in the story "Socks for Supper" (Level 2). Tell what you want to trade and what happened when you traded it."
3. "Suppose that you are off on a trip to see the panda in its native habitat in China ("Panda," Level 3) What would you need to know to make the trip. How could you find out? How could you put this information into a travel article for your hometown newspaper?"

How easily such critical-level questions can slide into a composition assignment. But hold back a moment. New evidence and emphasis on composition suggest that there are some intervening things to do before you say, "Take out a sheet of paper and write about it."

ORAL COMPOSITION PROCESS

Especially in the primary grades, composition should begin orally and spontaneously. For example, after reading "The Elves and the Shoemaker" (Level 2) and answering questions about the story, you may ask students to suggest a list of things one would need to buy in order to make a pair of shoes. You can then suggest that the shopping trip be turned into a story about such an event, complete with the difficulties the shopper might encounter. Accept all contributions, and encourage every member of the group to contribute something to the story. As a followup, some children may perform the story as a puppet show while others illustrate the story.

Refining the Story   Gradually these spontaneous story-making sessions can be modified and enriched. After the warmup, two or three children can choose one of the story ideas and prepare to tell it before the group. Alternatively, the entire class can continue to work on a story, but this time you might add some oral editing, skillfully and unobtrusively.

Suppose, for example, that the group has just read "The Garden," one of Arnold Lobel's "Frog and Toad" stories (Level 2). Now the group is composing a story about what happens after Toad's seeds begin to grow in his garden. A main happening has been agreed upon: the seeds will grow into such large flowers that Toad's house will be covered. One child suggests as a first sentence for the story, "The flowers got so big that Toad couldn't find his house when he came home from the store."

Now you can help extend and refine the story, "Why had Toad gone to the store in the first place?"

Student 1: He went to buy a watering can.
Student 2: He bought some fast-grow food he saw on television.
Student 3: A dog on TV said, "Give your flowers a treat with Quick Grow!"
Teacher: Now let's go back and start the story.

Student 1: Next day, Toad went to the store. He bought some plant food to make his flowers grow. Then he bought a watering can.

Student 4: When he came back, he said, "Where's my house? All I can see is flowers!"

Student 3: A flower said, "This is my home now! I need a big place so I can grow."

Teacher: What did the flower look like— the one that said that?

Student 3: It was pink, and it had big green leaves.

As the story continues, you can ask questions to help students organize and amplify it. There must be a give-and-take: encouragement to take risks, to try out ideas, and to alter the story when a "better" way is discovered.

WRITTEN COMPOSITION PROCESS

Group stories first composed orally may be turned into dictated stories with the teacher writing on the chalkboard or on large charts. Provision has also been made in the ODYSSEY program for primary students to write brief selections on their own—not only stories but lists, letters, and brief nonfiction. Eventually, written composition becomes a major feature in the interaction-with-literature process.

Having a Purpose Before combining reading and writing, however, it is important to know *why* to encourage readers to be writers. One good reason is given by Frank Smith: "Writing can extend both our imagination and our understanding."[5] Frank Smith points out that

writing, unlike speaking, "overcomes limitations of memory and attention." That is, the writer may stop scribbling or word-processing long enough to refresh the memory or to scratch out and revise or, simply, to go get a drink of water, play hopscotch, and try to return with a refreshed mind. The permanence of writing permits such intervals, giving a "second chance" at thinking, an opportunity to reflect and to refine thought. It is no wonder that educators are equating good writing instruction with the teaching of higher-order thinking skills.

A second reason why readers should also be writers is that writing does indeed seem to improve the reader's ability to interact with literature. The improvement takes the form of higher-level responses based on hierarchies of response to literature as well as richer composition based on a wide variety of criteria.[6,7]

A third reason is the student's purpose, intrinsic to the composition itself. The composition, if it is ever to get off the round, must have a valid reason for being: to settle once and for all the case for or against Rumpelstiltskin ("Rumpelstiltskin," Level 3), to find Rufus M. a well-earned list of interesting books to read ("Rufus M.", Level 3), to prepare a glossary of jargon for an aspiring baseball star ("Return of a Ball Player," Level 6), or to recall a memorable personal experience.

Frank Smith has suggested that writing can have three purposes—"as communication, record, and art." To have a spe-

---

5. Frank Smith, *Writing and the Writer* (New York: Holt, Rinehart & Winston, 1982), 1, 34.

6. D. Eileen Tway, *A Study of the Feasibility of Training Teachers to Use the Literature Rating Scale in Evaluating Children's Fiction Writing,* (Ph.D. diss., Syracuse University, 1970.)

7. James William Calder, *The Effects of Story Structure Instruction on Third-Graders' Concept of Story, Reading Comprehension, Response to Literature, and Written Composition,* (Ph.D. diss., University of Washington, 1984.)

cific purpose within those three categories—and, usually, an audience at whom the purpose is directed—must be part of the composition process, both from the teacher's perspective and the child's. **Publishing,** the final stage of the composition process, is also considered to be an integral part of writing programs that emphasize process. Those students who publish and share their writing are concerned with a wide audience in a positive way.

Prewriting The ODYSSEY program provides many ideas to stimulate written composition. Some ideas are in the students' books as activities following longer prose selections. Others are in this Teacher's Edition. Don't try to use them all. Try, instead, to present them as options to students. When feasible, invite students themselves to choose a topic and suggest purpose and audience. Such decisions, when shared with students, begin the **prewriting** process.

Prewriting should usually begin with oral warmup to stimulate ideas through interaction. Working in pairs or small groups, students can **brainstorm:** they are encouraged to say anything relevant to a potential composition. To make a brainstorming session pay off, however, requires a few "rules" and procedures.

1. Each person should be given a fair share of time to make a contribution—no one is left out.
2. Each idea is to be accepted for the moment—no one's idea is to be scorned or ignored.
3. Someone should be designated as "recorder" to tape, write a list, or simply remember the ideas.
4. At some point, usually after three to six minutes, call a halt and have students review and evaluate what has been said.

Prewriting also may include a kind of visual plan called **diagraming.** In one kind of diagraming activity, teachers may have students write a composition topic or theme idea in the center of a sheet of unlined paper. Here is an example, a topic idea based on the story "Steal Away Home" (Level 5). In the story, Obie and Amos are two children who are escaping from slavery with the help of the Underground Railroad. The students' assignment is to write dialogue for a scene in which the two characters are traveling from one "station" to another.

(What Obie and Amos talked about)

After the topic is placed in the center, have students group subtopics around this center, like spokes on a wheel or satellites around a planet. Lines and arrows can be added to show connections, including cause and effect. This type of diagram—called clustering, mapping, or composition-wheeling—is a visual, holistic, one-page guide to help the writer in the drafting and revising stages to come.

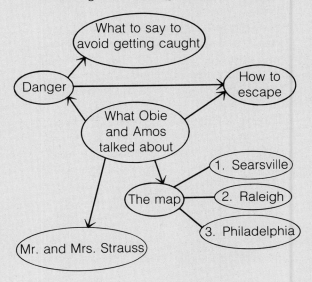

Taking notes and making lists are also included in prewriting to make the journey through the composition process more pleasant and productive. A pre-written word list, or *word bank,* can begin with descriptive adjectives, verbs, or figures of speech that first come to mind: a cat, for instance, is *furry/soft/velvety.* Farther down, the list may become more daring: the cat is a *furry-footed, soft secret-keeper.* During the writing, the student can draw from this word bank, selecting items that are fresh, accurate, and vivid.

Sometimes, especially at the primary level, students need a sentence "frame" to help them generate the word bank. This frame is a fairly simple sentence that contains a blank—for example, "The cat in my story is a _____ cat." Then the student lists as many appropriate words as possible to fill the blank. The same device can be used to generate a clause bank—for example, "My story is about a cat that _____."

At all levels, but with a challenging increase in complexity at intermediate grades, prewriting can include practice in **sentence combining, expansion,** and **reduction,** although these techniques are also useful throughout the writing process. For example, suppose a student has written three sentences: "My cat is pretty and brown. He can close his eyes. He can keep a secret." These sentences can be combined into one: "My pretty, brown cat can close his eyes, keeping a secret." Sentence expansion may include adding adjectives such as "velvety" or "furry-footed" to the description of the cat (both terms borrowed, incidentally, from the word bank above) or adding a larger unit such as, "My pretty brown cat with ears that turn to hear a whisper . . ."

Sentence reduction, of course, is the opposite—deleting excess words and phrases. It is well to teach students, even during prewriting, that a sentence can be too long or that trite extra words are unnecessary baggage. Suggest that students give too-long sentences better "weight" by reducing them.

Finally, for the student who just cannot get started, you might suggest a prewriting activity called **freewriting,** or quickwriting: "Write down anything that comes to mind about your topic. Fill a page! Don't stop to fix it up."

Composing The purpose of writing a first draft is to get the writer's ideas down on paper as quickly and fluently as possible, with no concern for correctness. Therefore, it is best never to ask that the first draft of a story, a play, a poem, or a nonfiction composition be a finished product. Composing—creating—is a tough enough job without the added burden of correct mechanics (spelling, punctuation, paragraphing, and neat handwriting)! Give students a feeling of the tentative nature of first-drafting. They should feel free to scratch out or scribble in. If the first draft is written on every other line, then ongoing revision and later revision will be easier, using the empty in-between lines.

Some students tire quickly during the first-draft stage of the written composition process. Let them take a brief break and then return to the task, reading over what they've done. Encourage them to do such reading with a "reader's eye," as if they are seeing the work for the first time—as a reader, not a writer. Explain that the ability to read one's own work from a reader's (not a writer's) viewpoint is part of an author's craft. It helps a writer make the composition interesting and clear.

If the writer gets "stuck" during the first-draft process, the writer should have a conference either with the teacher or with another student. During the conference, the writer should tell the purpose or the intention of his or her work and the audience for whom he or she is writing; the advisor might then suggest that a return to the prewriting diagram stage is one way to "get unstuck."

Revising   The trial and error of the writing process is a form of *revising*—editing for content and style. Some students stick to the task, editing as they go along or redrafting. Others need help early.

Generally, editing needs to be taught— and taught gradually. It is self-criticism, but criticism with a constructive purpose: to go over one's original creation with a listener's ear and a reader's eye to figure out how the content and style can be improved.

Editing includes cutting unnecessary language and revising sentences and words that lack force or fail to say exactly what is intended. For example, the teacher who asked the student to describe the flower in the discussion about Toad's garden was helping the child expand, hence edit, his or her first oral draft. The child's original version, "A flower said, 'This is my home!'" might therefore become "A big, pink flower stood tall and said, 'This is my home.'" Subsequently, when the child is learning to edit written expression, the same sense of "How can I improve this?" ought to prevail.

Editing for content, style, tone, unity, clarity, and coherence is all part of the revising process, as is proofreading for errors in grammar, usage, and mechanics. It has been suggested that teachers need to provide models for editing and proofreading; otherwise, some students remain puzzled about how to begin. Sharon Fox and Virginia Allen suggest this procedure: "On the blackboard or an overhead transparency a teacher could write a composition. Insertions, crossing out, arrows leading to additional sentences written in the margins, and the sign for beginning a new paragraph could be illustrated."[8] Without such a model, some students may think that revising means that the composition must be copied over and over.

It has also been suggested that students be taught to confer with each other and to help edit each other's drafts. This peer conferencing and peer editing should be done, of course, at the writer's invitation. It must be guided. It should begin on a positive note—"What do you think you are saying in your composition"—before moving to suggestions—"How might you make this composition clearer."

Useful Questions or Revising   The following questions have helped many writers at different levels in the past. Select from the list, adapt it, and add to it to make it your own. Give this or a similar list to students to use in revising their own compositions and in peer editing, depending on the grade level.

Revising Nonfiction Structure
- Can readers find the main idea(s) and supporting ideas in your writing? Should you "signal" them by underlining, by numbering, by adding heads, or by some other means?
- Is the organization clear? Does the composition have unity and coherence?
- Are connections clear? Are there places where you should add transitions and transitional phrases, such as *so, therefore, if—then, because, since?*
- Is the tone appropriate for the purpose and audience?

---

8. Sharon E. Fox and Virginia Garibaldi Allen, *The Language Arts: An Integrated Approach* (New York: Holt, Rinehart & Winston, 1983): 228.

Revising Story Structure

- Does your story start in an exciting place?
- Does someone have a problem or a goal in your story?
- Is there an interesting solution or attempt at a solution of the problem?
- Does your story have an end? Is the ending satisfying?
- Would a certain scene be more interesting if you expanded it?
- Is there a scene that is too long?
- Would some of the story be lost if the scene were shortened?
- Is the tone of the story appropriate for the purpose and audience?

Revising Conversation

- Does the dialogue "sound" like spoken language?
- Is there conversation in your story that is just "filler" and could be left out?
- Is there a place where conversation needs to be added to increase suspense or to move the story along?

Revising Sentences

- If you read your sentences aloud, do they have *cadence*? That is, do they read smoothly without making the reader stumble and have to go back to get the meaning?
- Are your sentences varied in length and complexity for added interest?
- Do your sentences flow smoothly? Have you used appropriate transitional words and expressions?
- Does each sentence have the precise words to carry its meaning?
- Can one sentence be combined with another to make the meaning clearer? (Note: Language arts textbooks provide sequences and practice in sentence combining and expanding. Emphasis in editing may be placed on the skills concurrently taught in the language arts text used in the class.)

Revising Words

- Can you make your writing style more direct by striking out empty words such as *very* and *a lot* and by using *active* rather than *passive* voice?
- Have you chosen colorful, vivid words that carry specific meanings?
- Can you use a more specific descriptive term by finding a synonym in a thesaurus?

Other ideas for improving compositions are included in some of the teaching plans in this Teacher's Edition. These suggestions may involve, for example, developing characterization through direct description, improving style through fresh figures of speech, and experimenting with point of view through first-person writing.

Final Drafting and Publishing To insist that all writing be perfect in mechanics can be stultifying. Yet correct spelling, punctuation, paragraphing, and all the other rudiments of acceptable form must be taught and applied. Therefore, most authorities recommend that writers do a careful proofreading before preparing a *final draft*—the final copy of a written composition. This final draft, with emphasis on correct form, is prepared when the work is considered worthy by its writer and the teacher. The result is a composition *product* as distinguished from the *process* that has dominated earlier drafts.

Not all composition process needs to become product, however, One authority, Donald Graves, suggests that about one out of every five compositions can be treated as product—that is, written into a final draft with correct mechanics so that it can be read easily and enjoyed by others. A simplified set of proofreaders' marks can be used to guide this final drafting, including marking for deletion, insertion, new paragraph, and the term *stet,* which means "do not make the change formerly indicated." These aids to editing and proofreading are in most dictionaries. To aid spelling, students may use an alphabetized list of words frequently used but sometimes misspelled. A recent source of such a list is Robert Hillerich's *A Writing Vocabulary of Elementary Children.*[9] A class dictionary is also a useful tool.

Should students' written products be "published"? Of course! To publish means to make public—not necessarily to be printed, bound, and sold in multiple copies across the counter. Publishing one's composition includes reading it aloud to an audience of peers, putting it on a bulletin board or in a class notebook or periodical for others to read, or sometimes binding a group of class composition products into an anthology to be placed more or less permanently in the school library. Numerous ideas for publishing are to be found in *Teaching Writing in K–8 Classrooms* by Iris M. Tiedt, et al.[10]

The complete recursive composition process—an open-ended, circular process of prewriting, composing, and revising into a final product for publishing— parallels that of professional authors, the writers of literature whose works comprise the ODYSSEY program. By recapitulating this process, students not only learn how to write but come to a fuller understanding, appreciation, and enjoyment of good literature and the skillful authors who have created it.

9. Robert L. Hillerich, *A Writing Vocabulary of Elementary Children* (Springfield, Ill.: Charles C. Thomas, 1978).

10. Iris M. Teidt et al., *Teaching Writing in K–8 Classrooms: The Time Has Come* (Englewood Cliffs, N.J.: Prentice-Hall, 1983), 196–200.

Additional Readings

Burrows, Alvina Treut, Doris C. Jackson, and Dorothy O. Saunders. *They All Want to Write.* Hamden, Conn.: Library Professional Publications, 1984. This fourth edition of a classic book, an ethnography of guiding written composition in elementary school, is a guide to the spirit as well as to technique.

Freeman, Ruth H. "Poetry Writing in the Upper Elementary Grades." *The Reading Teacher* 37 (December 1983): 238–242. An ongoing poetry composition program is described, beginning with simple unrhymed forms.

Graves, Donald H. *Writing: Teachers and Children at Work.* Exeter, N. H.: Heinemann, 1983. A step-by-step account, with straightforward advice to the writing teacher, based on boundless enthusiasm and experience—a "must" for the teacher of written composition.

Hennings, Dorothy Grant, and Barbara Moll Grant. *Written Expression in the Language Arts: Ideas and Skills.* 2d ed. New York: Teachers College Press, 1981. Sequenced topics and activities, including a rich variety of examples, make this a most helpful guide.

Temple, Charles, and Jean Wallace Gillet. *Language Arts: Learning Processes and Teaching Practices.* Boston: Little, Brown, 1984. Chapters 6 through 9 present a detailed discussion of the composition process, including the teaching of mechanics; see pages 238–249 for "Modeling and Teaching the Writing Cycle."

Tiedt, Iris M., et al. *Teaching Writing in K–8 Classrooms: The Time Has Come.* Englewood Cliffs, N. J.: Prentice-Hall, 1983. Helpful ideas to enhance the oral and written composition program are combined with theory on the process itself, including help with sentence-making, making word choices, editing, and evaluating.

Interpretive Reading and Dramatization

INTERPRETIVE ORAL READING

Sharing Interpretations To interpret a story or poem well requires practice and concentration. The interpretive activity should follow careful silent reading of the selection and incorporate insights gained through discussion. Interpretive oral reading usually implies an audience—one or more listeners to whom the reader presents his or her interpretation.

The key to interpretive reading is *concentration*. Readers must learn to concentrate on finding the image and the feeling they want to impart and to work steadfastly toward that goal in their oral reading. Listeners, too, must learn to concentrate their attention on the speaker in ways that make the speaker feel comfortable and show their interest and involvement. Here, then, are seven suggestions you can make to help the students in your class read aloud interpretively and listen attentively:

1. Find a selection, a stanza from a poem, or a scene from a story that you really want to read aloud to others.

2. Figure out why you have selected it. If it is funny, what makes it funny? the language? the action? the surprise? If it is scary, what makes it so? frightening words? a gradual buildup to a big scare?

3. Now visualize the images or the pictures behind the words. If you "see" the pictures in your mind as you read the selection aloud, your listeners will see them too. Sometimes it helps to tell yourself all about the pictures you imagine. Add ideas that the author did not tell you, using your imagination as you read.

4. If the story or poem has action, try imitating the action as you practice reading. Then leave out the movement and try to show the action with just your voice.

5. Practice reading until you do not have to look at the words all the time. Then read the selection to an empty chair approximately ten feet or more away from you. Look often at the chair as you read. If the chair were alive, could it hear you? Would it like hearing the selection the way you are reading it?

6. For intermediate grades: Identify the purpose of each scene in a story or stanza in a poem. Write one phrase that tells that purpose, for example, to scare, to surprise, or to win sympathy. Then, keep that purpose in mind as you read. Write the purpose on a sign and put the sign on your practice chair. Stop in the middle of your practice reading and ask yourself, "Am I reading to show that purpose?"

7. After you have the pictures and the purpose in mind, try experimenting with the volume and pace of your voice. Vary your voice from almost a whisper to almost a shout, from very fast to very slow. Then use some of this variety to help your listeners get the purpose in your reading.

Improving Oral Reading Interpretive oral reading improves with praise if the praise is specific. "You read that with a great deal of expression" is not specific enough; it does not tell the reader what he or she did effectively. A more useful comment might be, "I could hear the ghost rattling the dishes when you read that scene" or "I felt the sorrow of the man and woman when the girl told them she had to leave."

Interpretive oral reading also improves with good models. Most communities contain good models, so you may want to arrange readings by amateur or professional actors, senior citizens, or parents with time and talent for reading aloud. The request to "come and read to us" may bring surprising, pleasing results.

Improving Listening Skills   Listeners to interpretive oral-reading performances have opportunities to improve their listening skills by focusing their attention on the speaker, remaining quiet, and not providing distractions. Help students by adjusting seating and lighting to promote a good listening environment. A discussion of audience etiquette will also help.

CHORAL SPEAKING

Drawing Upon the Flow and Feel of Words   "Star light, star bright, first star I've seen tonight. . . ." These simple, clear words, memory-cued by rhythm and rhyme, invite instant playback. The invitation "Now say it with me!" puts the choral-speaking mechanism in motion.

Almost every rhymed and metered poem in the primary grades can be enhanced through choral speaking. In addition, shared speaking encourages participation without risk. Shyness, fear of making mistakes, and the embarrassment of forgetting lines are all overcome as one speaks with the group.

The technique is also an aid to reading and listening skills, particularly when used in the early years. As students recite together, they may rely partly on memory, partly on listening to others, and partly on print to guide them. In this way, the "difficult" words become familiar in print.

Avoiding the Sing-Song Pitfall   In choral reading, metered poetry may begin to sound "sing-song," a mere exercise in reciting rhythm without the intended interpretation of meaning. One way to avoid this pitfall is *not* to confine intermediate-grade choral reading to rhymed and metered poetry. An alternative is to let the sing-song pleasure of a metered poem run half its course, and then begin to introduce variety into the reading. Another way is to concentrate on the poem's meaning. You might begin by reading a few lines of a poem and asking questions like these: "Who is saying these lines? How should the lines be said? in a puzzled voice? in a sad voice? with a laughing tone? What is happening in the poem? How can we show this feeling with our voices?" Such attention to meaning, even with nonsense poetry, will help direct the rhythm and sound away from a sing-song pattern and toward vocal variety in pace and volume.

Another way to avoid sing-song interpretations is to divide the choral reading so that not *all* speakers read *all* of the lines. Some lines can be read in unison by all speakers, but other lines will be read by a subgroup or by one speaker.

PUPPETRY

Puppet shows hold fascination for children and adults. Students who a moment ago complained, "I can't think of what to say" are suddenly released when "it is the puppets who do the talking."

Buying and Making Puppets   Durable, inexpensive puppets can often be purchased in a toy department or store. Shop for the generic kind—an all-purpose bear, a basic bird, a human face that can be decorated or manipulated to fit a specific role. Avoid puppets that promote stereotyping and the "cute" puppets that call attention to themselves but would not fit into a story.

There is an advantage in making puppets, however. The students' attention is directed to features that show character traits in a specific story, play, or poem. In order to leave time for using the puppets in a production, select one of the following easy-to-make puppets.

1. Hand puppets   A simple hand puppet may be no more than an old sock stretched over the hand and adjusted so that the curved palm of the hand opens and closes like a mouth. The face of the hand puppet can be dabbed on with tempera paint or constructed from yarn, buttons, and sewn-on shapes of cloth.

2. Stick puppets   A stick puppet may consist of a painted or cut-paper face on a flat surface such as a paper plate stapled or pasted on the end of a tongue depressor.

3. Fist puppets   A fist puppet is more elaborate than those mentioned above. The fist puppet's head is modeled out of *papier-mâché* or other lightweight material, such as cotton or crushed paper with heavy paper covering. Features are applied with poster paint. The puppet's eyes should be larger than life to provide emphasis. A cardboard cylinder big enough to fit over the index finger is embedded at the neck of the puppet. The puppet's costume can be cloth that is cut and sewn to be gathered at the puppet's neck with sleeves that fit over the puppeteer's thumb and fifth finger.

Practice and Performance   Give students time to experiment with their newly constructed puppets—to play with voice and movement. When they are ready to perform, they may present the puppet show as Story Theater, where one or more readers read the story while puppeteers manipulate the puppets to show the action. The puppeteers may also perform the story on their own, using creative dramatics techniques to improvise dialogue and gesture. Finally, scripts may be selected or prepared. Some students may read the speeches while other students manipulate the puppets; or the puppeteers may speak the puppets' dialogue as they manipulate them.

READERS THEATRE

In Readers Theatre—the term is usually spelled that way, without an apostrophe—students read orally from scripts that are often based on selections from literature. Play scripts, then, are especially suitable for reading with this technique, since characters' speeches are already indicated. The technique is also adaptable for use with stories and poems that contain considerable direct conversation.

Specialists in the Readers Theatre technique indicate that selections may be abridged or occasionally paraphrased for script purposes. They warn, however, that scripts are to be used only for specific performance; to circulate scripts extensively or to use them for wide public performance is against the copyright law.

How It Works   Similar to actors in a play, the performers in Readers Theatre "take roles"; they speak lines assigned to characters or to one or more narrators. But unlike actors, Readers Theatre performers do not move about a stage; they hold scripts in hand or place them on music stands or desks. A few gestures and changes in position are permitted if these help the interpretation, but the real effect of the literary selection must come from the readers' oral interpretation of characters and narration. Hence the suggestions presented earlier for interpretive oral reading are appropriate for Readers Theatre practice as well.

The prospect of a Readers Theatre performance is highly motivating to students. Once roles are assigned, they do not need to be told to practice their oral reading. They will do so on their own, especially when they can practice with a partner or a "dialogue director" who can give instant feedback on whether the character is "coming through" in the reading.

Importance of the Director   The presentation can be improved by a good director who tells the readers how an audience might receive their efforts. Who should be the director? a student? the teacher? a parent volunteer? Any one of these will do if he or she can bravely but not threateningly stop the rehearsal at almost any point to offer advice: "I didn't *hear* how angry the two trolls were when Prince Lini refused them. Try that again." ("Half a Kingdom," Level 4). Of course, the director must find a balance between expecting too much in a performance and permitting flaccid, unthinking reading. Students respond to direction that asks for, but does not demand, a lively, varied interpretation.

Finally, the finished production may be performed for an audience. Performers may sit or stand side by side, facing the audience, or they may position themselves so that two opposing characters face each other, the narrators off to one side and slightly closer to the audience. The audience, the performance area, and the likely arrangement of readers should be decided upon before final rehearsals begin, so that the readers feel they are working toward a well-planned, polished performance.

STORY THEATER

Interpretive oral reading is combined with "acting out" in Story Theater. One or more students read aloud the selection, which should be a story or a poem with plenty of action. Simultaneously, a group of "players" performs the actions described in the reading. In addition, players may sometimes act as scenery. For example, several may portray a wall, a tree, or the window of a house.

How It Works   Story Theater begins with attentive reading and discussion of the story to be presented. Movement, or mime, can be encouraged as a natural extension of inference questions: "Show us how the lizard moves his head from side to side. Show how the hawk soars over the land, looking for the ring" ("The Wedding of the Hawk," Level 6). Roles are assigned or chosen by volunteers. Players develop their parts as they listen to the oral readers' rendition of the story; oral readers practice their skill until they can vary their pace to accommodate the pace of the players. The final performance, then, is a combination of oral reading and mimed action.

After its completion, the performance should be evaluated by the participants, using questions such as the following: "Which segments in the reading gave life to the story? What did the players do to make certain actions vivid? When a player was present but not specifically mentioned in a moment of action, what did he or she do? Did the player freeze, standing still so that attention was directed to the action, or did the player react to what was happening? Would a different response have been more effective?"

The critique, or evaluation, may be followed by a second performance, and students may then note improvements.

Choosing Appropriate Selections For primary-grade children, Story Theater works well with nursery rhymes and other simple action poems. It seems especially suited to folk tales that highlight action and do not contain a great deal of dialogue. Intermediate-level students, however, may wish to experiment with Story Theater productions in which players speak lines of dialogue.

CREATIVE DRAMATICS/ IMPROVISATION

Creative dramatics may begin soon after a story or a poem is read. During the discussion that follows, the teacher says, "*Show* us what you mean." A student gestures, mimes a series of actions, or speaks a line in a certain way to demonstrate a character or a description. From such a simple, brief beginning can come the activity often called *creative dramatics*. Creative dramatics is especially valuable for developing skills of inference, as students must infer the actions and motives that characters would be likely to display within the framework of the story. The inferring activity shapes and implements both action and motive. It thus goes a step beyond the more passive inference brought forward through discussion.

First Steps Creative dramatics develops gradually. Begin by having students identify *one* crucial scene they would like to play. Then have them "try on" characters and develop gestures, facial expressions, and a manner of speech for each. Lines of dialogue may be quoted directly from the story, but memorizing should not get in the way of the playing. Instead, encourage players to *improvise* dialogue in the spirit of the story and scene.

Once the improvisation is under way, there may be a tendency for the scene to go on and on. If this happens, stop the action. (A signal from you, such as the single word "Curtain," can be used to stop the action without embarrassing anyone.) Immediately ask students to evaluate the playing: "What was strong in the playing? What seemed to be going wrong?" At this point, ask the group, players and observers alike, to reread the scene.

Insight into Character Geraldine Siks, an expert on creative dramatics procedure, offers a further suggestion: Have each player identify first the *big purpose* of his or her character in terms of the entire story, and then the character's *little purpose* in the scene that is being played. In addition, character traits and emotions should be discussed.[11] During this discussion, the focus should be on the characters, not the players. Say, for example: "The old man must show that he is terrified of the sea monster," not "You should act more terrified when you look at the sea monster."

Following evaluation, the scene should be replayed. Further evaluation should note any improvements in the playing.

Need for Brief but Frequent Sessions
The single-scene sessions should be brief, perhaps no longer than ten minutes

---

11. Geraldine Brain Siks, *Drama with Children* (New York: Harper & Row, 1977), 119.

in primary grades and fifteen minutes in intermediate grades. Frequent sessions, perhaps two per week, are recommended by most experts as the best way to move from creative dramatics to meaningful dramatic interpretation.

From Scene to Story At all levels, dramatizing a single scene can lead to playing an entire story once the improvisation process runs smoothly. When an entire story is dramatized, pace and structure become more important than ever. The story must progress without having dialogue or action distract from its central focus.

Winifred Ward, perhaps the best-known expert in the field of creative dramatics in schools, advises that planners and players must "concentrate on essentials," shortening or omitting scenes that contribute to the written story but do not move the drama forward. Scenes themselves often require "tightening," which involves highlighting the essential movement and dialogue while omitting the nonessential. Ward's basic evaluation question at this point is "Did the scene *move*?"[12] Attention must also be directed to the clear presentation of the story's problems in an early scene and to the buildup through successive scenes to a climax and solution.

Using Drama in the Content Areas

Just as creative dramatics can help make story plots come alive through activity, a similar technique called *dramatic play* can enliven the study of content areas such as social studies and mathematics.

Dramatic play begins by identifying a setting or situation and finding out as

much about it as brief time permits. For example, the illustrations for "Ambassador to the Enemy," a chapter from the historical-fiction novel *Caddie Woodlawn*, (Level 5) can be studied along with information about pioneer life described in the students' social studies textbook. From this information, students can compose a still-life scene of American pioneers in the mid-1800s. Each student decides on a character in the scene and describes the activity of the character, including the objects that the character may be using. At a given signal the scene comes to life. Students, playing characters, create speech, action, and inter-action extemporaneously. Emphasis is on the setting and the situation—not on creating or recreating a plot.

After a brief portrayal, usually less than three minutes, the playing is stopped and evaluated: "Is it authentic? What else is needed?" Replay the scene and evaluate again. When the setting is unfamiliar—as it often is with historical periods such as those in eighteenth-century America ("To See Boston at Last," Level 6) or seventeenth-century Japan ("The Master Puppeteer," Level 6)—students may seek additional information beyond the literary selection and the social studies text, all with an eye to making the scene authentic.

Dramatic play may also include acting out and solving mathematics story problems implicit in a literary selection such as "It Pays to Advertise" (Level 4). Story problems arising from this tale of a boy and his lemonade stand could include the following: "How much would you have to charge if you bought frozen lemonade and lemons at the price advertised in today's newspaper's shopping guide?" Set the scenes: the store and the lemonade stand. Then have the students "play" the problem, deciding money amounts and

---

12. Winifred Ward, *Playmaking with Children from Kindergarten Through Junior High School*, 2d ed. (New York: Appleton-Century-Crofts, 1957), 138.

lemonade amounts during the enactment.

At first, dramatic play may seem difficult and a bit silly; but, with persistence, it can become an effective tool for using drama to interconnect literature and the content areas. The key to its success is to emphasize authenticity: how characters in a removed setting act, what they handle, what they see, and what concerns and problems they have. In this way, it adds the glow of realism to "subject matter." As one of its greatest proponents, Dorothy Heathcote, has remarked, "Suddenly you are walking into the time of the event."[13]

PLAY PRODUCTION

Information Presentations   In the classroom, a play script may be presented informally without scenery, costumes, or memorization, and with minimal movement. An informal presentation provides practice in characterization and timing. It also improves speaking skills, especially if readers must project their voices to an audience. The informal presentation can be enhanced if it is recorded on tape as a "radio play" with background music and sound effects. The tape may then be played for the readers' enjoyment and evaluation.

Formal Productions   Formal production based on a play script requires much more time and planning, and it deserves an audience. It may also require a budget. Still, the excitement of a formal production of a play often makes the effort worthwhile. So, too, do the other rewards: the literary learning that results from extended close work with the play script, the confidence that arises from success-

fully portraying characters and incidents, and the poise that comes with performing in a company before an audience.

Preparing Young Students for Play Productions   Students at the primary level need informal experience in drama before attempting a formal play production. Both Story Theater and creative dramatics should come first. Then, when a play script is before the students and the decision is made to present it as a play, they need to become aware of its requirements. Maxine McSweeny[14] reported one group's suggestions for play performance, which were written on the chalkboard by the teacher:

- Know exactly what to say and do. [They can't make it up in front of an audience.]
- Act so the audience can see what they do.
- Speak so the audience can understand what they say.
- Make the play's story live for the audience.

Suggestions for a Successful Production   Once a class has had some experience with formal play production on a small scale, the following suggestions may help to guide more extensive productions.

1. Make sure the class has had sufficient experience in oral interpretation and movement before they try to perform a play that requires extensive dialogue and a succession of scenes.

2. Make sure the class likes the play script. Talk it over. Ask them to explain the dramatic appeal: "What might an audience like about this play?"

---

13. Dorothy Heathcote, "Learning, Knowing, and Languaging in Drama," *Language Arts,* 60 (September 1983): 695–701.

14. Maxine McSweeny, *Creative Children's Theatre for Home, School, Church, and Playground* (Cranbury, N.J.: A. S. Barnes, 1974), 131.

3. Hold try-outs for all facets of the production, not just for acting roles. Ask for volunteers to make scenery (drawn, painted, constructed, or hung as a backdrop), to be in charge of props, or to act as dialogue coaches. The actors themselves must be selected carefully, of course. Have them try out by improvisation rather than by reading lines. Ask pairs of students to assume the characters from the play and then to compose speeches and movements to fit a particular scene.

4. With class participation, make a schedule for rehearsals. The first session should consist of reading lines, with attention to oral interpretation of character. The second session should begin the *blocking* of action, determining characters' movements about the stage in each scene. In general, movement must be motivated, and a character should not move while another is speaking. "Stage business"—the use of props and gestures—is included in the blocking of action. At this point actors may carry scripts but they should also devote attention to memorizing lines. Subsequent sessions give practice, scene by scene, in dialogue and action.

5. When planning scenery, costumes, and lighting, suggest rather than strive for actuality. Setting may be suggested by scenery sketched on wrapping paper or merely be a backdrop consisting of a curtain or drape. An item of costume, such as a hat or an appropriate jacket, can suffice to designate a character. Lighting need not require footlights or spotlights, but the playing area should be clearly visible to an audience. The playing area itself can be a cleared area in the classroom if a raised stage is not available.

6. Set aside time for a dress rehearsal—a session in which the entire pro-duction receives a run-through without interruption.** During this final rehearsal, the director may keep notes so that he or she can comment on the production afterward. The comments should be mainly positive, to encourage the players and crew to do their best. If the performance is to run smoothly, few changes should be made in the production at this point.

7. Plan to present a formal production before an audience. Besides offering a means for appreciating the considerable efforts of the cast, crew, and director, the production of a play is intended to provide entertainment for others. Some groups plan more than one performance, for increased experience before an audience.

A Word About Royalties   Some plays, if presented formally, require payment of royalties. Be sure to check the title and copyright pages of a play script for a royalty statement before deciding to put the script into production.

A Sense of Accomplishment   Allot time when the production is over for evaluating what was learned, what was especially satisfying, and what might be done "next time" to make the production process flow more smoothly. Teachers and other adults involved need to remember that play production in schools is for education, appreciation, and pleasure. A good question to consider is this: "Ten years from now will this play be recalled by my students with pleasure and a sense of real accomplishment?"

Also remember that theater experience with literature is *direct* experience with literature. As author Tove Jansson has a wise character say in *Moomin's Summer Madness,* "A theatre is the most important sort of house in the world, because that's where people are shown what they could be if they wanted, and what they'd like to be if they dared to, and what they really are."[15]

Additional Readings

Coger, Lesley Irene, and Melvin R. White. *Readers Theatre Handbook: A Dramatic Approach to Literature.* 3d ed. Glenview, Ill.: Scott, Foresman, 1983. This handbook contains definitions and "rules" for successful productions, with helpful case studies of how the procedures have succeeded in schools.

McCaslin, Nellie. *Creative Drama in the Classroom,* 3d ed. New York: Longman, 1980. This edition gives reasons for using pantomime, improvisation, and creative dramatics. It is rich in examples of how to use drama in the classroom.

Provenmire, E. Kingsley. *Choral Speaking and the Verse Choir.* Cranbury, N.J.: A. S. Barnes, 1975. Definitions, procedures, and materials for verse choir are presented, with discussion focused on each age level.

Sebesta, Sam. "'Reading with More Expression' in the Elementary School." *Readers Theatre News* 9 (Spring/Summer 1982): 10–11. The author explains how oral interpretation and reading as a search for meaning in literature may go hand in hand in the classroom.

Siks, Geraldine Brain. *Drama with Children.* 2d ed. New York: Harper & Row, 1983. Types of drama, including a clear definition of Story Theater, are described in Chapter 3. The book contains ample activities—procedures and goals for each, with designated age levels.

15. Tove Jansson, *Moomin's Summer Madness* trans. Ernest Benn (New York: Avon Books, 1955), 105–106.

Literature and the Content Areas

TEXT STRUCTURE

There is renewed interest in the tie between literature and the content areas of the curriculum. Topics in literature overlap those in almost all the subject areas—social studies, science, health, mathematics, music, and art—that fact has long been noted. But recent evidence points to the importance of another connection: *text structure*—how written communication is organized and how it delivers its message. Literature is a key to help students unlock the complexities of text structure.

Structure in Nonfiction and Fiction

Informational nonfiction often is organized by patterns of logic. A stated main idea is accompanied by supporting evidence, or the evidence may be presented alone, leaving readers to infer the main idea. There are, of course, other patterns of logic—other text structures for informational nonfiction. What matters most is how clearly and consistently the patterns are followed to help the reader get the message.

Some kinds of nonfiction (a biography, a description of how things work) and nearly all works of fiction are organized by time sequence. For most young readers, text structure made up of a sequence of events is easiest to follow.[16] However, young readers still may have difficulty getting the intended messages from their reading. Connections among events, in-

16. Nancy Marshall, "Discourse Analysis as a Guide for Informal Assessment of Comprehension," in *Promoting Reading Comprehension* ed. by James Flood (Newark, Del.: International Reading Association, 1984): 79–96.

cluding cause-effect or effect-cause, may evade them, or they may have trouble clustering events to arrive at a generalization.

Patterns such as these are used in content-area textbooks, reference materials—and in literature; but the clarity and consistency of such patterns of text structure are most evident in literature.

Literature as Models of Structure

Authors of literature are successful messengers: their text structures bear the message home to their readers. Generally, authors of literature are free to explore a structure and topic as fully as they and their readers wish. Author Laura Ingalls Wilder, for instance, devotes several pages to the problems that beset the Ingalls family as they cross a swollen creek on their journey west ("Crossing The Creek," Level 4). Authors may also experiment, at a leisurely pace, with a combination of text structures. Janet Chenery, the author of the realistic fiction story "Wolfie" (Level 3), for example, combines time-sequence fiction about three children and their pet wolf spider with a remarkable amount of logically structured information about the wolf spider, including comparison-and-contrast diagrams.

Literature, then, affords students excellent models of text structure. When students are guided in their reading of these models, they become better able to tackle the structures of textbooks and other sources designated as content-area material. These content-area texts often are more mixed in structure and loaded with more information within a limited space than most works of fiction. Hence literature bridges the way to understanding them.

A similar case can be made in regard to sentence structure. Writers of literature are almost by definition masters of the sentence form. They shape a sentence to a point. Incidentally but effectively, they entice young readers to explore a widening variety of sentence structures.

Writers of literature also provide good models of *diction* or word choice. Writers of stories, poetry, and literary nonfiction choose their words with care—for accurate meaning, the right shade of meaning to fit the tone and context, for connotation, rhythm, and sound. Such qualities should not be confined to "artistic" or "literary" style. They are essential to communication, especially to the fine craft of writing and reading in the content areas.

What can be done to teach these aspects of text: text structure, sentence structure, and diction? The following list provides several teaching suggestions.

1. Provide good literary models showing structure and word choice at their best.

2. Provide good models of text processing. "Think out loud" to show students how a skilled reader skims the titles and content of an informational selection to discover its purpose and organization. Show diagraming techniques—diagrams of content within a selection. Read rich but possibly unfamiliar sentence structures aloud to students and, at times, ask them to echo the reading to "get the taste" of new structures and terms.

3. Give special attention to activities that teach students about text structure. Many such activities and the objectives they are designed to achieve are included in the ODYSSEY program.

USING LITERATURE SPECIFIC TO CONTENT AREA TOPICS

The Social Studies Facts and generalizations from the social studies are seen more clearly against a tapestry of literature. For best results, bring that tapestry to students before, during, and after they encounter a social studies topic. Begin a unit with rich schema-setting literature— the illustrated folklore of a continent to be studied, easy and exciting biographies, historical fiction that says "you are there," modern fiction that affords a visit to a distant place. Encourage deeper reading as the unit progresses. A social studies text reference to a famous historical figure, a crucial incident, or an intriguing custom can and should motivate a search for literature that tells more. When a social studies unit has been completed, related literature may keep the unit topic alive in the students' minds, to show students that there is an immediate application of their newly acquired social studies knowledge.

Interest is the prime reason for allying literature with the social studies. Social studies topics begin with the students' environment but soon extend to "expanding communities," increasingly distanced from readers' immediate experience. This is as it should be: education should expand one's horizons. But these journeys to distant places and times must have relevance and excitement—hence the need for literature to help make them so. As Dorothy Grant Hennings points out, especially in regard to interest aroused by folklore as a background for social studies, readers discover "basic problems of living that human beings have struggled with from earliest times."[17]

In ODYSSEY, fiction and nonfiction selections related to social studies content at each grade level have been included, with questions and activities to help read-

17. Dorothy Grant Hennings, "Reading Picture Storybooks in the Social Studies," *The Reading Teacher*, 36 (December 1982): 284–289.

ers bridge the connection between literature and subject matter. The range of topics in the social studies is vast; to find additional literature relevant to a topic often requires use of reference sources. The annual *Subject Guide to Children's Books in Print* and *Adventuring with Books* are two good places to start.

Science   Natural science and the other sciences are provinces of literature, as both fiction and nonfiction selections in ODYSSEY attest. What can pertinent literature add to science content? First, literature supports our sense of wonder. Literature helps us explore and expand our wonderings about the world through the eyes of gifted authors and illustrators. Second, literature fosters an appreciation of accuracy and quest for accuracy. Word denotations and precise detail in literature sharpen the reader's perceptions—like a fast walk on a crisp morning. Third, literature helps us synthesize experiences. It may show, for example, how ingenuity of invention confronts natural disasters ("Changes, Changes," Level 1) or how human survival may be based on understanding and using the natural environment ("Bando," Level 5).

At one time there was concern that nonscientific literature might actually harm a child's development of science concepts. Hens, pigs, and spiders do not really talk—but in literature they sometimes do! Such concern has abated. Children, even at an early school age, are apparently able to see the distinction between "real" and "make-believe"—or to note the distinction when their teachers help them do so. A fascinating anecdotal article by Frances A. Smardo goes further to point out that fanciful "nonscientific" stories are just the right contrast for arousing interest in finding out "how it really is"—hence for scientific investigation.[18] By the same logic, science fiction—even when it presents a future world that may not "come true"—inspires hypothesis making and substantiated conjecture that are rooted in science.

As for informational literature devoted to science itself—there is a wealth of it. Teachers can investigate accuracy and coverage of informational science selections by reading reviews in *Science Books & Films,* published five times a year by the American Association for the Advancement of Science. A monthly column in *The Horn Book Magazine,* "Views on Science Books," discusses selections recommended on the basis of literary merit as well as scientific content.

Mathematics   Sometimes it is hard to see the relevance of a content area to one's life, even when the area is mathematics and one is preoccupied with saving money to buy a baseball glove ("It Pays to Advertise," Level 4). Some children have trouble seeing the connection between story problems in the arithmetic book and the "story problems" of real life. One study showed the superior results in mathematics problem solving when children made their own "math stories" based on their own needs.[19] Perhaps these "math stories" could even be made from the situations and characters children meet in literature, for these stories, too, may add both context and interest to mathematical problems. Many of the mathematics objectives and extending activities in the ODYSSEY program are based on this likelihood.

Literature also offers selections with more direct application to mathematics, ranging from simple counting rhymes to complicated literary mathematical puzzles. These connections are discovered as teachers and children explore literature; a list of 32 such items, of interest to various age levels, can be found in a recent article which shows their application to teaching measurement, geometric concepts, size, time, and money calculations.[20]

Health   Try a "Tasty Lit" course, as one school did: match a folklore item with a cooking item, the recipe based on the ethnic origin of the folk tale.[21] Figure out all the forms of exercise the characters get on the pages of *Where the Clouds Go* (Level 1)—and emulate them! Plan a treat for Paddington to offset his penchant for sugar ("Paddington Goes to the Hospital," Level 4), or find out what Beth can do about her allergy ("An Allergy Is a Bothersome Thing," Level 5). The possibilities are wide and challenging when it comes to incorporating literature into the health curriculum. They include direct use of informational literature from the expanding list of new materials on nutrition, safety, and health maintenance. ODYSSEY selections and activities provide a start. Encourage students to pursue health-related topics further in their reading.

Art   The visual arts offer teachers and students a great variety of activities: drawing and painting, paper cutting, sculpting and modeling, constructing and printmaking. Any one of these can stir the

---

18. Frances A. Smardo, "Using Children's Literature to Clarify Science Concepts in Early Childhood Programs," *The Reading Teacher,* (December 1982): 267–273.

19. Robert W. Wirtz and Emily Kahn, "Another Look at Applications in Elementary School Mathematics," *Arithmetic Teacher,* 30 (September 1982): 21–25.

20. Nancy J. Smith and Karla Hawkins Wendelin, "Using Children's Books to Teach Mathematical Concepts," *Arithmetic Teacher,* 29 (November 1981): 10–15.

21. Nancy K. Cochran, "How I Teach Boys and Girls: Nutrition and World Literature," *Forecast for Home Economics,* 26 (January 1981): 59.

students' imaginations and provide them with a visual means of responding to literature.

The teacher's choice of which art activity will enhance a literary experience can be guided by class discussions of a particular selection. For example, if the discussion focuses on the *setting,* then students might sketch the setting or visualize it through collage. As they reread a description of a setting in a story or a poem, urge the students to develop a mental image. Then using pencil, crayon, pastel, charcoal, or another sketching instrument, they can sketch quickly on paper the scene in their imaginations. Later, details may be added and the scene may be finished with tempera paint, water color, chalk, or another medium.

Characters in literature also may fire the imagination. Following a discussion of a main character's traits, invite students to model that character from clay. Encourage them to represent what the character was like and the impression that character made upon the readers rather than on how the character looked. Finished clay figures, dried, or baked in a kiln, can be displayed against a painted or constructed background of the story's setting. Intermediate-grade students might sculpt figures from plaster of paris blocks.

In addition to individual art projects, you may sometimes wish to encourage group projects in response to literature. For example, students could create a mural or a large map of a "journey" story, labeling each place and major event in the story. Students also could make an *accordion book* by the following method: the class identifies the main events in the story; each student sketches one of the events; the sketches are arranged in order and then connected by loose stitching or metal rings. The result is a visual display of the story sequence.

Two visual art forms, *collage* and *mobile,* add variety to the literature-and-art program. Both can help students respond to literature holistically. A *collage* is a combination of textures (cloth, foil, small flat objects) and cut-out images (news photos, parts of magazine ads, etc.) arranged on a flat surface. Its effect is to mirror and augment the tone and mood of stories and poems. A collage can also reveal a theme—not just of one selection but of many related works. For example, themes of meeting challenges, forming relationships, and relating to the natural world may all be subjects for collages.

A *mobile* is also a combination of items, but now the pieces (pictures, objects) are suspended by string or wire, and balanced so that they seem to hang in the air, turning so that the viewer sees a constantly shifting pattern. Try a mobile made of folk characters and objects important in folk tales. Use this mobile as an introduction to "folk tale trivia" or literary allusion. Bring it out from time to time and ask students to identify each item and the folk tale from which it came.

Music The rhythms and sounds of words have their counterparts in the rhythms and sounds of music. One study shows that soft classical background music during reading aids comprehension.[22] A language arts professor comments: "With a little guidance, children can see that the composer has created an impression through rhythm and increased tempo in much the same way that a writer may use a contrast in sentence lengths to develop a sense of quickness or calm."[23]

22. Colleen N. Mullikin and William A. Henk, "Using Music as a Background for Reading: An Exploratory Study," *Journal of Reading,* 28 (January 1985): 353–358.

23. Dianne Monson, "The Literature Program and the Arts," *Language Arts,* 59 (March 1982): 254–258.

Poems with strong rhythms or pleasant-sounding lines can inspire song making. To create songs from poems, have the students read a poem several times to bring out the rhythm, phrasing, and mood. Use choral speaking techniques to do this. Then have them investigate beat and sample melodies, progressing line-by-line through the poem. When the final song version is put together, tape the melody or quickly notate it above a written version of the poem.

Musical instruments can be used to create sounds that will heighten the mood for oral reading or any performance of literature. A "signature tune," for instance, may announce the entrance of each character in the telling of a folk tale. Such tunes can be composed on a homemade xylophone, recorder, or kalimba. To stress the rhythm in a poem, use rhythm sticks, various types of drums, sand blocks, and maracas. Musical instruments may also be used to help establish the setting of a story or a play.

Listening to music may also enhance literary appreciation. To seek a literal tie between a literary selection and a musical selection is unnecessary. For example, no composer has written a symphony, ballet, or specific program music to accompany the Norwegian folk tale "The Three Billy Goats Gruff" (Level 1, Reader), yet children can find the troll and the setting of the drama in numerous works of the Norwegian composer Edvard Grieg. Played before, during, and after the reading of a selection, such music adds impact while developing the students' listening abilities.

A "suite" of music selections (segments from works of several composers) can be collected to accompany a unit in the ODYSSEY program. The "Tell Me the Name" unit in Level 3, for instance, with its variety of moods, might stimulate a search for music that matches those moods. One such "suite" might include Mussorgsky's "Pictures at an Exhibition" to accompany J. R. R. Tolkien's poem "Oliphaunt" and Richard Strauss's "Till Eulenspiegel's Merry Pranks" to accompany the tales of "Rumpelstiltskin" (Level 3). But that's only one opinion. Let children themselves search for music that makes a "suite" connection.

A list of composers whose works can parallel the moods and structures of literature encompasses the whole history of music. Note-worthy among Western composers might be the following: Leonard Bernstein, Benjamin Britten, Cecile Louise Chaminade, Aaron Copland, Manuel de Falla, Gian Carlo Menotti, and Igor Stravinsky—as well as those in the classical tradition and modern composers of popular music. Folk music of many cultures should also be included. Students should have exposure to the composition and instrumentation of Asian music. Of special interest is the close tie between North American Indian music and the story tradition it supports. *A Cry from the Earth* by John Bierhorst (Four Winds Press, 1979) is an excellent source for this material.

These are only a few of the boundless opportunities to promote literary appreciation and response through the visual arts and music. Boundless, too, is the pleasure to be gained.

Additional Readings

Barron, Pamela Patrick, and Jennifer Q. Burley, eds. *Jump Over the Moon.* New York: Holt, Rinehart and Winston, 1984. Selected articles help set criteria for biography, counting and alphabet books, historical fiction and other materials pertinent to the content areas.

Davies, Rita. "How the Arts Can Be Central to Classroom Learning." *Learning* 13 (January 1985): 25–27. A teacher writes of using visual arts and music to explore a theme presented by poetry.

Dupuis, Mary M., ed. *Reading in the Content Areas: Research for Teachers.* Newark, Del.: International Reading Association Clearinghouse on Reading and Communication Skills, 1984. Experts on seven content areas (mathematics, health, science, social studies, foreign language, English, music) identify skills and strategies most pertinent to their areas. The booklet includes substantial annotated bibliographies to help teachers pursue the topics further.

Gaitskell, Charles D., and Al Hurwitz. *Children and Their Art: Methods for the Elementary School.* 4th ed. New York: Harcourt Brace Jovanovich, 1982. This book presents a synthesis of child development and art development, with examples applicable to combining visual arts and literature.

Miccinati, Jeannette Louise, Judith B. Sanford, Gene Hepner. "Teaching Reading Through the Arts: An Annotated Bibliography." *The Reading Teacher* 36 (January 1983): 412–417. Thirty-three selections, well summarized, to help the teacher bring music, art, and drama together with reading of literature.

Monson, Dianne L. and the Committee on the Elementary School Booklist. *Adventuring with Books* Urbana, Ill: National Council of Teachers of English, 1985. Selected, annotated book lists arranged under topics relevant to the social studies, with age-level designations, make this book a most useful tool for the social studies teacher and student.

Smardo, Frances A. "Using Children's Literature as a Prelude or Finale to Music Experiences with Young Children." *The Reading Teacher* 37 (April 1984): 700–705. Research findings on this topic are accompanied by a breezily annotated list of children's literature to use with dance, singing, and musical instruments.

Taub, K. Deborah. "The Endearing, Enduring Folktale." *Instructor* XCIV (November/December 1984): 61–70. Excellent resources, including folklore selected from many regions, show how such literature augments learning (and teaching) in the content areas.

Taylor, Gail Cohen. "Music in Language Arts Instruction." *Language Arts* 58 (March 1981): 363–367. A review of recent writing on music as an aid to story enjoyment; includes a list of resources for teachers.

A Strategy for Decoding

To grow into truly independent readers, children must become increasingly skillful at decoding unfamiliar words they encounter in print. Since genuine skill results from extensive practice, you may wish to use the following strategy to help children decode some of the unfamiliar words they encounter in selections in this book. In so doing, you will not only help children achieve an immediate objective—decoding a particular word in a selection—but also contribute to their achieving a broader goal—developing a genuine decoding skill.

This strategy is useful in helping children identify only those words that are unfamiliar in print, but are familiar in speech—words that are not in their "reading vocabularies," but are in their "listening and speaking vocabularies." Such words are numerous, especially with young children. The strategy encourages children to take advantage of both phonics clues and context clues in identifying unfamiliar printed words and often enables children to "decode" such words even before they have learned all of the sound–letter relationships required for complete phonic analysis.

Work through the following decoding strategy step by step with the children:

1. Select a word that is in the children's speaking and listening vocabularies, but is likely to be unfamiliar to them in print.

Example: fruit

2. Create a sentence that includes that word and no other unfamiliar words. The sentence should contain one of the following strong context clues:
   a. a synonym for the unfamiliar word,
   b. an antonym for the unfamiliar word,
   c. a definition of the unfamiliar word, or
   d. any other strong context clue (such as a modifier or an example)

Example: She took an **apple** from the fruit basket.

3. Display the sentence to the children with a blank in place of the unfamiliar word.

Example: She took an apple from the ___ basket.

4. Ask the children to read the sentence aloud and try to identify the missing word. Tell them to think of words that make sense in the sentence.

Example: She took an apple from the grocery, food, fruit basket.

5. Write the first letter of the unfamiliar word in the blank. Ask the children to read the sentence again and try to identify which word or words from step 4 now fit in the blank.

Example: She took an apple from the f___ basket. (Either *food* or *fruit* could fit in the sentence.)

6. Write the second letter of the unfamiliar word in the blank. If necessary, ask the children to read the sentence again to identify the word.

Example: She took an apple from the fr___ basket.

7. Repeat this procedure until a pronounceable sound (consonant–vowel combination) appears. Write the consonant–vowel combination in the blank and pronounce the partial word.

Example: She took an apple from the frui basket.

8. If the children still have not identified the word, repeat the procedure, adding a letter each time until the children correctly identify the word. If they identify the word before you write all the letters, complete writing the word in the blank.

Example: She took an apple from the fruit basket.

9. Review by asking:
• Does the word make sense in the sentence? What clues in the sentence helped you decide?
• Do the sound combinations match the letters in the word?

Example: Both *food* and *fruit* make sense in the sentence, but the sound–letter combinations of the word *food* do not fit the sound–letter combinations written in the blank.

Poetry and the Teacher

Myra Cohn Livingston

I am myself,
of all my atom parts I am the sum.
And out of my blood and my brain
I make my own interior weather,
my own sun and rain.
Imprint my mark upon the world,
whatever I shall become.

Eve Merriam, "Thumbprint"

ROBERT FROST has written that a poem "begins in delight and ends in wisdom." The Irish poet James Stephens tells us that "What the heart knows today the head will understand tomorrow." In these words both poets suggest one of the most meaningful ways of introducing children to poetry: to infect with *delight,* stress the *joy,* approach through the *heart,* and know that wisdom and understanding will follow. It makes all the difference.

Children grow into poetry, beginning with Mother Goose. From the first time they hear rhyming verses that tell a small story, that play with words, that move along with bouncing rhythms, that stress rhyme, they are affirming a basic need to listen with both heart and movement—to respond with pleasure.

Jack be nimble,
Jack be quick,
Jack jump over
The candlestick.

Even nonsense poems allow them to test their own knowledge of what is true and what is not, to improve their self-images, and to be able to laugh both at others and at themselves:

Far and few, far and few,
Are the lands where the Jumblies live:
Their heads are green, and their hands
are blue;
And they went to sea in a sieve.

Edward Lear, "The Jumblies"

New discoveries, thoughts, dreams, and widely ranging emotions surround children as they grow up. Poetry mirrors their experiences through a more sophisticated handling of imagery, rhythm, and sound. What distinguishes poetry from other forms of literature is a rhythm that almost invites our bodies to move, our fingers to tap, our feet to dance; combinations of words that make us wish to repeat them aloud; rhymes, oftentimes, that encourage us to make up our own series of sounds; and a sort of irresistible music that engages heart, mind, and body. From the simplest folk rhyme to the ballad, from the traditional to the most experimental contemporary poem, poetry gives children room where their emotions and imaginations may run free.

DISCOVERING POETRY

The delight of poetry is in discovery: a new image, a different way of looking, the pleasure of words and rhythms used well, a humorous idea, an eccentric person, a striking metaphor. The delight is in the freedom to choose from among so many kinds of poems the ones that speak to us. The delight is in becoming familiar with riddles and limericks, haiku and counting rhymes, ballads and shape poems. The delight remains so long as children are able to come to a poem and find something of themselves and their world mirrored, extended, or even stretched. The delight allows them to act out the stories in pantomime or dance, to sculpt, to illustrate, to chant the words aloud, alone or with others, to try writing poems of their own, to respond in individual ways to the poetry they hear and read.

In the ten books of the ODYSSEY series, teachers will find verse and poetry to bring delight and pleasure. Here are traditional verses that have long been favorites of young readers, juxtaposed with verse by contemporary poets who write for today's young people. A mixture of light and serious verse spanning centuries and cultures has been selected within the thematic strands to afford a wide choice for both teacher and student. It may certainly happen that some of the selections will not appeal to every child or teacher. All of us hear a different tune. Some enjoy rhyming verse and ordered meter, while others prefer a freer, more open approach to poetry. Humorous verse, limericks, and riddles appeal to some; poetry with a more serious tone, a different mood, to others. Fortunately there are enough poems for all. Both teachers and students should always feel free to pick and choose what is meaningful to them as individuals.

It is here, I believe, that the wisdom and understanding of which Robert Frost and James Stephens spoke become important. Wisdom is *not* the message given by a poem to a reader; wisdom is *not* didacticism cajoling, exhorting, or instructing the reader of a poem to behave in a certain fashion; wisdom is *not* high-flown sentiments in lofty diction. Nor is wisdom achieved by tearing apart a poem to find what figures of speech, what symbolism it may contain. Rather, wisdom is acquired by knowing that as we read poetry we grow in understanding. Wisdom is found by relating our thoughts and emotions as individuals to ourselves and to others about us, to other cultures, other centuries, other places. Wisdom comes in knowing that the best poetry has something to say for each of us if we first make the commitment to find the delight. Wisdom also implies that *com*prehending is not nearly so important as *ap*prehending. As John Ciardi has pointed out, it is important that we never ask "*What* does a poem mean?" but rather "*How* does a poem mean?" For Ciardi, the skillful combination of idea, form, words, and rhythm separates real poetry from mere pleasantries put into verse form.

Most likely we will not want to speak to children about methods of delighting or wisdom and understanding. What we can do is try to show them that poetry is part of life. Poetry has something to say about the way we view ourselves, our world, and everything in that world from a drop of rain to mirrors in the Fun House to our feelings about ourselves. Poetry can be funny, it can be sad. It is not, as many believe, a unit of study we get once a year filled with iambic pentameter and some poems to memorize.

Because of the increasing number of fine poetry anthologies available, it is possible for teachers in all grades to relate poetry to almost any subject. History might be studied using some of the folk poetry of America. Numerous poems deal with science and math. The ODYSSEY Teacher's Editions offer a wide variety of suggestions for integrating poetry with other arts—painting, dancing, creative writing, and dramatics, to name just a few.

Our most difficult job as teachers today may well lie in the need to elicit imaginative responses. In a world that promotes an unusual amount of passivity, reliance on mass media, and a great deal of programmed response, teachers need to touch the imagination of each child, to encourage this individual reaction to what is heard or read. In a single classroom there may be but a handful of children who respond to a given poem, but this reaction should be praised and nurtured. What happens when a poem and the right listener, the right reader, come together can be magic.

SHARING POETRY IN THE CLASSROOM

It will come as no surprise to teachers that few children today hear nursery rhymes at home. The classroom may well be the first place children hear poetry, and the teacher may well be the first person who reads poetry to them aloud. No matter what age or level of the students, poetry should be read aloud as often as possible.

Many of the poems in the ten ODYSSEY readers are suitable for individual and choral reading. Students can organize group readings of poems or memorize them for the joy of it. Many balk at the idea of memorization, but if a student especially likes a poem, the results can be wonderful! Whole classes have put on poetry programs to entertain other classes until the entire school becomes infected with the joy of performing. Again, if imagination is encouraged by the teacher, the students benefit not only from their personal response to poetry but grow with their hearts and minds to bring its enjoyment to others. Here are a few suggestions to help you get started.

1. *Choose poems you like and those you think your class will like.* Teachers cannot elicit enthusiasm for work they themselves do not enjoy. Be aware that riddles, limericks, and light verse will always be received well, but that other kinds of poetry will help young people grow in their perceptions and relationships with others.

2. *Encourage students to find verses and poems and share them with the class.*

3. *Experiment with different ways of reading the sounds and rhythms of poems.* One way to read a poem is to read each line as a separate idea followed by a pause.

Who has seen the wind? (pause)
Neither you nor I: (pause)
But when the trees bow down their
       heads (pause)
The wind is passing by.

               Christina Rossetti,
               ''Who Has Seen the Wind?''

Another way is to pause at the punctuation in a line. In this stanza, then, the question mark at the end of line 1 indicates a pause, as does the colon at the end of line 2. In the third line, however, one could either pause after the word *heads* or read the last two lines as one long sentence. There is no right or wrong.

4. *Don't be afraid to make mistakes when you read poems aloud.* Everyone does. If you flub a reading, pick up and start again—this will help minimize the students' embarrassment when they make mistakes in their own readings. Both teacher and students can learn together.

5. *Read with your heart rather than your head.* If you wish to laugh as you read, do so. When a poem is sad, don't hide your sadness; let it enter your voice just as you would let happiness.

Children know what emotions are—do not underestimate their ability to know if you are reading with honesty. They would much rather have a flawed, sincere reading from you than the perfectly enunciated recitation on a tape or record.

Don't be afraid to make the leap. Leave your head in arithmetic, in history, in social studies, in science; and bring your heart and sense of delight to poetry! You may astound yourself; you will astound your students—and together you will begin a love for poetry that you may never before have imagined possible.

Myra Cohn Livingston, ODYSSEY's poetry consultant, is Poet-in-Residence for the Beverly Hills Unified School District and a Senior Instructor at UCLA Extension. The author of thirty books, she has received many awards for her poetry, including the National Council of Teachers of English Award for Excellence in Poetry for Children, which was awarded her in 1980.

Bibliography

Books About Poetry

Ciardi, John. *How Does a Poem Mean?* Boston: Houghton Mifflin, 1959.

Hughes, Ted. *Poetry Is.* New York: Doubleday, 1970.

Kennedy, X. J. *An Introduction to Poetry.* 4th ed. Boston: Little, Brown, 1978.

Individual Poets

Bodecker, N. M. *Hurry, Hurry, Mary Dear! and Other Nonsense Poems.* New York: Atheneum, 1976.

Gasztold, Carmen Bernos de. *Prayers from the Ark.* New York: Viking Press, 1962.

Giovanni, Nikki. *Spin a Soft Black Song.* London: Leonard Hill Books, 1971.

Hughes, Langston. *Don't You Turn Back.* New York: Alfred A. Knopf, 1969.

Kennedy, X. J. *The Phantom Ice Cream Man: More Nonsense Verse.* New York: Atheneum, 1979.

Merriam, Eve. *Finding a Poem.* New York: Atheneum, 1970.

Moore, Lilian. *Think of Shadows.* New York: Atheneum, 1980.

Sandburg, Carl. *Wind Song.* New York: Harcourt, Brace, 1960.

Silverstein, Shel. *Where the Sidewalk Ends.* New York: Harper & Row, 1974.

Starbird, Kaye. *Don't Ever Cross a Crocodile.* Philadelphia: J. B. Lippincott, 1963.

Worth, Valerie. *Still More Small Poems.* New York: Farrar, Straus & Giroux, 1978.

Anthologies

Behn, Harry, trans. *Cricket Songs.* New York: Harcourt Brace Jovanovich, 1964. Haiku attuned to young people.

Benedetti, Mario, ed. *Unstill Life: An Introduction to the Spanish Poetry of Latin America.* Translated by Darwin J. Flakoll and Claribel Alegria. New York: Harcourt Brace & World, 1969.

Bierhorst, John, ed. *In the Trail of the Wind: American Indian Poems and Ritual Orations.* New York: Farrar, Straus & Giroux, 1971.

Bontemps, Arna, ed. *Hold Fast to Dreams: Poems Old and New.* Chicago: Follett, 1969. Poems by Black Americans.

Brewton, John E., and Blackburn, Lorraine A., comps. *They've Discovered a Head in the Box for the Bread and Other Laughable Limericks.* New York: Harper & Row, 1978.

Livingston, Myra Cohn, ed. *O Frabjous Day! Poetry for Holidays and Special Occasions.* New York: Atheneum, 1978.

Mackay, David, ed. *A Flock of Words: An Anthology of Poetry for Children and Others.* New York: Harcourt Brace Jovanovich, 1970. A splendid collection for middle grades and older readers.

Folk Literature and the Teacher

Barre Toelken

'Twas on a Thursday evening
late in the fall of the year. The
weather was wild outside. Rain fell
and the wind blew till the walls of
the cottage shook. There they all
sat around the fire, busy with this
thing and that. But all at once,
something gave three taps on the
windowpane—tap! tap! tap!

*East O' the Sun and
West O' the Moon,* a
Norwegian folk tale

SOMETIMES, in our rush to expose students to the best and most lasting examples of literature, we strive to present all the famous and well-known authors without recognizing that our students, and we ourselves, already come equipped with a fund of literary experience learned from our own families, friends, regional and ethnic groups. Even though the word *literature* is based on a Latin term meaning "letters" or "writing," the creation of stories, rituals, poetry, songs, drama, and games is as old as humankind itself: only in the most recent few minutes on history's clock has literary expression had much to do directly with the written word. But just as the ancient Greeks recited poems about epic adventures of centuries past, we continue oral traditions today as we tell jokes, legends, proverbs, riddles, and tales, using figures of speech and slang and varying our vocal tones to indicate such abstractions as sarcasm,

parody, love, stress, and commitment. In other words, much of the *quality* of our expressions, much of the *feel* of situations that bring us to laughter or give voice to our anxieties, continue to be expressed orally and often in the shared, inherited forms we call *folklore*.

Folklore provides a broad and complex field of study, but for practical purposes we can say that it is made up of informally learned beliefs, customs, mores, expressions, gestures, and observances that we come to know not through the formal channels of education, but by everyday associations with the people closest to us. We do not learn these primarily through print or other official channels; rather, they come to us in the jokes we hear from our families and friends, the gestures we pick up from those around us, the customs we use at birthday parties and religious holidays, the foods we eat at festival times, the lullabies we sing to our children, and the games we learn from each other. Folklore is also made up of the different narrative forms it takes as it is passed along: riddles, jingles, counting-out rhymes, folk songs, jump-rope rhymes, folk tales, legends, myths, and fables. The word *folklore,* then, simply refers to any traditions that people actually share, perform, or recall.

An important element in every type of folklore is the use of repetition. We find repetition in all literature, of course, but written literature tends to reduce or hide it in order to avoid redundancy, while folklore tends to emphasize it in order to produce a more recognizable structure and sense of direction. In northern Europe and among European Americans, the most common organizational and structural device is the use of three-part repetition. We look forward to the third occurrence because we know that something different or important will happen there. For example, the glass slipper in *Cinderella* cannot really fit the foot of the first sister, for it would destroy all our expectations, get rid of suspense, and make the story pointless. The key thing to remember is that different cultures use different kinds of repetition. Some, like many Native American tribes and several cultures in Asia, use a four-way repetition, which suggests a circle of the four directions instead of a linear movement toward a surprise ending. A few groups, like many of the Pacific Northwest Indian tribes, use the number five to suggest a cluster of stability (five villages, five chiefs, five adventures). We must always look for the way repetition is actually employed in folklore before we can see beyond the repeated patterns into the unstated assumptions of the culture whose game, legend, myth, or folk tale we and our students seek to understand.

Because folklore is transmitted orally, it "takes form" when it is actually being shared—when someone tells a story or a joke, when children jump rope, or when we sing "Happy Birthday to You" to someone. We can always learn something by looking beyond the words and into the situation where they come to life. Thus we understand the meaning of a folk expression only when we understand its context, including the customs and values which are its cultural "surroundings."

One important function of folklore is that it helps us reexperience and demonstrate the depth of connection with our closest groups. In some societies, the individual is encouraged to become quite independent from family and culture. At the same time, this very independence can be loaded with emotional uncertainty, alienation, and even fear. Folklore traditions compensate for the potential isolation an individual might feel by supplying a surrounding of familiar, shared values and expressions that make cultural life meaningful and stable. In other cultures, folk traditions are precisely what bind individuals together into a functioning group.

Beyond this, there is a practical reason for including a serious look at folklore in any introduction to literature: our students and we ourselves already know what's going on in it. Since our students already know and use counting and jump-rope rhymes, jokes, and word games, it should not be difficult to engage them in meaningful conversations about context, meaning, and usage—matters that, after all, not only help them understand their own expressions better but might well serve as a way of presenting written literature as closely related to what they already know. Students who can recognize metaphors in their own speech are less likely to find the metaphors of others strange. Instead of fighting the use of slang, we can profitably discuss it to see what it accomplishes. (What we find is that slang often does the same thing that poetry does: it says things with more power.) We can probe with our students which slang terms are powerful and which ones are not.

Students who see that their own jokes and games have structure and meaning will be more aware of structure and meaning in other kinds of literature. Students can easily talk about jump-rope games and rhymes in terms of structure, word play, and rhythms as well as the way they parody stock situations in the adult world and in their own. Customs determining who gets to keep a found object, who may go first in a game, who must be "it," as well as customs determining "correct" behavior in the group, are all expressed with specific traditional phrases, many of which use rhyme or metaphor. Ask students to discuss "dibs," "finders keepers," and the like, and it will be more natural to move to a discussion of word play, rhythm, metaphor, parody, and expressive joy in all literature.

Too often we assume that "real literature" is so far beyond our students that they cannot possibly understand its meanings and styles. A discussion of their own folklore, should help them see that literary expression is not foreign to the experience of ordinary human beings.

Indeed, many of the most powerful and lasting pieces of literature in all languages have been based on the topics, structures, and styles of oral literature, and many of them existed first as oral literature long before they were written down. We think of *Beowulf,* the *Iliad,* the *Odyssey, El Cid,* the Yugoslav epics, the English and Scottish popular, or folk, ballads, and the great, powerful myths of all major cultures. We recall, too, that Willa Cather, Chaucer, Shakespeare, T. S. Eliot, George Eliot, Langston Hughes, and others too numerous to mention have utilized folklore in their works to gain the tremendous literary power that comes from using familiar references to worlds of perception they and their audiences were already immersed in, their shared sense of reality, their concepts of the human cultural situation, that they learned from childhood onward.

As teachers, we can help students recognize, rather than avoid, these culturally shaped resources, these familiar codes that they themselves may apply to the deeper perception and enjoyment of literature. Students can more easily see the relationship between themselves and literature when they can see and hear what they have in common with poets—and that makes one fine place to start.

Barre Toelken is director of the Folklore and Ethnic Studies Program and professor of English at the University of Oregon. A Fulbright Research Professor in 1979—80 and a past president of the American Folklore Society, Dr. Toelken is a consultant on folklore for the National Endowment for the Arts, as well as a consultant on Native American culture for school districts throughout the country.

Bibliography

Professional Readings in Folklore

Brunvand, Jan Harold. *The Study of American Folklore.* 2d ed. New York: W. W. Norton, 1978. This basic textbook on folklore genres in America has separate descriptive and illustrative chapters on folk tales, myths, folk songs, customs, games, crafts, and so on.

Knapp, Mary, and Knapp, Herbert. *One Potato, Two Potato: The Folklore of American Children.* New York: W. W. Norton, 1978.

Opie, Iona, and Opie, Peter. *The Lore and Language of School Children.* London: Oxford University Press, 1959.

Toelken, Barre. *The Dynamics of Folklore.* Boston: Houghton Mifflin, 1979.

Folklore Anthologies for Children

Emrich, Duncan. *The Hodgepodge Book.* New York: Four Winds Press, 1972.

Lomax, Alan. *The Folk Songs of North America.* Garden City, N.Y.: Dolphin Books, 1975.

Thompson, Stith, ed. *One Hundred Favorite Folktales.* Bloomington, Ind.: Indiana University Press, 1968.

Resource Center

About the Authors and Illustrators

These notes present some information about the authors and illustrators in this book about whom biographical material was available. You may wish to read them aloud as you introduce the selections.

Andersen, Hans Christian (1805–1875) A failure as an actor, singer, dancer, and writer for adults, Hans Christian Andersen became successful only when he began writing children's fairy tales. In 1835 he wrote four short tales for the daughter of the secretary of the Academy of Art. Those tales, *The Tinderbox, Little Ida's Flowers, Little Claus and Big Claus,* and *The Princess on the Pea,* as well as his other fairy tales, are read world wide today and have made him immortal.

Baylor, Byrd A lifetime resident of the Southwest, Byrd Baylor says, "I just write about whatever I care about myself— which usually turns out to be some part of the Southwest . . . All the people and places I love most are very free spirited, and that is the feeling I'd like to have in whatever I write."

Behn, Harry As careers, Harry Behn wrote movie scenarios, taught school, and ran a little theater, but privately he enjoyed entertaining his three children with his poems. Twenty years later, his almost forgotten poems were published. When asked where he got the ideas for his writing, he said, "All of my stories and poems derive from dreams."

Bond, Michael See page 325 of the pupil's textbook for the feature about this author.

Byars, Betsy Though Betsy Byars had written articles for many magazines, writing only became her main interest when she began writing for children. Her own children sparked this interest. She has even used many of their experiences and activities in her books, especially in the story *The Midnight Fox.* This personal connection has made that story her favorite.

Ciardi, John /chär′•dē/ When he was already a famous poet and translator, John Ciardi decided to write for the children around him. He began writing poems as a game for his nephews and then for his children, but he says, "Now I write for myself. My children are in a hurry to grow up, I'm not; so I write for my own childhood."

Cleary, Beverly See page 285 of the pupil's textbook for the feature about this author.

Cohen, Barbara For her writing, Barbara Cohen uses her own childhood memories and stories that friends and relatives have told her about their youth. She has also drawn on the richness of her Jewish heritage for such stories as *The Carp in the Bathtub* and *Bitter Herbs and Honey.*

Cousins, Margaret Margaret Cousins enjoys writing and history. She combines these two interests successfully in many of her books, such as *Ben Franklin of Old Philadelphia* and *We Were There at the Battle of the Alamo.* Throughout her writing, she seeks to entertain, which makes her books so readable. She has said that she "wanted to write books for children, because the books I read as a child meant so much to me . . . I lived out on the prairie and did not know other children so that these worlds of books enriched my life and gave me a taste for literature and the wish to write. . . ."

dePaola, Tomie As a young boy Tomie dePaola made two promises to himself: one, that he would never tell children anything that was not true; two, that he would become an artist and a writer. He accomplished both of these goals and today has been recognized for his beautiful illustrations and his imaginative stories. His book *Strega Nona* was a Caldecott Honor Book in 1976 and also an American Library Association Notable Book in that year.

Estes, Eleanor Though she always wanted to become a writer, Eleanor Estes /ehs′•tēz/ said, "I never really decided to write for children. It just happened that I did." She filled her warm and funny stories with many memories of her own childhood. Often, in the middle of the night, she would remember what someone said or did. She wrote these memories down and later used them in the stories she wrote.

Field, Rachel (1894–1942) Rachel Field was the first woman to win the Newbery Medal (1924) for *Hitty: Her First Hundred Years.* She was not always a success, however: "I wasn't one of those children who are remembered by their . . . teachers as particularly promising. I was more than ten years old before I could

read. I was . . . lazy and behind . . . in everything except drawing pictures, acting in plays, and . . . poetry . . . ."

Froman, Robert Robert Froman is the author of a number of children's science and mathematics books. His personal interest in haiku led him to write poetry for young people. He believes children have a natural, spontaneous appreciation of poetry in all its forms. Robert Froman says that he hopes his poems will lead readers to the beauty and excitement of poetry.

Hancock, Sibyl See page 489 of the pupil's textbook for the feature about this author.

Hayes, William D. Born in Goliad, Texas, William D. Hayes is a writer, artist, and cartoonist who co-authored *Mexicali Soup* with Kathryn Hitte. His cartoons have been published in national magazines and newspapers.

Heide, Florence Parry Florence Parry Heide lives in Kenosha, Wisconsin, with her husband and five children. Among other books, she has written *Giants Are Very Brave* and *The Shrinking of Treehorn.* She has also collaborated with her daughter Roxanne on a series of mysteries for young readers.

Hitte, Kathryn Kathryn Hitte (hit) is a contributor of fiction, nonfiction, poetry, and plays to reading textbooks and anthologies published in the United States and Canada. Of her desire to become a writer she says: "I cannot remember when I did not want to be a writer. . . .Of course it's fun to write, and when a story is going well it becomes truly exciting. . . ."

Hughes, Langston See page 219 of the pupil's textbook for the feature about this poet.

Hughes, Ted English poet and novelist Ted Hughes believes that "Poets write poems to amuse themselves, partly." He has written *Poetry Is,* an informal introduction to poetry for young readers; *Nessie, The Mannerless Monster; Moon-Whales and Other Poems;* and many other works for children. He also has had a program for children on British television.

Kennedy, X. J. Poet X. J. Kennedy says that "writing verses and stories has preoccupied me since the age of nine or ten. . . ." While his children were growing up he would make up stories and verses to divert them. He kept the ones they liked in his drawer, later to be used as a collection of nonsensical verses. In his development as a writer, he has received a great deal of support from poet Myra Cohn Livingston. He uses an X in his name to distinguish him from ". . . the better-known Kennedys."

Lear, Edward (1812–1888) Edward Lear was an Englishman who spent a great deal of his life alone with his imagination. As a professional artist, he taught landscape painting to Queen Victoria. To amuse children he knew, he made drawings and wrote limericks. These limericks, accompanied by his drawings, were published, became very popular, and are loved to this day.

Livingston, Myra Cohn Myra Cohn Livingston began writing poetry at the age of five and has kept a journal since she was ten years old. She writes at any time of the day or night. She also spends her time teaching, listening to and playing music, going to bookstores and the beach, and caring for her family. In 1980 Myra Cohn Livingston won the National Council of Teachers of English Award for Excellence in Poetry for Children.

MacGregor, Ellen (1906–1954) Ellen MacGregor began writing children's books in 1946, but her accounts of Miss Pickerell's science-fantasy adventures began in 1950—first as a magazine story

and then as a book. Ellen MacGregor held strong opinions about science fantasy: "It's such a satisfying form of literature . . . . Stories like that are so refreshing with their combination of delightful absurdity and utter logic. . . ." In all her stories, the scientific information is accurate, yet she managed to explain such things as weightlessness in space, atomic energy, and carbon-14 testing so that anyone could understand them. Though Ellen MacGregor wrote only a few books about Miss Pickerell before her death, Dora Pantell picked up the story thread and has continued the series.

McGovern, Ann Ann McGovern feels strongly that children's books should have both heroes and heroines of all races. She is the author of *Black Is Beautiful, Runaway Slave: The Story of Harriet Tubman,* and many other books.

Mowat, Farley Canadian nature writer Farley Mowat has been intimately involved with the outdoors since he went birdwatching in the Arctic as a young boy. He is most interested in natural things and in people who try to live in harmony with nature.

Norris, Leslie Leslie Norris is best known for his poetry, about which he says, "My poetry is an attempt to recreate, not to describe." His talent for using simple language to express common experiences has helped to create his style. *Merlin and the Snake's Egg* is a collection of his poems that includes "Buying a Puppy," the poem reprinted in the student's text.

Pantell, Dora Though Miss Pickerell was created by Ellen MacGregor, Miss Pickerell's adventures have continued under the direction of writer Dora Pantell. By sifting through boxes of notes and story plans left by Ellen MacGregor, Dora Pantell was able to write many new Miss Pickerell books, including *Miss Pickerell on the Moon, Miss Pickerell Harvests the Sea,* and *Miss Pickerell Goes to Mars.* The new adventures capture the spirit of the original books and continue to teach young people interesting scientific facts.

Sandburg, Carl (1878–1967)   Though Carl Sandburg might be called the American grandfather of poetry, he was always interested in arithmetic too. In his student days Carl Sandburg was selected as a candidate for the United States Military Academy at West Point. He left after two weeks, however, because he had failed the tests in arithmetic and grammar! Later in his life, Carl Sandburg won the Pulitizer Prize twice: once for his biography of Abraham Lincoln (1939) and another time for his *Complete Poems* (1950).

Schwartz, Alvin   Alvin Schwartz first became interested in folklore when a child. He enjoyed knowing and telling all the jokes, riddles, and silly songs that were popular. At that time, he says, he never realized that "these games, songs, jokes, tales, and customs were often very old, that ordinary people like me had created them." Now he collects folklore from the folk, especially from children and the elderly.

Sobol, J. Donald   In addition to the well-known Encyclopedia Brown series for young readers, Donald J. Sobol has written adult mysteries and a syndicated newspaper series "Two-Minute Mystery." In 1976 he won the Mystery Writers of America Edgar Allan Poe Award. About his books for children, he comments, "I have tried to write the kind of books I wanted to read when I was a boy but could not find."

Spier, Peter   When Peter Spier was working on the watercolor pictures for his picture book *The Erie Canal,* he traveled to the area where the canal used to be. There he visited the Canal Museum in Syracuse, New York, to learn as much as possible about what life was like and how the area looked in the days of the canal. You can see the results of his visit and research in his fine illustrations.

Steig, William   William Steig has been a successful cartoonist and artist most of his life but only began writing and illustrating books for children when he was in his sixties. In 1970 he won the Caldecott Medal for *Sylvester and the Magic Pebble.*

Tresselt, Alvin   Alvin Tresselt credits his older sister for nurturing his love of nature. She taught him "the joys of the seed catalog, and the satisfaction of planting seeds and tending them as they grew." He has written over forty children's books, including the Caldecott Medal winner *White Snow, Bright Snow.*

Van Leeuwen, Jean   Jean Van Leeuwen often uses humor to make a serious point, and she tries to recreate certain remembered experiences from childhood. She started writing books for very young children and is now also writing for girls in their teens. She says she will continue to write as long as she has something to say that will benefit children of all ages. Among her humorous children's books are *Benjy and the Power of Zingies, The Great Cheese Conspiracy,* and *The Great Christmas Kidnapping Caper.*

White, Anne Terry   Anne Terry White has been a teacher, a social worker, and an editor, as well as a writer. She speaks Russian and French, and loves to travel. Though most of her writings are on historical subjects, she also has adapted many classic stories and books for children, including *Aesop's Fables.*

White, E. B. E. B. White, best known to adults as an essayist, columnist, and editor, began writing stories for children only after moving to a farm in Maine. That's where the story about Wilbur the pig was born. As E. B. White was feeding his own pig, he began feeling sorry for it and started thinking of ways to save it. A large spider was in the barn too. Soon the pig and the spider became the main characters of *Charlotte's Web.* E. B. White's other works for children include *Stuart Little* and *The Trumpet of the Swan.* He has said that although all of his stories are imaginary, he believes there is always some truth in them about how people and animals act and feel.

Wilder, Laura Ingalls See page 161 of the pupil's textbook for the feature about this author.

Williams, Garth Artist Garth Williams was working for *The New Yorker* magazine when E. B. White asked him to illustrate *Stuart Little.* It was the first book he ever illustrated, and he has been illustrating children's books ever since. He says that he starts by looking at a real animal and draws it over and over again until it looks like it has the human qualities he wants.

Wilson, Beth P. Beth Wilson was inspired to pursue writing at an early age. As a child, she wrote detailed letters to her favorite aunt. Her aunt looked forward to receiving them because they painted a vivid picture of people and places. Beth Wilson feels that authors have a responsibility to society to write books that will help people understand each other better and bring all people closer together.

Worth, Valerie Valerie Worth is the author of the story *Curlicues: The Fortunes of Two Pug Dogs,* as well as several poetry collections, including *Small Poems* and *More Small Poems.* Her interests in astronomy and gardening often provide subject matter for her poetry.

Poetry for Reading Aloud

The following poems are recommended as related reading in the teaching lessons for this level.

THE MOON'S THE NORTH WIND'S COOKY (WHAT THE LITTLE GIRL SAID)
A poem by Vachel Lindsay

The Moon's the North Wind's cooky.
He bites it, day by day,
Until there's but a rim of scraps
That crumble all away.

The South Wind is a baker.
He kneads clouds in his den,
And bakes a crisp new moon
    that. . . greedy
North . . . Wind . . . eats . . . again!

From
THE JUMBLIES
A poem by Edward Lear

And all night long they sailed away;
    And when the sun went down,
They whistled and warbled a moony song
To the echoing sound of a coppery gong,
    In the shade of the mountains brown.
"O Timballoo! How happy we are

When we live in a sieve and a crockery-jar!
And all night long, in the moonlight pale,
We sail away with a pea-green sail
  In the shade of the mountains brown."
    Far and few, far and few,
      Are the lands where the Jumblies
      live:
  Their heads are green, and their
      hands are blue;
  And they went to sea in a sieve.

They sailed to the Western Sea, they did,—
  To a land all covered with trees:
And they bought an owl, and a useful cart,
And a pound of rice, and a cranberry-tart,
  And a hive of silvery bees;
And they bought a pig, and some green
    jackdaws,
And a lovely monkey with lollipop paws,
And forty bottles of ring-bo-ree,
  And no end of Stilton cheese.
    Far and few, far and few,
      Are the lands where the Jumblies
      live:
  Their heads are green, and their
      hands are blue;
  And they went to sea in a sieve.

PUBLIC LIBRARY

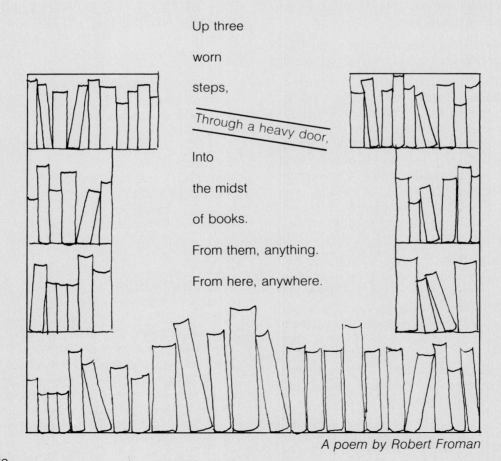

Up three

worn

steps,

Through a heavy door,

Into

the midst

of books.

From them, anything.

From here, anywhere.

A poem by Robert Froman

Music for a Song in Level 4

OLD JOE CLARKE
A folk song

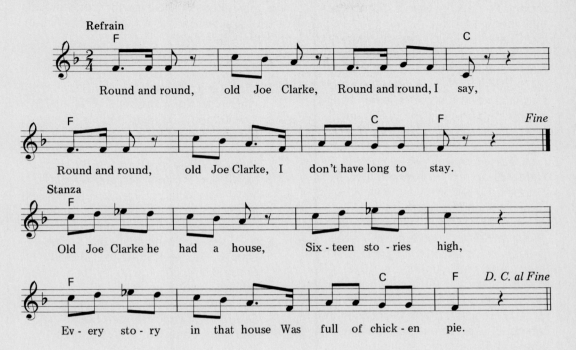

Round and round, old Joe Clarke, Round and round, I say,

Round and round, old Joe Clarke, I don't have long to stay.

Old Joe Clarke he had a house, Six-teen sto-ries high,

Ev-ery sto-ry in that house Was full of chick-en pie.

I went down to Old Joe Clarke's
And found him eating supper;
I stubbed my toe on the table leg
And stuck my nose in the butter.

I went down to Old Joe Clarke's
But Old Joe wasn't in;
I sat right down on the red-hot stove
And got right up again.

Professional Resources for the Teacher

Baskin, Barbara H., and Harris, Karen H. *Books for the Gifted Child.* New York: R. R. Bowker, 1980. An annotated list of almost 150 books for gifted children from kindergarten to upper grades, accompanied by several chapters on the historical and social problems of the gifted child.

Cianciolo, Patricia Jean, ed. *Picture Books for Children.* Chicago: American Library Association, 1973. This list of picture books is annotated with story synopses and art critiques. Categories of interest include Me and My Family, Other People, The World I Live In, and The Imaginative World.

Cullinan, Bernice E., et al. *Literature and the Child.* New York: Harcourt Brace Jovanovich, 1981. Along with selections of outstanding books, this book discusses criteria in choosing books for children and presents many practical teaching ideas.

Huck, Charlotte S. *Children's Literature in the Elementary School.* 3d rev. ed. New York: Holt, Rinehart & Winston, 1979. A reliable, comprehensive aid for understanding children's literature, for becoming familiar with classic and contemporary books, and for using books in the classroom.

Larrick, Nancy. *A Parent's Guide to Children's Reading.* 4th rev. ed. New York: Doubleday, 1975. An annotated listing of recommended books.

Livingston, Myra Cohn. *When You Are Alone/It Keeps You Capone: An Approach to Creative Writing with Children.* New York: Atheneum, 1973.

Lukens, Rebecca J. *A Critical Handbook of Children's Literature.* Glenview, Ill.: Scott, Foresman, 1976. Discusses the elements used to evaluate all literature—character, plot, setting, theme, point of view, style, and tone—and relates them to examples from children's books.

Moffett, James and Wagner, Betty J. *Student Centered Language Arts and Reading. K–13: A Handbook for Teachers.* 2nd ed. Boston: Houghton Mifflin, 1976.

Recommended Reading for the Student

Most of the books recommended in this bibliography are available in hardcover. Some materials, however, are listed as paperbacks because they were originally published in that form or because a hardcover version was not available for review. All of the books are divided into the categories of **easy, average,** and **challenging,** which indicate the reading levels of these books. The category **read aloud** indicates books that a teacher might read to the students.

Easy

George, Jean Craighead. *The Wounded Wolf.* New York: Harper & Row, 1978. A wounded wolf searches for shelter as hungry animals hunt him down.

Matsutani, Miyoko. *The Witch's Magic Cloth.* English version by Alvin Tresselt. New York: Parents' Magazine Press, 1969. The Witch of the Mountain threatens villagers until a brave old woman climbs the mountain to meet her.

Sobol, Donald J. *Encyclopedia Brown Carries On.* New York: Four Winds Press, 1980. Ten mysteries for Encyclopedia Brown to solve.

———. *Encyclopedia Brown Tracks Them Down.* New York: Bantam Books, 1981. Ten more cases for Encyclopedia Brown and his readers to solve.

Average

Bodecker, N. M. *The Lost String Quartet.* New York: Atheneum, 1981. Everything goes wrong for Sidney Periwinkle and his Daffodil String Quartet as they try to get to their concert on time.

Cerf, Bennet, ed. *Out on a Limerick.* New York: Harper & Row, 1960.

Gág, Wanda. *The Sorcerer's Apprentice.* New York: Coward, McCann & Geoghegan, 1979. Although hired by a magician as a helper, a young boy secretly learns spells and finally matches his skill with his master's.

Greenfield, Eloise. *Daydreams.* New York: Dial Press, 1981. An appealing poem about a child who daydreams. For poetry lovers and dreamers.

Hildick, E. W. *The Case of the Four Flying Fingers*. New York: Macmillan, 1981. The five McGurk detectives investigate the Galloping Garbage Gang and find themselves involved with a master burglar.

Lurie, Alison, reteller. *Clever Gretchen and Other Forgotten Folktales*. New York: Thomas Y. Crowell, 1980. Brave and resourceful heroines outwit adversaries and rescue friends and family in these fifteen entertaining folk tales.

Steig, William. *C D B!* New York: E. P. Dutton, 1968. A collection of letter puzzles with illustrations.

Winthrop, Elizabeth. *Journey to the Bright Kingdom*. New York: Holiday House, 1979. In this adaptation of a Japanese folk tale, Kiyo brings her blind mother into a mythical underground kingdom, hoping her sight will return long enough to see her daughter's face.

Wiseman, Ann. *Making Things: The Hand Book of Creative Discovery*. 2 vols. New York: Little, Brown, 1973 and 1974. Over 150 arts and crafts projects with step-by-step directions.

Challenging

Adamson, Joy. *Pippa, the Cheetah, and Her Cubs*. New York: Harcourt, Brace & World, 1970. A cheetah raised in captivity is reeducated to return to her natural jungle life.

Fenner, Carol. *Gorilla Gorilla*. New York: Random House, 1973. A story that contrasts a gorilla's life in Africa with its new life in a zoo.

Fritz, Jean. *The Cabin Faced West*. New York: Coward, McCann, 1958. Ann Hamilton adjusts to the rugged life she must live with her family on the western frontier.

Langton, Jane. *The Fledgling*. New York: Harper & Row, 1980. Through the guid-

ance of a mysterious Canadian goose, a young girl magically learns to fly.

Manning-Sanders, Ruth. *A Book of Ghosts & Goblins*. New York: Methuen, 1968. A collection of ghost stories from around the world.

North, Sterling, *Little Rascal.* New York: E. P. Dutton, 1965. The adventures of a boy raising an orphan raccoon.

Palmer, Robin. *Dragons, Unicorns, and Other Magical Beasts*. New York: Henry Z. Walck, 1966. Ten tales about imaginary and frightening beasts.

Read Aloud

Lear, Edward. *The Complete Nonsense Book*. New York: Dodd, Mead, 1962. Many examples of nonsense poetry including the poem "The Owl and the Pussycat."

Related Media

The following key is used to identify the media listed below: **C**—cassette; **F**—film; **FS**—filmstrip; **R**—record. The catalog number immediately following each title should be used when ordering from the company identified in the entry.

Aesop's Fables CL 851-C Chicago: Clearvue, Inc. Eight **FS** with cassettes.

Livingston, Myra Cohn. "An Introduction to Poetry." *The Writing of Poetry*. New York: Harcourt Brace Jovanovich Publishers, 1980. **FS** with cassette.

"Old Joe Clarke." *Dueling Banjos from the Movie "Deliverance"* (S/B) 2683. New York: Warner Bros. **R**

Notes

Notes

Notes

Notes

Notes

Notes

Notes

Teaching Plans

The teaching material for this book is divided into two sections: the
Teaching Plans on pages T83–T226 and the annotated material (in blue)
on the student–book pages. The Teaching Plans provide complete,
suggested strategies for teaching each selection. The annotations provide on–page help and information, including both skills labels and answers for the questions posed in the student's book. The inclusive page
numbers for each title indicate the student–book pages on which that selection and any annotated material can be found. To introduce your students and their parents to this book, you may wish to use Copying
Master 1 "Use a Table of Contents" (for the students) and ODYSSEY
Home Letter 1 (for the parents), which you will find in the Teacher's
Edition, Part II.

UNIT OVERVIEW

1 Problems and Puzzles
pages 12–79

Theme: Challenges to be met and
problems to be solved.

Selections
The Case of the Missing Roller Skates
   (story)
Where R U? (letter puzzles)
Puzzle (poem)
Concrete Cat (poem)
Mingled Yarns (poem)
The Princess on the Pea (story)
Arithmetic (poem)
It Pays to Advertise (story)
An Eskimo Birthday (story)
CONNECTIONS: Meeting Nature's
   Challenges
Problems (poem)
BOOKSHELF

_____

*Note that the copying masters indicated here are
from the Teacher's Edition, Part II.

Unit Materials

Home Letter   Home Letter 2 may be
sent home at the beginning or the end of
the unit.

Copying Masters for Evaluation*
Copying masters 2, 6, 10, and 13.

Copying Masters for Enrichment*
(Optional) Copying masters 3, 4, 5, 7, 8,
9, 11, 12, 14, and 15.

Introducing the Unit

To introduce the students to this unit have
them open their books to pages 12 and 13.
Ask: ☐ *What are the boys and girls standing
in?* (a maze) ☐ *What are some words you
would use to describe a maze?* (Lead students
toward words like confusing, twisting, difficult.) ☐ *Would you say that a maze is a*

puzzle? What are some of the things they have in common? (Possible responses: confusing, difficult, need solutions, both are problems) □ What is the name of this unit? (Problems and Puzzles) □ What would you expect the stories and poems in this unit to be about? (Lead students toward the conclusion that all will involve problems or difficulties.) □ Are mazes or puzzles sometimes fun? (yes) □ Some stories and poems in this unit will be funny and some will be mysterious, but all will tell you about difficulties and problems.

Unit Projects and Activities

Brainstorming **(Easy)** Present students with a problem or difficulty that affects the class—for example, how to keep the classroom clean, how to maintain good conduct all day—and have them **brainstorm** ideas that will lead to a solution. List the suggested ideas on the chalkboard.

Illustrating Phrases **(Average)** Have the students think of phrases that are used every day that are not to be taken literally—for example, raining cats and dogs, chip on your shoulder, split personality, a frog in your throat. Then have them select two phrases to illustrate. Display the illustrations to the class and have the class say what the phrases are.

Writing Directions **(Challenging)** Divide the class into small groups. Have each group choose a place in the school building and write a set of directions on how to get to the place from the classroom. You may wish to have the groups exchange sets of directions and actually follow the directions to see if they are correct.

The Case of the Missing Roller Skates

pages 14–23

Objectives

Literature/Comprehension
● **Identifying elements of plot—sequence and development**

● Identifying clues to a mystery's solution.

Vocabulary
● Using context clues to identify words.

Materials

For Evaluation

LITERATURE/COMPREHENSION copying master 2, "Solve Encyclopedia's Problem."

For Enrichment (Optional)

HEALTH/COMPREHENSION copying master 3, "Write the Main Idea."

COMPREHENSION/STUDY SKILLS copying master 4, "Find the Facts."

Summary of the Story

While Encyclopedia Brown is having a tooth pulled in Dr. Vivian Wilson's office, Sally Kimball's roller skates disappear from the waiting room. After some investigation, Encyclopedia and Sally question Billy Haggerty, the prime suspect. Billy gives himself away by knowing more than he should.

1 PREREADING

Key Vocabulary Words

corridor: a hallway. (page 17)
lead (lĕd): a clue. (page 19)

Introducing the Vocabulary

Write the key vocabulary words on the chalkboard. Have the students locate the words in the story, pronounce them, and infer their meanings from context. Call students' attention to the specific definition of *lead. Ask:* □ *What are some other meanings of the word?* (Possible responses: to show the way, to guide) □ *Can the word be pronounced a different way? What does that word mean?* (Possible response: metallic element used in pencils) □ *How do you know which is the correct way to pronounce the word?* (Possible response: see how it is used in the sentence)

Introducing the Story

Previewing and Predicting *Ask:* □ *Has anyone ever read any Encyclopedia Brown stories? Can you tell what kinds of stories they are from the title of this story?* (mysteries) □ *What makes a story a mystery?* (Possible response: contains an event or crime that is secret and needs to be solved) □ *How does the story writer help us solve the mystery?* (Possible response: by giving clues within the story)

Relating to Students' Experiences *Ask:* □ *Did you ever have something "disappear"? Did you misplace it or was it taken? How did you go about solving the mystery?* (Possible responses: tried to remember where it was seen last, asked friends if they had seen it)

2 READING

Setting a Purpose for Reading

Have the students look for clues as they read "The Case of the Missing Roller Skates." Have them see if they can solve the mystery before they finish the story.

Planning a Reading Strategy

Have the students read the selection silently, through the bottom of page 21. At this point, stop and elicit clues that will help solve the theft. List these clues on the chalkboard. Then have the students read the final page and compare their findings with Encyclopedia's reasoning.

3 POSTREADING

Reviewing the Story

The following question may be used to review the story. *Ask:* □ *Did you think that Billy had stolen the skate? Why or why not?* (Accept any answer that the student reasonably supports.)

After the students have finished reading the story, have them complete the review questions on page 23 in their books. The questions can be assigned as independent written work or can be answered orally during a class discussion. You may also wish to assign the activity on the same page.

Discussing the Story

You may want to use the following questions to discuss the selection further. *Ask:* □ *What steps did Encyclopedia Brown take to solve this mystery?* (He decided that the thief was not an adult; he checked every office in the building; he trapped Billy into saying that Dr. Vivian Brown was a man and a dentist.) ☐ *Why might the words* clever *and* cautious *be applied to Encyclopedia and Sally in their dealings with Billy Haggerty?* (Possible responses: They did not accuse Billy of the crime. They asked him questions and let him show his guilt through his own words.)

Evaluating the Story

To evaluate the student's recognition of the elements of plot, use **EVALUATION** copying master 2. **Objective: Identifying elements of plot—sequence and development.**

Extending the Story

Identifying Character Traits **(Easy)** Have the class look through the selection and **brainstorm** about the qualities of a good detective, using Encyclopedia Brown as an example. Write the word *detective* on the chalkboard and then **cluster** the appropriate qualities around it. For example:

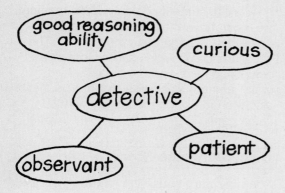

Holding a Treasure Hunt **(Average)** Plan a treasure hunt in the classroom. First divide the class into four groups. Provide each group with approximately four objects (such as magazines, postcards, shells, small musical instruments) to hide. Have each group write clues to help the other groups find the objects. (For example, a clue for a shell hidden in a shelf of books might read like this: "Although it used to be an animal's house, it is covered by books right now.") After each group has written its clues, have it exchange clues with another group and begin the search. The first group to locate all the hidden objects is the winner.

Extending Students' Understanding of Services and Payments **(Challenging)** Ask the students to imagine that Encyclopedia Brown decided to charge for his services. Have the class **brainstorm** to determine what factors he might consider in setting a fee. Some possible responses include: what other detectives charge, how much he feels his time is worth, and how much people can afford to pay. Then have the class break up into groups of four or five and, using similar criteria, decide what they would charge if a neighbor asked them to take care of his or her house for a week. Some of the chores include watering plants, feeding the cat, and bringing in the mail. Have the students be prepared to explain to the neighbor why they have set that specific fee.

Optional Copying Masters for Enrichment

The following copying masters may be assigned as independent classroom work or as home activities to be completed with or without parents' help.

HEALTH/COMPREHENSION copying master 3. **Objectives:** Identifying the main idea in a paragraph; reviewing good oral health habits.

COMPREHENSION/STUDY SKILLS copying master 4. **Objectives:** Distinguishing between fact and opinion; interpreting advertisements.

Related Reading

The following books can be used to extend the selection.

The House on Blackthorn Hill: A Hidden Clue Mystery by Andrew Bromberg. Greenwillow Books, 1982. Break the code and solve the mystery in these stories about a new detective team, Amanda and Sherlock Jones. (Challenging)

The Young Detective's Handbook by William Butler. Little, Brown, 1981. Readers have opportunities to solve crimes and learn about observation, reporting, etc., at the scene of a crime. (Challenging)

Sebastian Supersleuth and the Crummy, Yummies Caper by Mary Christian. Macmillan, 1983. The world's greatest four-legged detective goes underground, passing as an ordinary dog to foil dog-nappers. (Average)

Incognito Mosquito, Private Insective by E. A. Hass. Lothrop, Lee & Shepard, 1982. Incognito presents five cases here and challenges the reader to solve each wacky crime. (Average)

The Curse of the Egyptian Mummy by Pat Hutchins. Greenwillow Books, 1983. On an apparently innocent camping trip, Sam and his friends discover an Egyptian curse and clues to a mystery. (Challenging)

Einstein Anderson Sees Through the Invisible Man by Seymour Simon. Viking Press, 1983. The boy detective, much like Encyclopedia Brown, presents mysteries to puzzle out; but in this case, each crime has some scientific reason that leads to its solution. (Challenging)

Encyclopedia Brown and the Case of the Secret Pitch by Donald J. Sobol. Lodestar Books, 1965; Bantam paperback, 1978. Spanish Edition: *Encyclopedia Brown y la jugada secreta*. Barcelona: Editorial Molino, 1977. Encyclopedia Brown challenges the readers to solve the mystery quickly. For the reader who is not quite successful, the solutions are printed in the book. (Average)

Encyclopedia Brown Takes the Cake: A Cook and Case Book by Donald J. Sobol and Glen Andrews. Four Winds Press, 1983. Not only is Encyclopedia Brown solving cases but now he's learning to cook. His recipes are included along with answers to the mysteries. (Challenging)

Encyclopedia Brown's Second Record Book of Weird and Wonderful Facts by Donald J. Sobol. Delacorte Press, 1981; Dell paperback, 1982. This book contains funny records such as the Losers' Hall of Fame and funnier facts like the chicken with contact lenses. (Average)

Where R U?

page 24

Objectives

Decoding
- Decoding letter puzzles.

Composition
- Writing letter puzzles.

Materials

For Enrichment (Optional)

VOCABULARY copying master 5, "Find the Hidden Words."

1 PREREADING

Introducing the Puzzles

Previewing and Predicting Write "What do U C?" and "I C D B" on the chalkboard. *Ask:* □ *What do these lines say?* (What do you see? I see the bee.) □ *Now look at the title of the letter puzzles in your book. What does it say?* (Where are you?) □ *Let's look at the letter puzzles to figure out the answers to the question "Where R U?"*

2 READING

Planning a Reading Strategy

Allow the students time to examine the letter puzzles silently. Then ask volunteers to read each puzzle aloud and explain it.

3 POSTREADING

Extending the Puzzles

Writing Puzzles **(Challenging)** Have the students write letter puzzles. Suggest that they first write out the alphabet and the numbers 1 to 9 to see which characters can be used alone or combined to stand for words. (Suggestions: B, C, G, I, O, R, U, W, Y, 1, 2, 8)

Optional Copying Master for Enrichment

The following copying master may be assigned as independent classroom work or as a home activity to be completed with or without parents' help.

VOCABULARY copying master 5. **Objective:** Identifying words using clues and definitions.

Puzzle

page 25

Objectives

Literature
- Enjoying a concrete poem made up of questions.

Comprehension
- Making comparisons.

1 PREREADING

Introducing the Poem

Previewing and Predicting Draw ◎ on the chalkboard. *Ask:* □ *What do you see?* (Possible responses: a doughnut, a tire, a worm biting its tail, what you see when you look down a straw) ☐ *The poem "Puzzle" is made up of questions about a picture drawn by the poet. Do you see what the poet sees?*

2 READING

Planning a Reading Strategy

Read the poem aloud to the students. Ask them to create a picture in their minds as you read each question and to compare it with the picture given.

3 POSTREADING

Discussing the Poem

You may want to use the following questions to discuss the poem. *Ask:* ☐ *Which of the pictures in the poem did you think the drawing looked like?* (Some students may think the drawing looked more like another picture than it did the frozen puddle.) ☐ *Why did you think so?* (Accept any answer the student reasonably supports.) ☐ *Have you ever seen "pictures" in a cloud in the sky? How is this poem similar to seeing pictures in a cloud?* (The poet sees pictures in a frozen puddle that has been hit by a rock.)

Extending the Poem

***Making Inferences* (Average)** Have a volunteer put a line drawing that can have several interpretations on the chalkboard. Have students suggest ideas and list them on the board. Then have each student write a poem, following the format of the poem in the book.

***Writing Comparisons* (Challenging)** Read Vachel Lindsay's poem "The Moon's the North Wind's Cooky" to the class.

(The poem is on page T71 of this book.) *Ask:* ☐ *What is the moon called?* (a cooky) ☐ *Why is the moon compared with a cooky?* (because it sometimes looks as if bites are taken out of it) Have the students write their own comparisons to complete the sentence "The moon is . . ."

Related Reading

The following books can be used to extend the selection.

Un–Frog–Gettable Riddles by Joanne Bernstein and Paul Cohen. Albert Whitman, 1981. These jokes and riddles are all on one subject—frogs. (Average)

The Hink Pink Book by Marilyn Burns. Little, Brown, 1981. Pages full of humorous drawings add to a special kind of riddle book. The answers must be two words that rhyme. (Challenging)

How to Read & Write Poetry by Anna Cosman. Franklin Watts, 1979. Some good examples of "shape" or "concrete" poems are included in this collection. (Challenging)

Seeing Things: A Book of Poems by Robert Froman. T. Y. Crowell, 1974. Smoke disappearing and a spider spinning a web are some of the "shapes" presented in poems. (Easy)

Street Poems by Robert Froman. McCall's, 1971. Poems shaped like pictures, called "street poems" or "concrete poems," make up this collection. (Average)

A Book of Puzzlements: Play and Invention with Language by Herbert Kohl. Schocken, 1982. Letter and word puzzles, riddles, play songs, codes, and pictograms fill this book. (Challenging)

Fooling Around with Words by Ruthven Tremain. Greenwillow Books, 1976. Riddles, rebuses, spoonerisms, tongue twisters enliven this collection. (Average)

Teapot, Switcheroo, and Other Silly Word Games by Ruthven Tremain. Greenwillow Books, 1979. Pig latin, palindromes, eponyms, and word trivia are included here. (Easy)

Concrete Cat

page 26

Objective

Literature
- Enjoying a concrete poem.

1 PREREADING

Key Concept Word

concrete poem: a poem written in a shape.

Introducing the Vocabulary

Before the children begin reading, ask them to look at the poem, "Concrete Cat." *Ask:* ☐ *What does the word* concrete *mean to you?* (Besides building or paving material, elicit the meaning *existing* or *real* referring to something that can be seen or touched.) ☐ *A poem written in a shape of an object is called a concrete poem.*

Introducing the Poem

Providing Background: *Ask:* ☐ *What do you notice about the shape of this poem?* (It is in the shape of a cat.) ☐ *What do the words*
of the poem describe?* (a cat, litterbox, dish, mouse) ☐ *Why is this concrete poem in the shape of a cat?* (Possible response: because the poem is about a cat)

2 READING

Planning a Reading Strategy

Have the students read the poem silently. Tell them to be sure to study the arrangement of the letters in the words and their word positions in the poem.

3 POSTREADING

Discussing the Poem

You may want to use the following questions to discuss the poem. *Ask:* ☐ *Why is the poem called "Concrete Cat"?* (because it is in the shape of a cat) ☐ *In what ways did the poet write the words to make the cat shape?* (The students should point out word arrangements such as the curve of the *tail* and the two *paws*, and the letter arrangements of *eAr, eYe, moUth*.) ☐ *Why might someone say that seeing a concrete poem is as important as reading it?* (Possible response: because the words make the shape of the object that the poem is about.)

Extending the Poem

Writing Concrete Poems (Average)
Have the students write concrete poems. Begin by suggesting ideas for poems, such as a daisy, car, or chair. Elicit suggestions from the students as well. Choose one suggestion and, as a group, work out a concrete poem for it. Then have the students do their own poems. You may wish to make a bulletin board display of the completed concrete poems.

Mingled Yarns

page 27

Objective

Literature
- Identifying combinations of familiar stories and rhymes in a poem.

1 PREREADING

Key Vocabulary Words

genii: in Arabian stories, supernatural beings with magical powers who can take human or animal form. (page 27)
blubber: to weep loudly. (page 27)

Introducing the Vocabulary

Write the key vocabulary words on the chalkboard. Assist the students in pronouncing the words. (See page T58 for a decoding strategy.) Have them use the glossary at the back of the book to find the meanings of the words. Point out the multiple meanings of *blubber* (to weep; the fat of a whale). Have volunteers use each word in a sentence.

2 READING

Setting a Purpose for Reading

Say: ☐ *"Mingled Yarns" means mixed–up stories. Read the poem to figure out which stories and poems the poet has mixed together.*

Planning a Reading Strategy

Have a volunteer read each section aloud. After each section is read, pause and have the students write what stories they think are mixed together.

3 POSTREADING

Discussing the Poem

Have the students verify their ideas. *Ask:* ☐ *What stories and poems are mixed together?* (George Washington and the cherry tree and "Pinocchio"; "Jack Be Nimble" and "Jack and the Beanstalk"; "Aladdin and His Magic Lamp" and "Mary Had a Little Lamb.") ☐ *Which word gave the poet the idea to mix the yarns in the third part?* (lam*p*, lam*b*)

Extending the Poem

Drawing Characters **(Average)** Have the class **brainstorm** to come up with characters from stories or poems. Have each student choose at least two characters and combine them in a drawing. Have the drawings displayed. The class then has to guess which characters have been depicted.

Related Reading

The following books can be used to extend the selection.

Who's Zoo by Conrad Aiken and John V. Lord. Atheneum, 1977. Strange half–breed animals, like the camelephant, exhibit all the less admirable qualities of humans. (Average)

Arm in Arm by Remy Charlip. Four Winds Press, 1980. This collection of odds and ends includes shape poems, playlets, mirror images, and riddles. (Easy)

Did Adam Name the Vinegarroon? by X. J. Kennedy. Godine, 1982. Imaginative animals, extinct animals, and even star constellation animals are included in these animal verses. (Average)

The Princess on the Pea

pages 28–31

Objectives

Literature
● Detecting humor in a fairy tale.

Literature/Comprehension

● **Identifying elements of plot— sequence and development.**

Materials

For Evaluation

LITERATURE/COMPREHENSION copying master 6, "Fill in the Events."

For Enrichment (Optional)

LITERATURE copying master 7, "Mark It Fiction or Nonfiction."

SOCIAL STUDIES/STUDY SKILLS copying master 8, "Read the Graph."

Summary of the Story

A prince has not been able to find a genuine princess. When a rain–soaked princess arrives one stormy night, the Queen invites her to stay and puts a pea under her bedding. After the young woman complains of a poor night's sleep, the prince asks her to marry him, reasoning that only a true princess could be so sensitive.

1 PREREADING

Introducing the Story

Providing Background *Say:* ☐ *Hans Christian Andersen was a Danish storyteller who wrote many stories. You may have read some of them like "The Ugly Duckling" or the "Emperor's New Clothes." One of the things that makes his stories so popular is that they are humorous or funny. We are going to read another popular story by Hans Christian Andersen.*

Previewing and Predicting Have the students make a list of descriptions or qualities that come to mind when they think of a princess. They should keep the list until they have finished reading the selection.

2 READING

Setting a Purpose for Reading

As the students listen to the selection, have them pay particular attention to the descriptions of the princess and to the events that help to make the story humorous.

Planning a Reading Strategy

Read the story to the students. Exaggerate the humor of the story. Then have the students skim the story themselves and find the actual description of the princess.

3 POSTREADING

Reviewing the Story

The following may be used to review the story. *Say:* ☐ *Let's compare the list you made earlier describing a princess with what you have found in the story.* (Do comparative lists on the board with the ideas coming from the students.) ☐ *Do you think that the princess in the story is funny? Why or why not?* (Accept any answer that the student reasonably supports.)

Discussing the Story

You may want to use the following questions to discuss the selection further. *Ask:* ☐ *What events or ideas in this story were funny to you?* (Possible responses: a King answering a knock at the city gate; a real princess being out in the rain; the princess sleeping on twenty mattresses; the idea that someone could feel a pea under so many mattresses; a pea being placed in a museum) ☐ *Do you think this story could have really happened?* (Probably not; too many events in the story are unlikely.) You may want to point out that some of the humor of the tale results from the unlikelihood of the events really taking place.

Evaluating the Story

To evaluate the student's understanding of story sequence, use **EVALUATION** copying master 6. **Objective: Identifying elements of plot—sequence and development.**

Extending the Story

Using Story Theater (Easy) Have the students interpret the story through Story Theater. (See page T46 for Story Theater techniques.) *Ask:* ☐ *In which places in the*
story *would facial expressions be especially effective?* (Possible response: when the Queen thinks that it won't take long to find out if the girl is a real princess) ☐ *What kind of an expression would you use?* (Possible response: unbelieving, scornful)

Writing Story Endings (Average) Have the class discuss other possible tests for a real princess. List these on the chalkboard. Then have each student write a **rough draft** of a new story ending, using one of the class's suggestions as a test. Have pairs of students **share** and critique each other's rough drafts; then have the students write a **final version** of their story ending.

Sharing Reading (Challenging) Have students be storytellers to children in kindergarten or first grade. Have the students choose several fairy tales, practice reading them with expression, and then share them with the lower—level class.

Optional Copying Masters for Enrichment

The following copying masters may be assigned as independent classroom work or as home activities to be completed with or without parents' help.

LITERATURE copying master 7. **Objective:** Distinguishing between fiction and nonfiction.

SOCIAL STUDIES/STUDY SKILLS copying master 8. **Objective:** Interpreting information on a graph.

Related Reading

The following books can be used to extend the selection.

The Snow Queen by Hans Christian Andersen, retold by Amy Erlich. Dial

Press, 1982. A little girl's love lets her win out over the obstacles put in her path by the wicked Snow Queen. She succeeds in rescuing her friend held captive in the ice palace. (Average)

The Steadfast Tin Soldier by Hans Christian Andersen. Little, Brown, 1983. Adapted from the *Yellow Fairy Book* by Andrew Lang. This is the story of endless love—the love of a one-legged tin soldier for a beautiful dancing ballerina doll. (Easy)

Petrosinella: A Neapolitan Rapunzel by Giambattista Basile. Frederick Warne, 1981. Spanish Edition: *Petrosinella* (New York: Lectorum Publishers). Petrosinella, which means parsley, is held captive in a tower in the woods, but her long golden hair becomes her rescue ladder. (Challenging)

The Little Humpbacked Horse by Margaret Hodges. Farrar, Straus & Giroux, 1980. This Russian fairy tale concerns a man, who is considered to be a fool, and his little horse. They surprise everyone by being smarter than they seemed. (Challenging)

Aladdin and the Wonderful Lamp retold by Andrew Lang. Viking Press, 1981. Gorgeous pictures show the Persian setting for the story of a boy who found a magic lamp and a magic servant. (Average)

Beauty and the Beast by Marianna Mayer. Four Winds Press, 1978. Spanish Edition: *La Bella y la Bestia* (New York: Lectorum Publishers). The opulent illustrations showing a rich medieval life-style are an outstanding feature in this story of love conquering all. (Average)

Arithmetic
pages 32–33

Objectives

Literature
- Enjoying a descriptive poem.

- Recognizing that a poem can be written without rhyme.

Materials

For Enrichment (Optional)

VOCABULARY/MATHEMATICS copying master 9, "Read Forward and Backward."

1 PREREADING

Introducing the Poem

Relating to Students' Experiences Ask the students to describe arithmetic. Lead them beyond the responses "hard/easy" by asking them for examples of why it is hard/easy. Continue the discussion by *asking:* ☐ *What do you like about arithmetic? What do you dislike about it?* (Accept any answer that the student reasonably supports.) Point out that in the poem, Carl Sandburg gives his ideas about arithmetic.

2 READING

Setting a Purpose for Reading

Tell the students that as they read the poem they should think about which of the poet's ideas best agrees with their own description.

Planning a Reading Strategy

Read the poem aloud to the students. (You may wish to refer to the article "Poetry and the Teacher" by Myra Cohn Livingston on page T60 in the front of this book for information and techniques on sharing poetry.) They should be prepared to tell which part they like best and why.

3 POSTREADING

Discussing the Poem

You may want to use the following questions to discuss the poem. *Ask:* □ *Which description of arithmetic did you like best? Why?* (Accept any answer that the student reasonably supports.) □ *Read the lines of the poem that show that arithmetic is easy or enjoyable.* (Lines 3, 6, and 11; it is easy when the answer is right or when you are playing games.) □ *Read the lines that show that arithmetic can be troublesome.* (Lines 1, 8, 13, and 22; it is troublesome when answers are wrong or you forget how to solve a problem.) □ *What part of the poem seemed funniest to you? Why?* (Accept any answer that the student reasonably supports.)

Extending the Poem

Adding Illustrations **(Easy)** Have the students select one section (stanza) of the poem and illustrate it on plain drawing paper. Have them copy the section of the poem at the bottom of their drawing. Display the works throughout the room.

Writing a Poem **(Average)** Explain that this poem is written in free verse, which means that lines can be as long as the poet wants and that the lines do not have to rhyme. Have the students choose activities or school subjects and write free verse poems about them.

Optional Copying Master for Enrichment

The following copying master may be assigned as independent classroom work or as a home activity to be completed with or without parents' help.

VOCABULARY/MATHEMATICS copying master 9. **Objective:** Identifying and writing palindromes in language and mathematics.

Related Reading

The following books can be used to extend the selection.

Speak Up: More Rhymes of the Never Was and Always Is by David McCord. Little, Brown, 1980. This collection of poems is by an award-winning children's poet. (Average)

Rainbows Are Made by Carl Sandburg. Edited by Lee Bennett Hopkins. Harcourt Brace Jovanovich, 1982. This collection contains seventy of Sandburg's poems, grouped by subject and each headed by Sandburg's own definition of the poem. 1982 ALA Notable Book. (Challenging)

Zero Is Not Nothing by Mindel and Harry Sitomer. Harper & Row, 1978. This attention-grabbing book shows how important ZERO is whether you're playing ball, timing a race, weighing yourself, or counting your money. (Easy)

666 Jellybeans! All That? by Malcolm Weiss. Harper & Row, 1976. Number puzzles and tricks lead into the ideas behind algebra—and you won't even know it! (Average)

It Pays to Advertise

pages 34–49

Objectives

Literature/Comprehension
- **Identifying elements of plot—sequence and development.**

Comprehension
- Recognizing a problem in a story.
- Predicting the outcome of a story.

Vocabulary
- Choosing the meanings of multiple—meaning words.

Content Area (Social Studies)
- Recognizing the free enterprise system.

Materials

For Evaluation

LITERATURE/COMPREHENSION copying master 10, "Solve Benjy's Problem."

For Enrichment (Optional)

SOCIAL STUDIES/MATHEMATICS copying master 11, "Figure Out Benjy's Profit."

SOCIAL STUDIES copying master 12, "Decide What Will Happen to the Price."

Summary of the Story

Benjy is trying to earn money to buy a baseball mitt. His first venture, a carwash, fails. His mother makes several suggestions on ways to improve business which Benjy follows in his next venture, a lemonade stand. Although this business makes money, Benjy and his friend Jason learn about an expense of business—overhead. At the end of this excerpt, Benjy still needs more money for the mitt and is planning his next venture.

1 PREREADING

Key Vocabulary Words

invest: to put money into business. (page 43)
employee: a person hired by another. (page 47)

Introducing the Vocabulary

Write the words *invest* and *employee* on the chalkboard. Use the words in sentences and have the students suggest the word meanings. (Sentence suggestions: Since my dad hired me last month, he has hired two other employees. If you invest in that business, you might make a great deal of money.)

Introducing the Story

Previewing and Predicting *Say:* ☐ *You want to buy something but you don't have all the money to pay for it. What do you do?* (Possible responses: borrow the money, earn the money) ☐ *How can you earn the money you need?* (Possible responses: mow lawns, wash cars, run errands) ☐ *In the story you are going to read, Benjy is faced with a similar problem. See if it is as easy as Benjy originally thinks to earn enough money to buy what he wants.*

2 READING

Setting a Purpose for Reading

Tell the students to read the story to find out how Benjy decides to earn money, and what problems he encounters in trying to run a profitable business.

Planning a Reading Strategy

You may want to break the reading into two sections. End the first section of silent reading on page 44, where Jason says, "It looks like you get your mitt tomorrow." At this point you may want to review the events of the story to date, and to question students on whether they think Benjy has earned enough to get his baseball glove. Then have the students read the rest of the story silently to find out if their predictions are correct.

3 POSTREADING

Reviewing the Story

The following questions may be used to review the story. *Ask:* ☐ *What problem did Benjy have to face?* (earning enough money to buy a baseball glove) ☐ *What steps did Benjy take to try to solve his problem?* (He tried to earn money—first by having a carwash, and then by setting up a lemonade stand.)

After the students have finished reading the story, have them complete the review questions on page 49 in their books. The questions can be assigned as independent written work or can be answered orally during a class discussion. You may also wish to assign the activity on the same page.

Discussing the Story

You may want to use the following questions to discuss the selection further. *Ask:* ☐ *What helpful advice does Benjy's mother give him about setting up a business? Find the lines in the story.* ("You have to have something to sell that people want to buy" page 37; "You have to advertise" page 37; "You have to invest money to make money" page 43.) ☐ *Benjy learned that you have to invest money to make money. What does this mean?* (Possible response: You need to spend some money for such things as supplies and advertising in order to make the product and attract the buyers.) ☐ *Give some examples of how businesses invest money to make money.* (Possible responses: Buy better machines, hire more employees, find new ways of doing things more efficiently.)

☐ *Do you think Benjy will solve his problem and earn enough money for the glove? Why or why not?* (Possible responses: yes, because he is persistent and will work until he makes the money somehow; no, because it is just too much money for a person his age to make)

Evaluating the Story

To evaluate the students' understanding of plot, use **EVALUATION** copying master 10. **Objective: Identifying elements of plot—sequence and development.**

Extending the Story

Writing an Ending **(Easy)** Discuss with the students whether they think Benjy will achieve his goal and get his baseball glove. Tell them to consider the following points: How did Benjy manage to earn the money he needed? Was he satisfied with the baseball glove once he got it? What did Benjy learn from his experience? Have the students **brainstorm,** using these and their own ideas to develop several possible endings to the story. You may want to **list** these on the chalkboard. Then have the students **write a paragraph** describing one possible ending to the story. Some students might enjoy comparing their endings with the real ending of the novel *Benjy in Business.*

Writing a Paragraph **(Average)** Discuss with the students whether any of them have ever "gone into business" to earn money—or, if they were to start a business, what it would be. Then have them write brief paragraphs describing their real or imaginary businesses. For example, they may have set up a babysitting service, a lemonade stand, or a service doing yard work for neighbors. You may want to have students do Enrichment copying master 11, "Figure Out Benjy's Profit," before doing this activity. In that case, they could include information on what their costs, gross earnings, and profit were.

Compiling a Glossary **(Challenging)** Point out to the students the use of baseball terminology in the story. Have them skim the story to list all the baseball terms they can find. Then have them make a "baseball dictionary," including the words in this story as well as others they know. Have them alphabetize their dictionaries, having each new letter begin on a new page. Some other terms they may want to include are *bunts, bench jockeying, groove a pitch, put a foot in the bucket,* and *nothing ball.*

Optional Copying Masters for Enrichment

The following copying masters may be assigned as independent classroom work or as home activities to be completed with or without parents' help.

SOCIAL STUDIES/MATHEMATICS copying master 11. **Objective:** Calculating business costs and profits.

SOCIAL STUDIES copying master 12. **Objective:** Determining the effects of supply and demand.

Related Reading

The following books can be used to extend the selection.

Ferris Wheels by Norman D. Anderson and Walter R. Brown. Pantheon, 1983. This look at the amusement park ride shows the ways inventors work and how long a time it may take before they see results. (Challenging)

What to Do When Your Mom or Dad Says . . . "Earn Your Allowance!" by Joy Berry. Living Skills Press, 1982. After talking about allowances and what they should cover, the author lists responsibilities or household activities that could be used to earn an allowance. (Average)

The Shoemakers: Colonial American Craftsmen by Leonard Fisher. Franklin Watts, 1967. Shoemakers and cobblers, men who repaired shoes, were among the first tradesmen in the new Colony, since everyone needed shoes. At first shoes were only made to order; there were no ready-made shoes like the ones seen in stores today. (Challenging)

Department Store by Gail Gibbons. T. Y. Crowell, 1984. Colorful pictures show a day in a big department store, highlighting the different kinds of careers in merchandising. (Easy)

J. C. Penny: Golden Rule Boy by Wilma Hudson. Bobbs—Merrill, 1972. This book is an easy—to—read biography of the founder of a chain of stores who based his business on the *Golden Rule.* (Easy)

How to Grow a Hundred Dollars by Elizabeth James and Carol Barkin. Lothrop, Lee & Shepard, 1979. Amy wanted to sell some terrariums to make money for camp. This little book outlines just how to run a small business like Amy's. (Challenging)

The Purim Goat by Yuri Suhl. Scholastic Book Services, 1980. A boy teaches his goat to dance so he can earn enough money so the goat will not be sold. (Easy)

The Great Cheese Conspiracy by Jean Van Leeuwen. Dell paperback, 1973. Three mice, not too happy with the pickings at the theater where they live, decide to rob a cheese store. They soon discover real life is nothing like the gangster movies they have watched. (Challenging)

The Great Rescue Operation by Jean Van Leeuwen. Dial Press, 1982. One of the mouse gang—FATS—is missing, disappeared without a trace from the department store. Now Marvin the Magnificent and the other mice must start detecting! (Challenging)

An Eskimo Birthday

pages 50—71

Objectives

Literature
- Recognizing the interrelation of setting and plot.

Comprehension
- Finding details in a story.

- **Identifying causes in cause—and—effect relationships.**

Content Area (Study Skills)
- Scanning a story to locate details.

Content Area (Social Studies)
- Describing how traditions differ among individuals and groups.

- Recognizing how people adapt to their environment.

Materials

For Evaluation

COMPREHENSION copying master 13, "Write the Reason."

For Enrichment (Optional)

SOCIAL STUDIES copying master 14, "Watch the Weather!"

STUDY SKILLS copying master 15, "Travel by Map."

Background

The Eskimos today prefer to be referred to as Inuit (IN•oo•it), their American Indian name. The word *Inuit* means "people."

Summary of the Story

A fierce Alaskan snowstorm sends Eeka and her schoolmates home early. Although excited that it is her birthday, Eeka is worried about her father, who went out trapping and is overdue. Her father returns safely, but much to Eeka's disappointment, he was unable to bring back a fur to trim her new parka. At the party that evening, Eeka receives a surprise—two beautiful white foxskins from her grandfather.

1 PREREADING

Key Vocabulary Words

ruff: a high, full collar, in this case, made of fur. (page 52)

parka: a fur or cloth jacket or coat with a hood. (page 52)

mukluks: soft Eskimo boots made of sealskin or reindeer skin. (page 54)

caribou (kar'•ə•boō): a large North American deer closely related to reindeer. (page 64)

Introducing the Vocabulary

Write the key words on the chalkboard. Put lines between syllables in each word, e.g., par|ka. Put your hand under each syllable and assist the students in decoding the word part. Then have them pronounce the entire word. (See page T58 for a decoding strategy.)

Have the students practice their dictionary skills by looking up the words in the glossary at the back of the book. Ask for volunteers to use each word in a sentence.

Introducing the Story

Previewing and Predicting Say: ☐ *You know how it feels to want a special day, like your birthday, to be just perfect. In the story you are going to read, an Eskimo girl named Eeka wants her birthday to be special, but she has many disappointments and surprises before the day is over.*

2 READING

Setting a Purpose for Reading

Say: ☐ *As you read the story, notice the problems that face Eeka and her family. Also look for the main reasons why these problems existed.*

Planning a Reading Strategy

Because this story is long, it may be broken into two reading sessions. End the first session with the space break on page 60. After the students have finished reading the first section, you may want to review some of the problems Eeka faces on her birthday.

3 POSTREADING

Reviewing the Story

The following questions may be used to review the story. *Ask:* ☐ *What difficulties did Eeka face on her birthday?* (Possible responses: getting home from school; worrying about her father; being disappointed that there was no fur for her parka) ☐ *How was each problem solved?* (Possible responses: She used familiar landmarks to guide herself home; her father returned unharmed; Eeka's grandfather gave her a present of fox skins for her parka.)

After the students have finished reading the story, have them complete the review questions on page 71 in their books. The questions can be assigned as independent written work or can be answered orally during a class discussion. You may also wish to assign the activity on the same page.

Discussing the Story

You may want to use the following questions to discuss the selection further. *Ask:*
□ *What character besides Eeka does the author tell a great deal about?* (Grandfather)
□ *What kind of person is Grandfather?* (Possible responses: kind, humorous, loving)
□ *Find details from the story to support your description.* (Possible responses: kind, when he gives Eeka the fox skins; humorous, when he tells how he got lost in a storm as a child and when he gives the furs to Eeka, saying they aren't very good; loving, throughout the story, but especially when Eeka thanks him at the end) □ *How would you describe the setting of the story?* (Possible responses: far north in wintertime; very cold; stormy; small town)

Evaluating the Story

To evaluate the students' ability to identify causes, use **EVALUATION** copying master 13. **Objective: Identifying causes in cause–and–effect relationships.**

Extending the Story

Discussing Environments **(Easy)** Have the students compare traditions and customs of their lives with those of Eeka's. Some areas of discussion might include the following: How many generations of Eeka's family live together? Is this similar to or different from most families you know? How were the gifts Eeka received similar to or different from what you and your friends might receive? In what ways are Eeka's home the same as and different from the ones in your neighborhood? How was the school Eeka attended the same as or different from your school? Encourage the students to draw their observations from the story's illustrations as well as the text.

Writing a Letter **(Average)** Extend the discussion from the previous activity by having the students write a letter to Eeka, describing their last birthday celebration and comparing it to Eeka's. Try to keep students from making value judgments about Eeka's birthday by emphasizing the importance of respecting other cultures.

Making a Chart **(Challenging)** Have the students do research to find out more about Eskimo life, past and present. Have the students make a chart comparing old ways with new ways. Have them compare Eskimo life across the following categories: homes, transportation, customs, clothing, food, and education. Help the students set up their charts. Have them use information from the story and the library to fill in the chart.

Optional Copying Masters for Enrichment

The following copying masters may be assigned as independent classroom work or as home activities to be completed with or without parents' help.

SOCIAL STUDIES copying master 14. **Objective:** Recognizing how people adapt to different environments.

STUDY SKILLS copying master 15. **Objectives:** Interpreting information on a map; using a map key and compass rose.

Related Reading

The following books can be used to extend the selection.

Desperate Search by Matt Christopher. Little, Brown, 1973. A Persian cat and a dog are lost and their owners must ride out in a raging blizzard to find them in this story of friendship and survival. (Challenging)

Stone Fox by John Gardiner. T. Y. Crowell, 1980. In the dogsled race, no one believes he can beat the "Stone Fox," but one small boy is going to try. (Average)

Long Claws: An Arctic Adventure by James Houston. Atheneum, 1981. An Eskimo boy and girl are followed by a huge grizzly bear as they struggle across storm—swept tundra to bring back food for their family. (Challenging)

Songs of the Dream People: Chants & Images from the Indians & Eskimos of North America by James Houston. Atheneum, 1972. This collection contains chants and poetic images accompanied by illustrations reflecting the cultures from which they are drawn. (Average)

Alaska in Pictures by James Nach. Sterling, 1979. History, government, geography, and climate are among the topics shown and discussed in this book about Alaska. (Challenging)

The Changing Eskimos by Gerald Newman. Franklin Watts, 1979. This easy—to-read book about Eskimos covers their homes, clothing, tools, and crafts, (Easy)

Glaciers, Nature's Frozen Rivers by Hershell H. and Joan Lowry Nixon. Dodd, Mead, 1980. Why glaciers exist and how they form a part of our Earth's ecological balance are explained in this book. (Challenging)

Arctic Lands by Henry Pluckrose. Gloucester Press, 1981. The animals that live in the Arctic are shown in this book along with some of the plants that grow there. (Easy)

Eskimos by Susan Purdy and Cass Sandak. Franklin Watts, 1982. Besides a look at life in the Arctic, this book includes instructions to make some Eskimo items: a model kayak, a ceremonial mask, Eskimo dolls, even Eskimo games. (Average)

CONNECTIONS: Meeting Nature's Challenges

pages 72–77

Objectives

Content Area (Social Studies)
● Understanding how people adapt to their physical environment.

Content Area (Science)
● Describing environments of the far north and the desert.

1 PREREADING

Introducing the Selection

Previewing and Predicting *Ask:* ☐ *What did you find out about what it is like to live in Alaska by reading "An Eskimo Birthday"?* (Possible responses: It is very harsh, very cold; storms can be dangerous; you need to dress very warmly.) ☐ *What do you think it would be like to live in the desert?* (Possible responses: It would be very hot with very little water; you would probably wear very few clothes.)

2 READING

Setting a Purpose for Reading

Say: ☐ *In this selection you will read about people who live in places that have very harsh environments, like Alaska. As you read, notice how people find ways to live in these climates and conditions.*

Planning a Reading Strategy

Have selected students read the selection aloud. Refer to the pictures for clarification where appropriate.

3 POSTREADING

Reviewing the Selection

The following questions may be used to review the selection. *Ask:* ☐ *How have the Eskimos adapted to their surroundings?* (Possible responses: winter house has thick walls to keep out cold; door lets cold air in from below and vent lets hot air out from above; caribou skins used as clothing for warmth) ☐ *How have people of the Sahara adapted to their surroundings?* (Possible responses: clothing protects them from sun and wind; homes have thick walls to help maintain constant temperature; homes are painted white to reflect the sun's rays)

After the students have finished reading the selection, have them complete the review questions on page 77 in their books. The questions can be assigned as independent written work or can be answered orally during a class discussion. You may also wish to assign the activity on the same page.

Discussing the Selection

You may want to use the following questions to discuss the selection further. *Say:* ☐ *You have read about some of the challenges faced by people living in the far north and in desert areas. What other challenges from nature might these people have to meet?* (Possible responses: in the far north, getting enough food, living in darkness for long periods; in the desert, living without much water, getting food) ☐ *Is the environment in which you live closer to the Alaskan or Saharan environment? Explain.* (Accept any answer that the student reasonably supports.)

Extending the Selection

Making a Chart **(Easy)** Have the students make a chart, comparing the ways that Eskimos and people of the Sahara have adapted their housing and clothing to meet the challenge of their environments.

Making a Report **(Average)** Have four groups of students each choose a desert other than the Sahara, such as the Mojave Desert, the Gobi Desert in Mongolia, the Australian Desert, or the desert of the Arabian Peninsula. Have them use the encyclopedia to find out how people in other desert regions adapt to their surroundings. Have the students report their findings to the class, including locating the desert on a world map.

Doing Research **(Challenging)** Have the students do research to find out the answer to one of the following questions: In the far north, why are the days so short in winter and so long in summer? In the desert, why is it so hot in the daytime and so cold at night? Have them prepare written answers.

Related Reading

The following books can be used to extend the lesson.

Draw Fifty Buildings and Other Structures by Lee J. Ames. Doubleday, 1980. Famous buildings for shelter, business, or in honor of some event or person can be drawn following these instructions. (Challenging)

Charlie's House by Clyde Robert Bulla. T. Y. Crowell, 1983. Charlie, an English lad in the 1700's, wants to be his own master and live in a house he has built, so, at age twelve, he travels to America as an indentured servant. (Average)

Huts, Hovels & Houses by Timothy Fisher. Addison–Wesley, 1977. This make–your–own–shelter book includes: directions for building a house of cans, an inflatable three–room house, a dowel dome, a milk–carton house, snow houses, and a regular shed. (Challenging)

Homes: Shelter and Living Space by Joanna Foster. Parents' Magazine Press, 1972. This book gives an elementary look at shelter from caves to modern homes shaped like bubbles. (Average)

Skyscraper Book by James Giblin. T. Y. Crowell, 1981. Photos of skyscrapers plus a simple text show how these tall giants are built, the problems they create, and how people felt about the first "cloud–scraper" in 1884. (Easy)

The Weather Book by Ralph Hardy. Little, Brown, 1982. This illustrated guide to common and rather rare weather explains how weather works and how it affects our choices of clothing, shelter, work and more. (Average)

The Most Wonderful Dollhouse Book by Millie Hines. Butterick, 1979. Instructions are included for easy–to–make, inexpensive dollhouses with furnishings and doll families. (Challenging for working alone.)

Pyramid by David Macaulay. Houghton Mifflin, 1975; paperback, 1982. This award–winning book shows the tools, material, and labor force needed to engineer the giant tombs of the Egyptians. (Average)

Skyscrapers: A Project Book by Anne and Scott MacGregor. Lothrop, Lee & Shepard, 1981. Besides reading about the history of one kind of shelter from the first century to the present, we also learn how skyscrapers are constructed, and are given instructions for building a skyscraper model. (Challenging)

Let's Make a Tent by Jack Stokes. David McKay, 1979. This book contains simple instructions for building a Baker tent, a sort of lean–to style. (Easy)

See Inside a Castle by R. J. Unstead. Warwick Watts Press, 1979. Detailed illustrations show how people built strong houses for living and for protecting themselves against enemies. (Average)

Problems

page 78

Objectives

Literature
- Identifying the message in a poem.

- Recognizing that a poem can give insight into a universally shared feeling.

1 PREREADING

Introducing the Poem

Previewing and Predicting Discuss the title of the poem with the students. Point out that everyone has problems or troubles that he or she hopes to work out. Tell the students that in the poem they are about to read, the poet Calvin O'John has some valuable advice on problems.

2 READING

Planning a Reading Strategy

Read the poem aloud to the students. Then have them reread the poem silently, considering the advice of the poet.

3 POSTREADING

Discussing the Poem

You may want to use the following questions to discuss the poem. *Ask:* ☐ *What does the poem say about problems?* (Possible response: At the end of a day, some problems should be kept, while others can be forgotten.) ☐ *What do you think the poet means by keeping some problems and throwing some away?* (Possible response: Try to solve some problems, but forget those not worth worrying about.) ☐ *Why might this poem be a good ending for this unit?* (Possible responses: The unit is concerned with problems, and this is a short, direct poem on how to deal with problems; this is the end of the unit, just as the poem speaks of the end of the day; the poem sums up a reasonable way to handle problems.)

Extending the Poem

Writing a Paragraph **(Average)** Discuss with the students why some problems are "worth keeping." Help them understand that, for some problems, there is hope for solutions. **Brainstorm** with the students problems around the school that they think are worth solving (for example, lack of order in the cafeteria, pushing and shoving on way to classes). After **listing their choices** on the chalkboard, have them pick one and **write** their ideas of possible solutions to the problems.

Related Reading

The following book can be used to extend the selection.

Stopping by Woods on a Snowy Evening by Robert Frost. E. P. Dutton, 1978. Robert Frost's familiar poem is illustrated by artist Susan Jeffers. (Easy)

UNIT OVERVIEW

2 When The Moon Shines

pages 80–133

Theme: Illusions and transformations.

Selections
The Great Minu (folk tale)
The Ghost in the Attic (story)
What Night Would It Be? (poem)
LEARN ABOUT STORIES: Facts About
  Fiction
The Crane Maiden (folk tale)
When my canary (haiku)
What the Gray Cat Sings (poem)
CONNECTIONS: Animals as Symbols
BOOKSHELF

Unit Materials

Home Letter Home Letter 3 may be
sent home at the beginning or the end of
the unit.

Copying Masters for Evaluation*
Copying masters 16, 19, and 22.

Copying Masters for Enrichment*
(Optional) Copying masters 17, 18, 20,
21, 23, 24, and 25.

Introducing the Unit

Say: □ *When you get all dressed up in costume on Halloween and put on a mask you become someone or something else, don't you?
You changed or were transformed. Have you
ever scared anyone on Halloween?* (Most students probably have.) □ *Why was that per-*

---

*Note that the copying masters indicated here are
from the *Teacher's Edition, Part II.*

son scared? (Possible response: because he or
she didn't know who was behind the mask)

Have the students look at the picture on
pages 80 and 81. Ask a volunteer to read
the unit title. *Ask:* □ *What does the picture
make you think of?* (Possible responses:
Halloween, scary things, ghosts) □ *How
does the title fit in with the picture?* (Possible
response: When the moon shines on
Halloween, all kinds of scary things can
happen.)

Tell the students that in the selections
they will read in this unit, some things are
not exactly what they seem to be and
some things or people are transformed.

Unit Projects and Activities

Making Observations **(Easy)** Have the
students observe the phases of the moon
at least three nights a week for a month.
Have them draw what they see on a calendar (the kind that has white squares for
noting appointments) or have them make
their own calendars on construction paper
and show the phases on it.

Making an Oral Report **(Average)** Since
this unit is about transformations, have the
students do research on animals that exhibit some type of transformation. Ask students if they can name any of those animals and write their suggestions on the
chalkboard. You may need to add to the
list. (Suggestions: puff fish, butterfly fish,
flounder, arctic hare, chameleon, frog,
caterpillar) Have the students choose an

animal and find some information about it. Then have them share their findings with the class.

Writing a Paragraph (Challenging) Have the students think back to what they dressed as last Halloween. Tell them to write a paragraph giving hints to the identity by describing their costume and/or props. Allow students to read their paragraphs to the class and have class members guess the identity.

The Great Minu

pages 82–91

Objectives

Literature
● Identifying a story as a folk tale.

● Identifying a misunderstanding as the basis of humor in a story.

Comprehension
● Recalling details that support the main idea.

Vocabulary
● **Using context clues to identify words.**

Materials

For Evaluation

VOCABULARY/COMPREHENSION copying master 16, "Find the Meaning."

For Enrichment (Optional)

SOCIAL STUDIES/STUDY SKILLS copying master 17, "Read a Chart."

SOCIAL STUDIES/STUDY SKILLS copying master 18, "Learn About Ghana."

Summary of the Story

On a visit to the city of Accra, a farmer sees many fine things. Each time he asks who owns them, he is told, "Minu." Not realizing that "Minu" means "I don't understand," he assumes the Minu owns everything. When he asks whose funeral procession is passing, the reply is "Minu." Thinking that despite his wealth, Minu has died, the farmer returns home, content to lead a simple life.

1 PREREADING

Key Vocabulary Words

outskirts: the edge of a city. (page 86)
procession: a long line of people walking together in a slow and orderly manner. (page 90)
mourner: a person who expresses sorrow for someone who is dead. (page 90)

Key Concept Word

folk tale: a story, usually with an unknown author, containing legendary or magical elements; usually handed down orally among the people. (See Introducing the Story.)

Introducing the Vocabulary

Assist the students in pronouncing the key words (See page T58 for a decoding strategy.) Have the students find the words in context in the story and define each in their own words. Have them check their definitions by looking up the words in the glossary of the book.

Introducing the Story

Providing Background Locate Ghana on a world map. Tell students that this is the setting for the folk tale that they are going to read. *Say:* ☐ *Long ago, storytellers would travel from village to village to entertain people with their tales of good and evil. These stories would be told again and again by many people from generation to generation. These stories are called folk tales. We can discover many things about different cultures and ways of life when we read folk tales from other countries.*

Relating to Students' Experiences *Ask:* ☐ *Do you remember your first day in school? Were you excited? impressed with the large building? confused by new things your teacher said?* (Discuss the various responses.) ☐ *The farmer in the story you are going to read had new and exciting experiences also.*

2 READING

Setting a Purpose for Reading

Tell the students that the farmer meets many people on his trip to the city, but each time there is a misunderstanding. As the students read "The Great Minu," have them notice how all these misunderstandings add up to a surprise ending.

Planning a Reading Strategy

You may want to read aloud to the class the italicized introduction to the folk tale on page 83. Then have the students read "The Great Minu" silently.

3 POSTREADING

Reviewing the Story

The following questions may be used to review the story. *Ask:* ☐ *How do you know the farmer did not understand the people of Accra?* (The farmer never realized the "Minu" was not a person but a word meaning "I don't understand.") ☐ *What was the surprise ending of the folk tale?* (The farmer thinks that Minu has died, and decides to be content living the simple life of a farmer.)

After the students have finished reading the story, have them complete the review questions on page 91 in their books. The questions can be assigned as independent written work or can be answered orally during a class discussion. You may also wish to assign the activity on the same page.

Discussing the Story

You may want to use the following questions to discuss the selection further. *Ask:* ☐ *Why did the farmer want to leave his farm?* (Possible responses: He was bored; he wanted some excitement; he wanted to see something new.) ☐ *The farmer greeted several people on his way to Accra. Show how these people returned his greeting.* (Have students demonstrate the responses by smiling, nodding, and waving.) ☐ *Why did they not say hello?* (Possible response: They did not understand him.) ☐ *Do you think the farmer was sorry he went to Accra?* (Possible responses: probably not because he had seen that a rich man was no better off in death than a poor man)

Evaluating the Story

To evaluate story vocabulary, use **EVAL-UATION** copying master 16. **Objective: Using definitions and context clues to identify words; recalling details and making inferences.**

Extending the Story

Writing a Story Title **(Easy)** Ask the students to imagine that this folk tale was handed down to them without a title. Have the students rename the tale, trying to make the title different from the already existing one. Explain that a story title can tell the main idea, or can act as a "tease" to draw the reader into the story. Students may want to look at how other story titles in their books "fit" their stories before beginning this activity.

Performing a Play **(Average)** Assign parts to the students and have them act out the story. (See page T46 for Story Theater techniques.

Comparing Cultures **(Challenging)** (You may wish to do this after Social Studies copying master 18, "Learn About Ghana.") Have the students write a short report comparing life in Ghana to life in Alaska. Tell the students to use "An Eskimo Birthday" and "The Great Minu" as sources for their information. Before writing the report, have the students decide what categories to compare (such as climate, dress, food). Have them write an outline. The beginning of the report should compare the two life-styles. The final paragraph should suggest why the life-styles might be so different.

Optional Copying Masters for Enrichment

The following copying masters may be assigned as independent classroom work or as home activities to be completed with or without parents' help.

SOCIAL STUDIES/STUDY SKILLS copying master 17. **Objective:** Using and interpreting information from a chart.

SOCIAL STUDIES/STUDY SKILLS copying master 18. **Objectives:** Interpreting information on a map; using a compass rose; scanning a story for details.

Related Reading

The following books can be used to extend the lesson.

Beat the Story—Drum, Pum—Pum by Ashley Bryan. Atheneum, 1980. This Nigerian folk tale collection comments on many things—African animals, bad friends, and much, much more. (Average)

Star Boy by Paul Goble. Bradbury Press, 1983. When the Earth bride of the sky god made a hole in the sky, she could see her old Earth home and was unhappy. This story tells what happened to their child Star Boy and how the Sun Dance celebrates the Sun's blessing to the Earth. (Average)

Longhouse Winter: Iroquois Transformation Tales by Hettie Jones. Holt, Rinehart & Winston, 1972. These stories, only allowed to be told in winter by the Iroquois five—league nation, deal with changes—a chief becomes a robin, an evil person turns into a rattlesnake, and so on. (Average)

The Hundreth Dove and Other Tales by
Jane Yolen. Harper & Row, 1977;
Schocken paperback, 1980. Seven strong
stories tell of love, separation, loyalty, and
happiness. (Average)

*It Could Always Be Worse: A Yiddish Folk
Tale* by Margot Zemach. Farrar, Straus &
Giroux, 1977. Scholastic paperback, 1979.
A funny story in which a wise Rabbi helps
a man realize things could "always be
worse." (Average)

The Ghost
in the Attic

pages 92–103

Objectives

Literature
● Recognizing the relationship between
setting and mood.

Comprehension
● Identifying the unstated main idea of a
story.

● Identifying a character's feelings.

Vocabulary
● **Using context clues to identify
words.**

Materials

For Evaluation

VOCABULARY/COMPREHENSION
copying master 19, "Find the Words."

For Enrichment (Optional)

VOCABULARY/WORD ATTACK copying
master 20, "Add a Suffix."

STUDY SKILLS copying master 21,
"Study the Dictionary."

Summary of the Story

To terrify the local bully Peter Frost, the
Moffat children create a ghost in their attic. At first, Peter Frost is only slightly
shaken by the howls coming from the attic. Once in the dark attic, however, he is
thoroughly frightened when the ghost ca-
reens toward him. Not knowing that the
Moffats' cat is tangled in the rope attached
to the ghost and convinced the ghost is
after him, Peter Frost flees, leaving the
Moffats to laugh over their successful
prank.

1 PREREADING

Key Vocabulary Words

ominous: threatening; being an evil
omen. (page 94)
gaping: wide open. (page 94)
reproach: blame. (page 96)
blanched: turned pale. (page 96)
blustering: speaking in a noisy, boastful,
or bullying manner. (page 98)
careening: lurching; moving rapidly in an
uncontrolled way. (page 101)
bedlam: a place or condition of noise or
confusion. (page 102)

Key Concept

mood: the predominant feeling or tone
(See Discussing the Story on page
T111.)

Introducing the Vocabulary

Write the key vocabulary words on the
chalkboard. Also list the following on the
board: lurching, blame, threatening, paled,
wide open, boastful, noisy place. Have the
students find the key words in context in
the story. Have them read the sentence

and then find a word in the word list that could replace the key word. Have the sentence reread with the new word in place.

Call students attention to the words *blanched* and *blustering* and ask them which letters stand for the beginning sounds in each word. (bl) Remind the students that the *bl* in those words is a consonant cluster. (two consonant letters written together and reflecting the sound of both letters.) Ask the students if they can name any other consonant clusters. (Possible responses: cl, fl, br, dr, sm, st)

Introducing the Story

Relating to Students' Experiences *Ask:* □ *Have you ever wished you could play a trick on someone?* (Lead students to discuss who they would wish to trick and why. For example, they may wish to play a trick on a brother or sister just because it would be fun.) □ *Why might Halloween be a particularly good time to play a trick?* (Possible responses: People are more willing to believe in scary things on Halloween.)

2 READING

Setting a Purpose for Reading

Say: □ *In the story you are about to read, the Moffat children play a trick on a bully, Peter Frost. As you read the story, watch how the author uses descriptions of the sights, sounds, and smells of an attic to help the Moffats play a trick on Peter.*

Planning a Reading Strategy

Have the students read the story silently, noting that the use of language helps the reader to see and feel what the characters are experiencing.

3 POSTREADING

Reviewing the Story

The following questions may be used to review the story. *Ask:* □ *How did the author use description of the sights, sounds, and smells of an attic to have the Moffats scare Peter Frost? Look through the story to find examples to support your answer.* (sights: "pit of darkness" page 99; "head gaping horribly" page 100; "dragging its horrible chains" page 101; sounds: attic door falls open with a groan page 93; "hoarse whisper" page 99; "howl of reproach" page 96; seeing stuffed animals page 94; flashlights turning on and off pages 99–101; Jane calling out in a shrill voice page 101; smells: "strange musty smell" of attic page 93.)

After the students have finished reading the story, have them complete the review questions on page 103 in their books. The questions can be assigned as independent written work or can be answered orally during a class discussion. You may also wish to assign the activity on the same page.

Discussing the Story

You may want to use the following questions to discuss the selection further. *Ask:* □ *Was this a funny story or a scary story? Explain your choice.* (Most students will probably agree that it was both funny and scary.) □ *Do you think Peter Frost will try to get back at the Moffats? Why or why not?* (Possible responses: yes, people often want revenge when they are tricked; no, Peter Frost never wants to see the Moffats again.) □ *How did the Moffats' trick turn out even better than they had expected?* (Catherine–the–cat howled and was caught in Madame–the–ghost's sheets.)

☐ *One of the things that many selections in this unit have in common is that they describe making things seem different than they are—they describe creating illusions. What illusions are created in this story?* (Possible responses: a ghost made out of everyday objects; the attic transformed into a scary place)

Evaluating the Story

To evaluate the students' understanding of the story vocabulary, use **EVALUATION** copying master 19. **Objective: Using context clues to identify words.**

Extending the Story

Completing Sentences **(Easy)** Have the students **brainstorm** to list verbs on the chalkboard to complete the sentences below. Stress using colorful, descriptive verbs. When the students have **listed the verbs** have them choose one for each sentence. Have them **write** all the sentences on paper, title them "On Halloween," and illustrate one or more of the sentences.

> The ghosts (howl, cry).
> The bats (flutter, zoom).
> The moon (shines, glows).
> The cats (screech, yowl).
> The owls (hoot, stare).

Making a Chart **(Average)** Have the students skim the story and choose four or five words from the beginning, the middle, and the end that describe how Peter Frost's feelings changed. For example: In the beginning, Peter Frost was arrogant and jeering; in the middle, he was blustering, but shaking; by the end, he was scared. Then help the students set up a chart showing the change in feelings. The chart might look something like:

	Beginning	Middle	End
Peter's feelings	arrogant (p. 96)	blustering (p. 98)	scared (p. 97)

Describing Settings **(Challenging)** With the students, **brainstorm** to determine a list of elements that might be part of a setting for a Halloween story, for example, a foggy night, tree limbs groaning in the wind, or staggering footsteps on a deserted path. Have each student choose a few of the elements **listed** and **write** a paragraph describing a setting for a ghost story. Have pairs of students exchange paragraphs for criticism. Then have them **revise** the paragraphs as necessary.

Optional Copying Masters for Enrichment

The following copying masters may be assigned as independent classroom work or as home activities to be completed with or without parents' help.

VOCABULARY/WORD ATTACK copying master 20. **Objective:** Building vocabulary by adding suffixes to root words.

STUDY SKILLS copying master 21. **Objective:** Using a dictionary.

Related Reading

The following books can be used to extend the lesson.

Giant Cold by Peter Dickinson. E. P. Dutton, 1984. Spending the last night on a holiday island vacation, a boy dreams a Giant Cold has made the tropics a frozen wasteland and only he can bring back the warmth. (Challenging)

The Moffat Museum by Eleanor Estes. Harcourt Brace Jovanovich, 1983. The Moffats are setting up a special kind of museum, one filled with things that have memories for the Moffats themselves. (Challenging)

The Money Room by Eloise Jarvis McGraw. Atheneum, 1981. A diary and some old stock certificates make Scott and his sister think their great–grandfather has left money hidden somewhere. (Challenging)

What Night Would It Be?

pages 104–105

Objectives

Literature

- Recognizing sensory imagery in a poem.

- Examining ways in which a poet creates a mood.

1 PREREADING

Introducing the Poem

Previewing and Predicting Have the students look at the illustrations on pages 104 and 105. Ask them to guess what time of year they think it is. (autumn)

2 READING

Setting a Purpose for Reading

As the students listen to and read the poem have them think about the answer to the title question and what feelings that night often creates.

Planning a Reading Strategy

Read the poem aloud to the students. Emphasize the long vowel sounds in the first stanza particularly, contrasting with the repeated phrase "On the back . . ." Then allow time for them to read it silently. (See Extending the Poem for choral reading suggestions.)

3 POSTREADING

Reviewing the Poem

You may wish to use these questions to review the poem. *Ask:* ☐ *What word answers the question in the poem's title?* (Halloween) ☐ *What is the poet talking about when he says, "And what goes there / Rides a broomstick"?* (a witch) ☐ *Who are "the small men / with the lit grins / And with no chins"?* (jack–o'–lanterns)

Discussing the Poem

You may want to use the following to discuss the poem further. *Say:* ☐ *Think back to the story, "The Ghost in the Attic." What feeling was created in the story?* (being scared) ☐ *Did the words used in the story help create that feeling?* (You may wish to go back to the story and have the student pick out some of those descriptive phrases, such as "pit of darkness, head gaping horribly.") ☐ *Is the same feeling created in this poem?* (yes) ☐ *How does the poet make the reader feel the scariness of this night?* (Possible response: by asking question after question; by repeating lines; by the images he uses; by the rhythm of the poem)

Extending the Poem

Choral Reading **(Easy)** Have individuals each read a line and the rest of the class read the repeated lines. The students might add vocal interpretation to their readings, such as a crackling laugh after "broom—stick," a drawn—out "owl's hoo," and a scary "ghost's boo." Have the chorus raise their voices slightly for each repeating line. (See page T42 for further information on choral reading techniques.)

Writing a Poem **(Average)** Have the student write concrete poems. (See "Concrete Cat" on page 26.) Remind them that concrete poems are poems written in the shape of a particular object. They use words that suggest or describe the object to outline its shape. Suggest the shapes of a pumpkin, a bat, an owl, or a ghost. If students choose a pumpkin, they should write in black crayon on orange paper; a bat, white crayon on black paper; an owl, black crayon on tan paper; a ghost, black crayon on white paper. Display the finished poems on the bulletin board.

Writing a Report **(Challenging)** Have the students go to the library and research the origin of Halloween. Have them take notes on what they find and then prepare a report to be read to the class.

LEARN ABOUT STORIES: Facts About Fiction

pages 106–109

Objectives

Literature
- Identifying three types of fiction.
- Recognizing the variety of fiction.

1 PREREADING

Introducing the Selection

Providing Background Read aloud Robert Froman's poem "Public Library," which is on page T72 of this book. *Ask:* ☐ *What does the poem mean by "From them, anything. /From here, anywhere?"* (Possible response: Books introduce us to all sorts of places—both real and imagined.)

2 READING

Setting a Purpose for Reading

Say: ☐ *As you read this selection, think about the different kinds of stories you have read or can find at the library.*

Planning a Reading Strategy

After the students read pages 106–107 silently, have them read and prepare their answers for the book descriptions on pages 108–109.

3 POSTREADING

Reviewing the Selection

First ask volunteers to explain the answers to what kind of fiction each story (pages 108–109) is: (1) realistic fiction; (2) folk tale; (3) fantasy; (4) folk tale; (5) fantasy; (6) realistic fiction.

After the students have finished reading the selection, you may wish to assign the activity at the bottom of page 109. Have the students refer to the chart on page 107 when deciding on categories for their books.

Discussing the Selection

You may want to use the following questions to discuss the selection further. *Ask:*
□ *How is a folk tale different from a fantasy?* (Possible response: A fantasy has an author; a folk tale is retold by someone.) □ *How are folk tales and fantasy alike?* (Possible response: Both can use magic.) □ *What are some differences between realistic fiction and folk tales?* (Possible response: Realistic stories usually take place in the present, while folk tales take place in the past; the characters in realistic fiction are more true–to–life than those in folk tales.)

□ *What folk tale have you read in this unit?* ("The Great Minu")

□ *What kind of fiction would you call "The Ghost in the Attic" and why?* (realistic fiction because it takes place in the present, could possibly happen, main characters are realistic, has an author)

Extending the Selection

Making A Mobile (Easy) Have the students use drawings and magazine pictures to make mobiles for favorite books.

Some of the suspended mobile shapes should be reserved for brief comments about the books, as well as the titles and the authors. Other pictures should illustrate the setting, plot, and characters. (Review these elements, if necessary.)

Visiting the Library (Average) Have the students visit the library to find and read books in a category from which they have not chosen books before. Encourage them to ask the librarian if they need help.

Giving an Oral Report (Challenging) Ask volunteers to talk about their favorite books. Have the student begin the talk by writing the book's title and type of fiction on the chalkboard. The rest of the class should ask questions based on the facts listed in the chart on page 107. Encourage the students to explain why they enjoyed the books.

Related Reading

The following books can be used to extend the lesson.

The Mariah Delaney Lending Library Disaster by Sheila Greenwald. Houghton Mifflin, 1977. Mariah is more interested in making money than in reading books, much to the dismay of her writer–mother and publisher–father. (Challenging)

Libraries and How to Use Them by Jeanne B. Hardendorff. Franklin Watts, 1979. Understanding the organization of a library can be a help in locating information quickly. (Challenging)

The Puzzle of Books by Michael Kehoe. Carolrhoda Books, 1982. A simple photo–essay shows the work that goes into creating and printing a book. (Challenging)

The Crane Maiden

pages 110–122

Objectives

Literature
● Identifying the characteristics in a folk tale.

● Recognizing the transformation motif in a folk tale.

Comprehension
● **Identifying effects in cause–and–effect relationships.**

Content Area (Social Studies)
● Recognizing different cultures.

Materials

For Evaluation

COMPREHENSION copying master 22, "Tell What Happened."

For Enrichment (Optional)

COMPREHENSION/SOCIAL STUDIES copying master 23, "Plan a Trip."

VOCABULARY/COMPREHENSION copying master 24, "Find the Meanings."

Awards

The picture book *The Crane Maiden* was one of the Library of Congress Children's Books of the Year in 1968.

Summary of the Folk Tale

After freeing a crane from a trap, an old Japanese man is rewarded for his kindness when a young girl, Tsuru, comes to stay with him and his wife. Tsuru wants to help the poverty–stricken old couple celebrate the New Year. Advising the couple not to watch her, the girl weaves a beautiful bolt of cloth for the man to sell. Despite their promise, the old woman cannot resist peeking while Tsuru is weaving more cloth and is astounded to see a crane instead of the girl. Once seen in her true form, the crane maiden flies away, crying a single *koh* as her good-bye.

1 PREREADING

Key Vocabulary Words

maiden: a young unmarried girl. (page 110)
hearth: the fireside. (page 113)
kimono: a loose robe with wide sleeves and a sash, part of the traditional costume of Japanese men and women. (page 114)
shuttle: a device used in weaving to carry a thread from side to side between the threads that run lengthwise. (page 117)
bolt: a roll of cloth. (page 117)

Introducing the Vocabulary

Write the key words on the chalkboard. Assist the students in pronouncing them. (See page T58 for a decoding strategy.) Then have the students turn to page 113 in their books. Ask if they can identify any part of the picture using the words from the board. (maiden, hearth, kimono) Repeat with the picture on page 117. (kimono, bolt) Simply tell the students the meaning of *shuttle,* perhaps adding an illustration on the board.

Introducing the Story

Providing Background *Ask:* ☐ *Have you read a folk tale before in this book? What was its name?* (The Great Minu) ☐ *Where did that folk tale take place?* (Ghana, Africa) ☐ *Remember that a folk tale is a story told from generation to generation and is usually about good and evil. Sometimes a folk tale also contains some magic or a wish that comes true.*

Locate Japan on a world map. *Say:* ☐ *The folk tale we are going to read, "The Crane Maiden," is from Japan. The Japanese believe that the crane, a beautiful, tall white bird, brings good luck.*

Relating to Students' Experience *Say:* ☐ *The Japanese believe that the crane brings good luck. What do many people in the United States believe brings good luck?* (Possible response: rabbit's foot) ☐ *What does a black cat signify to some people?* (Possible response: bad luck)

2 READING

Setting a Purpose for Reading

Say: ☐ *In reading folk tales from other countries we learn something about different cultures, customs, and beliefs. Let's read "The Crane Maiden" from Japan and see in what way the crane brings good luck and the reason why.*

Planning a Reading Strategy

Call on students to read the story aloud. Explain the meanings of the underlined words at the appropriate times.

3 POSTREADING

Reviewing the Story

The following questions may be used to review the story. *Ask:* ☐ *In what way did the crane bring good luck?* (Possible response: By changing into a young girl who could help them, the crane saved the couple from poverty.) ☐ *Why did the crane choose the couple?* (Possible response: because the man was kind to it)

After the students have finished reading the story, have them complete the review questions on page 122 in their books. The questions can be assigned as independent written work or can be answered orally during a class discussion. You may also wish to assign the activity on the same page.

Discussing the Story

You may want to use the following questions to discuss the selection further. *Say:* ☐ *You have already talked about what lesson each character in the story may have learned. What lesson have you learned from this folk tale?* (Most students will probably say "Don't break a promise" or some equivalent statement.)

☐ *A change from one form to another is called a transformation. How is a transformation an important part of the story "The Crane Maiden?"* (First the crane is transformed into a girl; then the girl turns into a crane again.) ☐ *We said earlier that the Japanese believe that a crane brings good luck. How does the crane bring good luck in this story?* (Possible response: The couple gets a kind and helpful daughter who weaves beautiful cloth for them to sell.)

☐ *What are some things that you learned about Japanese customs from reading this folk tale?* (Possible responses: Respect is shown with a bow, porridge is eaten for meals, a bed is made of quilts, kimonos are worn, rice cakes are eaten to celebrate New Year's Day.)

Evaluating the Story

To evaluate the student's understanding of effects, use **EVALUATION** copying master 22. **Objective: Identifying effects in cause–and–effect relationships.**

Extending the Story

Writing a Story Ending **(Easy)** Have the students suggest other story endings or extend the story by telling what happened to the old couple after the crane maiden left. Were they unhappy? Did they go on as before? Had they learned a lesson?

Doing Research **(Average)** The crane is on the list of endangered species of the world. Have students locate information in the library about other endangered species and what is being done to save them. Have them report their findings to the class.

Preparing an Oral Report **(Challenging)** Begin the activity with a class **brainstorming** session on things mentioned in the story that made the students want to know more about Japan. Have the students do research on life in Japan. Some topics that may arise from the story are: birds of Japan, traditional clothes, relationships of children to parents, and folk tales of Japan. Then have the students **choose a topic** to explore further. Have them **report their findings** to the class. Students might tell if their research bears out the details in the story.

Optional Copying Masters for Enrichment

The following copying masters may be assigned as independent classroom work or as home activities to be completed with or without parents' help.

COMPREHENSION/SOCIAL STUDIES copying master 23. **Objectives:** Scanning a selection for details; drawing conclusions from a letter.

VOCABULARY/COMPREHENSION copying master 24. **Objective:** Recognizing the multiple meanings of words.

Related Reading

The following books can be used to extend the lesson.

Sweet and Sour: Tales from China by Carol Kendall and Li Yao–wen. Clarion Books/Seabury Press, 1979. The mystery and fascination of China surface in these twenty–four unusual tales, the oldest written over 2,000 years ago. (Challenging)

The Prince Who Knew His Fate translated by Lise Manniche. Metropolitan Museum of Art/Philomel/Putnam, 1981. In this ancient Egyptian tale, translated from the hieroglyphs painted on the walls of a tomb more than 3,000 years ago, a prince knows how he is to die. The actual hieroglyphic characters are printed along the bottom of each page. (Challenging)

Treasure Mountain: Folktales from Southern China by Catherine Sadler. Atheneum, 1982. This collection presents six tales that have been passed down by word of mouth over the years. Only lately have they been written. (Average)

Japan: Activities & Projects in Color by Claude Soleillant. Sterling, 1980. This book gives easy instructions for making many Japanese things: toys, costumes, food. Instructions for flower arranging are also included. (Challenging)

When my canary

page 123

Objectives

Literature

- Recognizing that haiku express feelings.

- Identifying the haiku form.

1 PREREADING

Introducing the Poem

Previewing and Predicting Explain that "When my canary . . ." is a short Japanese poem called a haiku (hī•kōo). Most often, a haiku expresses a thought about something in nature. It should create a picture in the reader's mind and give the reader a particular feeling.

2 READING

Setting a Purpose for Reading

As the students read the haiku, have them notice the feeling it gives them, as well as how a haiku can say so much in so few words.

Planning a Reading Strategy

Have the students read the haiku aloud once. Then have them read it silently, paying attention to the feeling expressed.

3 POSTREADING

Discussing the Poem

The following questions may be used to guide the discussion. *Ask:* ☐ *Why did spring end for the poet?* (because the canary flew away) ☐ *How did you feel when you read the poem? Happy? Surprised? Sad?* (Most students will probably feel sad.) ☐ *What do you notice about the title of the poem?* (It is the first line of the poem.) Explain that most haiku are titled this way.

Extending the Poem

Interpreting a Poem (Easy) During the week have the students draw pictures or cut pictures from newspapers or magazines that express feelings that they had while reading the poem. Encourage the students to read the poem several times. Ask for volunteers to show their pictures to the class.

Analyzing a Poem (Average) Explain the syllable structure of haiku to the students (five syllables in the first and third lines, seven syllables in the second line). Stress that in creating a haiku, a poet responds to a need to express a feeling, usually about something in nature. Have the students apply these criteria to the haiku in their books. You may wish to supply more poems for the students to analyze.

Writing a Poem (Challenging) Have the class **brainstorm** to think of things in nature that might be subjects for a haiku. **List** these on the chalkboard. Have the students **write** their own haiku, choosing subjects from the list they have compiled.

What the Gray Cat Sings

pages 124–125

Objectives

Literature
- Recognizing rhythm in a poem.
- Recognizing that repeated sounds contribute to a poem's tone.

1 PREREADING

Key Vocabulary Words

shuttle: a device used in weaving to carry a thread from side to side between the threads that run lengthwise. (page 124)

weft: in weaving, the threads carried by the shuttle from side to side across the fixed threads in a loom, also known as the *woof*. (page 124)

thrum: the ends of thread left on a loom after the cloth has been cut off: to pluck on, as a guitar; to strum. (page 124)

droning: making a continuous humming or buzzing sound with little variation. (page 124)

Introducing the Vocabulary

Write the key words on the chalkboard. Have the students look at the picture on page 125. Point out the loom, shuttle, and weft in the picture. Ask if students have ever heard of *shuttle* (a key word in "The Crane Maiden"). Have them look up the definitions of the other key words in the glossary.

Introducing the Poem

Providing Background Remind students that a transformation is a change from one form to another. *Say:* ☐ *Remember the folk tale "The Crane Maiden." What was the transformation or change in that story?* (The crane changed into a girl and then back again.) ☐ *We are going to read a poem that also contains a transformation.*

Relating to Students' Experiences *Ask:* ☐ *How many of you have ever heard a cat purr?* (probably most students have) ☐ *Close your eyes and think about the sound. What does it sound like?* (Have students approximate the purring sound.) ☐ *The sound is very steady, very droning, isn't it?* (yes) ☐ *The sound a loom makes when someone is weaving is a little bit like that. Think about the purring sound and the weaving sound when we read the poem.*

2 READING

Setting a Purpose for Reading

As the students listen and read, have them look for the transformation.

Planning a Reading Strategy

Read the poem aloud to the students. Emphasize the rhythm of the poem, while avoiding a singsong reading. Then have the students read it silently.

3 POSTREADING

Discussing the Poem

The following questions may be used to guide the discussion. *Ask:* ☐ *What is the transformation in the poem?* (A weaver is changed into a cat.) ☐ *What song did the* weaver sing? ("Pr–rrum, pr–rrum/Thr–ree thr–reads in the thr–rum/Pr–rrum!")

☐ *What does the gray cat sing?* (same song)

☐ *What is the purring sound of a cat similar to?* (noise of a weaving loom) You may wish to point out the similarities among the last five lines in each stanza to emphasize this point.

Extending the Poem

Making a List **(Easy)** Have the students reread the poem and make a list of the habits of cats that are mentioned or implied within the poem. If some students are not familiar with cats' habits, ask those students who know about cats to share that information with the class.

Preparing an Oral Report **(Average)** Point out to the students that cloth for clothes is not the only thing that is woven. Have students do research to discover other objects that contain woven materials and the uses for those objects. (Some suggestions: baskets, caned seats on chairs, spider's web, nest of the weaverbird)

Making a Headline **(Challenging)** Have the students make up newspaper headlines that would give a hint as to what happened to the weaver. Remind them that a headline is short and its purpose is to get people to read the article that follows it.

Related Reading

The following books can be used to extend the lesson.

Crickets and Bullfrogs and Whispers of Thunder by Harry Behn, selected by Lee Bennett Hopkins. Harcourt Brace Jovanovich, 1984. This book is a collection of Behn haiku. (Average)

Hello, Small Sparrow by Hannah Lyons Johnson. Lothrop, Lee & Shepard, 1973. This is a book of haiku, the nature poetry of Japan. (Easy)

CONNECTIONS: Animals as Symbols

pages 126–132

Objectives

Content Area (Social Studies)

● Understanding that animals have been used as symbols by many groups throughout history.

● Describing how customs differ among groups.

1 PREREADING

Introducing the Selection

Previewing and Predicting Say:

☐ *What do you think of when I say each of these things: the bald eagle, Smokey the Bear, the turkey, a black cat?* (Possible responses: America, forest fires, Thanksgiving, bad luck) Point out that animals often are used to stand for things. Remind them of the crane in the story "The Crane Maiden."

2 READING

Setting a Purpose for Reading

Say: ☐ *As you read this selection, notice what groups have used animals as symbols. Consider why such animals were chosen.*

Planning a Reading Strategy

First, call students' attention to the subheads within the selection. Point out to them that subheads give to the reader some ideas about the content of the selection. Then have selected students read the material aloud.

3 POSTREADING

Reviewing the Selection

The following question may be used to review the selection. *Ask:* ☐ *What are some of the groups that have used animals as symbols?* (early peoples; people of ancient Egypt, Greece, and Rome; American Indians; Vikings; people of the United States)

After the students have finished reading the selection, have them complete the review questions on page 132 in their books. The questions can be assigned as independent written work or can be answered orally during a class discussion. You may also wish to assign the activities on the same page.

Discussing the Selection

You may want to use the following questions to discuss the selection further. *Ask:* ☐ *In Japan the crane represents good luck. What might the symbols of ancient Greece and Rome represent?* (Possible responses: The owl of Athens might represent wisdom; the winged horse of Corinth might represent swiftness; the eagle of Rome might represent power.)

☐ *Why do you think the rattlesnake was used as a symbol for the young United States?* (Possible response: to tell other countries to beware of it and not try to take advantage of it because it was young and small)

☐ *Why do you think that the eagle is a fitting symbol for our country?* (Possible response: It is dignified and powerful.)

Extending the Selection

Making a Poster **(Easy)** Have the class discuss familiar symbols other than animals. Have them suggest symbols for holidays such as Halloween, Thanksgiving, and Valentine's Day. Have them make posters illustrating a variety of familiar symbols. Have them title their posters.

Writing a Paragraph **(Average)** Have the students do research to find out more about the totem poles of the Indians of the Pacific Northwest. Have the students write a paragraph describing what animals were used in these totem poles, and if possible, include information on what these animals stood for.

Making a Poster **(Challenging)** Have the students think of areas of modern life that use animals as symbols (e.g., sports teams, car names, city or town names). Have them choose one area and make a poster or a collage showing in what way the animal is used (e.g., advertising, logos, flags).

BOOKSHELF
page 133

Optional Copying Master for Enrichment

The following copying master may be assigned as independent classroom work or as a home activity to be completed with or without parents' help.

STUDY SKILLS copying master 25. **Objective:** Using an index.

3 Across the Land and Sea

pages 134–193

Theme: The excitement of journeys to new lands.

Selections
Building the Erie Canal (article)
The Erie Canal (folk song)
Crossing the Creek (story)
About LAURA INGALLS WILDER
CONNECTIONS: From Sea to Shining
  Sea
Kansas Boy (poem)
The Jumblies (poem)
Half a Kingdom (folk tale)
At Night May I Roam (chant)
BOOKSHELF

Unit Materials

Home Letter Home Letter 4 may be sent home at the beginning or the end of the unit.

Copying Masters for Evaluation*
Copying masters 27 and 31.

Copying Masters for Enrichment*
(Optional) Copying masters 26, 28, 29, 30, 32, 33, and 34.

Introducing the Unit

To introduce the students to the unit, *ask:*
☐ *Have you ever heard of a magic carpet? What does it do?* (Possible response: It lets someone fly to anywhere that person wants to go.) ☐ *Open your books to page 134–135.*

---

*Note that the copying masters indicated here are from the *Teacher's Edition, Part II.*

Do you see anything that looks like it might be a magic carpet? What? (the book that the children are on) ☐ *What do you think it means that the book is like a magic carpet?* (Possible responses: Books let us go to wherever we want to go; we can go to many places through reading books.) ☐ *What places have you gone to in the first two units of this book?* (Possible responses: Alaska, "An Eskimo Birthday"; Africa, "The Great Minu"; Japan, "The Crane Maiden")

Tell the students that in this unit, "Across the Land and Sea," they will be reading stories and poems about journeys to new lands. Explain that such journeys are often adventures for the reader as well as the characters in the stories and poems. Point out, too, that these may not only be adventures to new lands, but also to the past of our own land.

Unit Projects and Activities

Listing Ways to Travel **(Easy)** Divide the class into several groups. On a map point out two coastal cities. Have each group list all the ways they know that a person could travel between the two cities. See which group finds the most ways to travel. Then discuss the merits of all the ways of travel. (Examples: some may be faster; some cheaper; some more enjoyable, etc.)

Interviewing and Oral Reporting **(Average)** Divide the students into groups of two. Remind the students that everyone has exciting experiences to share. Have one of the students pretend to be a television reporter and ask the other to tell of something exciting that happened to him or her. Then have the reporter repeat the story for the rest of the class.

Making a Scrapbook (Challenging) Provide the students with travel magazines or travel posters. Have them cut out pictures which show places they would like to visit. Have them paste the pictures on a sheet of paper and write a paragraph telling why they would like to visit the place. Make a booklet to display the pictures and the writing.

Building the Erie Canal

page 136

The Erie Canal

pages 137–141

Objectives

Literature
● Recognizing that songs were sung to accompany work.

Content Area (Social Studies)
● Recognizing a major event in United States history.

Content Area (Music)
● Singing a folk song.

Materials

For Enrichment (Optional)

MUSIC/WORD ATTACK copying master 26, "Count the Syllables."

Awards

In 1970, the picture book *The Erie Canal* was one of the Library of Congress Children's Books of the Year.

Background

The Erie Canal was a revolutionary form of transportation in its day. Most transportation at this time was via boat on lakes and rivers. Roads were few and poor, and there were no cars or trains at that time. By connecting the Great Lakes to the Hudson River and thence to the Atlantic Ocean, the Erie Canal was responsible for New York City becoming the leading port in the nation. The Erie Canal is now part of the New York State Barge Canal System.

1 PREREADING

Key Vocabulary Word

canal: a waterway dug across land, and connecting already existing bodies of water. (page 136)

Introducing the Vocabulary

Write the word *canal* on the chalkboard. Ask the students to pronounce the word and verify their pronunciation. Ask them which letter spells the beginning sound. (c) Challenge the students to think of other ways to spell the sound /k/. (Possible responses: *ck* as in *ticket, ch* as in *anchor, cc* as in *occupy*) Have the students look up the meaning of the word *canal* in the glossary of the book.

Introducing the Article/Song

Providing Background Display a map of the New York and Great Lakes areas. Have a volunteer locate on that map the places indicated on the small map on page 136 in the student book. Point out on the large map the position of the Erie Canal in connecting the Atlantic Ocean via the Hudson River to the Great Lakes.

Previewing and Predicting Have the students look at the pictures on pages 138–139. Point out the mules pulling the barges along the canal. *Ask:* ☐ *Why do you think they needed mules to pull the barges?* (Possible responses: Barges could not move without something pushing or pulling them; mules were strong, hearty animals.) Tell the students that the men who led the mules used to sing songs as they were working and that they are going to read/sing one of those songs.

2 READING

Setting a Purpose for Reading

Say: ☐ *Read the article on page 136 to find out more about the Erie Canal. Then as you read the song, think about why people might have sung this song.*

Planning a Reading Strategy

Have the students read the article to themselves. Then have the students read the lyrics of the song on pages 138–141 together. Point out that two stanzas of the song are included on page 137, while only the first stanza is illustrated on pages 138–141. You may want to explain what a refrain is.

3 POSTREADING

Reviewing the Article/Song

The following questions may be used to review the selections. *Ask:* ☐ *What did you learn about the Erie Canal from the article on page 136?* (Possible responses: It took eight years to complete; it opened up the way west; immigrants helped to build it; horses, mules, and oxen pulled the boats and rafts.) ☐ *Why do you think people sang the song?* (Possible response: to pass the time when they were working)

Discussing the Article/Song

You may want to use the following questions to discuss the selection further. *Say:* ☐ *"I've Been Working on the Railroad" was sung by the people who built the railroads. The rhythm helped them keep up their hammering and digging. How do you suppose the rhythm of "The Erie Canal" helped the boatmen?* (Possible response: It kept them and their mules moving at a steady pace.) ☐ *Why do you think there were bridges at towns?* (Possible response: Roads crossed the canal there; people needed some way to get across the water.)

Extending the Article/Song

Singing a Work Song **(Easy)** Teach the students to sing "The Erie Canal." If possible, accompany the singing with a musical instrument. A student who has an instrument and can read music might like to accompany the class.

Writing a Diary Entry **(Average)** This may be done as a class activity. First discuss what a diary is. Then have the students study and discuss Peter Spier's illustrations. Have them think about what life on a barge was like. They may want to list on the chalkboard some of the things that happened, based on the song and the illustrations. Then have the students discuss what a diary of a boatman's child might include. Encourage motivated students to write an entry in the diary of a boatman's child living on the Erie Canal in the nineteenth century.

Preparing an Oral Report (Challenging)
Have the students do research to find out more about the Erie Canal. Some topics they may wish to consider are: the construction of the canal; how times have changed on the Erie Canal; and what kinds of cargo are shipped today on the Canal. Have the students report their findings to the class.

Optional Copying Master for Enrichment

The following copying master may be assigned as independent classroom work or as a home activity to be completed with or without parents' help.

MUSIC/WORD ATTACK copying master 26. **Objectives:** Recognizing syllables; dividing words into syllables.

Related Reading

The following books can be used to extend the lesson.

Folk Dancing by Lydia Anderson. Franklin Watts, 1981. This is an introduction to folk dancing with instructions on how to do–si–do and all the other moves of traditional dances. (Challenging)

The Village: Life in Colonial Times by James E. Knight. Troll, 1982. This book looks at life in the days a little earlier than the time of the canal, when people were settling towns and setting up stores and inns. (Average)

Life on a Barge: A Sketchbook by Huck Scarry. Four Winds Press, 1982. Canals found around the world, the barges which use them, and the people who operate the boats are all drawn here in the artist–author's style of filling every picture with hundreds of details. (Easy)

Canals by Cass R. Sandak. Franklin Watts, 1983. This simple but informative book discusses long ditches built to get cargo on boats from one body of water to another. (Easy)

Crossing the Creek
pages 142–160

Objectives

Literature
● Identifying words that describe setting.

● **Identifying character traits.**

Content Area (Social Studies)
● Describing pioneer life.

Materials

For Evaluation

LITERATURE copying master 27, "Tell About Story Characters."

For Enrichment (Optional)

SOCIAL STUDIES/STUDY SKILLS copying master 28, "Use the Map."

STUDY SKILLS copying master 29, "Find the Details."

Summary of the Story

Young Laura Ingalls and her family are traveling west over the prairie in a covered wagon. While they are crossing a creek, the water suddenly starts to rise. Though the family safely reaches the other side, Laura realizes that Jack, the family dog, has been left behind. Pa searches for Jack, but the family must move on without their beloved dog. As the family prepares for bed, Laura spots two green eyes in the near darkness. With gun in hand, Pa approaches the stranger, only to find Jack, who is happily reunited with the family.

1 PREREADING

Key Vocabulary Words

prairie: a large area of level or rolling grassy land, having few or no trees, especially the plains of the central United States. (page 143)

ford: a shallow place in a stream or river that can be crossed on foot, on horseback, or in a vehicle. (page 144)

Introducing the Vocabulary

Write the key vocabulary words on the chalkboard. Ask a volunteer to pronounce them. (See page T58 for a decoding strategy.) Have the students turn to page 151 in their books. *Say:* ☐ *This is a picture of a prairie. How would you describe a prairie?* (Lead the students to the definition above.) ☐ *Now turn to page 145 and look at the picture. The wagon is at a ford in the creek. What do you think a ford is?* (Lead the students to the definition above.)

Introducing the Story

Previewing and Predicting Locate Wisconsin and Kansas on a map of the United States. *Ask:* ☐ *If there were no cars or trains or planes, how would you get from Wisconsin to Kansas?* (Possible response: walk, ride a horse, wagon) ☐ *Do you think the journey would be easy? Why not?* (Possible responses: It is a long way to go on foot; something might happen to horse or wagon; it would take a long time.) ☐ *When you read the next story, pretend that you do not know about cars or trains or planes.*

Providing Background *Say:* ☐ *Today it is almost impossible to go where no one else has ever been. Even if you go into the wilderness, you will probably travel by road, or there will be a road nearby. Think about what it was like for the pioneers—no roads, no other people, no place to buy food, no way to know what dangers and adventures lay ahead.*

2 READING

Setting a Purpose for Reading

Say: ☐ *As you read "Crossing the Creek," remember that Laura and her family are making their way into a new land. Notice how the characters react to the dangers.*

Planning a Reading Strategy

Read the introductory paragraphs aloud to the students. Then have them read the selection silently. Since the selection is long, you may wish to divide the reading into two sections. Read through the bottom of page 150 as the first section.

3 POSTREADING

Reviewing the Story

The following questions may be used to review the story. *Ask:* ☐ *What dangerous situation did the Ingalls face?* (crossing a swift–running creek) ☐ *How did the characters in the story react in dangerous situations?* (Possible responses: Mary was afraid and hid; Laura was afraid but also wanted to see what was happening; Ma was cautious but brave; Pa was brave and faced the situation calmly.)

After the students have finished reading "Crossing the Creek," have them complete the review questions on page 160 in their books. The questions can be assigned as independent written work or can be answered orally during a class discussion. You may also wish to assign the activity on the same page.

Discussing the Story

You may want to use the following questions to discuss the selection further. *Ask:* ☐ *Although both Laura and Mary are good pioneers, each behaves differently. How would you describe Laura? Mary?* (Possible responses: Laura is brave, curious, caring; Mary is obedient, nervous, scared.)

☐ *Reread the last two paragraphs on page 130. How is this conversation important to the rest of the story?* (Possible response: It is important because just the opposite happens, and Jack is not all right.) Explain to the students that this is a clue or hint that suggests what will happen later. This technique is called foreshadowing; it adds to the suspense of the story.

Say: ☐ *The author uses many descriptions to help the reader visualize the setting. Skim the story to find words that make the prairie seem mysterious and even a bit frightening.* (Possible responses: "endless empty land"; "wind was mourning"; "the long wailing howl from the dark prairie")

☐ *The theme of this unit is adventure and suspense. How do you think "Crossing the Creek" fits in with this theme?* (Possible responses: The whole experience is an adventure; there is great suspense when they are crossing the creek and when they think Jack is a wolf.)

Evaluating the Story

To evaluate students' understanding of character traits, use **EVALUATION** copying master 27. **Objective: Indentifying character traits.**

Extending the Story

Improvising Travel Experiences **(Easy)** Have groups of four students decide on an adventure that Ma, Pa, Laura, and Mary might have today. For example, they might have a flat tire in the desert or get lost on a mountain hike. Ask the groups to discuss how each character would act. Then have the groups act out the adventure for the rest of the class. (See page T42 for improvisation techniques.)

Preparing for a Journey **(Average)** Ask the students to find books and articles to read about frontier life. Then have them list items they would need for a trip in a covered wagon. First, have them determine the approximate size of the wagon and decide what food, utensils, and tools they would take. Also have the students tell what in the list is most important. *Ask:* ☐ *If you had to lighten the load in the wagon by leaving two things behind, what would they be? Why?* Lead the class in a discussion of the things which were necessary for a long trip.

Writing a Paragraph **(Challenging)** Have the students write a paragraph from the point of view of Jack, the lost dog. Remind them to write as if Jack is telling the story. Ask them to tell how Jack felt when he was lost, what he thought about when he was alone, and how he felt when he saw the Ingalls family again.

Optional Copying Masters for Enrichment

The following copying masters may be assigned as independent classroom work or as home activities to be completed with or without parents' help.

SOCIAL STUDIES/STUDY SKILLS copying master 28. **Objectives:** Obtaining information on a map; using a map key and compass rose.

STUDY SKILLS copying master 29. **Objective:** Scanning a paragraph to find details.

Related Reading

The following books can be used to extend the lesson.

Children of the Wild West by Russell Freedman. Clarion Books, 1983. With the aid of frontier photographs, the author shows life in the American frontier lands from 1840 to the early 1900's. (Challenging)

The Laura Ingalls Wilder Songbook: Favorite Songs from the "Little House" Books by Eugenia Garson and Herbert Haufrecht. Harper & Row, 1968. This collection contains edited words and music for 62 songs and ballads, with an explanation as to the place in the stories where the songs appeared. (Challenging)

Seasons of the Tallgrass Prairie by Carol Lerner. William Morrow, 1980. Plant life of the American prairie is described season by season. (Average)

An Orphan for Nebraska by Charlene Joy Talbot. Atheneum, 1979. Orphaned on the journey to America in 1872, a young Irish boy makes his way to Nebraska where he learns the printer's trade. The story is based on actual happenings. (Challenging)

The Little House Cookbook: Frontier Foods from Laura Ingalls Wilder's Classic Stories by Barbara Walker. Harper & Row, 1979. More than 100 recipes are presented, each one preceded by a paragraph on the food's origin, use, and taste. (Challenging)

CONNECTIONS: From Sea to Shining Sea
pages 162–169

Objectives

Content Area (Social Studies)
● Describing the influence of geography on the settling of America.

● Describing how people use their physical surroundings.

● Locating regions on a map.

● Using a map to identify a route.

1 PREREADING

Introducing the Selection

Relating to Students' Experiences Have the students read the title of the selection. *Ask:* ☐ *Is this phrase familiar to you? Where have you heard it before?* (It is the last line of the first stanza of the song "America the Beautiful.") ☐ *What does the phrase mean?* (Possible responses: from the Atlantic to the Pacific; from the east to the west; from one border to the other)

Providing Background *Say:* ☐ *The first settlers to come to America were the American Indians, thousands of years ago. The first Europeans arrived nearly 500 years ago, with Christopher Columbus. Yet settlement did not begin until about 400 years ago. The United States has been settled by people from many nations, including Europeans, Africans, and Asians.*

2 READING

Setting a Purpose for Reading

Say: ☐ *As you read this selection, notice how geography helped and hindered the settling of America.*

Planning a Reading Strategy

Have selected students read the selection aloud. Use the maps within the selection to call students' attention to the places and areas discussed.

3 POSTREADING

Reviewing the Selection

The following questions may be used to review the selection. *Ask:* ☐ *How did geography influence the settling of America?* (Possible responses: On the Atlantic Coastal Plain, settlers moved up rivers; the Appalachian Mountains were a barrier to further westward settlement for a while; the desert created great hardships to people coming from Mexico.) ☐ *How did geographical features influence how people made a living?* (Possible responses: The Interior Plains were rich in farm and grazing land, so people were farmers or ranchers; the mountains contained coal and petroleum, so people were miners; the coasts had good harbors, so people engaged in fishing and shipping.)

After the students have finished reading the selection, have them complete the review questions on page 169 in their books. The questions can be assigned as independent written work or can be answered orally during a class discussion. You may also wish to assign the activity on the same page.

Discussing the Selection

You may want to use the following questions to discuss the selection further. *Ask:* ☐ *Why is this selection entitled "From Sea to Shining Sea"?* (Possible response: because our country stretches from the Atlantic Ocean to the Pacific Ocean.) On a large map of the United States have the students locate areas mentioned in the song and in the selection. Have them trace a particular route described in the selection.

☐ *Why did settlers move up river valleys on the Atlantic Coastal Plain?* (land was cheaper) Explain to the students that there were no roads at the time, and it was easier to travel up rivers by boat than to walk across land.

☐ *Why did people want to move west?* (Possible responses: People wanted more room or were seeking wealth.)

☐ *How did the discovery of gold in California influence settlement?* (Many people moved west to California.)

Extending the Selection

Singing **(Easy)** With the class, sing *America the Beautiful.* Have the students think of regions of the United States that correlate with each line. For example, "amber waves of grain" would refer to the plains regions.

Writing a Diary **(Average)** Have the students imagine they are moving west from Mississippi. Have them write an entry in their diary, describing some of the regions they have seen, and telling why they are moving west.

Doing Research **(Challenging)** Have the students do research on one of the following topics: Daniel Boone and the Wilderness Trail; the Oregon Trail; Spanish settlement in the Southwest; the California Gold Rush. Or, the students may wish to choose another topic that interests them. Then have the students present a report to the class explaining how that topic is related to the settlement of America.

Related Reading

The following books can be used to extend the lesson.

The Pioneers by Marie and Douglas Gorsline. Random House, 1982. The American West comes to life in the 1800's in this account of pioneer travel to Oregon. (Average)

How the Settlers Lived by George Laycock. David McKay, 1980. This description gives details on the living conditions, homes, clothes, and recreation of early settlers in the 1800's. (Average)

The Wonderful World of Maps by James F. Madden. Hammond, 1982. Readers are introduced to maps through simple text and full-color illustrations and maps. (Easy)

When Windwagon Smith Came to Westport by Ramona Maher. Coward-McCann, 1977. Based on fact, the book tells of an inventin' man who devised a wagon with a sail that was supposed to "sail" across the great plains in the 1850's. (Challenging)

Cumberland Gap & Trails West by Edith McCall. Children's Press, 1980. An abundance of pictures show pioneers as they struggled across the continent to settle the West. (Average)

Wagons Over the Mountains by Edith McCall. Children's Press, 1980. The "ships of the prairie" was what history named the wagons that pulled family and belongings across the "waves" of prairie grass and up over the treacherous Rocky Mountains in the early days of our country. (Challenging)

Mississippi Sternwheelers by Pam and Gerry Zeck. Carolrhoda Books, 1982. Photographs and text show transportation on the Mississippi from Huck Finn log rafts to the big paddle boats that were the royalty of river travel in the 1800's. (Average)

Kansas Boy

pages 170–171

Objective

Literature
● Recognizing and enjoying fantasy in poetry.

1 PREREADING

Introducing the Poem

Relating to Students' Experiences *Say:*
☐ *You do not have to travel far to have an adventure; you can have one even at home. Have you ever pretended that you lived someplace else and that you were someone else?*
You may want to discuss what it would be like if students lived in the desert or on an island. Have them picture it in their minds and imagine who they would be.

2 READING

Setting a Purpose for Reading

Say: ☐ *In the following poem, a boy living on the Kansas prairie has an exciting adventure as he imagines himself as someone he would like to be. Notice how this adventure differs from the Kansas boy's life.*

Planning a Reading Strategy

Read the poem aloud once to the students. Have them close their eyes and try to imagine the fantasy the Kansas boy is having. Then have the students read the poem aloud together.

3 POSTREADING

Reviewing the Poem

The following question may be used to review the poem. *Ask:* ☐ *How did the boy's life differ from the adventure he dreamed of?* (Possible responses: He was a farm boy in Kansas, far from the ocean; he dreamed of being a sailor.)

Discussing the Poem

You may want to use the following questions to discuss the poem further. *Ask:* ☐ *The boy "walks . . . as sailors walk." Can someone demonstrate that walk? Why do you suppose he has these dreams?* (Possible responses: People like to imagine adventures; he dreams about the sea because he's never seen it.) ☐ *Writers often compare things to make each thing appear clearer. When things are compared, the author is showing how they are alike. What "waves" are compared in line 4?* (the waves of corn growing and the waves of the ocean) ☐ *What things are compared in the last line of the poem?* (Possible responses: the gulls and the crows; shouts and dreams)

Extending the Poem

Using a Map **(Easy)** Display a map of the United States. Point out Kansas on the map. Lead the students in a discussion of why someone living in Kansas might never see sailing ships. Then have the students examine the map and make a list of states which border oceans or gulfs.

Writing Sentences **(Average)** Have the students select at least six words or groups of words from "Kansas Boy" which relate to the sea. (Examples: sea, sailors, waves, oceans, ships, spray, salty, sailed, coast, sea winds, white gulls.) Then have the students write sentences using the words they have found.

Using Description (**Challenging**) Have the students do a **clustering activity** to generate paragraphs about their fantasy place. First have them write the name of their fantasy place on a piece of paper and circle the name. Then have them use their senses to write as many words or phrases as they can think of to describe what their place is like. These words/phrases are clustered around the circled word(s). For example:

Finally have the students use these words/phrases to **write a paragraph** about their fantasy place.

The Jumblies
pages 172–175

Objectives

Literature
- Interpreting nonsense poetry.
- Distinguishing between sense and nonsense in poetry.

Materials

For Enrichment (Optional)

LITERATURE/COMPREHENSION copying master 30, "Finish the Rhymes."

1 PREREADING

Key Vocabulary Word

sieve: a utensil made of wire mesh or metal with many small holes, used for straining. (page 172)

Key Concept Word

nonsense: actions that convey an absurd meaning or no meaning.

Introducing the Vocabulary

Write the word *sieve* on the chalkboard and pronounce it. Have the students look up the definition in the glossary. Ask a volunteer to draw a picture of one on the chalkboard. Discuss what a sieve is used for (draining spaghetti or vegetables, rinsing fruits or lettuce).

Introducing the Poem

Providing Background *Say:* ☐ *Like many other characters in this unit, the Jumblies are traveling. Their journey is just a little different, however. Since you know that a sieve is a kitchen strainer, you will understand from the first line why this journey is a little strange.*

Relating to Students' Experiences *Ask:* ☐ *Have you ever heard anyone say to someone who was doing something silly "Stop that nonsense!" or "This is nonsense"? What do you think that person meant?* (Lead the students to conclude that what the other person was doing made no sense at all; that it was silly.) ☐ *You might want to say "This is nonsense" after you read "The Jumblies."*

2 READING

Setting a Purpose for Reading

Say: ☐ *As you read about the Jumblies' adventures, watch for things that might make you say "This is nonsense."*

Planning a Reading Strategy

First read the poem aloud as the students follow in the book. See page T71 in the front of this book for two more verses of "The Jumblies." You might read these fourth and fifth verses to the students before you read the sixth, and last, verse on page 175. After the initial reading, have the class do a choral reading of the poem. Assign one student to be the narrator, another student to read the dialogue of the Jumblies, and a third student to read the part of "every one." Have the entire class read the refrain, the last four lines of each stanza. (See page T47 for choral reading techniques.)

3 POSTREADING

Reviewing the Poem

The following questions may be used to review the poem. *Ask:* ☐ *What are some of the things that would lead you to conclude that the poem is nonsense?* (Possible responses: The Jumblies went to sea in a sieve; their heads were green and their hands were blue; they wrapped their feet in pink paper to keep them dry.)

Discussing the Poem

You may want to use the following questions to discuss the poem further. *Ask:* ☐ *Why is it silly to think that the Jumblies could sail in a sieve?* (Possible responses: because a sieve could not float; it does not keep out water) ☐ *In the second verse, people are saying that ". . . it's extremely wrong / In a sieve to sail so fast." Why is their advice nonsense?* (Possible responses: because speed will not keep a sieve from sinking) ☐ *Why is Jumblies a good name for these characters?* (Possible response: because they are jumbled, or mixed up; they do foolish things)

☐ *Were you surprised by the end of the poem? Why or why not?* (Possible responses: yes, because the Jumblies had a successful adventure, came back, and now everyone else wants to go; no, because in a nonsense poem, it makes sense for the ending to be something unexpected)

Extending the Poem

***Creating a Drama* (Easy)** Divide the students into small groups. Have them make Jumblies stick puppets (see T45 for puppetry techniques). Have each group create a short play using dialogue from the poem. Then have each group perform their play for the rest of the class.

Writing Sentences (Average) Ask the students to pretend to be Jumblies. Tell them that someone asks, "Why is your head green, and why are your hands blue?" Have the students write sentences to answer the questions.

Using Research Skills (Challenging) Ask the students to find information about different kinds of sailing vessels. Have them check with the librarian for help with their research. Then have the students choose one kind of ship and write at least one paragraph about it. Encourage the students to tell about the ship's history and its main uses.

Optional Copying Master for Enrichment

The following copying master may be assigned as independent classroom work or as a home activity to be completed with or without parents' help.

LITERATURE/COMPREHENSION copying master 30. **Objectives:** Identifying rhyming words; completing nonsense rhymes.

Related Reading

The following books can be used to extend the lesson.

Otter Nonsense by Norton Juster. Philomel/Putnam, 1982. These animal puns and ridiculous pictures make a challenging but funny book. (Easy)

The Pelican Chorus and the Quangle Wangle's Hat by Edward Lear. Viking Press, 1981. The first of these poems tells about the Nile; the other describes a creature whose hat was 102 feet wide! (Average)

Half a Kingdom
pages 176–191

Objectives

Literature
● Recognizing the characteristics of a folk tale.

● Recognizing the tone of a story.

Literature/Comprehension
● **Identifying solutions to problems in a story.**

Materials

For Evaluation

LITERATURE/COMPREHENSION copying master 31, "Solve the Problem."

For Enrichment (Optional)

MATHEMATICS copying master 32, "Divide the Kingdom in Half."

COMPOSITION copying master 33, "Imagine and Write an Adventure."

Awards

The picture book *Half a Kingdom* was one of the Library of Congress Children's Books of the Year in 1977 and a Children's Choice in 1978.

Summary of the Story

When Prince Lini disappears in a cloud of fog, the king offers half of his kingdom to the person who brings him back. Signy, a peasant girl, finds the prince asleep in a cave. Learning that he is under the spell of trolls, Signy discovers how to awaken him, and together she and the prince trick the trolls, making them disappear forever. They return to the king, who reluctantly gives Signy half his kingdom. She and the prince decide to marry and rule together.

1 PREREADING

Key Vocabulary Words

peasant: a poor farmer. (page 179)
troll: in folk tales, a troublesome creature, either dwarf or giant who lives in caves, in hills, or under bridges. (page 180)

Introducing the Vocabulary

Write the key vocabulary words on the chalkboard. Ask the students to pronounce the words, and verify their pronunciation. Have the students find the words in context in their books. Have them read the words aloud in context and infer the meaning of each word. At this point you may wish to present pictures of each word, if you can obtain these from the library. The students may wish to modify their definitions, based on these visual aids. Finally have the students check the glossaries in their books to verify the definitions of the words.

Introducing the Story

Previewing and Predicting Ask: □ *Do you know anything about a folk tale? Let's turn back to page 107 and reread some of the characteristics of a folk tale.* (Have the students read silently.) □ *What are some of the things that you already know about "Half a Kingdom" before you even read it?* (Lead students to put the characteristics of a folk tale in their own words.) □ *Have you read any other folk tales in this book?* ("The Great Minu," "The Crane Maiden")

2 READING

Setting a Purpose for Reading

Say: □ *As you read the next folk tale, notice its likenesses and differences from the folk tales you have read.*

Planning a Reading Strategy

Have the students read the story silently. After the initial reading, point out the frequent use of dialogue in the tale. Assign roles to two groups of students to read the dialogue between Signy and Lini on pages 183–184, and between Lini and the trolls on pages 185–186. Have the students try to bring out the humor in both scenes.

3 POSTREADING

Reviewing the Story

The following questions may be used to review the story. *Ask:* □ *How is this a typical folk tale?* (Possible responses: An ordinary person has her wishes granted; most characters act only one way; some magic happens; it contains the words "retold by.") □ *In a typical folk tale, a king would do anything to get his son back. In this story, though, the king does not want to give up half his kingdom for his son. What other things in this story are different from the usual folk tale?* (Possible responses: A prince is held prisoner; a woman finds him and helps him escape; Prince Lini is reluctant to return home.)

After the students have finished reading "Half a Kingdom," have them complete the review questions on page 191 in their books. The questions can be assigned as independent written work or can be answered orally during a class discussion. You may also wish to assign the activity on the same page.

Discussing the Story

You may want to use the following questions to discuss the selection further. *Ask:*
☐ *How would you describe the character Signy?* (Possible responses: brave, resourceful, honest) ☐ *By making a woman the rescuer in the tale, the author has done something unexpected. Often that which is unexpected is also humorous. What other examples of humor can you find in this story?* (Possible responses: Signy looks "near and narrow" for the Prince instead of "far and wide"; the trolls chant "Fie, Foo, Fum, Firl" because they smell a girl, instead of the usual giant's chant "Fee, Fi, Fo, Fum"; Signy plays a game of checkers before deciding to marry the Prince.)

☐ *There is a serious side to this folk tale, too. Look back at the conversation between Signy and Lini on pages 184–185. What is the tale saying that might be understood as a moral?* (Possible response: It's not fair for the rich not to work and the poor to have to work too hard.)

Evaluating the Story

To evaluate the students' story comprehension, use **EVALUATION** copying master 31. **Objective: Identifying solutions to problems in a story.**

Extending the Story

Making Reward Posters (Easy) Have the students make posters offering a reward for information about Prince Lini. Remind them to write specific information on their posters. Some students may wish to illustrate their posters with a picture of Prince Lini.

Writing a Newspaper Report (Average) Have the students pretend to be one of the friends traveling with Prince Lini when he disappeared. Have them write a report for a newspaper telling about the incident. Be sure that they include information that answers the questions who, what, when, and where.

Writing an Alternate Ending (Challenging) Have the students imagine that Signy refused to marry Prince Lini. Have them write another ending for the story. Encourage them to use dialogue and to have Signy tell the Prince why she will not marry him.

Optional Copying Masters for Enrichment

The following copying masters may be assigned as independent classroom work or as home activities to be completed with or without parents' help.

MATHEMATICS copying master 32. **Objective:** Using models to figure equivalent fractions.

COMPOSITION copying master 33. **Objectives:** Using details to describe an object; describing characters and a story setting; writing an adventure story.

Related Reading

The following books can be used to extend the lesson.

Clever Gretchen and Other Forgotten Folktales retold by Alison Lurie. T. Y. Crowell, 1980. These folk tales are not usually remembered and include heroines who are witty and brave, can defeat giants, answer riddles, and rescue friends.

Prince Ring: Icelandic Fairy Tale. Creative Education, 1983. This story of magic and nobility is set in the lands of the far North. (Average)

Zlateh the Goat and Other Stories by Isaac Bashevis Singer. Harper & Row, 1966. Seven stories depict life in a small Polish village. A lesson can be learned from each one. Spanish Edition, *Cuentos audios de la aldea Chelm.* (Average)

At Night May I Roam

page 192

Objective

Literature

● Recognizing that repetition and echo can give a poem cohesion.

1 PREREADING

Introducing the Poem

Providing Background *Say:* ☐ *"At Night May I Roam" is a song of the Sioux Indians. Maybe it expresses a wish that each of you might make.*

2 READING

Setting a Purpose for Reading

Say: ☐ *As you read "At Night May I Roam," notice the use of repetition in both stanzas (parts) and how the second stanza (part) echoes the first.*

Planning a Reading Strategy

Have the students read the poem silently. Then have the class do a choral reading of the poem. Have one group of students repeat the words "may I roam" while another group reads the rest of the words in each verse. See page T43 for choral reading techniques.

3 POSTREADING

Discussing the Poem

You may want to use the following questions to discuss the poem. *Ask:* ☐ *What was the effect of the repetition and echo in the chant?* (Possible responses: helped the chant hold together as a whole; created a hypnotic effect) ☐ *Why might a person sing this poem?* (Possible responses: might want to have the freedom to roam wherever he or she wishes; might want to enjoy nature at all times of day)

Extending the Poem

Researching Information **(Easy)** Ask the students to bring books, pictures, and objects that relate to American Indians. Where appropriate, have the students tell something about what they have brought. Then place all the materials in an interest center for the class.

Writing Poetry **(Average)** Have the students study the structure of "At Night May I Roam," noticing which words are repeated and which ones change from one stanza to another. Then have the students think of a time of day when they would like to roam. Ask the students to add a third stanza to the poem, using their own ideas.

Writing Short Biographies (Challenging)
Have the students consult the school librarian or other teachers to find information about famous Sioux Indians (Suggested names: Crazy Horse; Red Cloud; Sitting Bull; Gall; Spotted Tail). Ask the students to write a short biographical sketch of one of these famous persons. Ask for volunteers to read their biographies to the rest of the class.

Related Reading

The following books can be used to extend the lesson.

North American Indians by Marie and Douglas Gorsline. Random House, 1978. Bright–colored pictures show ways many of the different tribes lived, emphasizing their individual style of housing, clothing, and more. (Easy)

The Trees Stand Shining: The Poetry of the North American Indians selected by Hettie Jones. Dial Press, 1971. Just translated and written down in the last century, these poems are really songs in which the American Indians told their feelings about the world in which they lived. (Average)

BOOKSHELF

page 193

Optional Copying Master for Enrichment

The following copying master may be assigned as independent classroom work or as a home activity to be completed with or without parents' help.

STUDY SKILLS copying master 34. **Objectives:** Using the outside guides of the library card catalog; using the inside guides of the library card catalog.

4 *When Paths Cross*
pages 194–267

Theme: The relationship between contrasting points of view and personal growth.

Selections
The Lion and the Mouse (fable)
The Monkey and the Crocodile (fable)
Guess Who My Favorite Person Is (story)
Some People (poem)
Hope (poem)
Dreams (poem)
About LANGSTON HUGHES
The Escape (story)
Sound of Sunshine, Sound of Rain (story)
CONNECTIONS: The Turkey or The Eagle
Mexicali Soup (story)
BOOKSHELF

Unit Materials

Home Letter Home Letter 5 may be sent home at the beginning or end of the unit.

Copying Masters for Evaluation*
Copying masters 35, 38, 42, 45, and 48.

Copying Masters for Enrichment* (Optional) Copying masters 36, 37, 39, 40, 41, 43, 44, 46, 47, 49, 50, and 51.

Introducing the Unit

To introduce the students to the unit, have them read the unit title and look at the picture on pages 194–195. To begin the dis-

cussion, *ask:* ☐ *What is happening in this picture? Do you recognize these characters?* (Many students will be able to identify Peter Pan and Captain Hook about to do battle with each other.) ☐ *How does this picture relate to the unit title?* (Possible responses: Peter Pan's and Captain Hook's paths have crossed; Peter Pan and Captain Hook meet.) ☐ *What might happen when people's paths cross?* (Possible responses: Friendship could result, or conflict could result.) ☐ *What happened between Peter Pan and Captain Hook?* (They disagreed.)

Tell the students that in this unit they will be reading fables, stories, and poems about meetings between people and between animals. When people's paths cross, one result may be contrasting points of view, or different ideas about the same thing. Explain that this kind of meeting need not be unpleasant but instead may provide an opportunity for growth and learning.

Unit Projects and Activities

Completing Sentences **(Easy)** Explain to the students that growing and changing is part of the theme of this unit. Discuss with the students ways in which they have grown and changed. Encourage suggestions about personal as well as physical growth. Then write this sentence on the chalkboard: "Once I was _____, but now I am _____." Have each student think of three ways in which he or she has changed. Have them rewrite the sentences, using the instances they have thought of.

Keeping a Journal **(Average)** Ask the students to keep a journal to write down some of their thoughts after completing each of the selections in the unit. At the end of the unit, divide the students into small groups and have the students share some of the things which they have written. Afterwards, discuss any changes which anyone has made during the study of the unit.

Writing a Letter **(Challenging)** Have the students write a letter to a friend or to a well–known public figure. The letter should tell the person about those things that the student thinks the person should *never* change. Then lead the class in a discussion of good qualities which we like to find in people.

The Lion and the Mouse

pages 196–199

Objectives

Literature
● Identifying characteristics of a fable.

● **Identifying the theme (moral) of a fable.**

Comprehension
● Recognizing the meaning of proverbs and fables.

Materials

For Evaluation

LITERATURE copying master 35, "Write the Moral."

For Enrichment (Optional)

VOCABULARY/DECODING copying master 36, "Find the Silent Letters."

COMPREHENSION copying master 37, "Tell About the Fable."

Summary of the Fable

A Lion catches a Mouse but sets her free when she promises to repay him. Days later, the Lion is caught in a hunter's net. The Mouse gnaws through the ropes to free the Lion, proving that little friends may turn out to be great friends.

1 PREREADING

Key Vocabulary Words

thrashing: swinging, rolling, or moving around wildly and rapidly. (page 198)
gnaw: to chew. (page 198)

Key Concept Words

fable: a brief story that teaches a lesson.
moral: the lesson at the end of a fable.

Introducing the Vocabulary

Write these sentences on the chalkboard: My dog likes to *gnaw* on a bone. The fish was *thrashing* around in the net. Have a student read each sentence. *Ask:*
▢ *What other word could you use in the sentence instead of* gnaw? (Possible responses:

chew, bite) ☐ *What word could you use instead of* thrashing? (Possible responses: twisting, tossing) Read each sentence with a synonym in place of the underlined word.

Call students' attention to the word *gnaw*. Remind them that some words have letters that are not pronounced. These letters are called "silent" letters and the *g* in *gnaw* is one of them. Challenge students to think of other words beginning with the sound /n/ spelled *gn*. (Possible responses: gnu, gnash, gnome)

Introducing the Fable

Providing Background *Say:* Long ago in ancient Greece, a man named Aesop wrote many stories to teach lessons or morals. In these stories, called fables, animals with human personalities are usually the main characters. A fable usually ends with a statement of the lesson or moral.

Relating to Students' Experiences Ask if students have ever read or heard a fable. If so, have volunteers retell it. Students will probably be most familiar with "The Hare and the Tortoise" and "The Ant and the Grasshopper."

2 READING

Setting a Purpose for Reading

Direct the students to read the fable to find what lesson Aesop was trying to teach.

Planning a Reading Strategy

Have the students read the fable silently. Point out that the lesson or moral, at the end of the fable, is set in a different kind of type to make it stand out from the rest of the fable.

3 POSTREADING

Reviewing the Fable

The following questions may be used to review the fable. *Ask:* ☐ *What is the moral of the fable?* (Little friends may prove to be great friends.) ☐ *Put the moral into to your own words.* (Possible response: Someone you don't think much about may help you a great deal.)

Discussing the Fable

You may want to use the following questions to discuss the fable further. *Ask:* ☐ *What is a fable?* (a story that teaches a lesson or moral) ☐ *Would you say this fable is long or short?* (short) ☐ *Why do you think fables are so short?* (Possible response: The lesson can get lost in a long story.) ☐ *Who are the main characters in this fable?* (Lion and Mouse) ☐ *If the Lion were human, how would you describe him? Use examples from the fable to support your answer.* (Possible response: proud, lazy) ☐ *How would you describe the Mouse? Use examples from the fable to support your answer.* (Possible responses: loyal, brave)

Evaluating the Fable

To evaluate the students' understanding of the fable, use **EVALUATION** copying master 35. **Objective: Identifying the theme (moral) of a fable.**

Extending the Fable

Making a Chart **(Easy)** Review the elements of a fable presented in the discussion section: fables are brief; fables are told to point out a moral; fables usually have characters that are animals with human characteristics. Then have the students make a chart showing the general characteristics of a fable and how this fable exemplifies these characteristics.

Story Theater **(Average)** Assign parts to the students and have them act out the fable. (See page T46 for Story Theater techniques.)

Rewriting Morals **(Challenging)** Ask the students to quote morals or proverbs, such as "Look before you leap," "A stitch in time saves nine," or "Don't count your chickens before they hatch." (You may also wish to use the morals on the **EVALUATION** copying master.) Then have them rewrite the proverbs or morals in their own words.

Optional Copying Masters for Enrichment

The following copying masters may be assigned as independent classroom work or as home activities to be completed with or without parents' help.

VOCABULARY/DECODING copying master 36. **Objective:** Using phonic analysis to decode words.

COMPREHENSION copying master 37. **Objectives:** Identifying elements of plot—sequence of events; making inferences.

The Monkey and the Crocodile

pages 200–205

Objectives

Literature
- Identifying the characteristics of a fable.

Literature/Comprehension
- Creating an ending to a fable, given characters, setting, and situation.

- **Identifying elements of plot—sequence and development.**

Content Area (Social Studies)
- Applying the moral of a fable to personal experience.

Materials

For Evaluation

LITERATURE/COMPREHENSION copying master 38, "Complete the Events."

For Enrichment (Optional)

COMPOSITION copying master 39, "Write a Fable."

VOCABULARY copying master 40, "Find the Meaning."

Summary of the Fable

Crocodile is always trying to catch Monkey. In this story, he climbs on a rock in a river, knowing that Monkey must cross the river there to return to his tree. Monkey spies Crocodile and, pretending to surrender, tells Crocodile to open his mouth wide. Knowing that Crocodiles close their eyes when they open their jaws, Monkey escapes by jumping on Crocodile's head and whisking up into his tree.

1 PREREADING

Key Vocabulary Words

whisked: moved quickly and lightly. (page 204)
cunning: cleverness in getting something. (page 204)

Introducing the Vocabulary

Write the words *whisked* and *cunning* and their definitions on the chalkboard. Have the students pronounce the words and read the definitions. Then have them choose which word belongs in each of these sentences: The cat _____ after the mouse. You will have to have great _____ in order to win the prize. Then have the students create their own sentences using the words *whisked* and *cunning*.

Introducing the Fable

Providing Background Review with the students the characteristics of a fable. *Ask:* ☐ *What is a brief story that teaches a lesson or moral called?* (fable) ☐ *Who are usually the main characters of a fable?* (animals) ☐ *Let's list on the board the characteristics of a fable.* (brief, has a moral or teaches a lesson, usually animal characters)

Relating to Students' Experiences Have the students recall the previously read fable "The Lion and the Mouse." *Ask:* ☐ *Who were the main characters?* (Lion and Mouse) ☐ *What was the moral of the fable?* (Little friends may prove to be great friends.) Have the students retell the story that led to the moral.

2 READING

Setting a Purpose for Reading

Say: ☐ *Every fable has a moral. Read "The Monkey and the Crocodile" and look for the moral of this story. Be prepared to state it in your own words.*

Planning a Reading Strategy

Have selected students read the fable aloud. You may wish to assign parts similar to what is done in a play. Have one student read the monkey's words, one student read the crocodile's words, and one student be the narrator.

3 POSTREADING

Reviewing the Fable

The following questions may be used to review the fable. *Ask:* ☐ *What would you say the moral of the fable is?* (Lead students along the lines of "thinking things through before acting.") ☐ *What events led up to the moral?* (Lead students to retell the fable in their own words.) ☐ *Which character would you say was smarter? Why?* (Possible response: the monkey, because he outsmarted the crocodile)

After the students have finished reading the fable, have them complete the review questions on page 205 in their book. The questions can be assigned as independent written work or can be answered orally during a class discussion. You may also wish to assign the activity on the same page.

Discussing the Fable

You may want to use the following questions to discuss the fable further. *Ask:*
☐ *What words would you use to describe the Monkey's personality?* (Possible responses: smart, cunning, thoughtful) ☐ *How would you describe the Crocodile's personality?* (Possible responses: gullible, greedy, wicked)

☐ *The Monkey saved himself by noticing that Crocodile was on the rock. When have you saved yourself or someone else by noticing that something was unusual?* (You might help students by giving a suggestion, such as noticing an approaching car before crossing a street.)

Evaluating the Fable

To evaluate the students' understanding of the story order, use **EVALUATION** copying master 38. **Objective: Identifying elements of plot—sequence and development.**

Extending the Fable

Preparing an Oral Report **(Easy)** Have the students **brainstorm** to determine what elements of this fable's storyline might be verified through research. Some possibilities include: Do crocodiles like to eat monkeys? Do crocodiles close their eyes when they open their mouths? What do crocodiles and monkeys like to eat? Then have the students do research in an encyclopedia or book about these animals to find out the answers to these and other questions. Students may also be interested in finding out more about other habits of these animals. Have the students share their information with the class.

Writing Headlines **(Average)** Have the students write alliterative headlines proclaiming the victory of the monkey in this fable or the mouse in the previous fable or the predicament of the crocodile or the lion. (For example, Mighty Monkey Maneuvers Magnificently)

Making Comparisons **(Challenging)** Have students **brainstorm** to come up with human traits that can be applied to animals. Have them use a format such as "as busy as a bee." They should be able to explain why they associate the trait with a particular animal. (Possible responses: as stubborn as a mule, as sly as a fox, as eager as a beaver, as wise as an owl)

Optional Copying Masters for Enrichment

The following copying masters may be assigned as independent classroom work or as home activities to be completed with or without parents' help.

COMPOSITION copying master 39. **Objective:** Writing a fable.

VOCABULARY copying master 40. **Objective:** Recognizing multiple meanings of words.

Related Reading

The following books can be used to extend the lesson.

Fabulas de Esopo by Aesop. Barcelona: AFHA International, 1976. Beautiful illustrations accompany this collection of fables told in Spanish.

The Hare and the Tortoise and the Tortoise and the Hare by William Pene du Bois and Lee Po. Doubleday, 1972. The stories of the famous duo are told here in both Spanish and English. (Average)

Three Rolls and One Doughnut: Fables from Russia retold by Mirra Ginsburg. Dial Press, 1970. These fables and riddles from all corners of Russia are good for a chuckle and some serious thinking too. (Average)

Tales from Aesop retold by Harold Jones. Franklin Watts, 1982. Old–fashioned fairy tale–like pictures give a good feeling of the agelessness of the famous stories with morals. Spanish Edition: *Fabulas de Esopo* Lectorum Publishers. (Challenging)

Fables by Arnold Lobel. Harper & Row, 1981; paperback, 1983. Each of these fables has a surprise moral. (Easy)

Guess Who My Favorite Person Is

pages 206–215

Objectives

Literature
● Recognizing characters' points of view as expressed through imagery.

● Recognizing that imagery depends on careful observation and vivid language.

Content Area (Social Studies)
● Recognizing that people have different points of view.

Awards

The book *Guess Who My Favorite Person Is* was a Children's Choice in 1978.

Summary of the Story

Two girls meet in an alfalfa field and play the "tell–me–what–your–favorite–thing–is" game. To play the game, they take turns describing their favorite colors, sounds, tastes, and smells. After agreeing that their favorite time of day is "now," the new friends walk back to the road together.

1 PREREADING

Introducing the Story

Relating to Students' Experiences If possible obtain the record from the musical "The Sound of Music" and play the selection "My Favorite Things." Ask the students what some of their favorite things are. Encourage them to be as descriptive as possible when telling about their favorite things.

Previewing and Predicting *Say:*
☐ *Though I may like strawberries best while you like apples, neither of us is making a wrong choice. Each person has certain likes and dislikes. In this story, two girls become friends even though they learn that each other's choices and ways of looking at things are different.*

2 READING

Setting a Purpose for Reading

Have the students leaf through the story. Then *ask:* ☐ *Do you notice anything unusual about the way this story is written?* (Some students may notice that it is written in short lines of unequal length, almost as if it were poetry.) ☐ *This story is similar to poetry in another way: In it the author uses vivid language and careful observation to describe things in the world. She creates "word pictures," images so clear that you can picture them in your mind. As you read, look for these word pictures.*

Planning a Reading Strategy

Read the story aloud to the students, emphasizing the phrasing and imagery, as if the selection *were* poetry. Ask the students to close their eyes and try to imagine the setting and the word pictures described by the friends. Then have the students reread the selection silently.

3 POSTREADING

Reviewing the Story

The following questions may be used to review the story. *Ask:* ☐ *What word pictures did you notice in the story?* (Possible responses: ". . . the blue on a lizard's belly . . ." page 210; ". . . dark reddish brown that's good for mountains and for rocks" page 210; ". . . about a thousand bees buzzing in all the fields around." page 211)

After the students have finished reading the selection, have them complete the review questions on page 215 in their books. The questions can be assigned as independent written work or can be answered orally during a class discussion. You may also wish to assign the activity on the same page.

Discussing the Story

You may want to use the following questions to discuss the selection further. *Ask:* ☐ *How can you tell that the girls have differing ideas or views when they are choosing ladybugs?* (Possible response: They do not understand each other's choice of a favorite ladybug.) ☐ *Which girl do you think was the older? Why?* (Possible response: the one who was telling the story, because in the beginning she refers to the other girl as "this little kid") ☐ *Who do you think is the "favorite person" in the title of the story? Why?* (Possible response: the younger girl, because the two girls became friends as they told each other their "favorites") ☐ *Which of the "word pictures" describe your favorite things?* (Accept any answer that the student reasonably supports.)

Extending the Story

Graphing Favorites (Easy) Do this as a class activity. Have the class play the "tell—what—your—favorite—thing—is" game for a topic such as school subjects, activities, or kinds of reading. Begin by having students list their favorite of whatever topic is decided upon. Then list the choices on the chalkboard. For example, if "school subjects" was chosen, the list would include Reading, Math, Science, Social Studies, and so forth. Collect the student votes, and make a mark on the chalkboard beside each subject for each vote. Then have the class make a bar graph on a large piece of poster board (see below). The left column should list the subjects. On the bottom write "Number of Students' Favorites" and number each blank. Each blank should be the equivalent of one student. Title the graph "Students' Favorites: (add topic)."

Students' Favorite School Subjects

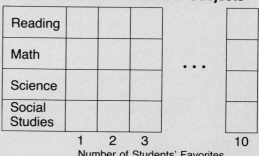

Number of Students' Favorites

Introducing Classmates (Average)

Divide the students into pairs. Have them share some of their interests with each other. For instance, each might tell of a hobby, a favorite food, a favorite sport, etc. After sharing interests, have the students stand before the rest of the class and introduce their partners, using the phrase: I would like you to meet my friend, _____. He/she likes _____.

Writing a Character Description (Challenging)

Have the students choose one of the characters in "Guess Who My Favorite Person Is" to write about. Tell them to give the character a name and to write a description of her. Encourage the students to include how the character looks; what she likes to do; how she relates to others; and whether she would be a good friend to have.

Related Reading

The following books can be used to extend the lesson.

Hawk, I'm Your Brother by Byrd Baylor. Charles Scribner's Sons, 1976. In this poignant story, a boy grows and changes because of his relationship with a hawk. (Average)

Everyone Needs a Rock by Byrd Baylor. Charles Scribner's Sons, 1974. The author tells how everyone needs some place to call his or her own, a place to think and ponder. Peter Parnall's beautiful pictures give a feeling for nature. (Easy)

Ramona and Her Father by Beverly Cleary. William Morrow, 1977. When Ramona's father loses his job, the whole family feels the effect. Ramona begins to understand about people's hopes, dreams and self-esteem. (Challenging)

Honey, I Love: And Other Love Poems by Eloise Greenfield. T. Y. Crowell, 1978. One charming, run-on poem focuses on laughing, home life, and friends, while the rest are poems on music, jump rope, train rides, anything you might love. (Easy)

Baseball Fever by Johanna Hurwitz. William Morrow, 1981. A very young boy is a baseball nut: he knows everything there is to know about it. It takes a special occasion for his father to realize different things matter to people, and these things may not be so foolish as others think. (Average)

The Covered Bridge House and Other Poems by Kaye Starbird. Four Winds Press, 1979. In these poems Kaye Starbird pays tribute to the people and beauty of New England. (Challenging)

Some People

page 216

Objectives

Literature
- Understanding and interpreting figurative language.

Comprehension
- Recognizing comparisons.

1 PREREADING

Key Vocabulary Word

shrivel up: to wrinkle and dry up. (page 216)

Introducing the Vocabulary

Write the key phrase on the chalkboard and pronounce it. *Ask:* ☐ *Have you ever seen a prune or a raisin? If I told you that a prune is a shriveled-up plum, could you tell me what shriveled-up means? What?* (Possible response: dried up) ☐ *Does anyone know what a raisin is?* (a shriveled or dried-up grape)

Introducing the Poem

Relating to Students' Experiences *Say:* ☐ *When you read "Guess Who My Favorite Person Is," you saw how the author can create pictures using words. And you might have created some of your own "word pictures." Poets can create vivid pictures with only a few words. One way they do this is by comparing two different things. For example: If a poet says "The grass is like velvet" or "the lake is as shiny as a diamond" you can picture what the poet is describing.*

2 READING

Setting a Purpose for Reading

Say: ☐ *Read this poem and identify the two comparisons presented in it.*

Planning a Reading Strategy

Read the poem aloud to the students. As you read, try to give expression to the words as though one person were talking to another.

3 POSTREADING

Reviewing the Poem

The following question may be used to review the poem. *Ask:* ☐ *What two comparisons did you find in this poem?* ("thoughts . . . like leaves all brown and dried"; "thoughts as thick as fireflies")

Discussing the Poem

You may wish to use the following questions to discuss the poem further. *Ask:* ☐ *How does the poem say you feel when you are with people you enjoy?* ("Your thoughts [are] as thick as fireflies/All shiny in your mind!") ☐ *What does that mean?* (Possible response: You can think of lots of things to share and talk about.) ☐ *How does the poem say you feel when you are with people you do not enjoy?* (". . . feel so tired inside,/Your thoughts begin to shrivel up/Like leaves all brown and dried!") ☐ *What does that mean?* (Possible response: You have nothing to share with some people; they aren't interesting to you.) ☐ *What is being said in the poem?* (Possible response: that for every person, some people are more exciting to know than others)

Extending the Poem

Making Comparisons **(Average)** Review the comparisons in the poem, and explain that these are comparisons that use the words *like* or *as*. Then have the students complete the following: smile like a _____; frowns like a _____.

Hope
Dreams

pages 217–218

Objectives

Literature
- Relating a poem's title to its meaning.

- Understanding and interpreting figurative language.

Vocabulary
- Choosing meanings for multiple meaning words.

Materials

For Enrichment (Optional)

LITERATURE copying master 41, "Make Comparisons."

1 PREREADING

Key Vocabulary Word

fast: tightly. (page 218)

Introducing the Vocabulary

Write the words *hold fast* and *run fast* on the chalkboard. Ask if *fast* means the same thing in both phrases. (no) Discuss the multiple meanings of the word *fast*. Have the students suggest synonyms for *fast* in the phrases on the board. (Possible responses: firmly, solidly, tightly, quickly, speedily)

Introducing the Poems

Relating to Students' Experiences *Say:*
☐ *Everyone has hopes and dreams. What kinds of hopes and dreams do you think many people your age have?* (Possible responses: hope they will do well in school, dream about being a sports star or astronaut)

2 READING

Setting a Purpose for Reading

Say: ☐ *As you read these two poems, see if you can tell why the poet thinks hopes and dreams are important.*

Planning a Reading Strategy

These poems are brief and may be read one after the other. Ask for a volunteer to read each poem. Then have the students reread the poems silently.

3 POSTREADING

Reviewing the Poems

The following question may be used to review the poems. *Ask:* ☐ *Why does the poet think hopes and dreams are important?* (Possible responses: They make life worth living; they give people something to look forward to.)

Discussing the Poems

You may want to use the following questions to discuss the poems further. *Ask:*
☐ *What does the poet hope for in the first poem?* (the end of his loneliness) ☐ *The second poem is called "Dreams." What kinds of*

dreams are discussed in the poem, dreams we have at night or dreams about what to do or be? How do you know? (Possible response: dreams about what to do or be, because those dreams often show hopes for life and for the future) □ *To what does the poet compare life without dreams?* ("... a broken–winged bird/That cannot fly"; "... a barren field/Frozen with snow.")

Extending the Poems

Making a Wall of Heroes **(Easy)** Have the students bring pictures to class of persons they admire. The heroes may be persons from any historical period. If a student does not have a picture of the admired person, ask him or her to print the person's name on a card. Make colorful construction paper frames for the pictures or cards and display them around the room. Allow each student to tell something about the dreams or accomplishments of his or her hero.

Making a List **(Average)** Ask the students to write lists of things that persons can do when they feel lonely. Have the students read their lists to the class.

Writing a Paragraph **(Challenging)** Ask the students to write at least a paragraph under the title "My Hopes and Dreams." Encourage the students to write about the good things which they hope will happen to them, their friends, and their family.

Optional Copying Master for Enrichment

The following copying master may be assigned as independent classroom work or as a home activity to be completed with or without parents' help.

LITERATURE copying master 41. **Objectives:** Identifying similes; writing similes.

The Escape

pages 220–229

Objectives

Literature
● Identifying a character's changing moods.

Comprehension
● Recognizing a sequence of events.

● **Identifying causes in cause–and–effect relationships.**

Materials

For Evaluation

COMPREHENSION copying master 42, "Write the Reason for Wilbur's Feelings."

For Enrichment (Optional)

COMPOSITION copying master 43, "Use Colorful Words."

VOCABULARY copying master 44, "Find the Right Word."

Awards

The novel *Charlotte's Web* was on the American Library Association Notable Children's Books list in 1952 and was a Newbery Honor Book in 1953.

Summary of the Story

Boredom and a persuasive goose convince Fern's pet pig, Wilbur, to try a brief taste of freedom. He escapes from his pen, but Mrs. Zuckerman, Fern's aunt, quickly spots him. Although the barnyard animals shout suggestions to help a frightened Wilbur avoid capture, he suc-

cumbs to the temptations of Mr. Zuckerman's pail of slops and returns to his
pen.

them appreciate the dialogue of the
goose. Then have them read the remainder of the story silently.

1 PREREADING

Introducing the Story

Providing Background *Ask:* □ *Has anyone ever read or heard of the book* Charlotte's
Web? *Can anyone tell us about it?*

Say: □ *In this section from the book,
Wilbur the pig finds a sure cure for his boredom—and more excitement than he can
handle.*

Relating to Students' Experiences *Ask:*
□ *Do you ever get bored with your routine,
your schedule of things you have to do every
day?* (Accept any answer that the student
reasonably supports.) □ *What do you do so
that you do not get bored?* (Accept any answer that the student reasonably supports.)

2 READING

Setting a Purpose for Reading

Say: □ *Usually when we read about an escape, the person or creature who escapes is
happy to be free. As you read about Wilbur,
notice how his escape differs and how he feels
about his escape.*

Planning a Reading Strategy

Since this is a challenging selection, you
may want to read the first part of the selection (through the end of the first paragraph on page 223) aloud to the students.
Use expression and intonation to help

3 POSTREADING

Reviewing the Story

The following question may be used to review the story. *Ask:* □ *What was unusual
about Wilbur's escape from his pen?* (Possible
responses: He did not really want to be
free; once he was free, he wished he were
back in his pen.)

After the students have finished reading
the story, have them complete the review
questions on page 229 in their books. The
questions can be assigned as independent written work or can be answered
orally during a class discussion. You may
also wish to assign the activity on the
same page.

Discussing the Story

You may wish to use the following questions to discuss the selection further. *Ask:*
□ *Wilbur wanted to do something different
because he was bored. After he was out of his
pen, though, he changed his mind. Why?* (Possible responses: because he did not like being chased; he was tempted by food; he did
not know what to do outside his pen.)
□ *Why did the other animals want Wilbur to
escape?* (Possible responses: because they
wished they were free; they enjoyed the
commotion.) □ *Do you think Wilbur has
grown or changed as a result of his escape?
Explain.* (Possible responses: Yes, when he
is bored again, he will remember how
frightening the escape was and find another
way to escape from boredom; maybe he will
remember the pail of slops and decide to escape again in the hopes of getting some
food.)

Evaluating the Story

To evaluate students' understanding of causes, use **EVALUATION** copying master 42. **Objective: Identifying causes in cause–and–effect relationships.**

Extending the Story

Writing Alternative Titles **(Easy)** Ask the students to write another title for the selection. Ask them not to use the word *escape* in the new title. Have the students read their titles to the class and tell why they chose the new titles.

Writing a Paragraph **(Average)** Have the students pretend to be the goose in the story. Then have them write a paragraph from the goose's point of view, telling Wilbur why he should not have gone back into his pen.

Researching Pigs **(Challenging)** Have the students make a list of facts about pigs. Encourage the students to consult the librarian or other knowledgeable persons for help. Encourage them to find little–known facts to share with the class.

Optional Copying Masters for Enrichment

The following copying masters may be assigned as independent classroom work or as home activities to be completed with or without parents' help.

COMPOSITION copying master 43. **Objective:** Identifying and using synonyms.

VOCABULARY copying master 44. **Objectives:** Identifying words by their meaning; identifying words using context clues.

Related Reading

The following books can be used to extend the lesson.

The Story of Arachne by Pamela Espeland. Carolrhoda Books, 1980. In this ancient myth of the origin of spiders, poor Arachne spins better than the Queen of the Gods, but discovers this was not wise at all! (Average)

The Spider by Margaret Lane. Dial Press, 1983. Fascinating information is presented about different kinds of spiders and the ways they live. (Easy)

Wonders of Pigs by Sigmund A. Lavine and Vincent Scuro. Dodd, Mead, 1981. The text focuses on how pigs were first tamed and how the different breeds were developed, but also includes a little about pigs in folklore and stories. (Challenging)

Spider Magic by Dorothy H. Patent. Holiday House, 1982. Wolf spiders, tarantulas, even spiders that look like ants are described, particularly the special body parts that make it possible for them to spin, leap, or walk on water! (Average)

Stuart Little by E. B. White. Harper & Row, 1945. When the Littles' son was born, even the doctor was surprised to see he was definitely NOT a person but a perfect little mouse. Heroic, loving, helpful and full of wit and wisdom—that's Stuart Little. (Challenging)

Sound of Sunshine, Sound of Rain

pages 230–245

Objectives

Literature
- Identifying descriptive language.
- **Identifying character traits.**

Comprehension
- Comparing points of view in a story.
- Recalling facts and details about the senses.

Materials

For Evaluation

LITERATURE/COMPREHENSION copying master 45, "Tell About Story Characters."

For Enrichment (Optional)

SOCIAL STUDIES/STUDY SKILLS copying master 46, "Map the Park."

MATHEMATICS/STUDY SKILLS copying master 47, "Figure Out the Time."

Summary of the Story

Because he is blind, a young boy has learned to enjoy the textures and sounds of his world. On pleasant days his sister takes him to a nearby park. Even though she tells him the park is ugly and dirty, he loves to spend his time there. One day the boy meets Abram, the ice cream man, who shares the boy's feelings about the park. As their friendship grows in the days that follow, the boy comes to learn that beauty can be found everywhere.

1 PREREADING

Introducing the Story

Providing Background Review point of view with the students. Point of view is the vantage point from which a story is told. Tell the students that in "Sound of Sunshine, Sound of Rain," the story is told from the first person point of view, that is, a character in the story tells the story *as he experienced it.* When a character within the story tells the story, he or she uses the pronoun *I* to describe his or her thoughts, feelings, and actions.

Previewing and Predicting *Ask:* ☐ *What are our five senses?* (sight, hearing, taste, smell, touch) ☐ *The story that we are going to read is called "Sound of Sunshine, Sound of Rain." Which of the senses do you think the story will deal with?* (hearing, touch) Point out that often when we lose one of our senses, our other senses become stronger.

2 READING

Setting a Purpose for Reading

Say: ☐ *In* "Sound of Sunshine, Sound of Rain," *people see the same place in very different ways. As you are reading the story, examine the different ways that people "see."*

Planning a Reading Strategy

Have the students close their eyes and listen as you read the first seven paragraphs of the story to them (pages 231–232). Have the students try to imagine that they lack the use of their sense of sight and that the experiences and sensations described by the boy are theirs. Then have them read the remainder of the story silently.

3 POSTREADING

Reviewing the Story

The following question may be used to review the story. *Ask:* ☐ *What might be some different ways that people can "see"?* (Possible responses: People can see exactly what is there; people can see more beauty in something than is actually there; people can see less beauty in something than is actually there.)

After the students have finished reading the story, have them complete the review questions on page 245 in their books. The questions can be assigned as independent written work or can be answered orally during a class discussion. You may also wish to assign the activity on the same page.

Discussing the Story

You may want to use the following questions to discuss the story further. *Ask:* ☐ *What words would you use to describe the boy's sister and mother?* (Possible responses: sister—impatient, loud; mother—understanding, warm, soft) ☐ *How would you describe Abram?* (Possible responses: friendly, understanding, generous) ☐ *The boy's sister and Abram both explained their feelings about the park. Whose ideas do you think the boy agreed with? Why?* (Possible response: Abram's, because the boy thought the park was a beautiful place)

☐ *Look at the three subheads in the story. What is described in each part?* (Possible response: The section entitled "Morning Voices" is about morning at the boy's house and getting to the park; the section entitled "A New Voice" describes his first meeting with Abram; the section entitled "Something Special" describes Abram giving the boy the balloon and the boy's feelings about the balloon.)

☐ *Look at the paragraph describing the dream on the middle of page 240. How has the author made you feel what the boy is dreaming?* (Possible response: The way she has described his being tumbled in a net seems very real and possibly frightening.)
☐ *When the boy's sister finds him, he is all tangled up in his blanket. To what part of his dream does this refer?* (trying to get out of the net)

☐ *Do you think the boy will find happiness? Why or why not?* (Possible responses: no, because he is too dependent on others and he does not live in a beautiful world; yes, because he is attempting to be independent and because he is trying to see beauty in his world.)

☐ *Remember that poets often describe things by using comparisons. The author of this story uses comparisons also, to help the reader see as the young boy might see. Choose a section from the story and find the comparisons that the author uses.* Examples: page 231 "voice . . . warm and soft as a pillow . . . little and sharp and high like needles flying . . ."; page 234 "her nails, little and sharp, like her voice"; page 238 "his voice is kind and soft as fur." ". . . is soft as a sweater."

Evaluating the Story

To evaluate students' understanding of character traits, use **EVALUATION** copying master 45. **Objectives: Identifying character traits; recalling details to support statements.**

Extending the Story

Identifying Sounds and Objects (Easy)

Tape—record sounds, such as vending machine noise and a whistling tea kettle. Bring in such objects as a hairbrush, a piece of sandpaper, and seashells, and put them in paper bags. Have students take turns trying to describe the objects after touching them only and the sounds without knowing what they are. Urge them to compare the objects to other things as the boy did in "Sound of Sunshine, Sound of Rain."

Writing a Paragraph (Average)

Have the students write at least one paragraph describing an ideal park. Encourage them to include: what kinds of plants should be there; where it should be located; what kinds of equipment should be there; and what kinds of rules it should have for its use.

Writing a Paragraph (Challenging)

Ask the students to write a paragraph explaining one of the following passages from the story: Abram's comparison of people and balloons (bottom, page 240); Abram's discussion of colors (top, page 243); if and how the boy has changed at the end of the story, or how the title is related to the story. Have them begin by jotting down thoughts, and then ordering them into a **first draft**. Have them **edit** their first draft and write a **final draft**. (See page T36 at the front of this book for techniques to use in teaching written composition.

Optional Copying Masters for Enrichment

The following copying masters may be assigned as independent classroom work or as home activities to be completed with or without parents' help.

SOCIAL STUDIES/STUDY SKILLS copying master 46. **Objectives:** Using a map key and compass rose to draw a map; marking a route on a map.

MATHEMATICS/STUDY SKILLS copying master 47. **Objective:** Interpreting a schedule to calculate minutes, seconds, and hours.

Related Reading

The following books can be used to extend the lesson.

The Gift by Helen Coutant. Alfred A. Knopf, 1983. A young girl seeks the perfect gift for her elderly friend who has lost her sight and learns that she can share her sight (the perfect gift) with the blind woman. (Easy)

Oliver Hyde's Dishcloth Concert by Richard Kennedy. Little, Brown, 1977. A fiddler, grieving over his wife's death, refuses to come and mingle with the other people in the town. A friend coaxes him to fiddle for a wedding, but Oliver will only do it if the friend and everyone else will do as Oliver asks. (Average)

Mine for a Year by Susan Kuklin. Coward-McCann, 1984. In this moving and heartwarming book with photographs, a boy spends a year working with a puppy before the dog starts training to be a guide dog. (Challenging)

The Balancing Girl by Bernice Rabe. E. P. Dutton, 1981. The story is about a girl who is very good at balancing things—even though she is in a wheelchair. (Average)

Hang Tough, Paul Mather by Alfred Slote. Harper & Row, 1972; Avon paperback, 1975. Paul Mather loves baseball, but he has only a few months of ballplaying before his dreaded leukemia makes it impossible for him to play. Spanish Edition: ¡Coraje, campeón! J. B. Lippincott, 1979. (Challenging)

The New Boy Is Blind by William E. Thomas. Julian Messner, 1980. Problems of a blind child as he enters a school environment are handled well here, and answers are given to questions students will be sure to ask. (Average)

The Seeing Stick by Jane Yolen. T. Y. Crowell, 1977. This modern Chinese legend tells about an emperor's blind daughter who is helped by a wise old man and his ideas. (Average)

CONNECTIONS: The Turkey or the Eagle?

pages 246–249

Objectives

Content Area (Social Studies)
- Identifying a national symbol.

- Recognizing individuals' rights to have differing opinions.

1 PREREADING

Introducing the Selection

Relating to Students' Experiences *Ask:* □ *What is a symbol?* (something that stands for something else) □ *What symbols can you think of that stand for the United States or its government?* (Possible responses: the flag, Uncle Sam, the eagle, the White House)

Providing Background *Ask:* □ *What is the name of this unit?* ("When Paths Cross") □ *What has that meant in most of the selections that you have read in this unit?* (Possible response: People disagree or hold different points of view; people or animals play tricks on one another; arguments.)

2 READING

Setting a Purpose for Reading

Have the students read the selection to see how the disagreement about our national symbol was resolved and why the eagle was chosen.

Planning a Reading Strategy

Have selected students read the selection aloud. Tell students to think about which symbol they would have chosen and why.

3 POSTREADING

Reviewing the Selection

The following may be used to review the selection. *Ask:* ☐ *Who decided that the eagle would be the official symbol of the United States?* (Congress in 1782) ☐ *Why was the bald eagle chosen?* (Possible responses: can be found only in North America; is beautiful and independent)

After the students have finished reading the selection, have them complete the review questions on page 249 in their books. The questions can be assigned as independent written work or can be answered orally during a class discussion. You may also wish to assign the activities on the same page.

Discussing the Selection

You may want to use the following to discuss the selection further. *Ask:* ☐ *What qualities were to be represented in the national symbol?* (Possible responses: independence, justice, freedom, equality, pride) ☐ *What characteristics does the wild turkey possess that made it a consideration for the national symbol?* (Possible responses: beautiful, a true American bird, smart, useful, independent)

Extending the Selection

Drawing Flags (Easy) Have the students find out what the different flags of the United States, since the country's beginning, have looked like. They should draw each flag and label the flag with the dates as to when it was used.

Preparing an Oral Report (Average) Have students select other symbols of the United States and have them prepare a report that tells the origin, use, and/or meaning of each symbol. (Suggested symbols: the National Anthem, the Liberty Bell, the flag, the Statue of Liberty, the Pledge of Allegiance, the White House)

Locating State Symbols (Challenging) Have the students find out if their state has a state flag, animal, flower, and/or motto. If you have students in your class who were not born in America, you may wish to have them share the information about the symbols of their native lands—flags, songs, etc.

Mexicali Soup

pages 250–266

Objectives

Literature
● Identifying changes in the characters' points of view.

Comprehension
● **Making inferences.**

Content Area (Social Studies)
● Describing how traditions and customs differ among individuals and groups.

Materials

For Evaluation

LITERATURE/COMPREHENSION copying master 48, "Solve Mama's Problem."

For Enrichment (Optional)

VOCABULARY/WORD ATTACK copying master 49, "Add a Prefix."

MATHEMATICS/SOCIAL STUDIES copying master 50, "Find the Better Buy."

Summary of the Story

As Mama is marketing for the ingredients to make Mexicali Soup, a meal that originates from her family's home in the mountains of Mexico, she meets each of her children. Learning that she is going to make Mexicali Soup, each child asks her to omit a different vegetable so the soup will be more like the food eaten by city people. When Mama returns home, she banishes the family from the kitchen and prepares the soup according to their wishes. Much to the family's surprise, the soup has become nothing but hot water.

1 PREREADING

Introducing the Story

Relating to Students' Experiences *Ask:* □ *Is there a favorite food or dish at your house, perhaps one that came from the country where your family or ancestors onced lived? Describe the food (dish). With what country is the food associated?* (Accept any answer that the student reasonably supports.)

Previewing and Predicting *Say:* □ *In the next story a Mexican family has moved to a large city in the United States. Mexicali*

Soup is the favorite meal of this family. See if you can guess what will happen to the soup as you read the story.

2 READING

Setting a Purpose for Reading

Say: □ *The recipe for the soup in the story changes. See if you know how the soup changes before you read the end of the story. But the soup is not the only thing that changes in the story. As you read, also notice the characters who change and how they change.*

Planning a Reading Strategy

Before beginning the reading, pronounce the Spanish names in the story.

Read the first two paragraphs aloud to the students. Use an expressive tone to help the students appreciate Mama's cheerful mood. Then have the students finish reading the story silently.

3 POSTREADING

Reviewing the Story

The following questions may be used to review the story. *Ask:* □ *How did Mama's mood change through the story?* (Possible response: She was cheerful in the beginning, then sad and angry, and finally satisfied.)

□ *What caused her mood to change?* (Possible response: She was cheerful when she thought about making the soup; then everyone complained about something in it; she figured out how to satisfy everyone, including herself.)

☐ *Did any other characters change? Explain.* (Possible response: Some students will think that Mama changed her family's point of view.)

After the students have finished reading the story, have them complete the review questions on page 266 in their books. The questions can be assigned as independent written work or can be answered orally during a class discussion. You may also wish to assign the activity on the same page.

Discussing the Story

You may want to use the following questions to discuss the story further. *Ask:* ☐ *How did Mama trick her family?* (by removing everything from the soup but the water) ☐ *Look at page 259, where Mama begins to hum in the kitchen. Why do you think she begins to sing?* (Possible response: She has thought of a way to teach her family a lesson, and it makes her feel good.)

☐ *What did the family think of the soup when they lived in the mountains?* (They thought it was "the best soup in the world.") ☐ *Why did the family want to change the soup?* (Possible responses: They didn't want to be different; they wanted to be like city people; they thought they could improve the soup.)

☐ *The title of this unit is "When Paths Cross." What paths crossed in this story?* (Possible responses: Mama's and the rest of her family's; the "old" ways and the "new" ways.) ☐ *What do you think was learned?* (Possible response: The new ways are not always better.)

Evaluating the Story

To evaluate the students' understanding of the story, use **EVALUATION** copying master 48. **Objectives: Identifying sequence and development; recalling details; making inferences.**

Extending the Story

Finding and Listing Spanish Names **(Easy)** Provide students with maps of the United States and have them examine the names on the maps to find at least ten names of cities, rivers, or mountains that reflect the Spanish heritage of the United States. Tell the students that most of these will be found in the West and Southwest. Tell them that most of the Spanish names will begin with *San, Santa, El, Los, Las,* or *Del.* Have the students list the names they found; indicate whether they are cities, rivers or mountains; and tell in what state they are located.

Improvising **(Average)** Have volunteers improvise the dinner-table scene and what might happen after Mama's speech. (See page T47 at the front of this book for improvisation techniques.)

Writing Recipes **(Challenging)** Have each student write a recipe for a favorite dish. To help them with the style, provide cookbooks or recipes from a newspaper. Point out the two parts of most recipes: the first lists the ingredients, and the second part describes how to prepare the dish. Have students suggest reasons for these two sections. (Possible response: The first part is helpful for the cook to gather the ingredients.)

Optional Copying Masters for Enrichment

The following copying masters may be assigned as independent classroom work or as home activities to be completed with or without parents' help.

VOCABULARY/WORD ATTACK copying master 49. **Objective:** Building vocabulary by adding prefixes to root words.

MATHEMATICS/SOCIAL STUDIES copying master 50. **Objective:** Calculating unit prices; evaluating unit prices.

Related Reading

The following books can be used to extend the lesson.

The Wind in the Willows Country Cookbook by Arabella Boxer. Charles Scribner's Sons, 1983. Recipes for all kinds of occasions are accompanied by Ernest Shepard's marvelous pictures. (Challenging)

Poem Stew selected by William Cole. J. B. Lippincott, 1981. These poems are about all sorts of food, some good, some rather strange, but all funny. (Challenging)

The Fairy Tale Cookbook by Carol MacGregor. Macmillan, 1983. This cookbook contains recipes for stone soup, Ananse's baked yams, Strega Nona's magic pasta, and other goodies. (Challenging)

Mexico: Activities & Projects in Color by Claude Soleillant. Sterling, 1978. With drawings and photographs, the book describes how to make a Mexican party (fiesta), a piñata, jewelry, costumes, and all sorts of things including Mexican food. (Challenging)

Science Experiments You Can Eat by Vicki Cobb. Harper & Row, 1972. All these experiments with food produce edible results. Spanish Edition: *Experimentos científicos que se pueden comer.* (Challenging)

Cricket's Cookery by Pauline Watson and Cricket Magazine editors. Random House, 1977. With recipes in verse and witty sayings, this book includes a recipe for meatballs made with directions to a parody of the "Marine Hymn" and banana bread to the tune of "Oh, Susanna." (Average)

BOOKSHELF

page 267

Optional Copying Master for Enrichment

The following copying master may be assigned as independent classroom work or as a home activity to be completed with or without parents' help.

STUDY SKILLS copying master 51. **Objective:** Identifying author, title, and subject cards in a library card catalog.

5 What a Character!
pages 268–353

Theme: The actions of remarkable characters in humorous situations.

Selections
Spunky Ramona (story)
About BEVERLY CLEARY
My Sister Jane (poem)
CONNECTIONS: Folk heroes of the United States
Four Fearsome Critters (folklore)
There Was an Old Man with a Beard (limerick)
A Young Lady of Ealing (limerick)
Paddington Goes to the Hospital (play)
About MICHAEL BOND
LEARN ABOUT PLAYS: On Stage!
Digging into the Past (story)
Old Joe Clarke (song)
BOOKSHELF

Unit Materials

Home Letter Home letter 6 may be sent home at the beginning or end of the unit.

Copying Masters for Evaluation*
Copying masters 52, 56, and 59.

Copying Masters for Enrichment*
(Optional) Copying masters 53, 54, 55, 57, 58, 60, 61, and 62.

Introducing the Unit

To introduce the students to the unit, have them read the unit title silently and look at the illustration on pages 268–269. Ask

*Note that the copying masters indicated here are from the *Teacher's Edition, Part II*

students to suggest meanings for the word *character.* (Some students may say a character is a person in a play or story; others may know that a character can be a person who is different or unusual.) Ask a student to read the unit title, reminding him/her to use expression, as indicated by the exclamation mark. Then *ask:*
□ *What characters do you recognize in this illustration?* (Some students will be able to identify Mary Poppins, Paul Bunyan and his blue ox Babe, Alice in Wonderland, and Winnie the Pooh.) □ *Why do you think these characters are pictured with this unit title?* (Possible response: because all are very memorable.) □ *What might these characters have in common?* (Possible responses: They are all funny; they come from well–known stories.)

Tell the students that in this unit they will be reading stories, poems, and a play about remarkable characters who find themselves in unusual situations. Then allow some time for the students to look through the unit.

Unit Projects and Activities

***Making a Book Display* (Easy)** Have the students make a book display of remarkable characters in literature. You may want to begin this activity by having the class **brainstorm** about qualities or situations that make certain characters unforgettable. Then have each student select a book that they have read about an unusual character. Students who cannot think of a book may want to consult the

"Bookshelf" on page 353. Have the students arrange their books in a book display in the library or reading areas of the classroom. Entitle the display "What a Character!"

Writing Sketches **(Average)** Ask the students to write a character sketch of themselves. Have them mention some of their better qualities, things they can do very well, and things they are proud of. Tell the students to use their names as the title for their sketches. Ask for volunteers to read their sketches to the class and post the papers on the bulletin board or bind them together in a booklet so that everyone can read them.

Writing a Character Sketch **(Challenging)** Have the students write a character sketch of some remarkable person they know. They should begin by **outlining** their sketch to include a physical description of the person, the attributes that make the person remarkable, and examples of actions that display the attribute. Have the students write a **rough draft,** submit it to another student or small group of students for discussion, and then **revise** it. Remind the students that a character can be understood more easily by a reader when the writer describes the character's thoughts, words, and actions, rather than just using adjectives to tell about the character.

Spunky Ramona

pages 270–284

Objectives

Comprehension
- **Identifying character traits and feelings through action.**

- Recalling details.

Vocabulary
- Identifying words using context clues.

Materials

For Evaluation

COMPREHENSION copying master 52, "Tell About Story Characters."

For Enrichment (Optional)

VOCABULARY/COMPREHENSION copying master 53, "Choose the Best Word."

VOCABULARY/WORD ATTACK copying master 54, "Find the Compound Words."

Awards

In 1975, the novel *Ramona the Brave* was on the Library of Congress Children's Books of the Year List and one of the School Library Journal Best Books of the Year for Children.

Summary of the Story

Six–year old Ramona Quimby is reluctant to show her parents her first–grade progress report. She finally does reveal the report to them, but explodes at what she considers her teacher's unfairness by shouting a bad word. Her family's laughter makes Ramona cry, but they discuss her difficulties and reassure her. Reminded that she is "spunky," Ramona goes to sleep feeling better.

1 PREREADING

Key Vocabulary Word

spunky: courageous; spirited (page 270)

Introducing the Vocabulary

Write the vocabulary word on the chalkboard, and ask the students to pronounce it. Write the word in context on the chalkboard (see page 282). Have the students read the sentence aloud and tell the meaning of the word. Have them suggest synonyms for the word. (Synonyms: courage, spirit, pluck, boldness, fearlessness)

Introducing the Story

Relating to Students' Experiences *Say:* □ *This unit is about unforgettable characters. The story we are going to read is a part of a longer story about a girl named Ramona. Has anyone ever read anything about Ramona before? What is Ramona like?* (Accept any answer that the student reasonably supports.)

Previewing and Predicting *Say:* □ *Ramona is spunky; she has spirit and courage. She is also six years old, confused, and frightened by a teacher who does not seem to understand her.*

2 READING

Setting a Purpose for Reading

Say: □ *Read this story to find out why Ramona is so unforgettable. Look for things she says and does that show her personality and feelings, and for ways she solves her problems.*

Planning a Reading Strategy

Have the students read the selection silently. You may wish to do the suggested extending activity (see Extending the Story) using Story Theater techniques before you begin the discussion of the story.

3 POSTREADING

Reviewing the Story

The following questions may be used to review the story. *Ask:* □ *What words would you use to describe Ramona?* (Possible responses: spunky, spoiled, artistic, defiant) □ *Show examples from the story to support your descriptions.* (Accept any answer that the student reasonably supports.) □ *What were Ramona's problems?* (Possible responses: showing the progress report to her parents; not getting along with her sister; getting along with her teacher; dealing with the disappointment of the somewhat critical school report) □ *How did Ramona handle her problems?* (Possible responses: She tried to hide the progress report and drew pictures to forget her troubles; she got along with her sister at times, but seemed jealous of her, too; she did not seem able to get along with her teacher; she shouted what she thought was a "bad word" to express her disappointment about the report and her frustration at her family's seeming lack of understanding.)

After the students have finished reading the story, have them complete the review questions on page 284 in their books. The questions can be assigned as independent written work or can be answered orally during a class discussion. You may also wish to assign the activity on the same page.

Discussing the Story

You may want to use the following questions to discuss the selection further. *Say:* ☐ *Find examples of Ramona's spunk in the story.* (Possible responses: at first she refuses to bring her progress report to the table; she gives her own opinions.) ☐ *How do Ramona's feelings change during the story?* (Possible responses: She is angry and upset when her father asks for her progress report; embarrassed when everyone laughs at her; comforted when her family reassures her.)

☐ *How did each member of Ramona's family comfort her at the end?* (Possible responses: Her father reminded her that she had spunk; her sister recalled incidents when their parents had laughed at her and also explained why Mrs. Griggs might like a student like Beezus more than one like Ramona; her mother reassured her about her parents' love for her.)

☐ *Do you think Ramona is a likable character? Why or why not?* (Accept any answer that the student reasonably supports.)

Evaluating the Story

To evaluate students' understanding of character traits, use **EVALUATION** copying master 52. **Objectives: Identifying character traits; recalling details.**

Extending the Story

Writing About Character Differences **(Easy)** Remind the students that all people in families are different. In the story, Ramona and her sister Beezus were not alike. Have the students make a chart with the names of Ramona and Beezus at the top. Have the students write words or sentences under each name to show how the girls acted alike or different in different circumstances.

Enjoying Story Theater **(Average)** Have groups of students act out the dinner table scene using Story Theater techniques. Before they begin, discuss ways to emphasize the humor of the situation. For example, they may want to exaggerate Ramona's reactions as opposed to the calmness of the rest of the family. (See page T46 for Story Theater techniques.)

Writing a Letter **(Challenging)** Have the students pretend to be one of Ramona's parents and write Ramona's teacher about the progress report. Remind them to write about both the positive and the negative things that Mrs. Griggs said. After the students have written the letters, have them let another student read the letters to see if they are easily understood. Then have the students **revise** their letters and write a second draft if it is necessary.

Optional Copying Masters for Enrichment

The following copying masters may be assigned as independent classroom work or as home activities to be completed with or without parents' help.

VOCABULARY/COMPREHENSION copying master 53. **Objectives:** Identifying words by meanings; identifying words using context clues.

VOCABULARY/WORD ATTACK copying master 54. **Objective:** Identifying and writing compound words.

Related Reading

The following books can be used to extend the lesson.

Henry Huggins by Beverly Cleary. William Morrow, 1950. A typical small boy gets into all kinds of funny predicaments. Spanish Edition: *Henry Huggins* translated by Argentina Palacios. William Morrow, 1983. (Challenging)

Ralph S. Mouse by Beverly Cleary. William Morrow, 1982; Dell paperback, 1983. This book, the winner of the 1983 Golden Kite award, tells the story of a rather special rodent who is one of the author's most memorable characters. (Challenging)

Ramona the Pest by Beverly Cleary. William Morrow, 1968; Dell paperback, 1982. The pesky little girl who makes everyone laugh is at it again. Spanish Edition: *Ramona la chinche.* Lectorum Publishers, 1984. (Challenging)

Shark Lady: True Adventures of Eugenie Clark by Ann McGovern. Four Winds Press, 1979. When she was little, this independent lady knew she wanted to work with the life in the oceans. In this biography she tells of her special career. (Challenging)

Jefferson by Mary Francis Shura. Dodd, Mead, 1984. The kids on the block, each one special in his or her own way, plan a surprise birthday party for little Jefferson. His brother is worried, because every time Jefferson is involved, there's disaster. (Average)

My Sister Jane

pages 286–287

Objectives

Literature
- Enjoying a humorous character description in a poem.

- Identifying exaggeration.

Materials

For Enrichment (Optional)

LITERATURE copying master 55, "Find and Write Exaggerations."

1 PREREADING

Introducing the Poem

Providing Background *Say:* □ *If I said that someone has a heart as big as a house, you would know that I was exaggerating—or stretching the truth. If I said "I've told you that a thousand times," you would know that I was exaggerating. Can you think of other examples of exaggeration?* (Suggestions: heart of gold; weak as a kitten; sitting on top of the world)

2 READING

Setting a Purpose for Reading

Say: ☐ *In this poem, a boy describes his sister Jane. See if you believe everything he says.*

Planning a Reading Strategy

First, have the students read the poem silently. Then assign roles for a choral reading. Have the class read the refrain at the end of each stanza, and have different students take the role of the boy in each stanza. Encourage the students to use expression to convey the sense of Jane's strangeness. (See page T44 for choral reading techniques.)

3 POSTREADING

Reviewing the Poem

The following questions may be used to review the poem. *Ask:* ☐ *Did you believe everything the boy said about his sister Jane? Why or why not?* (Possible response: no, because no person can do or be the things he described about Jane)

Discussing the Poem

You may want to use the following questions to discuss the poem further. *Ask:* ☐ *The boy describes Jane as a crow. What crow–like things does she do?* (She stares like a crow, has thin crow legs, flies around the house.) ☐ *How do you know the boy is exaggerating?* (Possible responses: He will not tell anyone that Jane is a crow; she is disguised when people visit; she would not fly through the house or dance on the piano keys when visitors are present.)

☐ *Why do you think the boy compares Jane to a crow?* (Possible responses: He is teasing her; something about her may remind him of a crow and he is making up the poem for fun.)

Extending the Poem

Making a List **(Easy)** Remind the students that Jane displayed bad manners at the table by stabbing her food the way a crow would do. Have them make lists of good "non–crow" table manners. Have the students share their lists. Then lead the students in a discussion of good manners at other places and times.

Writing a Paragraph **(Average)** Have the students write a paragraph to persuade Jane not to act like a crow. Encourage them to give Jane some specific reasons why she should act differently.

Writing About Crows **(Challenging)** Have the students do simple research to find out about the habits of real crows. Ask the students to consult with their librarian for help with finding appropriate information. Then have the students write a summary of what they have learned and share the summary with the other students.

Optional Copying Master for Enrichment

The following copying master may be assigned as independent classroom work or as a home activity to be completed with or without parents' help.

LITERATURE copying master 55. **Objectives:** Recognizing exaggerations; writing exaggerations.

CONNECTIONS:
Folk Heroes of America

pages 288–295

Objectives

Literature
- Identifying a tall tale and its origin.

Comprehension
- Explaining likenesses in tall–tale heroes.

1 PREREADING

Introducing the Selection

Previewing and Predicting *Ask:* ☐ *What is the name of this unit?* ("What a Character") ☐ *What characters have you read about so far in this unit?* (Ramona and Jane) ☐ *Were they your average, everyday people?* (no) ☐ *Read the title of this selection. Do you think you will be reading about people like Patrick Henry or George Washington? Why or why not?* (Possible response: no, because they probably were not humorous characters like this unit includes)

Providing Background *Ask:* ☐ *What are the characteristics of a folk tale?* (If necessary refer the students back to the characteristics listed on page 107.) (Possible responses: Wishes are granted to ordinary people; most characters act only one way; some magic may happen; they were made up long ago and passed down orally.) ☐ *We are going to read about stories that have some of the same characteristics.*

2 READING

Setting a Purpose for Reading

Say: ☐ *Read this selection to find out what a tall tale is and why tall tales might have come about.*

Planning a Reading Strategy

After selected students have read a section of the selection aloud, have a student indicate on a map of the United States the part of the country referred to in each tall tale.

3 POSTREADING

Reviewing the Selection

The following questions may be used to review the selection. *Ask:* ☐ *What is a tall tale?* (Possible response: a story that contains a little bit of truth that is stretched) ☐ *Why do you think tall tales came about?* (Possible responses: for fun, to celebrate the outstanding features of an ordinary person, to show that some jobs were so difficult that they required extraordinary people)

After the students have finished reading the selection, have them complete the review questions on page 295 in their books. The questions can be assigned as independent written work or can be answered orally during a class discussion. You may also wish to assign the activities on the same page.

Discussing the Selection

You may want to use the following questions to discuss the selection further. *Ask:* ☐ *What do folk tales and tall tales have in common?* (Possible responses: They were passed down orally, some magic or something extraordinary is often involved, most characters act only one way.)

☐ *Which tall tale would you enjoy reading and why?* (Accept any answer that the student reasonably supports.)

Extending the Selection

Reading a Story (Average) Have the students find the tall tales of the heroes mentioned here or other famous tall tales. Point out to them that there are often many variations on the stories, so encourage them to bring in different versions of the same story. Have a storytelling time where students can read their tall tales to the rest of the class.

Creating a Tall Tale (Challenging) As a class, make up a tall tale. Help students select a person, an occupation, and exploits. Encourage them to use their imagination and really stretch the truth in telling the story. Write and revise the tale on the chalkboard. Then have volunteers create a book of the tale including illustrations.

Researching Regional Tall Tales (Challenging) Have the students find out about the songs, sayings, tales, and heroes of the region in which they live. They might interview older people in the community and ask them to tell about songs, sayings, or stories they heard as they were growing up. They might ask the librarian or the workers at the local historical society or history museum for help. Have the students present their findings to the class. Students may wish to collect their findings in a notebook, to be placed in the class library.

Related Reading

The following books can be used to extend the lesson.

The Lone Arthur by Arthur Coren. Little, Brown, 1978. A funny modern tall tale hero, Arthur handles all the bad guys like Smiling Sid and Tall Tom Tanner. Spanish Edition: *Arthur el solitario.* Barcelona: La Gaya Ciencia, 1981.

Horseshoe Harry and the Whale by Adele deLeeuw. Parents' Magazine Press, 1976. In American folklore this seven–foot Wyoming folk hero had legs that were so curved they looked like a horseshoe! (Average)

Febold Feboldson by Ariane Dewey. Greenwillow Books, 1984. According to folklore, Febold was the first farmer to come to the Great Plains and settle in what is now Nebraska. (Challenging)

Jim Bridger's Alarm Clock & Other Tall Tales by Sid Fleischman. E. P. Dutton, 1978. These stories grew around the legendary adventures of Jim Bridger, a scout and mountain man who actually lived in the 1800's. (Challenging)

Paul Bunyan Retold and Illustrated by Steven Kellogg by Steven Kellogg. William Morrow, 1984. This retelling of the super folk hero of the lumber camps is a funny, informative, full–color masterpiece for all ages. (Easy)

John Henry, the Steel–driving Man by C. J. Naden. Troll, 1980. This is a retelling of the story of the legendary railroad worker who pounded spikes in the early days of the railroad and who died "with his hammer in his hand." (Average)

Four Fearsome Critters

pages 296–299

Objectives

Literature
● Recognizing the role of imagination in creating fantasy characters.

Vocabulary
● Inferring word meanings from sentence context.

Awards

Kickle Snifters and Other Fearsome Critters was one of the School Library Journal Best Books of the Year in 1976 and a Children's Choice in 1977.

Summary of the Selection

Four creatures from American folklore and their strange habits are discussed. Those amazing animals may inhabit the woods or the mountains, but they are more likely to be found in someone's imagination.

1 PREREADING

Key Vocabulary Words

fearsome: scary. (page 296)
folklore: the stories, traditions, and superstitions of a group of people. (page 296)
bestiary: a book of fables about the habits of actual and mythical animals; this type of book originated in the Middle Ages. (page 299)

Introducing the Vocabulary

Remind students that it sometimes helps, when confronted with pronouncing an unknown word, to look for shorter words within it or to see if the word is made up of two known words. Write the key vocabulary words on the chalkboard. Ask the students to pronounce them and verify their pronunciation. (See page T58 for a further decoding strategy.) Then write these sentences on the chalkboard: The story of Paul Bunyan and his blue ox Babe is part of America's _____. On Halloween the _____ goblins come out. You can read stories about mythical beasts in the _____. Ask students which key word completes each sentence and then ask them to infer the meaning of the words.

Introducing the Selection

Relating to Students' Experiences *Ask:*
☐ *Have you ever thought you saw something in the dark and then looked again to find that nothing was there? You may be interested to know that you are not the only person this has happened to. When you read "Four Fearsome Critters," you will see what I mean.*

2 READING

Setting a Purpose for Reading

Say: ☐ *As you read about the four fearsome critters, think about what is real and what is imaginary about them.*

Planning a Reading Strategy

The rhythm and expression of this folklore lends itself to oral reading. Begin by reading the introductory section to the students. Have them read the remainder of the selection silently. Then ask for volunteers to read aloud about each of the four critters. Remind the students to use expression to help the listeners visualize the creatures.

3 POSTREADING

Reviewing the Selection

The following questions may be used to review the selection. *Ask:* ☐ *Was there anything real about each of the four fearsome critters you just read about?* (Possible response: Maybe the only thing about them that was real was the fear that created them.) ☐ *What was imaginary?* (Possible response: names of the creatures, what they do)

Discussing the Selection

You may want to use the following questions to discuss the selection further. *Ask:* ☐ *The author says these critters live only in people's imaginations. Why did people make them up in the first place?* (Possible responses: to explain something they did not understand; to entertain each other) ☐ *How do you think each of the critters came about?* (Possible responses: The hide-behind came about as an explanation of people disappearing or as a reason for the feeling of something being behind you when you're in a forest; the slide-rock bolter came about to explain things that might swoop down from mountain peaks; whing-whangs came about because of people's belief in creatures that are out only at night

and leave no traces of themselves; kickle snifters came about to explain the feeling of seeing unreal things when we are sleepy.)

☐ *Which creature did you think was most fearsome? Why?* (Possible response: Students may think the hide-behind is most fearsome because it could make people disappear.)

☐ *Which creature did you think was the funniest? Why?* (Possible response: kickle snifters, because they are small, harmless, and full of laughter)

Extending the Selection

Creative Writing **(Easy)** Help students put words together to create a **list** of their own critters, for example, trunk-scrunchers, tin-can crushers, or sneak-upons. Have the students form small groups. Have each group choose a critter and based on its name, **list** at least three characteristics of the critter. Then have each student **write a paragraph** that tells what each critter does and illustrate it with a picture of their critter.

Improvising **(Average)** Have pairs of students make up imaginary creatures and act out "incritterable encounters" with them. (Students may want to use the creatures they made up for the first activity.) See page T47 for improvisation techniques.

Making a Report **(Challenging)** Have the students do research and report upon a "fearsome critter" that has yet to be proven real or imaginary, such as Bigfoot or the Loch Ness Monster. Have them present their findings to the class in an oral report.

The following books can be used to extend the lesson.

Me and the Man on the Moon—Eyed Horse by Sid Fleischman. Little, Brown, 1977. A young boy figures out a way to stop some train robbers in this tall—tale mystery. (Average)

Kickle Snifters and Other Fearsome Critters by Alvin Schwartz. J. B. Lippincott, Bantam paperback, 1978. Try to top these strange critters from American folklore. (Easy)

Unriddling: All Sorts of Riddles to Puzzle Your Guessery, Collected from American Folklore by Alvin Schwartz. J. B. Lippincott, 1983. Short puzzling tales, riddle jokes, picture riddles, rebuses, and more can lead to hours of word fun. (Challenging)

Whoppers: Tall Tales and Other Lies collected by Alvin Schwartz. J. B. Lippincott, 1975. Here is another entertaining collection of all kinds of not—true tidbits, from one—liners to tall tales such as the one where the fish follows the fisherman home. (Average)

There Was an Old Man with a Beard

A Young Lady of Ealing

pages 300–301

Objectives

Literature
- Recognizing a limerick.

- Recognizing humor in limericks.

1 PREREADING

Key Vocabulary Word

limerick: a nonsense poem written in five lines, rhymed in a pattern as aa bb a and having a definite pattern of rhythm. (page 300)

Introducing the Vocabulary

Write the key word on the chalkboard. *Say:* ☐ *Rhythm and rhyme are two characteristics of some poems. The poems that you are going to read have a definite kind of rhythm and rhyme. This kind of poem is called a limerick.*

Introducing the Poems

Providing Background *Say:* ☐ *Besides having a definite rhythm and rhyme pattern, limericks are short, funny poems in five lines that usually start "There was a . . ."*

2 READING

Setting a Purpose for Reading

Say: □ *The limericks on these pages introduce you to two people and tell you some very strange things about them. As you read, notice what makes these limericks funny.*

Planning a Reading Strategy

Read the limericks aloud with the class for enjoyment. Then ask volunteers to read each of the limericks again.

3 POSTREADING

Reviewing the Poems

The following question may be used to review the poems. *Ask:* □ *What makes these limericks funny?* (Possible responses: The rhyming words are funny; unusual things happen to the people in the poems.)

Discussing the Poems

You may want to use the following questions to discuss the poems further. *Say:* □ *You have learned that humor can come from many sources; among these are exaggeration and nonsense. Would you say the humor in these limericks stems from exaggeration like in the poem "My Sister Jane" or nonsense like in "Four Fearsome Critters"?* (Most students will agree on nonsense.) Before asking the next question you may need to review where to look for rhyming words in a poem—most often at the end of a line. *Ask:* □ *Which lines rhyme in the first limerick?* (Lines 1, 2, and 5 rhyme; lines 3 and 4 rhyme.) □ *Which lines rhyme in the second limerick?* (the same as in the first.) □ *What rhyming pattern do you think limericks have?* (Lines 1, 2, and 5 rhyme; lines 2 and 4 rhyme.)

Extending the Poems

Reading Limericks (Easy) Have the student find examples of limericks in other books in the school library. Instruct them to select at least two to memorize and present to the class.

Writing a Paragraph (Average) Have the students imagine that they were present to see the young lady of Ealing try to walk on the ceiling. Have the students write a paragraph explaining what happened to the young lady. Tell the students that they may choose to make the incident either realistic or silly.

Writing a Limerick (Challenging) Review the rhyming pattern of limericks. Then tell the students that they also need an idea for a limerick. Have the students brainstorm to list funny situations, strange names or things that could not happen. Have them also make lists of words and names that rhyme. Tell the students that if they put a surprise in the last line of the limerick, it will make the limerick funnier. Have the students begin with the standard "There was a . . ." and then write limericks. Have them read them aloud and ask if they have the same rhythm as the limericks in the book. The students should revise to establish that rhythm. You may wish to explain the rhythm of limericks as follows: There are two rhythm patterns— in one, a pattern of three syllables, the accent is on the last syllable (˘ ˘ ′); in the second, a pattern of two syllables, the accent is also on the last syllable (˘ ′). Lines 1, 2, and 5 have the same rhythm pattern: one two–syllable followed by two three–syllable (˘ ′ ˘ ˘ ′ ˘ ˘ ′). Lines 3 and 4 consist of one two–syllable and one three–syllable pattern (˘ ′ ˘ ˘ ′).

Related Reading

The following books can be used to extend the lesson.

They've Discovered a Head in the Box for the Bread and Other Laughable Limericks by John Brewton and L. Blackburn. T. Y. Crowell, 1978. With pictures by Fernando Krahn, this collection includes familiar limericks, ones you finish yourself, and brand–new ones. (Challenging)

Six Impossible Things Before Breakfast by Norma Farber. Addison–Wesley, 1979. In this riotous collection of stories and poems are tall tales, poems about how to ride a unicorn, and stories such as the one about the bubbles that never burst. (Average)

Laughing Time; Nonsense Poems by William Jay Smith. Delacorte Press, 1980. This funny collection has poems about people, the alphabet, and all kinds of animals, one sillier than the next. (Average)

Flapdoodle: Pure Nonsense from American Folklore by Alvin Schwartz. J. B. Lippincott, 1980. Who can pass up stories and verse that tell about the impossible; wordplays; jokes and riddles with instructions on how to tell them; tricks to fool friends—all pure nonsense from American folklore. (Challenging)

Paddington Goes to the Hospital

pages 302–324

Objectives

Literature
- Identifying verbal and visual humor in a play.

Comprehension
- **Identifying causes in cause–and–effect relationships.**

Vocabulary
- Recognizing word play based on double meanings.

Materials

For Evaluation

COMPREHENSION copying master 56, "Write the Reason."

For Enrichment (Optional)

VOCABULARY/HEALTH copying master 57, "Find the Word That Fits."

VOCABULARY copying master 58, "Find the Meanings."

Summary of the Play

Paddington Bear goes to the hospital to deliver a basket of food to Mr. Curry, who claims to be suffering from a bad leg. A series of misunderstandings, first with a nurse, then with a psychiatrist and a doctor, and finally with Mr. Curry, keeps Paddington's visit to the hospital lively. After Paddington and the doctor successfully conspire to reveal Mr. Curry's sham illness, they share the basket of food originally intended for Mr. Curry.

1 PREREADING

Key Vocabulary Word

relapse: a falling back into an illness after improving. (page 304)

Introducing the Vocabulary

Write the key vocabulary word on the chalkboard, and ask the students to pronounce it. Have the students find the word in context in their books and read the sentence aloud. Have them infer the meaning of the word and then verify the meaning by checking the glossary in their books. Ask them which part of the word is a prefix and what that prefix means. (*re–* means back)

Introducing the Play

Previewing and Predicting *Say:*
□ *Sometimes some things are funny because people don't always understand what we say. If someone says, "There's the patient," and the next person says, "Patient? How long do I have to wait?", what is the misunderstanding?* (Lead students to the fact that the word *patient* had two different meanings.) You might want to use other examples that will appear in the play: head man (boss, doctor who deals with heads), head shrinker (slang for psychiatrist, a person who shrinks heads).

2 READING

Setting a Purpose for Reading

Say: □ *You are about to read a play about Paddington, a small brown bear from Peru who gets into one escapade after another. As you read this play, watch for the confusion that results when Paddington visits the hospital and the reasons for the confusion.*

Planning a Reading Strategy

Say: □ *Plays contain dialogue, or the speech between characters. Plays look different from stories, because each character's lines appear separately. Sometimes the author includes instructions to the reader or actor about what actions to perform or how to say the lines; these instructions are included in parentheses before the speech itself. In addition each scene in a play opens with a description of the setting.*

Read the introductory paragraph aloud to the students. Then have them read the play silently. Afterward have them do an informal presentation of the play. Assign roles, or have students volunteer for parts. You may wish to change actors midway through the play to allow for greater student participation. (See page T49 for information about play productions.)

3 POSTREADING

Reviewing the Play

The following question may be used to review the play. *Ask:* □ *What are some of the examples of the confusion that resulted when Paddington visited the hospital?* (Possible responses: The nurse thought Paddington needed to see a psychiatrist; the psychiatrist became frustrated in his encounter with Paddington; Paddington was mistaken for a medical student by Sir Archibald.)

After the students have finished reading the play, have them complete the review questions on page 324 in their books. The questions can be assigned as independent written work or can be answered orally during a class discussion. You may also wish to assign the activity on the same page.

Discussing the Play

You may want to use the following questions to discuss the selection further. *Say:*
☐ *The humor in this play depends on misunderstandings of words and on comical actions. If this play were on television, which parts would be funny even without the picture?* (Possible responses: the scenes with the receptionist and Mr. Heinz) ☐ *Which parts would still be funny without the sound?* (Possible responses: Paddington in a surgeon's gown; the joke on Mr. Curry)

☐ *Humor resulted when Paddington misunderstood the word* scruples. *What other words did he misunderstand?* (Possible responses: He did not know he had any reactions; when Sir Archibald asked him for his diagnosis, he thought it was a kind of food; when the nurse referred to him as a patient, he asked if he had to wait long.)

☐ *Did you think Paddington was a remarkable character? If so, why?* (Possible responses: yes, because he got into unusual situations; because he misunderstood people and that resulted in funny situations; because he never got angry or flustered when there was confusion all around him)

Evaluating the Play

To evaluate the students' understanding of cause and effect, use **EVALUATION** copying master 56. **Objective: Identifying the cause in a cause–and–effect relationship.**

Extending the Play

Interviewing a Character (Easy) Divide the students into groups of three or four. Have them think up interview questions to ask Paddington. (Examples: What did you think of Sir Archibald? Would you enjoy being a doctor?) Ask for volunteers to play Paddington, as students from the groups ask Paddington questions.

Illustrating Phrases (Average) In the play, a misunderstanding resulted when the nurse referred to Paddington as a patient, and he thought she said he would have to be patient. Write the following phrases on the board: a horse of a different color, a lively letter, a blue prince, a huge trunk, a palm reader. Have the students choose phrases and illustrate them. Then have the class see if there were any misunderstandings in how the phrases were illustrated, i.e., did all the students choosing a particular phrase select the same meanings of the words?

Making a Poster (Average) Have students make posters to be displayed in the classroom that answer the question "What kinds of food should I eat that will help me stay healthy and strong?" The students will first have to find the answers to the question and then plan their posters. You may wish to have students work in small groups on this project.

Investigating Careers (Average) Have the students choose a career in the health profession and find out as much as possible about that career (e.g., training needed, job opportunities, salary, working environment). If possible they should interview someone presently in that career and perhaps invite them to address the class.

After the students have investigated the career, have them briefly tell the class about it and whether or not they would consider pursuing that career. (Suggested careers: general practice doctor, pediatrician, hospital nurse, school nurse, physical therapist, physical education/health teacher, X–ray technician, dietitian, dentist, dental hygienist, paramedic.)

Writing a Scene for a Play (Challenging)
Have the students write a short dramatic scene to show Paddington in another situation. (Examples: Paddington going to the police station; to a baseball game; or to a library.) Have the students first write a summary of what will happen. Then have them create the dialogue. Encourage the students to write some stage directions for the actors. Then have several students perform some of the scenes for the class.

Writing Sentences (Challenging) Remind students that homophones are words that sound alike but are spelled differently and have different meanings. Have the students write sentences, preferably humorous, using at least one set of homophones in each sentence. Challenge them to write a sentence made up entirely (except articles) of sets of homophones. (Suggested homophones: bare–bear, ant–aunt, lone–loan, beat–beet, blue–blew, sent–cent, eight–ate, I–eye, fair–fare, hair–hare, heard–herd, knead–need, mail–male, pane–pain, pause–paws, pair–pear, read–reed, rose–rows, sail–sale, see–sea, sun–son, their–there, week–weak, one–won)

Optional Copying Masters for Enrichment

The following copying masters may be assigned as independent classroom work or as home activities to be completed with or without parents' help.

VOCABULARY/HEALTH copying master 57. **Objective:** Identifying words by their definitions.

VOCABULARY copying master 58. **Objective:** Identifying words with multiple meanings.

Related Reading

The following books can be used to extend the lesson.

Whatever Happened to Uncle Albert? And Other Puzzling Plays by Sue Alexander. Houghton Mifflin, 1980. Four mystery plays are presented complete with stage setting diagrams and suggestions for costumes and scenery. (Average)

Animals Should Definitely Not Act Like People by Judi Barrett. Atheneum, 1980. Animals trying to be people makes a funny book and proves what the author said in the beginning! (Easy)

A Bear Called Paddington by Michael Bond. Houghton Mifflin, 1960; Dell paperback, 1968. The Brown family found the bear sitting in the train station with a sign that said: "Please Take Me Home" around his neck—so they did. Spanish Edition, *El oso Paddington* (abridged). Barcelona: Plaza & Janes, 1982. (Average)

Complete Adventures of Olga da Polga by Michael Bond. Delacorte Press, 1983. This volume contains all the stories about the irrepressible guinea pig who learns to speak French, falls in love with a Russian prince, gets a new name, and dances ballet. (Challenging)

Paddington on Stage: Plays for Children by Michael Bond and Alfred Bradley. Houghton Mifflin, 1977. These short plays are based on the books about the sticky-fingered, accident-prone bear. (Average)

Let's Find the Big Idea by Bernice Wells Carlson. Abingdon Press, 1982. With ideas for puppets and props included, nineteen skits and plays based on fables and stories from all over the world teach lessons as well as entertain. (Average)

Plays Children Love: A Treasury of Contemporary and Classic Plays for Children by Aurand Harris and Coleman Jennings. Doubleday, 1981. Along with this collection of popular plays for children is a discussion about staging, rehearsing, and performing. (Average)

Bears of the World by Dorothy H. Patent. Holiday House, 1980. This book describes many different kinds of bears and the ways they adapt to their particular environment. (Challenging)

LEARN ABOUT PLAYS:
On Stage!

pages 326–329

Objectives

Literature

● Recognizing that plays and stories are written in different forms.

● Understanding that a play is meant to be performed.

1 PREREADING

Introducing the Selection

Relating to Students' Experiences *Ask:*
☐ *What plays have you seen on TV or on stage? What do you remember about those plays?* (Accept any answer that the student reasonably supports.) ☐ *What was different about seeing a play performed and reading a story?* (Lead the students to comment generally about sets and dialogue.)

2 READING

Setting a Purpose for Reading

Say: ☐ *You are about to learn more about plays and the written form they take. As you read, pay attention to the ways that plays and stories differ.*

Planning a Reading Strategy

Have volunteers read aloud the material on page 326. Read and discuss the material on page 327. Have the students read the fable on pages 328–329 silently. Then complete the activity at the bottom of page 329 as a class.

3 POSTREADING

Reviewing the Selection

The following question may be used to review the selection. *Ask:* ☐ *How do plays differ from stories?* (Possible responses: Plays are written in a different form; plays are meant to be performed; a play tells a story, only with dialogue; a story has descriptions—what the author tells the reader.)

Discussing the Selection

You may want to use the following questions to discuss the selection further. *Ask:* □ *How are plays and stories similar?* (Both have plots, settings, characters, and dialogue.) □ *Why do you think plays are written as they are?* (Possible response: Since they are meant to be performed, they give clear directions to the actors.) □ *If you were a writer and had an idea for a work that had a lot of dialogue, would you choose to write a play or a story?* (probably a play)

Extending the Selection

Making a List (Easy) Have the students select a character from the play "Paddington Goes to the Hospital." Then have them list everything that the character would need to play his or her part. Instruct the students to describe the costumes and the props needed by the character. Have the students read their lists to the class to see if others can think of anything else that the character would need.

Writing and Performing a Play (Average) Have the class work together to finish the play in their books on page 329. The play can then be performed with little preparation. Students may want to collect costumes (old hats, a cloak) and make props and scenery.

Writing Prose from a Play (Challenging) Have the students reverse the writing process they have used in this lesson by taking a page from "Paddington Goes to the Hospital" and rewriting it as if it were part of a story. Encourage them to choose a page that has stage directions and possibly a setting description as well as dialogue.

Digging Into the Past

pages 330–351

Objectives

Literature
● Identifying character traits.

● Comparing ways that characters respond to problems.

Literature/Comprehension
● Identifying elements of plot—sequence and development.

Content Area (Science)
● Understanding how information about the past is gained.

Materials

For Evaluation

LITERATURE/COMPREHENSION copying master 59 "Solve Miss Pickerell's Problem."

For Enrichment (Optional)

VOCABULARY copying master 60, "Find the Words."

SOCIAL STUDIES/STUDY SKILLS copying master 61, "Fill in the Chart."

Summary of the Story

Mr. Esticott takes Miss Pickerell down into the test pit of the digging site in Square Toe County to show her where the archeological discoveries have been made. The tour turns into a trial, however, when the shoring collapses and the two are temporarily trapped. Refusing to be intimidated by the situation, Miss Pickerell takes Mr.

Esticott on a further tour of the pit, both in search of an exit and of additional finds. They are finally rescued, but not before Miss Pickerell makes an important discovery.

1 PREREADING

Key Vocabulary Words

dig: an archeological excavation or its site. (page 331)

shoring: a group or system of supporting boards used to prevent something. (page 334)

intact: untouched; with no part missing. (page 340)

Key Concept Word

archeology: the scientific study of the life and culture of ancient peoples. Also spelled **archaeology.**

Introducing the Vocabulary

Ask: ☐ *Have any of you ever found an old arrowhead and wondered about the people who used it? Or have you ever seen pottery in a museum and wondered who found it and where? There is a science that looks for old things to tell us about how people lived years and years ago. This science is called* archeology. Write the word on the chalkboard. Then write the key vocabulary words on the board. Tell the students that those words are all related to archeology. Have them look at the words in the story context and infer the meanings.

Introducing the Story

Relating to Students' Experiences *Ask:* ☐ *Have any of you ever read a story about a character called Miss Pickerell? Can anyone tell us about her?* (Accept any answer that the student reasonably supports.) ☐ *The story we are going to read is a part of a longer story about Miss Pickerell.*

Previewing and Predicting *Ask:* ☐ *The Miss Pickerell books always deal with some aspect of a science. What particular science do you think "Miss Pickerell Goes on a Dig" deals with?* (archeology) ☐ *We will find out what archeologists look for and what they can tell about what they find.*

2 READING

Setting a Purpose for Reading

Say: ☐ *In the following story two people find themselves with a serious problem. Notice the difference in how they react to their problem.*

Planning a Reading Strategy

You may wish to divide the reading into two sections—the first one ending on page 340. Have selected students read the story aloud. Clarify the meanings of phrases where appropriate.

3 POSTREADING

Reviewing the Story

The following questions may be used to review the story. *Ask:* ☐ *What was the problem the two people faced?* (They were stuck in a cave–in.) ☐ *How were Miss Pickerell and Mr. Esticott's responses to their problem different?* (Possible responses: Mr.

Esticott was more afraid; Miss Pickerell tried to do something to solve the problem while they were waiting to be rescued.)

After the students have finished reading the story, have them complete the review questions on page 351 in their books. The questions can be assigned as independent written work or can be answered orally during a class discussion. You may also wish to assign the activity on the same page.

Discussing the Story

You may want to use the following questions to discuss the selection further. *Ask:*

☐ *How did Miss Pickerell figure out the importance of the rock she discovered by the hearth?* (When she found it, she knew it reminded her of another rock she had seen, that "came from another continent, and was centuries old." Then she guessed that because the workmanship was the same, maybe the descendants of the people who fashioned Professor Tuttle's rock once lived in Square Toe County.)

☐ *What adjectives can you think of to describe Miss Pickerell?* (Possible responses: unafraid, quick–thinking, courageous, determined)

☐ *Find examples in the story of ways Miss Pickerell showed courage and steadiness of mind in response to being trapped.* (Possible responses: When they are first trapped, she firmly states that "There must be a way out"; shortly afterwards, she says, "There must be *something* we can do to help ourselves"; she figures out which direction to expect the rescuers to come from; she lets the rescuers know where they are; she asks for light when their flashlight goes out.)

☐ *How would you have reacted in Miss Pickerell's situation? Would you have done anything differently?* (Accept any answer that the student reasonably supports.)

☐ *Why do you think this story is included in a unit about remarkable characters in funny situations?* (Possible response: Miss Pickerell is a remarkable character; the situation was funny in a way, because everything ended up all right.)

☐ *How did Miss Pickerell say scientists could tell how old the rock was?* (by measuring how much carbon–14 is left in the soot that was in the rock)

Evaluating the Story

To evaluate the students' understanding of the story, use **EVALUATION** copying master 59. **Objective: Identifying elements of plot—sequence and development.**

Extending the Story

Writing Sentences (**Easy**) Review with the students the words they used to describe Miss Pickerell in the *Discussing the Story* section. Then have the students write three sentences describing Miss Pickerell. For students who need a structure, you may wish to provide the following: Miss Pickerell was _____ because she (or when she) _____ .

Writing a Letter to an Editor (**Average**) Have the students pretend that they are Miss Pickerell. Ask them to write a letter to the local newspaper telling about the "find" of the rock that resembled Professor Tuttle's. Remind the students to explain the importance of the "find" clearly. Have the students notice Miss Pickerell's use of language in the story and try to write from her point of view, using words that she might use.

Researching Information about Archeology (**Challenging**) Have the students conduct research to find information about the methods of archeology or about jobs in archeology. Remind the students to consult with the librarian for help in finding information. Take time in class to share what the students have learned.

Optional Copying Masters for Enrichment

The following copying masters may be assigned as independent classroom or as home activities to be completed with or without parents' help.

VOCABULARY copying master 60. **Objective:** Using context clues to identify words.

SOCIAL STUDIES/STUDY SKILLS copying master 61. **Objectives:** Interpreting information from a chart; drawing conclusions.

Related Reading

The following books can be used to extend the lesson.

Mummies Made in Egypt by Aliki. Harper & Row, 1979. This wonderful picture book shows just how mummies were prepared and what the ceremony and burial rites meant. (Average)

Digging Up Dinosaurs by Aliki. Harper & Row, 1981. This well–illustrated book presents techniques used by paleontological expeditions. (Easy)

Monster Dinosaur by Daniel Cohen. J. B. Lippincott, 1983. This book attempts to straighten out the facts, theories, and folklore surrounding these long–gone giants. (Challenging)

Miss Pickerell to the Earthquake Rescue by Ellen MacGregor and Dora Pantell. McGraw–Hill, 1977; Archway paperback, 1980. Once more the indomitable lady rushes in and saves the day when nature goes on a rampage. (Average)

Going on a Dig by Velma F. Morrison. Dodd, Mead, 1981. With particular attention to American Indian sites, the author presents the methods archeology and paleontology experts use as they prepare for exploratory expeditions. (Challenging)

Ancient Greeks by Anton Powell and Patricia Vanags. Gloucester Press, 1978. Based in part on archeological findings, this book recreates a picture of life in ancient Greece, including a look at the original Olympic games as well as houses, clothes, jewelry, and foods. (Challenging)

Old Joe Clarke

page 352

Objective

Music
- Enjoying and singing a folk song.

1 PREREADING

Introducing the Song

Providing Background *Say:* ☐ *"Old Joe Clarke" is a folk song that has been played in the Ozark Mountains for a long time. Now it can be heard all across the United States, wherever people are square–dancing. Its words are just for the fun of it; there is no sense, except in having a good time.*

2 READING

Setting a Purpose for Reading

Say: ☐ *Read the lyrics of the song. Consider why people might enjoy singing and listening to it.*

Planning a Reading Strategy

Read the song aloud to the class. Then teach the class the melody, and have them sing "Old Joe Clarke" as a round, with all the students singing the chorus together. (The music for "Old Joe Clarke" is on page T73. Recordings of this song are also available. See page T75 for a discography.)

3 POSTREADING

Reviewing the Song

The following question may be used to review the song. *Ask:* ☐ *Why do you think people might enjoy singing and listening to "Old Joe Clarke"?* (Possible responses: It is funny; it is nonsense; it has a good beat.)

Discussing the Song

You may want to use the following question to discuss the selection further. *Say:* ☐ *People like to dance to this song. How could you dance or act out this song?* (Possible responses: Students might spin to "round and round"; they might pantomime stubbing their toes and sitting on a hot stove.)

Extending the Song

Using a Map **(Average)** Have the students find the Ozark Mountains on a map and measure the distance to the place where they are living. Ask the students to write a short paragraph telling how they think the song might have traveled to the rest of the country.

Researching Origins of Folk Dances **(Challenging)** Have the students conduct library research about folk dancing. Have them ask the librarian for help and have them write reports on what they have learned. Ask the students to be sure to include information about square dancing since "Old Joe Clarke" is a song used for square dancing.

Related Reading

The following books can be used to extend the lesson.

Singing Bee! A Collection of Favorite Children's Songs compiled by Jane Hart. Lothrop, Lee & Shepard, 1982. This collection of over 100 songs with musical accompaniment includes lullabies, Mother Goose rhymes, holiday songs, and much more for all ages. (Easy)

Pop Goes the Weasel & Yankee Doodle: New York in 1776 & Today, with Songs & Pictures by Robert Quackenbush. J. B. Lippincott, 1976. Adding some new verses, the author—illustrator shows scenes from the past and those of today for us to compare. Music for both songs is included. (Easy)

American Folk Songs for Children by Ruth Crawford Seeger. Doubleday, 1980; Doubleday paperback, 1980. In this collection are all the favorite folk songs that everyone should know. (Average)

BOOKSHELF

page 353

Optional Copying Master for Enrichment

The following copying master may be assigned as independent classroom work or as a home activity to be completed with or without parents' help.

STUDY SKILLS copying master 62. **Objectives:** Recognizing and using the Dewey Decimal system; obtaining information from a chart.

6 To Live with Animals
pages 354–416

Theme: Relationships between animals and humans.

Selections
The Carp in the Bathtub (story)
Buying a Puppy (poem)
Wol to the Rescue (story)
CONNECTIONS: How Animals Protect Themselves
The Black Fox (story)
frog (poem)
LEARN ABOUT POETRY:
Similes and Metaphors
BOOKSHELF

Unit Materials

Home Letter Home Letter 7 may be sent home at the beginning or end of the unit.

Copying Masters for Evaluation*
Copying masters 63, 67, and 70.

Copying Masters for Enrichment* (Optional) Copying masters 64, 65, 66, 68, 69, 71, 72, and 73.

Introducing the Unit

To introduce the students to the unit, have them read the unit title and look at the illustration on pages 354–355. To begin the discussion, *ask:* ☐ *What is happening in this picture?* (Most students will be able to

*Note that the copying masters indicated here are from the *Teacher's Edition, Part II.*

identify Noah's ark, with many kinds of animals entering the ark as Noah checks them off a list.) You may want to have students identify the animals in the picture.

Ask: ☐ *How do you think the picture relates to the unit title?* (Possible response: According to the story, Noah lived with animals for forty days and forty nights until the flood waters went down.) ☐ *What characteristics might a person need to live with animals?* (Possible responses: kindness, patience, interest in different kinds of beings, caring)

☐ *Why do many people like animals so much? What is interesting about animals?* (Possible response: They are alive; pet animals usually like us no matter what we do; they give affection; they are fun.)

Tell the students that in this unit they will be reading stories and poems about people and animals together. Some of the animals are pets, and some are wild. Students will have an opportunity to see the many ways people relate to animals, and animals to people.

Unit Projects and Activities

Making a Map **(Easy)** For a class project have the students draw a large map of their state or territory on a large piece of butcher paper. Then have them paste or draw pictures on the map to illustrate the various kinds of animals which live in their area. Conduct a **brainstorming session** to get a list of animals. Also have the students talk with adults who are knowledge-able of the area. Remind the students that insects, birds, and reptiles are also animals.

Using Facts (Average) Divide the class into an even number of groups. Have each group think of animals and write down facts about each on a card. Encourage the students to read to find facts that are not very obvious. Then pair the groups and have each group state facts for the other to guess the animal. See which group can guess the most animals with the fewest number of misses.

Writing About Extinct Animals (Challenging) Have the students find the names of extinct animals and do research to find information about them. Have the students check with the librarian and other teachers to find the information. Then have students write several paragraphs stating facts about the animal, including probable reasons for its becoming extinct. Have the students share the information with the rest of the class.

The Carp in the Bathtub

pages 356–373

Objectives

Literature
● Inferring motivations for characters' actions.

● Relating the main idea of a story to personal experience.

Comprehension
● Finding solutions to problems.

● **Identifying effects in cause–and–effect relationships.**

Vocabulary
● Acquiring knowledge of words of a particular tradition.

Materials

For Evaluation

COMPREHENSION copying master 63, "Tell What Happened."

For Enrichment (Optional)

SCIENCE copying master 64, "Finish the Food Chains."

COMPREHENSION copying master 65, "Find the Main Idea."

Awards

In 1972, the picture book *The Carp in the Bathtub* was one of the School Library Journal Best Books of the Year for Children.

Background

Passover (Pesach) has been celebrated each spring for over 3,200 years to commemorate the escape of the Jews from slavery in Egypt. On the first two nights of the eight–day holiday, family and friends gather for the *Seder,* a ceremonial meal of foods that symbolize the conditions of slavery and the exodus from Egypt.

Summary of the Story

Leah and Harry become fond of a live carp Mama brings home to make into *gefilte* fish for Passover. When Mama goes out, the children decide to save the fish and persuade their reluctant neighbor, Mrs. Ginzburg, to keep it in her bathtub temporarily. Papa learns what has happened and takes the fish home. The children mourn over their loss until a week later, when their father brings them a cat for a pet.

1 PREREADING

Key Vocabulary Words

Passover: A Jewish holiday celebrating the ancient Hebrews' freedom from slavery in Egypt. (page 358)

Seder (sā′•dər): the meal served on the first two nights of Passover, a Jewish holiday. (page 358)

gefilte fish (gə•fil′•tə fish): oval fish cakes or balls made from a white fish such as carp. (page 358)

Introducing the Vocabulary

Write the key vocabulary words on the chalkboard and have the students pronounce them after you. Share with the students the information in the Background section to explain the meanings of the words.

Introducing the Story

Relating to Students' Experiences *Ask:*
☐ *Have you read any stories in this book that showed life either in a different culture with different customs than yours or in earlier times? Look at the Table of Contents and see if you can name some.* (Possible responses: "An Eskimo Birthday," "The Great Minu," "The Crane Maiden," "Crossing the Creek," "Mexicali Soup") ☐ *The story we are going to read tells about the customs of a particular group of people more than one hundred years ago.*

2 READING

Setting a Purpose for Reading

Say: ☐ *In this story, Leah and her brother grow fond of a live fish Mama is keeping in her bathtub. But they have a problem. Read "The Carp in the Bathtub" to find out what the problem is and what they decide to do to solve their problem.*

Planning a Reading Strategy

Have selected students read the story aloud. Pronounce and explain the Hebrew and Yiddish words to the class as they come to them in the story. Call the class's attention to the art and how it contributes to the feeling of time over a hundred years ago.

3 POSTREADING

Reviewing the Story

The following questions may be used to review the story. *Ask:* ☐ *What was the problem Leah and Harry faced?* (Possible response: Even though they knew that the carp was to be cooked, it became their pet.) ☐ *How did they try to solve their problem about killing the carp?* (They tried to save the carp by taking it out of their apartment.)

After the students have finished reading the story, have them complete the review questions on page 373 in their books. The questions can be assigned as independent written work or can be answered orally during a class discussion. You may also wish to assign the activity on the same page.

Discussing the Story

You may want to use the following questions to discuss the selection further. *Ask:* ☐ *What did the parents think of when they thought of the fish?* (food) ☐ *What did the children think of the fish?* (Possible response: The fish is a friend and a pet.) ☐ *Look at page 371. How do the children justify their eating of chicken?* (They say they never met the chicken.)

☐ *How did Papa show his sympathy for the children's point of view?* (Possible responses: He tried to explain why they ate fish; he brought them an acceptable pet, a cat.)

☐ *Do you think Papa ever told Mama what the children did with her carp? Why or why not?* (Possible responses: He told her because he wanted her to know how much the children loved animals; he never told her because he did not want to upset her.)

Evaluating the Story

To evaluate students' understanding of cause and effect, use **EVALUATION** copying master 63. **Objective: Identifying the effects in cause–and–effect relationships.**

Extending the Story

Improvising Endings **(Easy)** Have groups of five students decide on new endings for the story. (For example, if Papa tells Mama about the fish, how does she react?) Tell them to begin with the scene where Leah and Harry meet Papa at the subway. Have each group improvise their new endings for the rest of the class. (See page T47 for improvisation techniques.)

Listening to Music **(Easy)** Obtain a copy of the soundtrack of the Broadway show "Fiddler on the Roof" and play all or part of it to the students. Explain to them that the play concerns Jewish life and customs in a time earlier than the setting of "A Carp in the Bathtub" and in a different country.

Listing Customs **(Average)** "The Carp in the Bathtub" mentions many Jewish customs and traditions. Have the students reread the story and list the things in the story that reflect Jewish traditions. Students may want to list these in the form of a chart, under the categories "Food," "Holidays," and "Other."

Making Books About Animal Care **(Average)** Have the students work in groups to find out about the care of a certain kind of pet. Ask the students to read about pet care and to talk with those who care for a number of the animals. Then have the students make booklets, telling how to train, feed, and care for the pet. Have the students illustrate their works with photographs or drawings and display the books for the class to read.

***Writing a Letter* (Challenging)** Have the students write Leah letters about beloved pets or treasured possessions that they had to give up. Urge them to describe for Leah what they valued most about the animal or object and why it was so hard to part with it. Ask them to consider what, if anything, they learned from the experience.

Optional Copying Masters for Enrichment

The following copying masters may be assigned as independent classroom work or as home activities to be completed with or without parents' help.

SCIENCE copying master 64. **Objectives:** Naming and sequencing parts of a food chain; predicting outcomes based on observed patterns.

COMPREHENSION copying master 65. **Objectives:** Identifying the main idea of a paragraph; writing details that support a main idea.

Related Reading

The following books can be used to extend the lesson.

Freshwater Fish and Fishing by Jim Arnosky. Four Winds Press, 1982. This illustrated book contains information about the most common fish, where they live, what they eat, and how to catch them. (Challenging)

Finders Weepers by Miriam Chaikin. Harper & Row, 1980; Dell paperback, 1982. Day-to-day life and preparation for special Jewish holidays make an entertaining story of family life. (Average)

Fish by Fiona Henrie. Franklin Watts, 1981. Keeping fish as a hobby can be lots of fun as this well-illustrated book shows. (Average)

Ella of All-of-a-Kind Family by Sydney Taylor. E. P. Dutton, 1978; Dell paperback, 1980. The series about the close-knit, happy-hearted Jewish family who live in New York early in the 1900s continues with a focus on Ella.

Buying a Puppy
pages 374–375

Objectives

Literature
- Recognizing a narrative poem.

- Identifying the speaker of a poem.

Comprehension
- Relating a poem's subject to personal experience.

Materials

For Enrichment (Optional)

SOCIAL STUDIES/STUDY SKILLS copying master 66, "Read a Road Map."

1 PREREADING

Introducing the Poem

Relating to Students' Experiences *Ask:*
☐ *If your parents told you to get a scrap of meat and an old towel, would you know why? The child in this poem doesn't know why either but is very happy when she finds out the reason. As you read, see if this poem reminds you of a day in your own life.*

2 READING

Setting a Purpose for Reading

Say: □ *You may know that a narrator is someone who tells a story. The poem you are about to read is called a narrative poem; like a narrator, it tells a story. As you listen and then read, see if you can determine the story in this poem.*

Planning a Reading Strategy

Read the poem aloud to the students. Then have selected students read stanzas of the poem aloud. Remind the students that since this poem tells a story they should use a tone of voice similar to what they would use when storytelling.

3 POSTREADING

Reviewing the Poem

The following question may be used to review the poem. *Say:* □ *In your own words, tell the story in this poem.* (Possible response: A father and his little girl drive to the country to pick out a puppy for her birthday present.)

Discussing the Poem

You may want to use the following questions to discuss the poem further. *Ask:*
□ *Who is telling the story in this poem?* (the child) □ *How do the child's feelings change during the poem?* (at first, bewildered, then hopeful, excited, and finally, happy) □ *At what point in the poem does she become hopeful?* (Possible response: in the sixth stanza, when she says: "Oh,/To have one, one of my own!")

□ *What do you think the girl named her puppy?* (Answers will vary.)

Extending the Poem

***Retelling a Narrative Poem* (Average)** Have the students write the story of the poem in paragraph form. Have volunteers read their paragraph before the class.

***Writing and Revising a Story* (Challenging)** Ask the students to write true or imaginary stories about their pets or about pets they would like to have. In keeping with the narrative objective, encourage them to write about something that happened or about something that could happen. (Examples: how they acquired the pet; what the pet has done to prove itself unusual; a time the pet got lost, etc.) Have each student read his or her story to another student. Have the other student suggest ways to make the story clearer or more understandable. Then have each student **rewrite** his or her story, using the suggestions of the person who heard it.

Optional Copying Master for Enrichment

The following copying master may be assigned as independent classroom work or as a home activity to be completed with or without parents' help.

SOCIAL STUDIES/STUDY SKILLS copying master 66. **Objectives:** Interpreting information on a map; using a map key and a compass rose.

Related Reading

The following books can be used to extend the lesson.

The Life of a Dog by Jan Feder. Children's Press, 1982. Written almost like a story, the book tells about a year in the life of a farm watchdog with pictures of many dogs. (Average)

Dogs by Fiona Henrie. Julian Messner, 1983. This book gives all the basic knowledge needed to select and care for a dog. (Challenging)

All About Dogs As Pets by Louis Saban. Julian Messner, 1983. The choice and care of your pet dog is presented with a look at the various breeds. (Challenging)

Wol to the Rescue

pages 376–383

Objectives

Literature
• Identifying realistic fiction.

• Distinguishing an animal's traits through its actions.

Literature/Comprehension
• **Identifying elements of plot— sequence and development.**

Vocabulary
• Recognizing how the choice of words makes a story vivid.

Materials

For Evaluation

COMPREHENSION copying master 67, "Put the Story Events in Order."

For Enrichment (Optional)

STUDY SKILLS copying master 68, "Use Guide Words."

VOCABULARY/WORD ATTACK copying master 69, "Identify the Sounds."

Awards

The novel *Owls in the Family* was one of the American Library Association Notable Children's Books in 1962.

Background

This story is about an owl who has become a pet. Emphasize to students that the owl was found when he was very young. Discourage them from touching wild animals unless in a controlled situation, such as a petting zoo.

Summary of the Story

Two boys, their dogs, and their pet owls, Wol and Weeps, are camping in a cave. During the day, Wol is the focus of fun as prairie chicks mistake him for their mother. At dusk, however, Wol proves his worth when he lets out a horned owl hunting scream just as two older boys begin to get rough with his master. Seeing Wol's white, ghostlike shape in the Hanging Tree, the tough boys run off in terror, and Wol has the last laugh since even his master is scared.

1 PREREADING

Introducing the Story

Providing Background Have the students turn back to page 107 in their books and reread the description of realistic fiction. Tell them that the story they are going to read is considered realistic fiction.

Relating to Students' Experiences *Ask:*
☐ *What stories have you heard or read of pets saving people?* (Students may be familiar with stories of Saint Bernard dogs rescuing

people caught in avalanches in the Alps, or of the dog Snowy performing rescues in the French series about Tintin.) ☐ *In the next story you will read about an owl that becomes a hero, but not in the way you might expect.*

2 READING

Setting a Purpose for Reading

Say: ☐ *As you read "Wol to the Rescue," look for actions or people who are realistic and the events in which they are presented.*

Planning a Reading Strategy

Have selected students read the story aloud. Point out to the class how the illustrations within the story enhance both its humorous incidents and its threatening incidents.

3 POSTREADING

Reviewing the Story

The following questions may be used to review the story. *Ask:* ☐ *What are the characteristics of realistic fiction?* (Story takes place in the present; it could have happened; main characters are like people you know; it has an author.) ☐ *What in the story did you think was realistic?* (Possible responses: The setting is the present; the events could have happened; the main characters are like known people; it has an author.)

After the students have finished reading the story, have them complete the review questions on page 383 in their books. The questions can be assigned as independent written work or can be answered orally during a class discussion. You may also wish to assign the activity on the same page.

Discussing the Story

You may want to use the following questions to discuss the selection further. *Say:* ☐ *Describe how Wol must have felt when the prairie chicks thought he was their mother.* (Possible responses: nervous, anxious, embarrassed) ☐ *Read the section of the story that shows how he felt.* (page 377, line 12, through page 378, line 12)

Ask: ☐ *Was Wol trying to protect his master when he saved him?* (Possible response: probably not; the boy said Wol probably thought the coyote's howl was "some kind of a challenge")

☐ *What incidents in the story show the boys' respect for nature?* (Possible responses: watching the prairie chicks hatch; being concerned that the mother hen find her chicks; liked to feel that they were living in the olden times when the prairie was less populated and civilized)

☐ *What facts about animals did you learn from the story?* (Possible responses: A prairie chicken has her nest on the ground; chicks just hatched will identify with another bird if their mother is not there; coyotes howl at night; owls scream to scare mice or rabbits.)

Evaluating the Story

To evaluate students' understanding of plot, use **EVALUATION** copying master 67. **Objective: Identifying elements of plot—sequence and development.**

Extending the Story

Making a List (Easy) As a class project, have the students find books and articles naming different kinds of owls. Make a heading *Owls* on a poster board or on the chalkboard. Have the students write down the names of different kinds of owls under the heading as they discover them.

***Creating Dialogue* (Average)** Have the students imagine that the two roughnecks in the story stopped to talk to each other after they had been scared away by Wol. Have the students write several sentences of dialogue portraying what the roughnecks might have said.

***Doing Research* (Challenging)** Have students research the characteristics and habits of horned owls. Have them verify the information in the story.

Optional Copying Masters for Enrichment

The following copying masters may be assigned as independent classroom work or as home activities to be completed with or without parents' help.

STUDY SKILLS copying master 68. **Objective:** Using guide words in a dictionary.

VOCABULARY/WORD ATTACK copying master 69. **Objective:** Using context clues to identify words; using phonic analysis to decode words.

Related Reading

The following books can be used to extend the lesson.

Snowy Owls by Patricia Hunt. Dodd, Mead, 1982. This close look at a most exceptional bird discusses the bird's defense trick, that of pretending to have a broken wing. (Challenging)

Listen to the Crows by Laurence Pringle. Harper & Row, 1976. Crows have always been thought of as smart birds, and this book studies them to see why. (Easy)

Orphans from the Sea by Jack Denton Scott. G. P. Putnam, 1982. Sometimes birds need our help and this book tells of people who work to rescue and heal orphaned or injured seabirds and other wild creatures. (Challenging)

Night Animals by Millicent E. Selsam. Four Winds Press, 1980. Few words and impressive photographs show the world of creatures, such as the owl, who do their living at night. (Easy)

Owls: Hunter's of the Night by Margaret W. Sadoway. Lerner, 1981. Good detailed information is presented about this nocturnal bird. (Challenging)

CONNECTIONS: How Animals Protect Themselves

pages 384–391

Objective

Content Area (Science)
● Identifying how animals defend themselves.

1 PREREADING

Introducing the Selection

Relating to Students' Experiences *Ask:*
☐ *Would you ever confront a scared skunk? Why or why not?* (Possible response: probably not, because it would spray) ☐ *Would you ever pick up a frightened porcupine? Why*

or why not? (Possible response: probably not, because you would get stuck with quills) ☐ *Why would a skunk or a porcupine do such things?* (Possible response: It is scared and just trying to protect itself.)

2 READING

Setting a Purpose for Reading

Have the students read the selection to find out ways in which animals can protect themselves from their enemies.

Planning a Reading Strategy

Have selected students read the selection aloud. Have students try to remember if they have ever seen any of the animals mentioned in the selection in their natural environment.

3 POSTREADING

Reviewing the Selection

The following questions may be used to review the selection. *Ask:* ☐ *Do you think that one method of protection is more effective than another? Why or why not?* (Possible response: no, because each method is designed for a particular animal; any method is effective as long as it protects the animal from its enemies.)

After the students have finished reading the selection, have them complete the review questions on page 391 in their books. The questions can be assigned as independent written work or can be answered orally during a class discussion. You may also wish to assign the activities on the same page.

Discussing the Selection

You may want to use the following questions to discuss the selection further. *Ask:* ☐ *What other animals have striking markings that help protect them?* (Possible response: jaguar, tiger) ☐ *Do you think the size of an animal ever protects it? Explain.* (Possible response: yes, for example the elephant and the whale; they have no natural enemies except man.)

Extending the Selection

Making a Chart **(Easy)** Have the students make a chart showing defenses and which animals use that defense. Encourage students to find more examples of animals that protect themselves in the ways listed.

Researching Other Defenses **(Average)** There are more ways for animals to defend themselves than are described in the selection. Have students research to find these other ways. (Suggestions: size, freezing in position, color, shape)

Researching Extinct Animals **(Challenging)** Animals often became extinct because they could not defend themselves properly. Have students research to find out why and when some animals became extinct and how their enemies overcame them.

Related Reading

The following books can be used to extend the lesson.

Porcupines by Wyatt Blassingame. Dodd, Mead, 1982. The life cycle and behavior of the porcupine helps it survive, even though it is small and slow and cannot hear or see very well! (Average)

Tricks Animals Play by Jan Clarkson. National Geographic, 1975. Color photos show opossums "playing dead" while other animals pull inside a shell, use bad smells, or camouflage themselves by blending into their environments. (Easy)

Animal Defenses by Anabel Dean. Julian Messner, 1978. Black–and–white drawings show the variety of weapons animals employ from sharp needle–like projections to poisons, stings, and other defenses. (Average)

Poisonous Snakes by George S. Fichter. Franklin Watts, 1982. How snakes use venom as a protective device plus other interesting facts are included in this study of these reptiles. (Challenging)

Alligators, Racoons and Other Survivors by Barbara Ford. William Morrow, 1981. Why some animals survive and not others (the alligator manages, but the crocodile has a hard time staying in existence) still puzzles scientists. (Challenging)

Killer Fish by Russell Freedman. Holiday House, 1982. How fish kill by biting, stinging, or shocking is explained in detail. (Average)

Killer Snakes by Russell Freedman. Holiday House, 1982. This study explains how cobras, sea snakes, vipers and other poisonous snakes defend themselves and survive. (Average)

Tooth and Claw: A Look at Animal Weapons by Russell Freedman. Holiday House, 1980. This description of animal protection covers sprays, teeth, claws, horns, poisons, and stings. (Easy)

Hunters and the Hunted: Surviving in the Animal World by Dorothy H. Patent. Holiday House, 1981. Animals must constantly struggle for survival, and their methods may surprise you. (Challenging)

Animal Attackers by Brenda Thompson and Cynthia Overbeck. Lerner, 1977. This discussion of the attack behavior of animals describes how they eat and protect themselves in a competitive world. (Easy)

The Black Fox

pages 392–411

Objectives

Literature
- Recognizing that a character's change in attitude causes changes in behavior.

- Using description to evoke a feeling.

Comprehension
- **Identifying a character's feelings.**

Content Area (Science)
- Acquiring facts about animals.

Materials

For Evaluation

COMPREHENSION copying master 70, "Tell Tom's Feelings."

For Enrichment (Optional)

STUDY SKILLS copying master 71, "Scan for Details."

VOCABULARY copying master 72, "Find the Right Word."

Awards

The novel *The Midnight Fox* was one of the Library of Congress Children's Books of the Year in 1968.

Summary of the Story

While visiting his aunt and uncle's farm, Tom sees a black fox several times. Each time he is still and silent but thrilled to see the wild, beautiful creature. The last time he sees her is the most exciting of all: after weeks of seaching, he finds her den and watches her kit play. Tom decides not to return, for fear the fox would move to a new location if she realized her den had been discovered.

1 PREREADING

Key Vocabulary Words

ravine: a long, deep hollow in the earth, usually formed by the action of a stream; a large gully. (page 401)
frenzy: a fit of wild or violent excitement, often with a burst of activity. (page 410)

Introducing the Vocabulary

Write the key vocabulary words on the chalkboard and assist the students in pronouncing them. (See page T58 for a decoding strategy.) Have the students find the words and their meanings in the glossary. Then have them read the words in the story context and supply a synonym for each word. (ravine—gully, frenzy—excitement)

Introducing the Story

Relating to Students' Experiences *Ask:*
☐ *What are some differences between pets and wild animals?* (Possible responses: People feed pets, but wild animals get their own food; pets live with or close to people, but wild animals usually keep away from people; people often love pets, but wild animals usually do not let people get close to them, physically or otherwise.)

☐ *Have you ever seen a wild animal in its natural environment? How did you react to it? How did it react to you?* (Discuss.)

2 READING

Setting a Purpose for Reading

Say: ☐ *In the next story watch how a wild animal helps change Tom's lonely summer into a surprisingly exciting one.*

Planning a Reading Strategy

You may wish to divide the reading into two sections. Have the students read to the break on page 401 for the first section. You might want to discuss the events in the story at that time before proceeding with the reading of the rest of the story.

3 POSTREADING

Reviewing the Story

The following questions may be used to review the story. *Ask:* ☐ *Tom's attitude toward being on the farm changed from the beginning of the story to the end. What caused that change?* (seeing the fox) ☐ *How did the fox change Tom's summer?* (Possible responses: Before he saw her, he was bored; afterwards he had an interest.)

After the students have finished reading the story, have them complete the review questions on page 411 in their books. The questions can be assigned as independent written work or can be answered orally during a class discussion. You may also wish to assign the activity on the same page.

Discussing the Story

You may want to use the following questions to discuss the selection further. *Ask:* ☐ *Tom felt bored and lonely during his first three days on the farm. How did his behavior show this?* (Possible responses: He stood quietly; he got in his grandparents' way; he looked through farm magazines.) ☐ *When he became interested in the fox, how did his behavior change?* (Possible responses: His days started to pass more quickly; he started observing animals and doing more exploring; he kept busy.)

☐ *Why do you think Tom liked the fox so much?* (Possible responses: It was exciting to see a wild creature in its natural environment; it was a free creature; he admired its independence.)

☐ *Remember that a poet sometimes uses comparisons to help us see things. Sometimes the comparisons use the words* like *or* as. *In this story the author uses comparisons to help the reader appreciate Tom's point of view and to create a feeling. For example, "...with a bound that was lighter than the wind—it was as if she was being blown away over the field..." (page 400). Find three more examples of comparisons on pages 400–402* (Possible responses: [seeing an animal in the zoo and a wild animal that is free] "was like seeing a kite on the floor and then, later, seeing one up in the sky ... pulling the wind" [page 400]; "The tree trunks were like statues in some old jungle temple..." [page 401]; "She came over the rocks as easily as a cat. Her tail was very high and full, like a sail that was bearing her forward. Her fur was black as coal..." [page 402].)

☐ *How might the story about the old man who flew be related to Tom's experience with the black fox?* (Possible response: Like the fox, the old man was free and he did not disturb nature when he flew.)

☐ *What facts did you learn about foxes by reading the story?* (Possible responses: They move quickly and quietly; they avoid con-

tact with human beings; they hide their dens and will move them if discovered; they provide food for their young.)

Evaluating the Story

To evaluate the students' understanding of story details, use **EVALUATION** copying master 70. **Objectives: Identifying a character's feelings in a story; recalling story details.**

Extending the Story

Making Headlines **(Easy)** Have the students cut out headlines from newspapers and use the lettering to make up headlines telling about something important that happened to them. Have them study the style of newspaper headlines before they begin the activity.

Making a List **(Average)** Ask the students to review the letter which Tom wrote to Petie about his farm chores. Then have the students list the chores which they do in and around their homes during the week. Next, have them select a "most favorite" and "least favorite" chore and write several sentences telling why they like or dislike the chore.

Making Dioramas **(Challenging)** Have the students do research on various animals' habitats. Then have them make dioramas of these environments. They may want to make a box diorama, with one open side and a painted background scene inside, or an open diorama, which is made by placing figures in front of a more open background. They may want to make clay objects, papier-mâché or salt–and–flour figurines, or paper cutouts to arrange in front of the backgrounds.

Optional Copying Masters for Enrichment

The following copying masters may be assigned as independent classroom work or as home activities to be completed with or without parents' help.

STUDY SKILLS copying master 71.
Objective: Scanning a story for details.

VOCABULARY copying master 72.
Objective: Using context clues to identify words.

Related Reading

The following books can be used to extend the lesson.

Wonders of the World of Wolves by Jacquelyn Berrill. Dodd, Mead, 1970. This outstanding book shows how the wild−dog family lived and survived all these years. (Challenging)

The Fox by Margaret Lane. Dial Press, 1982. Through this concise, informative book, the reader learns how the fox behaves and how it looks, sounds, and feeds. (Easy)

Foxes by Kay McDearmon. Dodd, Mead, 1981. Easy to read, with beautiful photographs, the book introduces red, gray, swift, and Arctic foxes. (Easy)

Why Animals Behave the Way They Do by Eugene J. Walter, Jr. Charles Scribner's Sons, 1981. Certain defense behavior of animals often plays a big part in their survival, the fox included. (Challenging)

frog
page 412

Objective

Literature
• Recognizing description in a poem.

1 PREREADING

Introducing the Poem

Relating to Students' Experiences *Say:*
□ *You have probably all seen a frog. Let's list some words on the board that would describe one.* (Possible responses: green, slimy, big eyes, long tongue, wet)

2 READING

Setting a Purpose for Reading

Say: □ *As you read "frog," see if the poet uses the same descriptive words that we listed on the board.*

Planning a Reading Strategy

Have the students read the poem aloud several times. You may wish to have different students read different stanzas in order to emphasize the number of descriptions included within the poem.

3 POSTREADING

Reviewing the Poem

The following questions may be used to review the poem. *Ask:* □ *What words does the poet use to describe a frog?* (Possible responses: spotted, green, mossy, gold–circled eyes) ☐ *Whose words are more descriptive?* (probably the poet's) ☐ *To what does the poet compare the frog? its color? its eyes?* (a stone thrown into the pond; moss on a stone; bright metal rings)

Extending the Poem

Making Lists **(Easy)** Have the students write a list, giving at least six things that might have caused the frog in the poem to jump into the water. Encourage the students to think of reasons that are not obvious or ordinary.

Writing an Acrostic **(Average)** Ask the students to use the letters *f, r, o,* and *g* to make an acrostic about a frog. Have the students write the letters vertically and write a word or a phrase beginning with each letter to describe a frog.
Example:
  Friendly
  Rowdy
  Old
  Green

Taking a Survey on Frogs **(Challenging)** Have the students ask several people outside the class: What do you like or dislike about frogs? Ask the students to take notes and compile reasons given by the people for liking and disliking frogs. Have the students share the information with the class. Lead a discussion on any unusual findings.

Related Reading

The following books can be used to extend the lesson.

Rabbits by Fiona Henrie. Franklin Watts, 1980. The author looks at rabbits in the wild and as pets. (Challenging)

The Dog Writes on the Window with His Nose and Other Poems collected by David Keredian. Four Winds Press, 1977. Written by famous poets, these small but perfect poems are mostly about animals. (Average)

LEARN ABOUT POETRY:
Similes and Metaphors

pages 413–415

Objectives

Literature
● Recognizing similes and metaphors.

● Recognizing why poets use similes and metaphors.

1 PREREADING

Introducing the Selection

Providing Background Have the students look at the title of the lesson. Point out that the word *simile* appears in the word *similar.* Both words come from the Latin word *simil* which means "one thing is like another." Explain that the word *metaphor* comes from the Greek word *meta,* which denotes "change or transformation." Tell the students to think of the change, or *metamorphosis,* of a caterpillar into a butterfly.

2 READING

Setting a Purpose for Reading

Say: □ *We have noticed in several poems and stories that we have read that the poets and authors often compare one thing to another. In this lesson we will learn the name for these comparisons. As you read, try to understand why poets and authors use comparisons.*

Planning a Reading Strategy

Have selected students read the selection aloud. You may wish to stop at each example of simile or metaphor and have the students explain the comparison in their own words.

3 POSTREADING

Reviewing the Selection

Ask: □ *Why do you think poets use similes and metaphors?* (Possible responses: to help us see something in a new way, to paint a picture for us) □ *How are similes and metaphors alike?* (Possible response: Both use comparisons to describe things.) □ *How are similes and metaphors different?* (A simile is usually introduced by the words *like* or *as*; a metaphor is usually introduced with the word *is*.)

□ *Look at the parts of the poems on pages 414 and 415. In the similes that the poets have used, are the two things compared ever really like each other?* (no) □ *Why do you think poets compare unlike things?* (Possible responses: They have something in common that is not usually thought of; it gives the reader a new way of looking at things.)

Extending the Selection

Completing Similes **(Easy)** Have the class brainstorm to complete similes such as: as red as a _____; as warm as a _____; as long as a _____. Encourage the students to think of unusual comparisons.

Finding Metaphors and Similes **(Average)** Have the students find similes and metaphors in other poems. Some examples found in this text include: "Puzzle," (page 25) "Kansas Boy," (page 170) "Dreams," (page 218) and "My Sister Jane," (page 286). Ask the students to write the lines that contain a simile or metaphor.

Writing Similes **(Challenging)** Have the students write at least six similes about themselves. Each sentence should begin with: I am like _____.

BOOKSHELF
page 416

Optional Copying Master for Enrichment

The following copying master may be assigned as independent classroom work or as a home activity to be completed with or without parents' help.

STUDY SKILLS copying master 73.
Objective: Alphabetizing book titles by author and title.

UNIT OVERVIEW

7 Tales of Texas

pages 418–498

Theme: Texas, Past and Present.

Selections
CONNECTIONS: Indians of Early Texas
The Legend of the Bluebonnet (story)
CONNECTIONS: Texas Wildlife
CONNECTIONS: The Spaniards in Texas
The Other Pioneers (poem)
CONNECTIONS: Texas Family Tree
The Alamo: Texans Fight for Freedom
Colonel Travis Draws the Line (story)
CONNECTIONS: Texas Cowboys
The Old Chisholm Trail (song)
Spindletop (story)
About SIBYL HANCOCK
CONNECTIONS: Texas Today
BOOKSHELF

Unit Materials

Home Letter   Home Letter 8 may be
sent home at the beginning or the end of
the unit.

Copying Masters for Evaluation*
Copying Masters 74, 77, and 80.

Copying Masters for Enrichment*
(Optional)   Copying masters 75, 76, 78,
79, 81, and 82.

Introducing the Unit

Have the students open their books to the
unit opener on pages 418–419. Explain
that each item is related to Texas and its
history. Have the students name the items

---

*Note that the copying masters indicated here are
from the *Teacher's Edition, Part II.*

they see and to express one thing about
Texas that each item brings to mind. Read
the unit title and *ask:* □ *How might Texas
have been different 50 years ago?* (Possible responses: fewer people, fewer cars, more
people living in the country) □ *How might
Texas have been different 500 years ago?*
(Possible responses: no cities, no cars, different people, fewer people) Tell the students that in this unit, they will read about
Texas as it was at various times in the
past, and as it is today.

Unit Projects and Activities

Marking a Map **(Easy)** Pin an outline map
of Texas on the bulletin board. As the students read the unit, have them paste
small paper cutouts on the map as symbols representing the facts they learn
about Texas, including events in Texas
history. For example, they might choose a
paper cutout of a fort to represent the battle of the Alamo, a cowboy hat to stand for
cowboys, and an oil derrick for oil. Have
them place each symbol on the appropriate spot on the map and make a map key
explaining the symbols.

Making a Texas Notebook **(Average)** For
each selection, have the students **write** a
paragraph summarizing what they have
learned about Texas. Have them assemble all their paragraphs in a notebook.
Some of the students may want to supply
illustrations for their notebooks—their own
drawings as well as photographs cut from
magazines. Have the students make title
pages and covers for their notebooks.

Doing Photo Research **(Challenging)**
Have the students find and bring in pictures of people, places, and things that represent Texas. The photos can be of an everyday person, or a particular geographic area, or a city. The photos can be from books, magazines, or travel posters. Select a wall or large bulletin board where these pictures can make up a mural that can be added to throughout the unit.

CONNECTIONS:
Indians of Early Texas

pages 420–421

Objectives

Comprehension
● Recognizing similarities and differences.

Study Skills
● Gaining information from a map.

Content Area (Social Studies)
● Identifying how Indians in Texas adapted to their physical environment.

Background

Ten main Indian groups lived in Texas before the advent of the settlers. They included three farming groups: the Wichitas of north central Texas, the Caddoes of northeast Texas, and the Jumanos of southwest Texas; two fishing groups: the Atakapans of the northern gulf coast and the Karankawas of the southern gulf coast; two plant-gathering groups: the Coahuilticans of the gulf coast and the Tonkawas of central Texas; and three buffalo-hunting groups: the Kiowas, the Lipan Apaches, and the Comanches. All three hunting groups roamed throughout west Texas.

1 PREREADING

Introducing the Selection

Relating to Students' Experiences Ask the students to think about where the food they eat comes from. Suggest a food such as bread and lead the students back to the grain that is its source. (Other suggested foods: hamburger, milk, cheese, eggs)

Previewing and Predicting *Say:*
☐ *Imagine you are stranded in a forest that has a stream running through it. What could you do to get food?* (Possible responses: fish, find berries and nuts, hunt rabbits)
☐ *Where would you find shelter?* (Possible responses: make a lean-to, dig a burrow)
☐ *People in earlier times found food and shelter in much the same way.*

2 READING

Setting a Purpose for Reading

Tell the students that the American Indians in Texas could be grouped into categories based on their similarities and differences. Have them read the selection to see what basis is used to categorize the Indian groups in Texas.

Planning a Reading Strategy

Have the students first look at the map at the opening of the selection and identify the symbol used on the map and map key. Then have the students read the selection silently.

3 POSTREADING

Reviewing the Selection

The following questions may be used to review the selection. *Ask:* ☐ *How were the Texas Indians grouped?* (Possible response: by how they obtained their food) ☐ *What was the relationship between how they got their food and where they lived?* (Possible response: The Indians used what natural resources were available where they lived.)

Discussing the Selection

You may want to use the following questions to discuss the selection further. *Ask:* ☐ *How might the lives of the Indians have been affected by the places where they lived, aside from how they obtained their food?* (Possible responses: Crafts would be related to skills needed for food gathering; houses would depend on available materials and on whether the tribe was nomadic; clothes would depend on work and weather; festivals would depend on other aspects of life.) ☐ *Are modern-day Texans affected by where they live? Why or why not?* (Possible responses: Yes, jobs depend on available resources; dress depends on climate. No, people can change whatever they have to to suit their needs.)

Extending the Selection

Finding Information in Books (Easy)
Have the students use books in the library to find out the names of the ten American Indian groups that lived in Texas. Suggest that they try to get at least the following information about each group: (1) name (2) category (i.e., farmers, fishers) (3) one interesting custom and (4) type of shelter the people built.

Finding Word Derivatives (Average)
Have the students use library references, maps, and books about Texas and Indians in Texas, travel guidebooks, Texas-oriented magazines, and other sources to find Texas place names that come from American Indian words. Suggest that they put the information in the form of a chart. For example:

Place Name	Indian Word	Meaning
Texas	Teyshas	friend
	Tejas	
	Tayas	

Researching and Reporting (Challenging)
Divide the students into ten groups. Have each group choose one of the ten American Indian groups and find out about the geography of the region in which that group lived. Suggest an atlas and pictorial guidebooks about Texas as sources of information. Each of the groups might then prepare a short report on the area they have researched. Suggest that the report describe temperature, rainfall, vegetation, and land forms such as mountains, desert, coastal forest, and so on. All ten reports can then be combined to make a class book titled, "Where the Indians Lived in Texas."

Related Reading

The following books can be used to extend the lesson.

Settlers and Strangers: Native Americans of the Desert Southwest and History As They Saw It by Betty Baker. Macmillan, 1977. American Indians of the desert Southwest are presented in a historical context. (Challenging)

Significant American Indians by Editors of Children's Press. Children's Press, 1975.

This book presents portraits of famous American Indians from 1530 to today. (Challenging)

Plains Indians by Christopher Davis. Gloucester Press, 1978. This book recounts the two-hundred-year story of the American Indians of the Great Plains, discussing their feelings for the land, their daily lives, cultures, and final decline. (Challenging)

Red Power on the Rio Grande by Franklin Folsom. Follett, 1973. The author presents details of the American Indian Revolution of 1680 when the Indians fought for their freedom from Mexico. (Challenging)

Indians of North America by Daniel Jacobson. Franklin Watts, 1983. This informative book discusses the various groups and their leaders, their culture, and everyday life. (Challenging)

Geronimo by Ronald Syme. William Morrow, 1975. This is a biography of the great American Indian chief. (Easy)

The Legend of the Bluebonnet

pages 422–433

Objectives

Literature
● Identifying a legend.

Comprehension
● **Identifying the causes in cause–and–effect relationships.**

● Making critical judgments.

Vocabulary
● Using context clues to infer word meanings.

Content Area (Social Studies)
● Describing Comanche traditions, customs, folkways, and religious beliefs.

Materials

For Evaluation

COMPREHENSION copying master 74, "Give the Reason."

For Enrichment (Optional)

VOCABULARY/WORD ATTACK copying master 75, "Find the Long Vowel Sounds."

VOCABULARY copying master 76, "Find the Right Word."

Summary of the Story

The Great Spirits have created drought and famine because the Comanches have been selfish. The Great Spirits offer to end the drought if the Comanches sacrifice their most prized possessions. Most of the

Comanches are unwilling to sacrifice the particular thing they hold dear. One little girl, however, sacrifices her doll. Bluebonnets spring from the ashes of the doll, and the drought ends.

1 PREREADING

Key Vocabulary Words

legend: a story, usually having some historical basis, telling a hero's exploits. (page 422)

drought: a long period of time without rain. (page 423)

famine: a great shortage of food. (page 423)

shaman: a person believed to have special powers and who performed sacred ceremonies for a people. (page 424)

Introducing the Vocabulary

Write the key vocabulary words on the chalkboard and have them pronounced. Ask the students to infer the meaning of the words from these sentences:

Because of the drought, people were asked to use water wisely.

Because of the lack of water, the crops did not grow and animals died. There was a famine.

The Comanches asked the shaman to pray and offer sacrifice.

(For a discussion of legend, see Introducing the Story.)

Introducing the Story

Providing Background *Say:* ☐ *Sometimes stories were made up to tell how something came to be the way it is, for example,* *how the rainbow came to exist or how a flower developed. The stories usually have a main character who is responsible for what happens. These stories are called legends. What do you think "The Legend of the Bluebonnet" tells about?* (the bluebonnet) ☐ *Does anyone know what a bluebonnet is?* (You may need to explain that a bluebonnet is a wildflower.)

Previewing and Predicting *Say:* ☐ *Think back to the story we read called "The Carp in the Bathtub." We learned about some of the traditions, customs, and celebrations of the Jewish people. In the story we are going to read now, we are going to learn about some of the traditions, customs, and celebrations of the Comanche Indians of many years ago.*

Relating to Student's Experiences Tell the students that "The Legend of the Bluebonnet" is about someone who gives up her most precious possession. Have the students think about what they consider their own most valued possession and what they might have done if they had been the girl in the story.

2 READING

Setting a Purpose for Reading

Say: ☐ *This legend is about a brave person who made a sacrifice to save her tribe. Read the story to find out why a sacrifice was necessary and what the reward was.*

Planning a Reading Strategy

First have the students look at the illustrations and ask them why the girl's name "She–Who–Is–Alone" seems an appropriate one. (She is alone or apart in most of the pictures.) Then have the students read the selection silently.

3 POSTREADING

Reviewing the Story

The following questions may be used to review the story. *Ask:* □ *Why was a sacrifice necessary?* (Possible responses: because there was a drought; because the Great Spirits were angry with the Comanches; because people were dying) □ *What was the sacrifice demanded by the Great Spirit?* (the most valued possession among the people) □ *What was the reward for the sacrifice?* ("Life will be restored to the Earth and to the People.")

After the students have finished reading the story, have them complete the review questions found on page 433 in their books. The questions can be assigned as independent written work or can be answered orally during a class discussion. You may also wish to assign the activity on the same page.

Discussing the Story

You may want to use the following questions to discuss the selection further. Direct the students' attention to the warrior and the woman mentioned on page 428. Remind them that the Great Spirits had asked the Comanche to sacrifice their most valued possessions. *Ask:* □ *Why were they so sure that the Great Spirits did not want their possessions?* (Possible responses: They were not really sure; they just didn't want to give them up because they were selfish.) □ *Did the Great Spirits want a particular object? Explain.* (No, they simply wanted the people to be less selfish.)

□ *What can you tell about the Comanche customs and traditions from reading this legend?* (Possible responses: They lived in tipis; they were buffalo hunters; they depended greatly on the yearly rain; they were guided by the Great Spirits; a shaman spoke to the Great Spirits for them.)

□ *A legend has a great person, or hero, as the main character. Why was She–Who–Is–Alone a great person?* (Possible responses: She gave up something valuable to save her people; she was unselfish.)

Evaluating the Story

To evaluate students' understanding of cause and effect, use **EVALUATION** copy master 74. **Objective: Identifying the causes in cause–and–effect relationships.**

Extending the Story

***Making an Oral Report* (Easy)** Have the students research the type of shelters used by different Indian tribes and then make an oral report to the class. Suggest that they bring pictures of the shelters if possible.

***Making a Model* (Average)** Some students may want to make a model of a Comanche tipi, using twigs for poles, thread for thongs to tie the poles together, and paper, cloth, or canvas for the buffalo–hide fabric of the tent itself. Suggest that the students do some research to find out how the Comanche actually constructed their tipis and what kinds of designs they painted on them.

***Inventing a Legend* (Challenging)** Suggest to the students that they make up a fanciful legend–like story of their own about the origin of some element of nature, such as the moon, fire, a nearby river, or some animal. Suggest that they compose this legend as a group, in serial fashion (the group sits in a circle and one student begins the story, stopping anywhere. The next student takes up where the first left off and so on around the group until the story reaches some conclusion).

Optional Copying Masters for Enrichment

The following copying masters may be assigned as independent classroom work or as home activities to be completed with or without parents' help.

VOCABULARY/WORD ATTACK copying master 75. **Objective:** Identifying spelling patterns of long–vowel sounds.

VOCABULARY copying master 76. **Objective:** Using context clues to identify words.

Related Reading

The following books can be used to extend the lesson.

The Girl Who Married a Ghost and Other Tales from the North American Indians collected by Edward S. Curtis and edited by John Bierhorst. Four Winds Press, 1978. This collection presents many fine tales, some scary, some funny, such as the trickster tale from the Comanches of Texas. The book is illustrated with photographs of American Indians from the groups represented in the tales. (Challenging)

The West by Jerry Jennings. Fideler, 1979. This book provides maps and charts, as well as information about the land, climate, and people of the area. (Challenging)

Thunder on the Tennessee by G. Clifton Wisler. Lodestar Books, 1983. Sixteen–year–old Willie joins the 2nd Texas Regiment and leaves his beloved Texas to fight for the Confederacy. (Challenging)

CONNECTIONS: Texas Wildlife
pages 434–443

Objectives

Comprehension
● Recognizing facts and details that support a main idea.

Content Area (Social Studies)
● Identifying wildlife of Texas.

1 PREREADING

Introducing the Selection

Relating to Students' Experiences *Ask:*
☐ *Have you ever seen animals, besides people's pets, as you were walking in the park, or in the desert, or in the mountains? What kinds of animals did you see?* (Allow students to share experiences.) ☐ *Did you know that you can find some kinds of animals in Texas that you can't find in many other states?* Continue the questioning, asking about plants in place of animals. Remind the students that they have already read about one kind of native plant—the bluebonnet.

2 READING

Setting a Purpose for Reading

Have the students read to find out what sorts of plants and animals are found in different parts of Texas. Have them think about what the different parts of Texas are like, based on the plants and wildlife each region supports.

Planning a Reading Strategy

Before students read, ask them to look at the pictures in the selection and see if they can name any of the plants or the animals. Then have the selection read aloud by selected students.

3 POSTREADING

Reviewing the Selection

The following questions may be used to review the selection. Have students indicate on a map of Texas the plants and animals found in the different regions. Then ask if that area is swamp or plains or mountains.

Ask: ☐ *What animals are extremely common in Texas?* (deer, coyotes, reptiles) ☐ *What animals found in Texas are rare?* (bison, whooping cranes, sea turtle, brown pelican)

After the students have finished reading the selection, have them complete the review questions on page 443 in their books. The questions can be assigned as independent written work or can be answered orally during a class discussion. You may also wish to assign the activity on the same page.

Discussing the Selection

You may wish to use the following questions to discuss the selection further. *Ask:* ☐ *Why do different plants and animals live in different areas?* (Possible response: Each plant or animal needs a different environment in which to live; one plant might need a great deal of rain where another might need it dry.) ☐ *How is the environment in west Texas different from the environment in east Texas?* (Possible responses: The west is hot and dry, proved by the fact that mesquite and cacti thrive there; vegetation is sparse and thorny; east gets rain, has thickets, and swamps.)

On the map of Texas, have the students look for mountains, plains, plateaus, and major bodies of water. Remind the students that such geographic features define different environments and that somewhat different plants and animals thrive in each environment. Have the students try to identify some of the different environmental regions of Texas. (Big Thicket region, coastal plains, central prairie, mountain ranges of west Texas, Rio Grande)

Extending the Selection

Listing Extinct and Endangered Species **(Average)** Have the students research the names of animals that used to live in Texas but have become extinct and those which still exist but whose numbers are diminishing to dangerous levels. Have them present their findings in the form of a chart with two main columns, one labeled ENDANGERED and the other labeled EXTINCT.

Making a Diorama **(Challenging)** Have the students make a diorama of a scene in one of the regions of Texas, showing typical landforms, vegetation, and animals. Indicate to the students that they must begin by researching the region that they have chosen so as to know what the area looks like and what life forms are found there. Then lead them through the following steps for making a diorama: 1) Set a cardboard box on its side so that the opening faces out. 2) Inside the box, paint the sky on the top and the upper sides. On the lower sides, paint a landscape stretching away from the foreground. 3)

Build a foreground with dirt, sand, rocks, and any other suitable materials. Trees, for example, might be made of real twigs for trunks and painted cotton for leaves, depending on the desired effect. Let imagination be the guide. 4) Place in the scene representations of selected animals. These can be cutouts from magazines or painted papier-mâché or clay models.

Related Reading

The following books can be used to extend the lesson.

Texas by Allan Carpenter. Children's Press, 1979. This study of the state includes the following content: maps; state seal, bird, tree, flag, and flower; history, geography, economics; points of interest; and landmarks. (Challenging)

The Sierra Madre by Donald Dale Jackson and Peter Wood. Time–Life, 1975. This description of the Sierra Madre section of Texas covers Big Bend National Park as well as parts of Mexico, and discusses the flowers, geography, and ecosystems of the area. (Challenging)

The Rio Grande by Ramond Johnson. Silver Burdett, 1980. Full–color illustrations show the geography and economic worth of this great river and present activities around and on it. This is part of the *Rivers of the World* series. (Challenging)

CONNECTIONS:
The Spaniards in Texas

pages 444–445

Objectives

Comprehension
- Finding details.

- Identifying a sequence of events.

Content Area (Social Studies)
- Describing the influence of Spanish culture on Texas.

- Identifying significant individuals and their contributions to Texas history.

1 PREREADING

Introducing the Selection

Providing Background Display a map of Texas and ask the students to name some cities in Texas. Write the names of towns with Spanish names, such as San Antonio and Corpus Christi, on the chalkboard. Point out that these names are Spanish. *Say:* □ *Many places in Texas have Spanish names. Why might that be?* (Possible response: Spain used to have control of Texas.) Tell the students that "The Spaniards in Texas" is about the time when Spain ruled Texas.

2 READING

Setting a Purpose for Reading

Have the students read the selection to find out when the Spaniards came to Texas and who came to the area they called New Spain.

Planning a Reading Strategy

Have selected students read the selection aloud. Assist them in the pronunciation of the proper names.

3 POSTREADING

Reviewing the Selection

The following questions may be used to review the selection. *Ask:* ☐ *What three groups of Spaniards came to Texas before 1821?* (Possible responses: explorers, gold–seekers, priests) ☐ *When the Spaniards were in charge of Texas and Mexico, they called the region New Spain. What was the area called after the Spanish colonists broke away in 1821?* (Mexico)

Discussing the Selection

You may want to use the following questions to discuss the selection further. *Ask:* ☐ *What effect do you think the Spaniards had on Texas?* (Possible responses: Early explorers opened the way for future settlers; Spaniards started towns, named many geographic features of Texas—rivers, mountains.)

☐ *Of the three groups of Spaniards written about in the selection who came to Texas, which group do you think had the most im-* *portant effect, and why do you think so?* (Possible responses: the explorers, because without them none of the others would have known Texas existed; the gold–hunters, because they were the biggest group; the priests, because they built something lasting—missions, some of which have grown into cities)

Extending the Selection

Making a Bulletin Board Display **(Easy)** Have the students find pictures of buildings built by the Spanish or that use Spanish–style architecture. Have them display their findings on the bulletin board and title the display "Spanish Architecture."

Making a Model **(Average)** Divide the class into small groups. Have each group research to find what buildings a mission consisted of. Then have the students make a model of a mission using material of their choice (e.g., clay, sticks).

The Other Pioneers

pages 446–447

Objectives

Comprehension
- Making inferences.

- Identifying the unstated main idea.

Content Area (Social Studies)
- Identifying Spanish contributions to Texas history.

1 PREREADING

Introducing the Poem

Previewing and Predicting *Say:* ☐ *We read earlier that Indian nations settled in Texas and then we read a legend that told us about one of them. We have just read about the Spanish coming to Texas. The poem "The Other Pioneers" will tell us a little more about them.*

2 READING

Setting a Purpose for Reading

Tell the students to look for the contributions made by the "other" pioneers as they read the poem.

Planning a Reading Strategy

Read the poem aloud to the students emphasizing the rhythm somewhat in order to make it easier to identify. Then have the class read it silently.

3 POSTREADING

Reviewing the Poem

The following questions may be used to review the poem. *Ask:* ☐ *According to the poet what pioneers were the first to come to Texas?* (the Spanish) ☐ *Why do you think they are called the "other pioneers"?* (Possible response: because most people think of the Saxons and Irish first) ☐ *What contributions did these pioneers make to Texas?* (Possible responses: plowed land; built towns, homes, and churches; sang songs; cleared brush; planted corn; gave their names)

Discussing the Poem

You may want to use the following questions to discuss the poem further. *Ask:* ☐ *What kind of people do you think these Spanish pioneers were?* (Possible responses: brave, industrious, willing to take chances) ☐ *What is the poet trying to say by repeating the names in the last six lines?* (Possible response: Spanish tradition is alive in Texas.)

Extending the Poem

Presenting a Reading (Average) Have groups of students prepare a choral reading of the poem "The Other Pioneers." (For choral reading techniques, see page T44 in the Teacher's Edition.)

Writing a Poem (Challenging) Review with the students the characteristics of a haiku (see "When my canary," page 123). Then have students write a haiku that expresses some of the same feelings expressed in "The Other Pioneers."

CONNECTIONS: Texas Family Tree

pages 448–450

Objectives

Comprehension
● Drawing conclusions.

Content Area (Social Studies)
● Identifying significant individuals and their contributions to Texas history.

1 PREREADING

Introducing the Selection

Previewing and Predicting *Say:* ☐ *In an area where you have French, Spanish, Mexicans, and Indians and that has vast amounts of undeveloped lands, what skills would people need to live and prosper?* (Possible responses: the ability to farm, the knowledge of languages, the ability to organize groups of people)

2 READING

Setting a Purpose for Reading

Suggest to the students that the history of a time can, to some extent, be seen through the lives of its leading figures. Have the students read to learn about each individual's role in the history of Texas.

Planning a Reading Strategy

Have volunteers read aloud about the different individuals. Assist with the pronunciation of the names where needed.

3 POSTREADING

Discussing the Selection

The following questions may be used to discuss the selection. *Ask:* ☐ *In what way was Doña Maria Calvillo's ranch like a small town?* (Possible responses: Several families lived there; people engaged in different occupations; food was grown and stored.) ☐ *Why do you think people were jealous of Juan Seguin?* (Possible responses: He was powerful in the government; he was in favor of Texan independence.) ☐ *Who designed the first flag of the Texas republic?* (Lorenzo De Zavala) ☐ *Why did the Spanish government finally help Father Francisco Hidalgo?* (Possible response: Spain was afraid that the French, who were helping him, would gain too much power.) ☐ *Why did Father Miguel Hidalgo start the Mexican Revolution?* (He saw how the Spanish rulers mistreated the Mexican people.) ☐ *What two valuable talents did William Goyens possess?* (He was a blacksmith, and he spoke several Indian languages.) ☐ *How did Padre Nicolas Balli trick King Phillip?* (He had food and fresh horses waiting for him.)

Extending the Selection

***Designing a Flag* (Easy)** Tell the students to pretend that they have been commissioned to design a new state flag. Have them execute their designs in color and display them around the classroom. Stress to the students that they should be able to explain why they chose the design they did.

***Preparing an Oral Report* (Average)** Have the students select one of the people presented in the selection and do further research into his or her life. Then have the students present their findings to the class as a first-person report, allowing the other students in the class to guess who the presenter is.

***Preparing a Family Tree* (Challenging)** Divide the class into several groups and have each group prepare a contemporary family tree following the style of the selection just read. Each group should compile their family tree into a booklet to be shared with other groups.

The Alamo: Texans Fight for Freedom

pages 451–453

Objectives

Comprehension
- Drawing conclusions

Content Area (Social Studies)
- Recognizing basic facts about the founding of Texas as a republic and a state.

- Identifying significant individuals and their contributions to Texas history.

Background

The movement for Texas independence included not only prominent settlers from the United States—Davy Crockett and Sam Houston had both served in the U.S. Congress, and Houston had also been governor of Tennessee—but many Mexicans such as Gaspar Flores, Placido Benavides, Jose Navarro, Jose Francisco Ruiz, and Lorenzo de Zavada. Navarro, Ruiz, and Zavada were among the signers of the Texas Declaration of Independence. Originally, Texans wanted autonomy as a state within Mexico. Santa Anna's response to Texan demands—jailing Stephen Austin, dissolving the legislature—made Texans both more militant and more radical in their demands for independence.

1 PREREADING

Introducing the Selection

Providing Background Remind the students that Spain ruled Texas for about 300 years. *Ask:* ☐ *Who ruled Texas after Spain lost control of it?* (Mexico) Explain that around the time Mexico took over, people who lived in Texas were beginning to think of themselves, not as Spaniards or Mexicans, but as Texans. *Ask:* ☐ *How do you think this made the people feel about Mexico?* (Possible response: made them want to break away) Tell the students that the 15 years of Mexican rule were probably the stormiest period of Texas history. Explain that "The Alamo: Texans Fight for Freedom" describes some of the people who played important roles in the search for independence.

2 READING

Setting a Purpose for Reading

Say: You have probably all heard the saying "Remember the Alamo." Read this selection to discover where that saying came from and what its deep meaning is.

Planning a Reading Strategy

Ask if any of the students have been to the Alamo. Elicit descriptions of it from them and ask what one thing they remember most about being there. Then have selected students read the selection aloud.

3 POSTREADING

Reviewing the Selection

The following questions may be used to review the selection. *Ask:* ☐ *What was the Alamo?* (an old mission turned into a fort) ☐ *Why was "Remember the Alamo" a battle cry?* (Possible responses: in memory of the people who lost their lives at the Alamo; represented the fight for independence)

Discussing the Selection

You may wish to use the following questions to discuss the selection further. *Ask:* ☐ *Why did the Texans want to be free of Mexican rule?* (Possible responses: settlers from the United States wanted to be part of the United States; Texans did not like Santa Anna; Texans did not like Mexican laws.) ☐ *When Texas was set up as a country, a new republic, and Sam Houston elected its president, what did that mean?* (Lead the students to discuss that since Texas was no longer under the government of Spain or Mexico, it had to establish its own government.) ☐ *Do you think all the problems facing Texas were over when it became independent? Explain.* (Possible response: no, because Mexico might still try to get it back)

Extending the Selection

Doing Research **(Easy)** Have the students use library books or their history books to find out what states made up the United States before 1836. Have them make a chart with the states and their dates of admission to the Union.

Preparing an Oral Report **(Average)** Soldiers were not the only people in Texas, and war was not the only way of life during the time Texas became a Republic. Many people and events contributed to its growing prosperity. Have the students select a person or topic and prepare a report to share with the class. Suggest the following: Henri Castro, John James Audubon, Ferdinard Linkheimer ("Father of Texas Botany"), the *Galveston News,* Texas Rangers, Alphonse de Saligny, the log cabin, Baylor University, Jane Long, Cynthia Parker.

Related Reading

The following books can be used to extend the lesson.

Texas: In Words and Pictures by Dennis Fradin. Children's Press, 1981. This book looks at our second largest state from the capitol to its magnificent rivers, history, national parks, and future. (Average)

The Story of the Alamo by Norman Richards. Children's Press, 1970. This simple telling explains the problems leading up to the Mexican War and the action involved. (Average)

The Valiant Few: Crisis at the Alamo by Lon Tinkle. Macmillan, 1964. This explanation of the Texan war for independence from Mexico centers on the battle at the Alamo and the ultimate Texas victory five weeks later at San Jacinto. (Challenging)

Colonel Travis Draws the Line

pages 454–463

Objectives

Literature
- Recognizing historical fiction.
- Determining the climax of a story.

Comprehension
- **Recalling details.**
- **Identifying elements of plot— sequence and development.**

Vocabulary
- Using clues to identify words.

Content Area (Social Studies)
- Identifying significant individuals and their contributions to Texas history.

Materials

For Evaluation

COMPREHENSION copying master 77, "Tell About Story Characters."

For Enrichment (Optional)

VOCABULARY copying master 78, "Match Words and Definitions."

SOCIAL STUDIES copying master 79, "Find the Main Idea."

Summary of the Story

Colonel James Bonham brings word to the Texans under seige in the Alamo that no help can be expected from outside. Colonel Travis realizes that staying in the Alamo is risking certain death. He calls the garrison together and draws a line on the floor, inviting all who are prepared to fight to the death to step across it. The response is halting at first, but when the desperately ill James Bowie asks to be lifted across the line the whole garrison crosses in a rush, except one French mercenary, who makes good his escape. The story ends with disaster impending.

1 PREREADING

Key Vocabulary Words

sentry: a soldier standing guard at a gate. (page 454)
volunteer: a person who freely chooses to join an armed force. (page 454)
recruit: a newly drafted member of an armed force. (page 455)
garrison: troops stationed at a military post or fort. (page 458)

Introducing the Vocabulary

Assist the students in pronouncing the key words. Then write the words on the chalkboard in a column. In another column write the following: all the troops, on guard duty, called to service, opposite of recruit. Have the students match each word with the phrase that tells about or defines it.

Introducing the Story

Previewing and Predicting *Ask:* ☐ *What happened to the Texan fighters in the Alamo?* (They all died.) Point out that, in a story about a famous event in history, a writer cannot keep the reader in suspense about how the story ends because everyone already knows the ending. Therefore the focus must be on some different point of interest. *Ask:* ☐ *What do you suppose might* *be a point of interest in the story of the Alamo?* (Possible responses: how the Texans felt and acted in those final moments; why they fought in the Alamo)

Relating to Students' Experiences Point out to the students that the narrator in this story is about their age. Suggest that, as they read the story, they try to imagine how they might have felt in his place and what they would have done if faced with his choice.

2 READING

Setting a Purpose for Reading

Tell the students that most good story plots build up to one dramatic moment called the climax, which is usually a key turning point and which helps determine the outcome of the story. Have the students try to determine what event constitutes the climax of this story.

Planning a Reading Strategy

Read the introduction aloud with the students. Then have the students read the story silently. Remind the students of the descriptions of the Alamo shared in the last selection and tell them to try to picture it as they read.

3 POSTREADING

Reviewing the Story

The following questions may be used to review the story. *Ask:* ☐ *What do you think was the climax of this story? Explain.* (Lead the students to conclude that the scene in which Colonel Travis draws the line is the climax because it represents the turning point in the action.) ☐ *How did Colonel Travis cause a turning point in the story?* (Possible response: By drawing a line, he forced all the men to make a decision.) ☐ *How did Jim Bowie's act prove to be a turning point?* (Possible response: without it, some of the garrison might have decided to leave.)

After the students have finished reading the story, have them complete the review questions on page 463 in their book. The questions can be assigned as independent written work or can be answered orally during a class discussion. You may also wish to assign the activity on the same page.

Discussing the Story

You may want to use the following questions to discuss the selection further. *Ask:* ☐ *Were the Texans in the Alamo volunteers or were they forced to be there?* (volunteers) ☐ *How do you know they were volunteers?* (Colonel Travis gave them the choice of leaving, but no one did except the Frenchman who fought for a salary.) Have the students point out at least two other instances in which someone in the story, by words or deeds, demonstrated that they were in the Alamo by choice. (Possible responses: Thirty-two recruits at the beginning of the story have to sneak past the Mexican army to get into the Alamo; Colonel Bonham comes back though Travis says he didn't need to.)

Point out the line on page 461, "The Alamo was not a place to fight for money." *Ask:* ☐ *What was the reason to fight at the Alamo, according to the story?* (love of Texas) Suggest that in addition to love of Texas, the fighters at the Alamo each had personal reasons for choosing to stay there and fight to the death. ☐ *What other reasons might there have been for people to stay* and *fight?* (Possible responses: for Bonham, friendship—he didn't want to abandon his friend Travis; for Travis, pride as a military leader, plus sense of duty—he felt that by delaying the Mexicans he could give the Convention in Washington–on–the–Brazos time to do its work; for the narrator's brother, a desire to live up to his father's ideals; for the narrator, a desire to be like his brother)

☐ *Does anyone remember what realistic fiction is? Remember "The Ghost in the Attic" was an example.* (If necessary, have the students turn to p. 107 to review the characteristics of realistic fiction.) ☐ *"Colonel Travis Draws the Line" is an example of historical fiction. What do you think historical fiction is?* (Possible responses: It's a story but uses events or people from history.) ☐ *What do you think are some characteristics of historical fiction?* (Possible responses: Events really happen; main characters really lived; story has an author; the author adds some imaginary events or people.)

Evaluating the Story

To evaluate students' recall of story details, use **EVALUATION** copying master 77. **Objectives: Recalling details; identifying elements of plot—sequence and development.**

Extending the Story

Preparing a Book List **(Easy)** Have the students prepare a list of books of historical fiction that they might enjoy reading. Encourage the students to use the card catalog in the library and to solicit the assistance of the school librarian.

Locating Memorials **(Average)** Remind the students that the Alamo has become a memorial commemorating a special historical event. Have the students locate other special memorials, not just in Texas but throughout the rest of the nation. The students should tell where the memorial is and what historical event it commemorates. If possible, have them display a picture.

Doing Research **(Challenging)** Have the students do research into the lives of Jim Bowie and Davy Crockett. Remind them to be aware of the distinction between facts and historical fiction.

Optional Copying Masters for Enrichment

The following copying masters may be assigned as independent classroom work or as home activities to be completed with or without parents' help.

VOCABULARY copying master 78. **Objective:** Using context clues to identify words.

SOCIAL STUDIES copying master 79. **Objective:** Identifying the unstated main idea of a paragraph.

CONNECTIONS: Texas Cowboys

pages 464–475

Objectives

Comprehension
● Distinguishing between fact and fiction.

● Identifying cause and effect.

Content Area (Social Studies)
● Understanding how people adapt to their physical environment.

● Identifying examples of the factors of production.

Background

Several factors came together in Texas after the Civil War to create a ranching boom. One factor was the large pool of available labor. Soldiers returning from the war needed work, and the Civil War had disrupted what had been the mainstay of the Texas economy—cotton farming.

Second, millions of cattle were running wild on the Texas prairie; the horses needed for herding them, all descended from animals brought to Texas by Spanish armies some 300 years earlier, were running wild as well.

Third, the growing cities in the North constituted lucrative markets for meat. Cattle could not be raised near the cities because ranching required more open grazing land than existed in the Northeast.

One key element tied all these factors together: the railroad. Tracks were built to Abilene, Kansas, just after the war, connecting to Chicago and points east. Driving cattle to Abilene was feasible—barely. Ranching entrepreneurs therefore hired cowboys to help them export the longhorn cattle, and thus the legendary cowboy era was born.

1 PREREADING

Introducing the Selection

Previewing and Predicting Find out if anyone in the class has ever seen any cowboy movies or television shows. *Ask:* ☐ *What do cowboys look like?* (Possible responses: big hats, boots, tall, wear guns) ☐ *What do they do?* (Possible responses: rope cattle, ride horses) ☐ *What kind of people are they?* (Possible responses: brave,

like to be alone, some are good, some bad) Tell the students that novels, movies, and TV shows present a storybook image of cowboys. Explain that a storybook image is a glamorous and exciting one but perhaps not quite a true picture of something.

2 READING

Setting a Purpose for Reading

Have the students read the selection to find out who cowboys really were and what their lives were like. As the students read, have them consider the differences between real and storybook cowboys, and ask them to decide why people created storybook images of cowboys rather than of farmers, or some other group.

Planning a Reading Strategy

Have selected students read the selection aloud. Call students' attention to the illustrations at the appropriate places in the selection and have them identify the animals, or articles of clothing, or activity described.

3 POSTREADING

Reviewing the Selection

The following questions may be used to review the selection. *Ask:* ☐ *How were real cowboys different from cowboys in movies and storybooks?* (Possible responses: Real ones spent more time working; their work was often grueling and boring; their lives were not as exciting; pistols were not for shooting each other.) ☐ *Why do you think people created a storybook image of cowboys and not farmers or ranchers?* (Possible responses: People did not have as much contact with cowboys to really know what they did; they knew what ranchers and farmers did.)

After the students have finished reading the selection, have them complete the review questions on page 475 in their books. The questions can be assigned as independent written work or can be answered orally during a class discussion. You may also wish to assign the activity on the same page.

Discussing the Selection

You may want to use the following questions to discuss the selection further. *Ask:*
□ *Since cowboy work was hard and dangerous, why did so many people choose this work?* (Possible responses: Few other jobs were available, some men had skills and qualities needed to be cowboys—e.g., ability to ride a horse, face danger—but none for safer, easier jobs.)

□ *Why was Texas a better place to raise cattle than Illinois or New York?* (Texas had more open range.) □ *How might working and living on the open range have felt?* (Possible responses: scary, lonesome, sometimes boring, exciting)

Extending the Selection

Inventing Brands (Easy) Show the students a number of sample brands such as the Circle T ⊤ , the Bar Fork ⅄ , and the EJ, Ɇ . After the students have deciphered how words were represented as symbols in brands, have them invent some ranch names and brands of their own. Point out that ideal brands were simple to make but hard to alter. Interested students might then go on to research and compile a list of actual Texas brands.

Making a Cowboy Scrapbook (Average) Have interested students keep a scrapbook in which they compile images of cowboy life in the modern world. Some of these can be actual cutouts of ads and illustrations that show cowboys; some may be words and phrases they have heard (such as *maverick* to mean someone stubbornly independent), or accounts of events based on a cowboy theme, or descriptions of clothes that derive from the storybook image of cowboy life.

Related Reading

The following books can be used to extend the selection.

American Cowgirls: Yesterday and Today by Sharon Cosner. David McKay, 1978. Along with the history of cowgirls and a description of a modern cowgirl's life— clothing, living conditions, work—are some chuckwagon recipes. (Challenging)

Cowboys by Marie and Douglas Gorsline. Random House, 1980. This book gives straightforward information on cowboys: their clothing, daily lives, and the way it really was in the Old West. (Challenging)

Famous American Cowboys by Bern Keating. Rand McNally, 1977. This book takes a look at the Texas cattle baron and the men who worked for him. Frederic Remington the artist, Will Rogers the cowboy entertainer, Richard King the cattle baron, and many others are highlighted. (Challenging)

Cowboys and Computers: Life on a Modern Ranch by Margaret G. Malone. Julian Messner, 1982. Today's cowboy comes equipped with rope, branding iron, pickup truck, and a computer to help keep an eye on things! (Challenging)

Rodeo by Elizabeth Van Steenwyk. Harvey House, 1978. These portraits are biographical sketches of eight women in rodeo competition. (Challenging)

The Black Mustanger by Richard Wormser. William Morrow, 1971. The Riker family has been hit with hard times and moves to Texas from up North. There, Mr. Riker attempts to capture a herd by branding cattle. When he breaks his leg, his son Dan must take over. Through his new friendship with Will Mesteño, the black mustanger, Dan is able to provide a living for his family. (Average)

The Old Chisholm Trail

pages 476–477

Objectives

Literature
● Enjoying a folk song.

Comprehension
● Making generalizations.

Content Area (Social Studies)
● Describing cultural traditions derived from the Texas cowboy era.

Background

The Chisholm Trail ran from ranches near San Antonio, Texas, to the cattle–shipping railroad center at Abilene, Kansas. Thousands of cattle were driven along this trail from around 1867 until the time when railroad lines were established in Texas some twenty years later.

1 PREREADING

Introducing the Song

Previewing and Predicting *Say:*
☐ *Remember the folk song "The Erie Canal" that you learned earlier this year. When was it sung?* (Possible response: when the men were working on the barges on the canal)
☐ *Did you find out anything about the men's job when you read the words to the song?* (You may wish to have students refer back to pages 137–141 to give specific answers.)
☐ *We are going to learn another folk song and it is called "The Chisholm Trail." When do you think the cowboys might have sung it?* (Possible responses: on a roundup or cattle drive.) ☐ *Do you think we will learn something about the cowboys' work?* (yes)

2 READING

Setting a Purpose for Reading

Have the students read the words of the song to discover how the cowboy prepared for his job as a cowpuncher.

Planning a Reading Strategy

Have the students read the words to the song first. Then teach them the tune to the song by singing the first verse to them a few times, encouraging them to join in and sing along with you as soon as they are able. Once all the students know the tune, divide the class into two groups. Have the groups sing alternate verses of the song, each group listening while the other sings. Have both groups—the whole class—join in on the chorus.

3 POSTREADING

Reviewing the Song

The following questions may be used to review the song. *Ask:* □ *When was this song probably sung?* (Possible response: during a cattle drive) □ *What two things did the cowboy own when he started herding the cattle?* (a ten-dollar horse and a forty-dollar saddle) □ *What else do you think the cowboy needed to help him do his job?* (Possible responses: his gun, a rope, some food while on the trail)

Discussing the Song

You may want to use the following questions to discuss the song further. *Ask:* □ *Would you say that the cowboy is happy or sad in verses 2–6? Explain your answer.* (Possible response: happy because he is going to be the best cowpuncher and the quickest-shooting cowboy) Point out in verse 1 that the cowboy says he is going to tell his troubles. *Ask:* □ *Do you think that the cowboy remained happy? Why or why not?* (Possible response: no, perhaps he got tired riding the trail, or maybe he was injured) You may wish to locate or have a student locate the remaining verses of the song to see if their ideas about the cowboy were correct.

Extending the Song

Making a Map (Easy) Have the students research the route that the Chisholm Trail took from San Antonio, Texas, to Abilene, Kansas. Then have them trace a modern-day map, and indicate the Chisholm Trail on it.

Exploring Cowboy Songs (Average) Direct interested students to look in library books for other cowboy songs. Suggest that any student who pursues this activity bring a copy of at least one song to class and, with the teacher's help, lead the class in a sing-along.

Listing Slang Words and Expressions (Challenging) Have the students make a list of slang words and expressions from cowboy life, such as cowpoke, six-shooter, buckin' bronco, vamoose, and dogie. Have them find out what each word means and, if possible, how it came into being.

Spindletop

pages 478–488

Objectives

Literature
● Identifying historical fiction.

Comprehension
● Distinguishing between factual and fictional details.

● **Identifying elements of plot—sequence and development.**

Content Area (Social Studies)
● Identifying major resources of a region of Texas.

Materials

For Evaluation

COMPREHENSION copying master 80, "Number the Events."

For Enrichment (Optional)

STUDY SKILLS copying master 81, "Scan for Details."

MATHEMATICS copying master 82, "Read a Graph."

Background

The first oil wells in the United States were drilled in Pennsylvania by Edwin Drake in the 1850s. In the late 1800s several attempts were made to drill for oil in Texas, but without much success. As the twentieth century began, prevailing wisdom held that no significant oil reserves existed anywhere in the United States except in the northeast. That wisdom was shattered in 1901 by the Spindletop gusher at Beaumont, Texas, which not only launched the multi–billion–dollar Texas oil industry, but is still producing significant quantities of oil and gas.

Summary of the Story

Jimmy's father and four other men had been drilling for oil at Spindletop, Texas. Recently, Jimmy had been going to the drilling site with his father. But his mother felt that the drilling site was a dangeorus place for a boy. She was right. One day an explosion spewed mud, rocks, and pieces of drill pipe out of the ground—the men had struck oil! The people of nearby Beaumont flocked to the sight. One of them accidently set fire to the oil field, but the oil workers managed to put the fire out. Ten days passed before the well finally stopped throwing out rocks. Jimmy's father then helped Curt, another of the oil workers, cap the well with pipes and valves.

1 PREREADING

Key Vocabulary Word

derrick: a tower built over the opening of an oil well, used to support drilling equipment and to lift and lower pipe. (page 480)

Introducing the Vocabulary

Write the key vocabulary word on the chalkboard. Have the students pronounce it and look up its meaning in the glossary of their books. Ask if they have ever seen a derrick and if so where. (Allow time for student discussion.)

Introducing the Story

Providing Background Tell the students that the story "Spindletop" opens in the year 1901. *Ask:* ☐ *What do you think was the biggest business in Texas at that time?* (ranching) ☐ *Where did most people in Texas live?* (ranches, farms, small towns) Emphasize that, in fact, Texas was not much different in 1901 than it had been at the height of the cowboy era. Tell the students that shortly after the events in this story, Texas began going through the rapid changes leading to the Texas of today.

Previewing and Predicting Tell the students that "Spindletop," like "Colonel Travis Draws the Line," is historical fiction. *Ask:* ☐ *What are the characteristics of historical fiction?* (Possible responses: The story is not true but some or all of the events really happened; main characters may have really lived; author adds some imaginary events or people.)

2 READING

Setting a Purpose for Reading

Have the students read the story about the discovery of oil in Texas. As they read, have them try to determine which parts of the story are historical fact and which parts are details added for the sake of the story.

Planning a Reading Strategy

Have selected students read the story aloud. After the entire story has been read, you may wish to select a certain scene to do as Story Theater. (For Story Theater techniques, see page T46 in this book.)

3 POSTREADING

Reviewing the Story

The following questions may be used to review the story. *Ask:* □ *What parts of the story do you think are really facts?* (Possible responses: The Spindletop well is in Beaumont, Texas; oil was first drilled there; how oil was drilled; a *christmas tree* was used to cap the well.) □ *What parts of the story do you think that the author created?* (Possible response: the characters and what they did and said; mother's birthday)

After the students have finished reading the story, have them complete the review questions on page 488 in their books. The questions can be assigned as independent work or can be answered orally during a class discussion. You may also wish to assign the activity on the same page.

Discussing the Story

You may want to use the following questions to discuss the selection further. *Ask:* □ *What hints are given early in the story that oil drilling might be dangerous?* (Jimmy's mother is worried, doesn't want him to go; Curt offered to cap the well because he did not have a family to support.)

□ *Why was it so important to Jimmy and his family that oil be discovered?* (Possible response: The family spent all their money to buy the land near Spindletop.) □ *Why did the drillers need a new drill bit?* (Possible response: Something sharp might get through the rock whereas a dull bit would not.) □ *Does fire still present a problem in oil wells? Explain.* (Possible response: yes, because the oil burns so easily and rapidly)

Evaluating the Story

To evaluate students' recall of story order, use **COMPREHENSION** copying master 80. **Objectives: Identifying elements of plot—sequence and development; recalling details.**

Extending the Story

Making a List **(Easy)** Have the students make a list of as many different products as they can discover that are made from oil. Suggest that they look in the library for books about oil to help them make the list.

Making a Bar Graph **(Average)** Direct the students to research the amount of oil other countries produce and how much each one produces. Have the students make a bar graph in which each different bar represents a country.

Writing a Plan (Challenging) A group may want to discuss and explore Captain Lucas's options just after oil has been discovered on his land and the well has been capped. Ask the group to consider what Captain Lucas should do to make money from the oil. Have the group write up a plan showing the general steps the Captain would have to take. Remind the students to take into account where potential buyers of the oil would be located. Have the group present their plan to the class, and then respond to questions from the other students.

Optional Copying Masters for Enrichment

The following copying masters may be assigned as independent classroom work or as home activities to be completed with or without parents' help.

STUDY SKILLS copying master 81.
Objective: Scanning to find details.

MATHEMATICS copying master 82.
Objective: Interpreting information on a graph.

Related Reading

The following books can be used to extend the lesson.

Oil and Natural Gas by Betsy Harvey Kraft. Franklin Watts, 1982. This book presents an overview of the formation, discovery, drilling for, and processing of petroleum and natural gas. It also covers the methods of worldwide distribution. (Challenging)

Energy from Fossil Fuels by Dale Rice. Raintree, 1983. How fossil fuels are formed, the discovery and continuing search for additional sources, and the future of fossil fuels is clearly and simply explained with many full–color photographs. (Challenging)

Oil by Alan Piper. Franklin Watts, 1980. This book describes the search for and production of oil on land and offshore; drilling disasters; transportation of oil (tankers and pipelines); and the problems of future production and maintenance of reserves. (Challenging)

See Inside an Oil Rig and Tanker by Jonathan Rutland. Warwick Press, 1979. Color photographs and diagrams tell the story of the search for oil and the procedures used in recovering the petroleum from the ground and transporting it to refineries and then to consumers. (Challenging)

The Story of Offshore Oil by Harry Edward Neal. Julian Messner, 1977. Through black–and–white photographs, the reader gets a look at the formation, location and extraction of offshore oil, the life of roustabouts, and the concerns of environmental groups. (Average)

CONNECTIONS:
Texas Today

pages 490–497

Objectives

Comprehension
- Identifying cause and effect.

Study Skills
- Gaining information from a map.

Content Area (Social Studies)
- Explaining the importance of economic interdependence within and among regions of Texas.

- Identifying major economic resources of regions of Texas.

1 PREREADING

Introducing the Selection

Previewing and Predicting *Ask:* □ *How do you think Texas is different today from what it was in the time of the cowboys?* (Possible responses: television, electricity, cars instead of horses and stagecoaches, oil more important now than cattle ranching, big cities)

2 READING

Setting a Purpose for Reading

Have the students read the selection to find out how Texas has changed and is still changing. As they read have them think about the reasons for the changes in Texas.

Planning a Reading Strategy

Have the students read the sections on ranching, farming, and industry silently. Then have selected students read the section on Texas cities aloud, while others locate each of the cities on a wall map of Texas as the information is being read.

3 POSTREADING

Reviewing the Selection

The following questions may be used to review the selection. *Ask:* □ *What things are the same in ranching today as what you read about in "Texas Cowboy"?* (Possible responses: Cowboys still do the work; cattle are still important.) □ *What things are different?* (Possible responses: Cowboys now ride in trucks or helicopters; short–horned cattle, sheep, and goats are raised now.) □ *What changes did the discovery of oil cause?* (Possible responses: Factories were built; cities grew up around the factories; most people live in cities and not in the country.)

After the students have finished reading the selection, have them complete the review questions on page 497 in their books. The questions can be assigned as independent written work or can be answered orally during a class discussion. You may also wish to assign the activity on the same page.

Discussing the Selection

You may wish to use the following questions to discuss the selection further. *Ask:* □ *In what ways did the discovery of oil and the building of refineries and factories lead to the growth of the cities?* (Lead the students to conclude that jobs were available, so that many people came.) ☐ *In what ways did the people working in the oil fields or refineries bring more people to the cities?* (Lead the students to conclude that other businesses— e.g., grocery stores, car repair shops, medical services—open up to serve newcomers, which means more jobs, which draws more people.)

Have the students study the location of the five major Texas cities on a Texas map (preferably one that shows topographical features as well as cities) *Ask:* ☐ *Where do most people in Texas seem to live?* (eastern half and near Gulf) ☐ *Why might that be?* (oil fields are mostly located in east; refineries are near Gulf for easier shipping; western half is ranching country, which is less conducive to growth of cities)

Have students discuss ways in which the changes in Texas may have made life better, and ways in which the changes may have made life worse. (Possible responses: better—more jobs, more money, more amenities; worse—more pollution, noise.)

Extending the Selection

Making a Presentation (Average) Ask the students how they would rather learn about something new—1) have somebody read about it to them; 2) see examples and pictures of it; 3) meet someone who is an expert in it; 4) see a movie or hear a record that deals with it. (They will probably choose 2–4.) Tell the students to keep those ways in mind as they prepare to share some information about a topic with the rest of the class.

Have the students choose some aspects of the topics suggested below and tell about this subtopic in Texas today.

Suggested topics: ethnic festivals, music (opera, classical, country–western), dancing, sports, art.

Related Reading

The following books can be used to extend the selection.

The Best Town in the World by Byrd Baylor. Charles Scribner's Sons, 1983. This book presents life in a small Texas town around the turn of the century. (Easy)

Pioneering on the Plains by Edith McCall. Children's Press, 1980. This book shows everyday life and transportation and survival in the Great Plains. (Challenging)

The Texans by David Nevin. Silver Burdett, 1975. Lots of pictures enrich this look at the people who settled, developed, and now live in Texas. Also included is information about early life, natural resources, national points of interest, and cattle ranching. (Challenging)

The South Central States by Harold Woods. Franklin Watts, 1984. The author traces the history of Texas, Oklahoma, Louisiana, and Arkansas, describing the geography, climate, natural resources, and industries for each state. (Challenging)

Notes

Notes

Notes

Notes

Notes

Notes

Across
Wide Fields

HBJ HARCOURT BRACE JOVANOVICH, PUBLISHERS
Orlando   San Diego   Chicago   Dallas

Across Wide Fields

ODYSSEY An HBJ Literature Program
Second Edition

The title of this book is from Ruth Lechlitner's poem "Kansas Boy" on page 170.

Sam Leaton Sebesta

Consultants

Elaine M. Aoki	Myra Cohn Livingston
Willard E. Bill	Daphne P. Muse
Sonya Blackman	Sandra McCandless Simons
Sylvia Engdahl	Barre Toelken

Acknowledgments

For permission to reprint copyrighted material, grateful acknowledgment is made to the following sources:

Atheneum Publishers: "Mingled Yarns" from *One Winter Night in August and Other Nonsense Jingles* by X. J. Kennedy (A Margaret K. McElderry Book). Copyright © 1975, 1977, 1978, 1979 by X. J. Kennedy.

The Bobbs-Merrill Company, Inc. and Faber and Faber Limited: "My Sister Jane" from *Meet My Folks* by Ted Hughes. Copyright © 1961, 1973 by The Bobbs-Merrill Company, Inc.

Corona Publishing Company, San Antonio, TX: From *The Boy in the Alamo* (Titled: "Colonel Travis Draws the Line") by Margaret Cousins.

Curtis Brown, Ltd.: "Old Joe Clarke" by Ruth Crawford Seeger from *American Folk Songs for Children.* Copyright 1948 by Ruth Crawford Seeger; renewed © 1976 by Michael Seeger.

Dial Books for Young Readers, a division of E. P. Dutton, Inc.: From *Benjy in Business* (Titled: "It Pays to Advertise") by Jean Van Leeuwen. Copyright © 1982 by Jean Van Leeuwen.

Dodd, Mead & Company, Inc.: Text adapted from *An Eskimo Birthday* by Tom D. Robinson. Copyright © 1975 by Tom Robinson. "There was an old man with a beard" from *The Complete Nonsense Book* by Edward Lear.

Doubleday & Company, Inc.: Four illustrations from *The Erie Canal* by Peter Spier. Copyright © 1970 by Peter Spier.

E. P. Dutton, Inc.: "Puzzle" from *Street Poems* by Robert Froman. Copyright © 1971 by Robert Froman. "The Case of the Missing Roller Skates" from *Encyclopedia Brown, Boy Detective* by Donald J. Sobol. Copyright © 1963 by Donald J. Sobol.

Eakin Press, P. O. Box 23066, Austin, TX 78755: Adapted from *Spindletop* by Sibyl Hancock, illustrated by Patty L. Rucker. Copyright © 1980, 1984 by Sibyl Hancock and Patty L. Rucker.

Farrar, Straus & Giroux, Inc.: "Frog" from *Small Poems* by Valerie Worth. Copyright © 1972 by Valerie Worth. "At Night May I Roam" from *In the Trail of the Wind,* edited by John Bierhorst. Copyright © 1971 by John Bierhorst.

Follett Publishing Company, a division of Follett Corporation: *The Great Minu* by Beth P. Wilson. Text copyright © 1974 by Beth P. Wilson. This story is based on "The Honourable Minu," originally published in *West African Folk Tales* by George Harrap & Company Ltd., London, England.

Harcourt Brace Jovanovich, Inc.: "Arithmetic" by Carl Sandburg from *The Complete Poems of Carl Sandburg.* Copyright 1950 by Carl Sandburg. Slightly abridged excerpt from "The Ghost in the Attic" in *The Moffats* by Eleanor Estes. Copyright 1941, 1969 by Eleanor Estes. "The Princess on the Pea" by Hans Christian Andersen, slightly adapted from *It's Perfectly True and Other Stories,* translated by Paul Leyssac. Copyright 1938 by Paul Leyssac; renewed 1966 by Mary Rehan. "When My Canary" from *Cricket Songs: Japanese Haiku,* translated by Harry Behn. © 1964 by Harry Behn.

Harper & Row, Publishers, Inc.: From pp. 16–23 and illustrations from pp. 20, 21 and a portion of the jacket from *Charlotte's Web* by E. B. White, illustrated by Garth Williams. Copyright 1952, 1980 by E. B. White. Illustrations copyright renewed 1980 by Garth Williams. From *Little House on the Prairie* by Laura Ingalls Wilder. Text copyright 1935 by Laura Ingalls Wilder; renewed 1963 by Roger L. MacBride. Adapted text from pp. 7, 28, 38, 39, 49, 60, 61, 62 in *Kickle Snifters and Other Fearsome Critters* by Alvin Schwartz (J. B. Lippincott Co.). Text copyright © 1976 by Alvin Schwartz. "What Night Would It Be?" from *You Read to Me, I'll Read to You* by John Ciardi (J. B. Lippincott Co.). Copyright © 1962 by John Ciardi.

Houghton Mifflin Company: "Paddington Goes to the Hospital" from *Paddington on Stage* by Michael Bond and Alfred Bradley. © 1974 by Alfred Bradley and Michael Bond.

Alfred A. Knopf, Inc.: "Hope" from *Selected Poems of Langston Hughes.* Copyright © 1942 by Alfred A. Knopf, Inc.: renewed 1970 by Arna Bontemps and George Houston Bass. "Dreams" from *The Dreamkeeper and Other Poems* by Langston Hughes. Copyright 1932 by Alfred A. Knopf, Inc.; renewed 1960 by Langston Hughes.

League of United Latin American Citizens: "The Other Pioneers" by Roberto Félix Salazar from *Lulac News,* July, 1939.

Ruth Lechlitner and POETRY: "Kansas Boy" by Ruth Lechlitner. Copyright 1931 by The Modern Poetry Association. Originally appeared in *Poetry*, November 1931.

Little, Brown and Company: "Concrete Cat" by Dorthi Charles from page 196 of *An Introduction to Poetry*, Fourth Edition, edited by X. J. Kennedy. Copyright © 1971, 1978 by X. J. Kennedy. From "The Texas Cowboy" by Arbie Moore in *American Folk Poetry An Anthology* by Duncan Emrich. First published in *Texas and Southwestern Lore*, 1927.

Little, Brown and Company in association with the Atlantic Monthly Press and the Canadian Publishers, McClelland and Steward Limited, Toronto: From *Owls in the Family* (Titled: "Wol to the Rescue") by Farley Mowat. Copyright © 1961 by Farley Mowat Ltd.

Lothrop, Lee & Shepard Company, a division of William Morrow & Co.: Adaptation of *The Carp in the Bathtub* by Barbara Cohen. Copyright © 1972 by Barbara Cohen.

Macmillan Publishing Co., Inc.: "Some People" from *Poems* by Rachel Field. Copyright 1924, 1930 by Macmillan Publishing Co., Inc.

McGraw-Hill Book Company: From *Miss Pickerell Goes on a Dig* (Retitled: "Digging Into the Past") by Ellen MacGregor and Dora Pantell. Copyright © 1966 by McGraw-Hill, Inc.

Eve Merriam: From "Metaphor" in *It Doesn't Always Have to Rhyme* by Eve Merriam. Copyright © 1964 by Eve Merriam. Published by Atheneum Publishers.

William Morrow & Company: From pp. 142–161, verbatim, in *Ramona the Brave* (Retitled: "Spunky Ramona") by Beverly Cleary. Copyright © 1975 by Beverly Cleary.

Calvin O'John, former student at the Institute of American Indian Arts, Santa Fe, New Mexico, a Bureau of Indian Affairs School: "Problems" by Calvin O'John from *The Whispering Wind*, edited by T. D. Allen. Copyright © 1972. Published by Doubleday & Company, Inc.

Parents' Magazine Press: Adaptation of *Mexicali Soup* by Kathryn Hitte and William D. Hayes. Text copyright © 1970 by Kathryn Hitte and William D. Hayes. Adapted from *The Crane Maiden* by Miyoko Matsutani. Text copyright © 1968 by Parents' Magazine Press. Adaptation of *Sound of Sunshine, Sound of Rain* by Florence Parry Heide. Text copyright © 1970 by Florence Parry Heide. Illustration copyright © 1970 by Kenneth Longtemps.

Prentice-Hall, Inc., Englewood Cliffs, NJ: Adapted from "The Monkey and the Crocodile" in *Jataka Tales*, retold by Ellen C. Babbitt. © 1912; renewed 1940.

G. P. Putnam's Sons: *The Legend of the Bluebonnet* by Tomie dePaola. Text and illustrations copyright © 1983 by Tomie dePaola.

Random House, Inc.: Text of "The Lion and the Mouse" from *Aesop's Fables*, retold by Anne Terry White. Copyright © 1964 by Anne Terry White.

Louise H. Sclove: "What the Gray Cat Sings" from *I Sing the Pioneer* by Arthur Guiterman. Copyright 1926 by E. P. Dutton and Co., Inc.; renewed copyright 1954 by Mrs. Vida Lindo Guiterman.

Charles Scribner's Sons: Adapted from the text of *Guess Who My Favorite Person Is* by Byrd Baylor. Copyright © 1977 by Byrd Baylor.

Simon & Schuster, Inc.: From *C D B!* by William Steig. Copyright © 1968 by William Steig.

Texas Folklore Society: From "The Texas Cowboy," contributed by Arbic Moore in *Texas and Southwestern Lore*, 1927.

Viking Penguin Inc.: "Buying a Puppy" from *Merlin & the Snake's Egg* by Leslie Norris. Copyright © 1978 by Leslie Norris. From *The Midnight Fox* (Titled: "The Black Fox") by Betsy Byars. Copyright © 1968 by Betsy Byars. All rights reserved.

Jerry Vogel Music Company, Inc.: "The Erie Canal" (text and melody line) also known as "Low Bridge, Everybody Down" or "Fifteen Years on the Erie Canal." Copyright 1912; renewed 1940. Copyright assigned to Jerry Vogel Music Co., Inc., 58 West 45th Street, New York, NY 10036. Reproduction prohibited.

Frederick Warne & Co., Inc.: "The Jumblies" by Edward Lear. From *Half a Kingdom* by Ann McGovern. Copyright © 1977 by Ann McGovern.

Art Acknowledgments

Chuck Bowden: 161, 219, 285, 325 (adapted from photographs from the following sources: 161, courtesy Harper & Row Publishers, Inc.; 219, courtesy UPI; 285, courtesy William Morrow and Company, Inc.; 325, courtesy Houghton Mifflin Company). Sybil Hancock, © Eakin Press: 489; Sharon Harker: 79, 103, 106–107 top, 108–109 top, 133, 160, 193, 267, 326–327 top, 326 bottom, 328–329 top, 328 top right, 329 bottom, 353, 413–414 top, 415 top, 416; Ron Himler: 411; Tony Kenyon: 324, 327 bottom, 328 top left, 328 bottom; Christa Kieffer: 413 bottom; Robert Masheris: 420, 444, 448–461 (adapted from photographs from the following sources: Daughters of the Republic of Texas; Texas State Library; Eugene C. Barker Texas History Center, University of Texas, Austin); Sarn Suvityasiri: 205, 266; Ed Taber: 106–107 bottom, 108–109 bottom, 383; John S. Walter: 74.

Cover: Tom Leonard.

Maps: Joanna Adamska Koperska.

Unit Openers: Mila Lazeravich, 1–6.
Phil Kantz, 7.

Photo Acknowledgments

HBJ PHOTO by Arthur Tress: 75.

RESEARCH CREDITS: Bruce Coleman, Inc., © Tom Brakefield: 73; Bruce Coleman, Inc., David deVries: 72 left; Bruce Coleman, Inc., Giorgio Gualco/U.P.: 72 right; Photo Researchers, Inc., © Dr. Georg Gerster: 76; Animals, Animals, Robert C. Fields: 249 right; Animals, Animals, Leonard Lee Rue: 249 left; Photo Researchers, Inc., © Tom Branch: 435 right; Photo Researchers, Inc., © Harold Hoffman: 435 left; Sullivan Association from *Texas Highways Magazine:* 491; Grant Heilman: 492; Photo Researchers, Inc., © Michael Murphy: 493 bottom; Rapho Div./Photo Researchers, Inc., © Sam C. Pierson, Jr.: 493 top; Photo Researchers, Inc., © Tom McHugh: 494 top right; Photo Researchers, Inc., © J. C. Stevenson: 494 top left; Michael D. Sullivan: 494 center; PhotoCorp Services, © Leo Touchet: 494 bottom left and right, 496.

Contents

5 What a Character! *269*

6 To Live with Animals 355

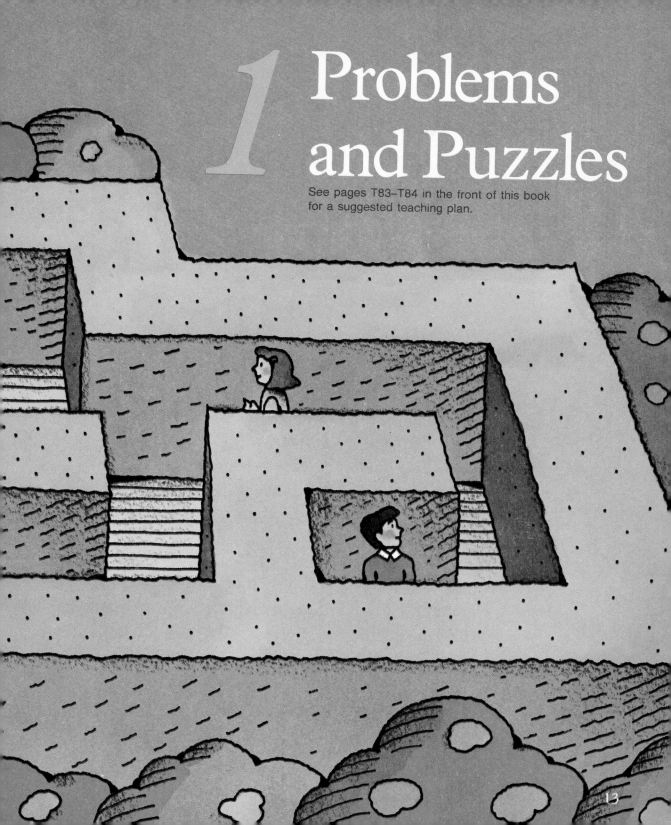

1 Problems and Puzzles

See pages T83–T84 in the front of this book for a suggested teaching plan.

See pages T84–T87 in the front of this book for a suggested teaching plan for this selection.

The Case of the Missing Roller Skates

A story by Donald J. Sobol

Illustrated by Bert Dodson

Reading Level Easy

Mr. Brown may be the Chief of Police of Idaville, but it is his son Leroy who puts the clues together and provides the solutions to many police cases. His success in solving his father's cases leads Leroy, also known as Encyclopedia Brown, to form his own detective agency with Sally Kimball as his partner. Then one day Encyclopedia finds that he himself is the victim of a crime.

Between nine and nine-thirty on Tuesday morning Sally Kimball's roller skates disappeared from the waiting room in Dr. Vivian Wilson's office.

And where was Encyclopedia Brown, boy detective? He was not ten feet away from the scene of the crime. He was sitting in a chair, with his eyes shut and his mouth wide open!

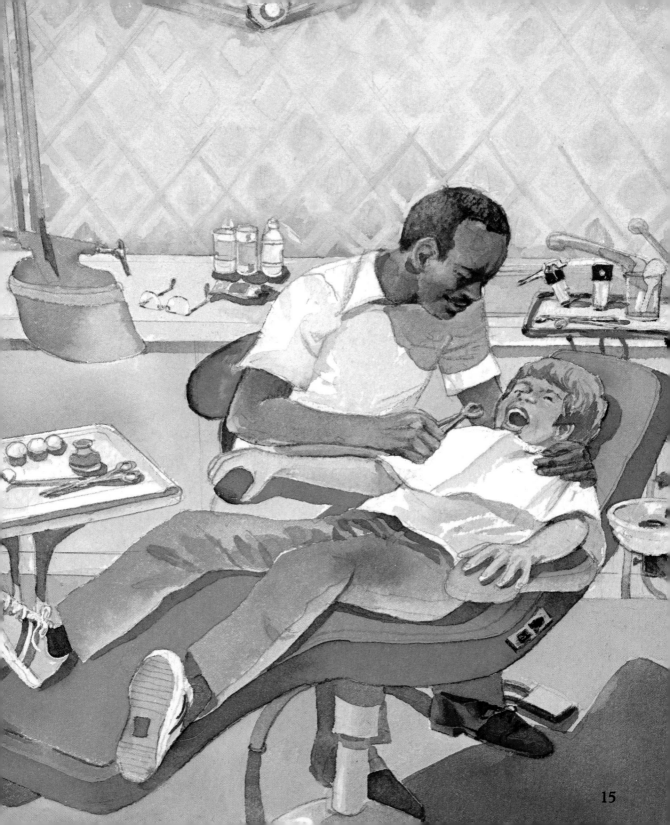

In a way, he had an excuse.

Dr. Wilson was pulling one of Encyclopedia's teeth.

"There!" said Dr. Wilson. He said it cheerfully, as if he were handing Encyclopedia an ice cream cone instead of a tooth.

"Ugh!" said Encyclopedia.

Dr. Wilson said, "All right. Hop down from the chair."

Encyclopedia hopped down and put the tooth in his pocket. He was going to give it to Charlie Stewart, who collected teeth and kept them in a flowered cookie jar.

Encyclopedia went into the waiting room. The chair on which he had left Sally's roller skates was empty!

He looked behind the chair. He dropped to his knees and looked under the chair.

"The skates—they're gone!" he exclaimed.

"Are you sure you brought them with you?" asked Dr. Wilson.

"I'm sure," answered Encyclopedia. "They were broken. I fixed them last night for my partner, Sally Kimball. I was going to take them over to her house on my way home from your office."

Dr. Wilson shook his head sadly. "I'm afraid you will never get them back."

But Dr. Wilson knew nothing about detective work. Encyclopedia liked the dentist, though he felt that Vivian was a better first name for a woman than a man.

"I'll find the skates," said the boy detective. He spoke with certainty. But he felt no such thing. What he felt was the blow to his pride; it hurt worse than his jaw. Imagine a detective being robbed!

In the <u>corridor</u> outside Dr. Wilson's office, Encyclopedia leaned against the wall. He closed his eyes and did some deep thinking.

Dr. Wilson's office was on the ground floor of the new Medical Building. The building had three floors and fifteen offices. All the offices were used by doctors or dentists.

What if the thief had followed him into the building in order to steal the skates? Then the case was closed. "I could spend the rest of my life looking through closets, school lockers, and garages all over Idaville," Encyclopedia thought.

But suppose the thief had simply come into the building to see a doctor. Suppose, on his way in, he had noticed a boy carrying a pair of roller skates. Well, that was something else!

Encyclopedia reasoned further. "The thief could be a grown-up, a boy, or a girl."

He ruled out a grown-up. First, because it was unlikely that a grown-up would steal an old pair of small skates. Second, because a grown-up would be too hard to catch. Too many men and women went in and out of the Medical Building every hour.

"I'll have to act on the idea that the thief is a boy or a girl," he decided. "It's a long chance, but the only one I have."

Leg work is walking from place to place to get information.

He opened his eyes. The case called for plain, old-fashioned police <u>leg work</u>!

Encyclopedia began on the ground floor. He asked the same question in every office: "Were any boys or girls here to see the doctor this morning?"

The answer was the same in every office: "No."

Things looked hopeless. But on the top floor he finally got a <u>lead</u>. The nurse in room 301 told him a boy named Billy Haggerty had been there this morning to have a sprained wrist treated.

Encyclopedia asked in the last two offices— just to be sure. Neither doctor had treated children that morning.

Billy Haggerty became suspect number one!

Encyclopedia got Billy Haggerty's address from the nurse in room 301. He hurried back to Dr. Wilson's office to use the telephone. He called Sally. He told her to meet him in front of the Haggerty's house in half an hour.

"We may have some rough going ahead of us," he warned.

But Billy Haggerty turned out to be only an inch taller than Encyclopedia, and shorter than Sally.

Billy drew himself up to his full height at Encyclopedia's first question: "Were you in Dr. Vivian Wilson's office this morning?"

"Naw," snapped Billy. "I don't know any Dr. Wilson."

"You didn't ask anyone about Dr. Wilson?" put in Sally.

"I never heard of him before you spoke his name," said Billy.

"Then you went straight to your own doctor on the third floor?" said Encyclopedia.

"Yeah. Dr Stanton in room 301. What's it to you?"

"Dr. Wilson's office is down the hall from both the stairs and the elevator," said Encylopedia thoughtfully. "You wouldn't pass his office going up or coming down."

"I don't know where his office is, and I don't care," said Billy. "It's none of your business where I was."

"We just want to be sure you weren't in Dr. Vivian Wilson's office this morning. That's all," said Sally.

"Well, I wasn't. I had a sprained wrist, not a toothache. So why should I go near his office?" demanded Billy. "I don't like snoopers. What are you after?"

"A pair of roller skates," said Encyclopedia.
"Do you mind returning them? You've given
yourself away."

WHAT GAVE BILLY AWAY?

21

See pages T85–T87 in the front of this book
for suggested postreading strategies.

Solution to
"The Case of the Missing Roller Skates"

Billy Haggerty said that he had never heard of Dr. Vivian Wilson and that he didn't know where his office was. But he knew too much about him.

He knew that Dr. Vivian Wilson was (1) a man, not a woman; and (2) a dentist, not a doctor.

When he was tripped by his fibs, Billy returned the roller skates to Sally.

Questions

1. Billy made two statements that showed he might be fibbing. What were they?

2. When did Encyclopedia first discover that he had a *problem?*

3. What did Encyclopedia do in the office building to try to *solve* the problem?

4. Why did the author put the *solution* after the story, not within it?

5. In this story, a *suspect* is a person who
   a. is the wrongdoer.
   b. might be the wrongdoer.
   c. is innocent, but is accused of being the wrongdoer.

6. Encyclopedia Brown has special skills. You'll find a clue to one of those skills in his name. What is that skill? Tell two other skills that Encyclopedia uses in his work.

Activity   Write an Advertisement

If Encyclopedia Brown had not found Sally's roller skates, he might have put an advertisement in a newspaper, offering a reward for their return. Write an advertisement for Encyclopedia. In your advertisement, tell what the skates looked like, and where and when they were last seen.

1. Literal/Details "I never heard of him before you spoke his name"; "I had a sprained wrist, not a toothache." (page 20)

2. Interpretive/Details (Inferred) He found he had a problem when he saw that Sally's roller skates were missing. (page 16)

3. Literal/Details He did some careful thinking and visited every office in the building. (pages 17–19)

4. Interpretive/Judgment Possible response: He wanted the reader to guess the solution before reading it. (pages 21–22)

5. Literal/Definitions b. (page 19)

6. Critical/Analysis His name probably comes from his ability to know about so many things, as if he were an encyclopedia. Other talents; ability to listen carefully; ability to observe closely; ability to be at the right place at the right time.

Where R U?

Letter puzzles written

and illustrated by William Steig

See page T88 in the front of this book for a suggested teaching plan for this selection.

I M N D L-F-8-R.

(I am in the elevator.)

D D-R S N D I-V.

(The deer is in the ivy.)

D C-L S N D C.

(The seal is in the sea.)

24

Puzzle

A poem by Robert Froman

See pages T88—T89 in the front of this book for a suggested teaching plan for this selection.

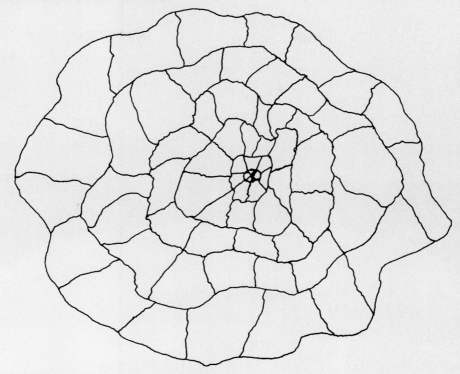

Map of a city with streets meeting at center?

Net to catch people jumping from a burning building?

Spider's web?

Burner on an electric stove?

Fingerprint?

No.

Frozen puddle after a hit by a rock.

Concrete Cat

A poem by Dorthi Charles

See page T90 in the front of this book for a suggested teaching plan for this selection.

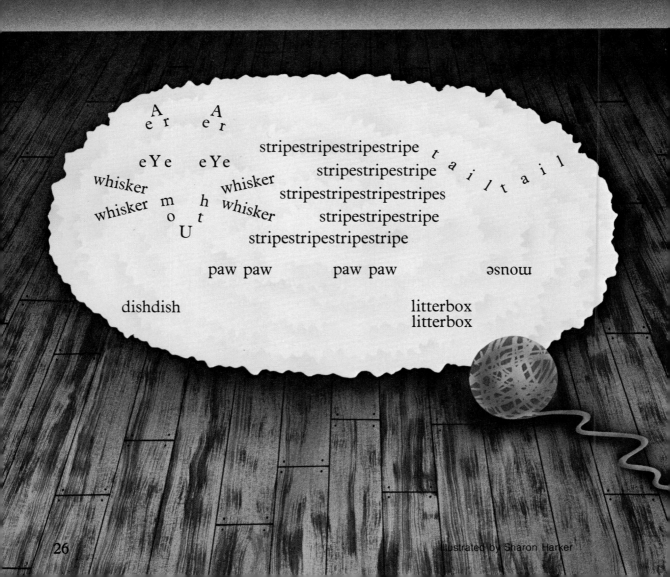

Illustrated by Sharon Harker

Mingled Yarns

A poem by X. J. Kennedy

See pages T91–T92 in the front of this book for a suggested teaching plan for this selection.

What stories are mixed together?

1) Whose cherry tree did young George chop?
   It was Pinocchio's.
   And every time George told a lie
   He grew an inch of nose.

2) Jack be nimble,
   Jack be quick,
   Jack jump over
   the beanstalk stick!

3) Aladdin had a little lamp,
   It smelled all keroseny.
   And everywhere Aladdin took
   His lamp jam-packed with genii.

   He took his lamp to school one day,
   Which made the teacher blubber
   And all the children laughed to see
   Young Al the old lamp-rubber.

Illustrated by Marie-Louise Gay

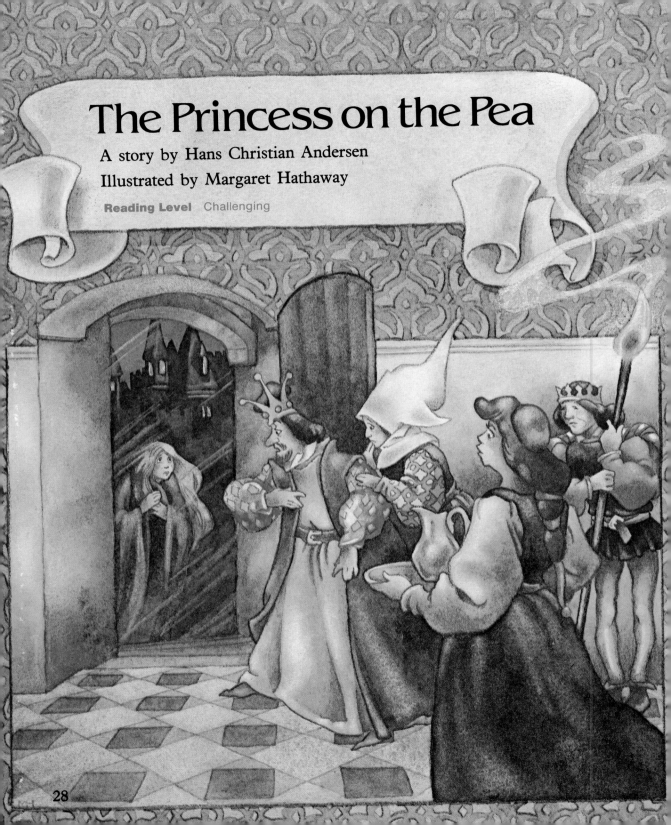

The Princess on the Pea

A story by Hans Christian Andersen

Illustrated by Margaret Hathaway

Reading Level Challenging

See pages T92—T94 in the front of this book for a suggested teaching plan for this selection.

Once upon a time there was a Prince; he wanted to get himself a Princess, but she must be a *real* Princess. So he traveled all over the world to find one, but in every case something was the matter. There were any number of Princesses, but he could never quite make out whether they were real or not—there always seemed to be a catch somewhere. So he came back home and was very unhappy, for he did so want to find a true Princess.

One evening a terrible storm came on; lightning flashed, thunder rolled, and the rain poured down in torrents—it was simply awful! Suddenly there was a knock at the city gate, and the old King went out to answer it.

It was a Princess standing outside, but what a sight the rain and bad weather had made of her! The water streamed down her hair and down her clothes, it ran in at the toes of her shoes and out at the heels, and yet she said she was a real Princess.

Bedclothes are coverings used on a bed.

Feather beds are comforters.

Eiderdown is fine, soft duck feathers that are often used to fill comforters.

"It won't take us long to find that out," thought the old Queen, but she did not say anything. She went into the bedchamber, took off all the <u>bedclothes,</u> and placed one pea on the bottom boards of the bed. Then she took twenty mattresses and put them on top of the pea, and after that she put twenty <u>feather beds</u> stuffed with <u>eiderdown</u> on top of the mattresses.

That's where the Princess was to spend the night.

See pages T93–T94 in the front of this book for suggested postreading strategies.

In the morning they asked her how she had slept.

"Oh, dreadfully badly!" said the Princess. "I hardly slept a wink all night. Whatever could have been in the bed? I was lying on something so hard that I'm black and blue all over. It was simply awful!"

So of course they could see that she was a real Princess, since she had felt the pea right through the twenty mattresses and the twenty feather beds. No one but a real Princess could have such a tender skin as that.

So the Prince took her for his wife, because now he knew that he had got hold of a real Princess.

And the pea was put on view in the museum, where it is still to be seen—unless somebody has taken it.

Arithmetic

A poem by Carl Sandburg

See pages T94–T95 in the front of this book for a suggested teaching plan for this selection.

Arithmetic is where numbers fly like pigeons in
   and out of your head.
Arithmetic tells you how many you lose or win if
   you know how many you had before you lost or
   won.
Arithmetic is seven eleven all good children go to
   heaven—or five six bundle of sticks.
Arithmetic is numbers you squeeze from your head
   to your hand to your pencil to your paper till
   you get the answer.
Arithmetic is where the answer is right and
   everything is nice and you can look out of
   the window and see the blue sky—or the answer
   is wrong and you have to start all over and
   try again and see how it comes out this time.

If you take a number and double it and double it
again and then double it a few more times, the
number gets bigger and bigger and goes higher
and higher and only arithmetic can tell you
what the number is when you decide to quit
doubling.

Arithmetic is where you have to multiply—and you
carry the multiplication table in your head
and hope you won't lose it.

If you have two animal crackers, one good and one
bad, and you eat one and a striped zebra with
streaks all over him eats the other, how many
animal crackers will you have if somebody
offers you five six seven and you say No no no
and you say <u>Nay</u> nay nay and you say <u>Nix</u> nix
nix?

Nay and *nix* are other
ways of saying no.

If you ask your mother for one fried egg for
breakfast and she gives you two fried eggs
and you eat both of them, who is better in
arithmetic you or your mother?

Illustrated by Sharon Harker

IT PAYS TO ADVERTISE

From the story *Benjy in Business* by Jean Van Leeuwen   Pronounced /lōō′·wən/.

Illustrated by Ted Carr   **Reading Level**   Easy

See pages T96–T99 in the front of this book for a suggested teaching plan for this selection.

More than anything else, nine-year-old Benjy
wanted a Clyde Johnson catcher's mitt. But how was
he going to get it?

Benjy's parents suggest that he work for the
money, so Benjy goes into business for the summer.
His first job — taking care of his baby sister — is too
tiring, and Benjy doesn't feel he has the strength to
take care of her long enough to earn the money he
needs. His second business venture — washing cars — is
a failure. Not only do Benjy and his friend Jason not
get much business, but it rains the entire afternoon.
Discouraged, Benjy sits down to the table with his
mother to find a solution. He just has to have that
catcher's mitt!

"Hot chocolate?" said his mother. "In the middle
of summer?"

Benjy watched the water roll from his hair down
his face to his shirt and then drip from his shorts
onto the kitchen floor. "Please?" he said.

"Well, all right," said his mother. "But get out of these clothes quickly before we have to bail out the kitchen."

When Benjy got back, she was just pouring the hot chocolate into his mug. "One marshmallow or two?" she asked.

"Two," said Benjy.

"Silly question," said his mother, smiling. She sat down across from him at the table. "Well, how did the car-wash business work out?"

"Terrible," said Benjy.

"That bad?" said his mother.

Benjy nodded. It was peaceful sitting in the kitchen drinking hot chocolate with the rain pouring down outside. And with just his mother for a change. Usually his sister was there, too, banging on her tray with her shoe or babbling away in her strange language. It was past time for her to be up from her nap—she must have overslept. Benjy told his mother about sitting by the mailbox for hours while all the cars went by without stopping, and keeping on adding things to his sign, and how when he finally got his first customer, it started to rain.

"That was bad luck about the rain," said his mother.

"It was bad luck about the whole day," said Benjy.

"What do you think went wrong?" asked his mother.

Benjy shrugged. "I guess no one wanted their car washed."

"Well," said his mother, "not enough people, anyway. Remember what your father said? You have to have something to sell that people want to buy." She looked out the window thoughtfully. "One other thing you might keep in mind if you want to be a businessman. People can't buy your service unless they know about it. You have to advertise."

"You mean like on TV and in the newspaper?" said Benjy.

"Not quite like that," said his mother. "But if you just have a sign on the mailbox, only people who happen to pass your mailbox will see it."

"I could make more signs," said Benjy. "And put them up on other roads, like they do for garage sales."

"That's what I mean," said his mother. "Then you can attract customers who don't live on our street."

"I could even put a sign on Route One Seventy-one," said Benjy.

"Well, maybe not there," said his mother. "Cars on the highway are usually going too fast to stop. Anyway, that's a suggestion if you decide to go into business again. It pays to advertise."

"Right," said Benjy.

Benjy didn't go into business again the next day. He thought he needed some time off. Besides, it was still raining.

He fished around under his bed and in his closet and a few other places and found all his baseball cards. Using two shoeboxes, he separated them into

this year's and last year's. Then he sorted this year's cards into piles according to teams and put rubber bands around them. That took most of the day. After that he copied Clyde Johnson's picture from last year's card, colored it with his colored pencils, and put it up on his bulletin board.

Looking at the picture made him think about the mitt again. He had to get it, and soon. Otherwise his

38

baseball career would never take off. But he still
needed $20.43. How was he ever going to get it?

The next morning Benjy went over to see Jason.
He was bound to have some ideas. Not that all of his
ideas were terrific, but he always had a lot of them.

"I've got it!" said Jason when he and Benjy were
hanging by their knees from the climbing bars of
Jason's swing set. "A worm farm!"

"A *worm* farm?" They were looking at the world upside down, with the worms on top. Something must have gotten jumbled inside Jason's brain.

"I'm not kidding," said Jason. "I read about it in a book. This kid digs up his backyard and makes pits and raises worms to sell. And he makes a fortune."

Benjy could just see his mother's face if he told her he was going to have a worm farm. He could also see his father's face if he told him he was going to dig pits in the backyard. This wasn't one of Jason's better ideas.

"It'll never fly," Benjy told him.

Jason let go with his hands and swung so his hair just brushed the ground.

"How about this?" he said, smiling upside down. "We open a gym in my basement, and we charge people to join. Like a health club. And they get to use my brother's barbells and his punching bag and all that stuff."

Too much blood must be rushing to Jason's head.

"Use your brother's stuff?" said Benjy. "Your brother won't even let *you* use his stuff."

"Oh, yeah," said Jason. "I forgot."

Maybe he'd do better right side up. Benjy did a quick <u>skin-the-cat</u> and went to sit in the shade.

Jason flopped down next to him. "Sure is hot," he said.

"The thing of it is," said Benjy, "that you have to have something to sell that people want to buy."

"Right," said Jason.

"If you were a customer, what would you like to buy?" asked Benjy.

"Right now," said Jason, "I'd like to buy a drink."

Benjy looked at him. Jason had done it again. He'd always known he could count on him for ideas.

"That's it," said Benjy.

"It is?" said Jason.

"Sure," said Benjy. "We can sell lemonade."

"Now, that is a good idea," said Jason.

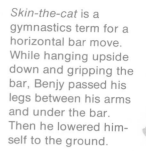

Skin-the-cat is a gymnastics term for a horizontal bar move. While hanging upside down and gripping the bar, Benjy passed his legs between his arms and under the bar. Then he lowered himself to the ground.

41

They made six signs on big pieces of cardboard, all with red arrows saying LEMONADE THIS WAY, and put them up on nearby corners. The seventh sign said LEMONADE HERE—15¢ A CUP. They stuck that one on the mailbox. Benjy's mother gave them a pitcher of lemonade and a stack of paper cups. She let them use an old card table for a lemonade stand, and Benjy got two folding chairs from the garage.

He sat down in one—just as Charlie Fryhoffer drove by without even looking.

"Oh, no," groaned Benjy. "This better not be like last time."

But it wasn't. In the first ten minutes three cars stopped. One was Mrs. Bolton with her two little kids and their two friends. She bought five cups. A man from Adams Air Conditioning bought two cups. And another woman in a station wagon with three kids bought four cups. "I saw your sign over on Laurel Lane," she said. "A cup of lemonade hits the spot on a day like this."

The woman is saying that lemonade is a welcome drink on a hot day.

As she drove away Jason stuck out his hand. "Congratulations, old pal," he said. "You're going to rake in a fortune.

Benjy grinned. "Same to you. It was your idea."

Money was jingling in his pocket. And the pitcher of lemonade was nearly empty. Already.

Benjy went to the house to get more.

"Already?" said his mother. "Business must be good."

"I'm going to rake in a fortune," he told her.

"In that case," said his mother, "you can pay me back for the lemonade. That's how it's done in business, you know. You have to invest money to make money."

"No problem," said Benjy. "I'll pay you when we close up the stand."

The second pitcher went fast too. And the third. Just about everyone on Benjy's street stopped at the lemonade stand. Mrs. Parkinson and a friend of hers and Mrs. Rosedale and Alex Crowley's mother and sister. And the mailman and the man who came to read the electric meters. And a lot of people Benjy had never seen before.

"Those signs are really working," said Jason.

"It pays to advertise," said Benjy.

To rake in a fortune is to make a lot of money.

43

His pockets were overflowing with money now. He needed a cash register. When he went to get the fourth pitcher of lemonade, he brought back one of his baseball-card shoeboxes. He dumped all the money into it.

"Wow!" said Jason. "It looks like you get your mitt tomorrow."

"Maybe," said Benjy.

He started counting it. But he'd only gotten to $2.50 when another car stopped, its brakes screeching.

Jason nudged him. "Look who finally decided to give us a break."

Benjy looked up. It was Charlie Fryhoffer.

"You guys got the right idea," he said, whipping out a comb and working over his hair. It was so long, Benjy didn't know how he could see where he was driving. He handed Charlie a cup of lemonade and Charlie drank it in one gulp and held out the cup for a refill. Then he tossed Benjy two quarters. "Keep the change," he said. And he took off down the road, his car clanking like a lawn mower.

"One of these days," said Jason, "his engine's going to fall out right in the middle of the road."

"If he doesn't drive into a tree first," said Benjy.

After Charlie Fryhoffer things quieted down a little. It was getting late in the afternoon and it wasn't as hot. Mrs. Bolton stopped again, but only to ask how they were doing. A man in a tan delivery van stopped and bought one cup. And then no one.

"Want to call it a day?" Jason asked.

"Not yet," said Benjy. "I've got to sell this last pitcher. I'm paying my mother for it."

"How about having a catch while we're waiting?" Jason suggested.

That sounded good to Benjy. He was tired of sitting in the folding chair. His legs felt like they were falling asleep.

Benjy got his mitt and a tennis ball. He let Jason use the old catcher's mitt that used to belong to his father. They took turns pitching a few.

Jason was wild. He walked two batters and then made a wild pitch.

But Benjy struck out the side. His fastball zipped right down the middle, and his change-up got the outside corner of the plate. Even his curve ball seemed to be curving a little.

"Nice throwing," said Jason.

"Thanks," said Benjy. There was a possibility that he might be a pitcher when he grew up instead of an outfielder. If he could just learn to throw a slider.

Then they gave each other high fly balls.

It was the last of the ninth and the Yankees were ahead, 1–0, on a homer by Clyde Johnson. But the Red Sox were threatening. They had two men on and two out and their cleanup hitter, Jim Barker, stepping up to the plate.

He swung on the first pitch. And it was a long fly ball out to deep centerfield. Clyde Johnson was racing back. Could he get there in time? He was all the way back, up against the centerfield wall. He leaped high in the air.

And he missed. Benjy tripped on a tree root and fell flat on his back. He heard a strange *clunk*. And then he heard Jason laughing.

Benjy looked up. There was the yellow tennis ball, in the pitcher of lemonade.

"Nice catch," said Jason.

"Nice throw," said Benjy. He picked himself up. "Well," he said, "we may as well call it a day."

Jason took the signs down and Benjy put everything away inside. Then they went up to Benjy's room to count the money in the shoebox. It came to $7.30.

"Looks like you don't get your mitt tomorrow," said Jason.

"No," said Benjy. "But at least I'm starting to get someplace."

He handed Jason a dollar.

"What's that for?" asked Jason.

"For helping," said Benjy. "A businessman has to pay his employees, you know."

You might want to have the students figure out how many 15¢ cups of lemonade Benjy sold if he had $7.30 at the end of the day.

He went downstairs to find his mother.

"How much do I owe you for the lemonade?" he asked.

"Well, it was fifty-nine cents a can and you used four cans," she said. "But I'll throw in the first one free. That comes to—let's see—a dollar seventy-seven."

Benjy counted out the money.

"Thanks," said his mother.

"Thanks for the free can," said Benjy.

He went back upstairs and counted what was left in the shoebox. Now it came to $4.53. Benjy stuffed it all into his monkey bank. Then he got his piece of paper and did some subtraction. Twenty dollars and forty-three cents minus $4.53 was $15.90. He still had $15.90 to go.

Benjy sighed. "Making money sure is tough work," he said to Jason.

Jason was looking through Benjy's baseball cards. "Yeah," he said. "Spending it is a lot easier." Then he looked up. "You know what you've got to do, Benjy? Start thinking big. Forget about stuff like lemonade, fifteen cents a cup. You need to go for big money."

Benjy nodded. That's what he needed, all right. Big money. "But what kind of business can a kid go into to make big money?" he asked.

"I don't know yet," said Jason. "But don't worry, I'll think of something. Hey, Benjy, want to trade your Jose Lopez? I'll give you two all-stars."

"No way," said Benjy.

See pages T97–T99 in the front of this book for suggested postreading strategies.

Questions

1. On the first page of the story, you find out that Benjy is all wet. What sentence later on tells you how Benjy got wet?

2. Why is Benjy so eager to make money?

3. Benjy's mother charged him for the lemonade. Should she have also charged him for making the lemonade? Tell why or why not.

4. Choose a word to complete each sentence.
   a. If Benjy's mother *bails out* a boat, she should use _____.
   b. If someone *bails out* a friend in debt, he or she could use _____.
   c. If a pilot *bails out* of a plane, he or she should use _____.

   a parachute   a bucket   money

Activity   Make a New Sign

Besides the lemonade, Benjy has decided to sell three healthful juices. Jason will bake three dozen oatmeal cookies to sell, too. For a small extra charge, Benjy and Jason will act out the most exciting play of this year's World Series.

All of these activities call for a new sign for their stand to advertise their new business. Hurry! Hurry! Read all about it. Design the sign for Benjv and Jason's new business.

1. Interpretive/Details (Inferred) "Well, how did the car-wash business work out?" (page 36) It was peaceful sitting in the kitchen drinking hot chocolate with the rain pouring down outside." (page 36)
2. Interpretive/Details (Inferred) Possible response: any of the sentences from the paragraph that begins "Looking at the picture made him think about the mitt again." (page 38)
3. Critical/Evaluation Possible responses: yes, because it is like a business and he should pay for what he gets; no, because it is all in the family and she must know that he wants to buy the baseball glove
4. Literal/Definitions a. a bucket; b. money; c. a parachute

See pages T99–T102 in the front of this book for a suggested teaching plan for this selection.

An Eskimo Birthday

A story by Tom D. Robinson

Illustrated by Sandy Rabinowitz

Reading Level Challenging

The Eskimo people live in a climate where it is below the freezing point for most of the year. Danger and death have been part of the Eskimos' daily life. Now that there are snow machines as well as dog teams, houses instead of igloos, electric lights, and stores, Eskimo life has changed. Still, many of the old people keep to the old ways while the young take on the new.

The strong wind that had brought the storm shook the windows of the little school with each gust. Often even the lights from the closest houses winked, then disappeared as swirls of snow were thrown against the side of the building.

<u>Eeka</u> kept looking, first at the storm, then at the clock above the blackboard. The hands seemed to be held back by giant weights. Only two-thirty—another whole hour to go! Oh, and it was such a special day! "My birthday," she muttered to herself, as she hit her desk softly with her clenched fist.

Pronounced /ē′·kə/.

Eeka had so hoped everything would go perfectly. It had been calm when her father had gone out to check his traps early in the morning. Her mother was home cooking a big meal for the party that night, and then there was the beautiful new parka her mother had sewn, complete but for the fur ruff and trimming.

The trapping season had been a poor one, but there was always the chance that this time, especially this time, her father would have luck and find some fox in his traps so the parka could be finished. Now the storm that had completely covered the village with snow took that slim chance away. Eeka sighed and stared out at the darkness caused by the storm and lack of winter sun.

Just then, the door to the classroom opened. The principal came in and whispered something to Eeka's teacher, and when he left, she quietly asked the children to listen.

"Because the storm seems to be getting worse, we're dismissing school early. Many of your parents are out in the hall, waiting to take you home. If your parents are not there, please be careful when you leave. And," she added, "you fifth graders make sure and take home any little ones who live close to you."

Eeka gave a squeal of delight. She threw her books into her desk and went running to the door.

After setting traps, a trapper must check them periodically to see if any animals have been caught.

"Eeka! Eeka!" called her teacher. "Slow down before you run over somebody."

Eeka slowed to a quick walk, while one of the other students explained, "It's her birthday and her mother is cooking for her. That's why she's in a hurry."

The teacher was smiling. "Well, happy birthday, Eeka, but save some energy for the walk home! I'd like to see you in one piece for your party."

Out in the corridor, Eeka found her first-grade cousin waiting for her by the coat hooks. Eeka slipped her old parka over her head, pulled the hood up tight around her face, and thrust her hands into her mittens.

Between the wind and her slippery <u>mukluks</u>, it took all of Eeka's strength to get the school door open. Once outside, the girls were blown sideways several feet by a strong gust before they could regain their balance.

When they were headed in the right direction, they both put their heads down and away from the wind that raged against their sides. Eeka looked up only to check that she was going the right way. Each time, the stinging blasts of snow made her forehead ache with cold.

Neither girl spoke. They would have had to shout to have been heard above the wind, and walking up and down the quickly forming drifts didn't leave much breath for talking. Once in a while, Eeka caught the glimmer of a light from one of the houses. Between that and having walked this way hundreds of times before, she was able to keep on a fairly straight line home.

Eeka's cousin lived right next door to her, so, when they got near their houses, Eeka just let go of the little girl's hand, and she slid down the small drift between the two buildings, stopping with a bump against the <u>storm porch</u> of her house. Her cousin disappeared inside her door.

Eeka looked for her father's <u>snow machine</u>, but it wasn't there. She stood looking past her house in the direction she knew her father had gone, and

A *storm porch* is an enclosed area passed through before entering the main rooms of a house. It protects the inside of the house in severe weather.

A *snow machine* is also called a *snow-mobile.*

wondered how he could ever find his way home in this weather.

Pulling a hand out of one of her mittens, she placed it over her nose to warm it up. With the other hand, she pushed the door open and entered the storm porch.

Inside the long, narrow building, Eeka carefully brushed all the fine snow from her parka and pants. The light from the single, bare bulb on the ceiling made scary shadows out of all her father's hunting gear that hung on the walls. Close by the inside door was a box which housed a female dog curled around her four new puppies. Eeka knelt down and let the mother lick her hand. It was a bad time for the pups to be born, these cold months, but her father wanted to build his team back up. His snow machine was old and a new one just cost too much. Eeka gave each puppy a pat.

Eeka was greeted by the smell of freshly baked pies and cakes as she entered the house, and a loud screech from her little brother. On seeing her, he threw his bottle over the side of the crib and held out his arms to be picked up. Eeka's mother was bustling about the stove. Bending down for a hug, she said, "Happy birthday, little one."

Eeka walked into the only other room of the house, the bedroom she shared with her mother and father. She put her parka on her bed. On her parents' bed lay the new parka her mother had sewn, a beautiful, dark blue velveteen. There was no telling now when the parka would be done. It seemed enough just to hope her father would make it home all right.

Eeka heard her brother screech again; so she
turned with a sigh and went back into the main
room to pick him up. Her grandfather was sitting
on the edge of his bed in the corner next to the
oil stove. He was slowly stripping bits of baleen to
use in making the shiny, black baskets he sold at
the store. They were small, but they brought a
good price when sold at the right time to the right
people.

He raised his head and looked at Eeka, his
white hair making his wrinkled, brown face seem
even darker. Then he looked at the clock.

"Did they let you out early because it's your
birthday?" he asked with a smile. His voice was
almost a whisper. "Schools sure have changed."

Apah is the Eskimo
word for *grandfather*.

Eeka laughed as she sat down and began to
bounce her brother on her knees. The warmth was
beginning to return to her cheeks. ''Not because
of my birthday, Apah. Because of the storm.''

''I remember coming home from Sunday school
once, when I was very little,'' her grandfather
began slowly. He had put his knife down and was
looking toward the window. ''It was away from
town—you know the place—up toward the little
lagoon. Anyway, it was stormy like this, and we
were trying to follow the row of whale bones back
to the village. Somehow we got lost and wandered,
it seemed like for hours.''

Eeka had heard most of her grandfather's stories, including this one, many times before, but they seemed to get better and better. When other old people came by to visit, they would talk with Grandfather about the way things were in the past. They usually spoke in Eskimo, so Eeka would sit close to her mother who would tell her everything that was being said.

"At first it was fun and then we got scared," Grandfather went on. "We stopped, and some of us started to cry while some of us started to pray. Suddenly, the clouds began to lift toward the south and the wind slowed down. We hadn't noticed the wind when we left the church, or we could have used it as a guide. We were way over on the north beach, almost out on the sea ice. People were looking all over for us. We never knew if it was our praying or our parents' shouting that drove the storm away."

"Well," laughed Eeka's mother, "I'm glad I don't have to worry about Eeka like Grandmother had to worry about you! She would take notice of the wind direction when going out in a storm."

Grandfather chuckled. "I guess children these days are a lot smarter in some things than we were. But," he added, "I'm not sure school gives them all the answers." His eyes were shining.

"It's Eeka's father I'm worried about," Eeka's mother said softly, as she began to dress the baby. A little frown crossed her face as she spoke. "We'd better hurry, Eeka, if we're going to get those things at the store for tonight. And bring the five-gallon can and the little sled so we can get some stove oil." She slipped the baby up under the back of her parka where he would ride safe and warm. Eeka put on her parka and went out to tie the can onto the sled.

The wind was at their backs as they walked to the store. Now and then, an extra strong gust would push them ahead, making them run for a few steps until they regained their balance. The light from a snow machine, or the outline of another figure, would appear close by them, then <u>dissolve</u> back into the snow and darkness. It wasn't as cold walking with the wind, but still Eeka and her mother were happy to see the lights of the new store and the warmth it offered.

Everyone greeted them when they got inside, most people calling out happy birthday to Eeka and kidding her about getting old. Eeka's mother took the baby out from inside her parka. She placed him in the shopping cart, which Eeka began pushing, following her mother up and down the aisles.

Here, *dissolve* means *disappear.*

As they moved down the back row of the
store, past the hardware, snow machine parts, and
rifles, Eeka and her mother came to the corner
where the furs hung. Eeka stared at the five fox
skins, all of them small and stained yellow with the
oil of the seals the foxes had feasted on. Her
mother walked over and looked at each one.

"They're too expensive, Eeka, and not nearly
good enough for your parka. There were two
others, big and pure white, but they were even
more money. Perhaps your father will bring some
home from his traps."

"It is probably too stormy for him to find his
traps," offered Eeka. "I'll just be glad for him to
get home."

As they walked up to the cash register, Eeka was again teased about its being her "special" day. She blushed and turned away, but she couldn't hide her smile.

Kegs are small barrels.

The men sitting on <u>kegs</u> and piles of rope near the check-out counter asked Eeka's mother many questions in Eskimo about Eeka's father—when he had left, the direction he had gone, how much gas he had with him, if he had a stove and a tent. Eeka wished at that moment that she'd listened more closely to her grandfather. He had tried to get her to speak Eskimo when she was younger, but she never seemed to have the time. And now, as the men spoke to each other in quiet tones, Eeka understood only that they were discussing a search party.

It seemed impossible to Eeka that in this great, white country one small man, also dressed in white, could be found in such a storm. How she wished he had never gone—and for her!

"Don't worry, little Eeka," her favorite uncle said, putting his big arm around her shoulders. "If your father's not back soon, we will go out and get him. We won't let him miss your birthday party." He smiled down at her, and Eeka began to feel much better.

The walk home was horrible! The wind that had pushed them over to the store now blew directly in their faces, some gusts making them stop completely. Both Eeka and her mother put their heads down, not daring to look up. Her mother pulled the sled, heavy with the stove oil and the fish. Eeka carried the rest of the things in a sack clutched tightly to her chest so it wouldn't blow away. Many times they turned their backs to the wind, resting and warming their noses and cheeks with a bare hand.

Whenever they did glance up to get their directions, the snow flew in their faces and made it almost impossible to see. As Eeka had done when coming home from school, they used drifts, oil drums, dog stakes, and the brief flicker of the light from a house to guide them.

Finally, when Eeka thought she was as cold as she could get, she saw the familiar shape of her house just ahead. And there, outside the little house, was her father—unloading <u>caribou</u> from his sled. He was home safe! Eeka nearly fell over a drift as she ran ahead to greet him.

Eeka's father had many things to do before he could finally come inside and warm up. First, he carried in a large piece of meat and placed it by the stove to thaw out so it could be used in caribou soup that evening. Then he and Grand-father had to unload the sled and cover the snow

machine. Finally, there was the oil to put in the drum alongside the house, and the four older dogs to be fed. Only then was he able to come in and get the hot cup of coffee that would start the wonderful heat flowing back into his body.

All this time, Eeka helped her mother unpack their groceries, anxiously waiting for a chance to see if her father had trapped a fox. When everything was put away, she crowded near him, but she couldn't bring herself to ask.

Then Eeka's father spoke to her.

"All my traps were covered by the snow, Eeka," her father said. "There was a bit of fur in one trap where a fox had been, but I think a wolverine beat me to him. Maybe he thinks he's found somebody who will feed him and he will return to the trap. The next thing he'll know, he will be a pair of new mittens for you, as punishment for having taken your fox." Eeka tried to smile, but it was hard not to look disappointed.

A *wolverine* (line 15) is a stocky, meat-eating animal of the weasel family, having blackish shaggy hair with white markings.

"Eeka," called her mother, "come and feed your brother. There is much to do before the party and it is almost time for people to come." Eeka was glad to be busy rather than have time to think about something that couldn't be helped. In fact, she was so busy that she was surprised when the door opened and the first of the guests walked in.

By the time all the people had arrived, the last cake had been iced and the caribou soup was done. Eeka and her mother laid a cloth out on the floor and put the food and dishes on it. People could help themselves, and eat either sitting on the floor or on one of the benches at the table.

When Eeka's mother called her to come open her presents, the girls began teasing about what they had brought. Eeka didn't like the idea of standing up in front of all the other people, but she was anxious to see what she had gotten.

Everyone had brought something, either an envelope with a card and money in it, or a present wrapped in a paper sack with a birthday message written across the outside. Eeka's mother insisted that she read every one before she opened it. Some were serious and some, like the message from her uncle, made people laugh until tears ran down their faces.

There were more things than Eeka had ever hoped to get—clothes from the store, a game, a deck of playing cards, a scarf knit by an aunt, a beautiful pair of caribou mukluks from her grandmother, and almost ten dollars from the envelopes.

Eeka was gladly just about to give up her place as the center of attention, when one of the women walked out of the bedroom and held the new parka up to Eeka.

"Here," she said, "put it on so everyone can
see the fine present your mother has made for you."

Eeka stared at the parka. Without a ruff or trim
it looked anything but nice. It was so lifeless!
Why? thought Eeka. Everything was going so well.
I hate that ugly thing! I hate it! But she blindly
shoved her hands into the sleeves and stood
there, head down, while everyone commented on
what a fine parka it was.

Suddenly, she could stand it no longer. Eeka turned to rush from the room, to take the parka off and hide the tears she knew would come if she had to hear another word.

She almost knocked her grandfather down as she spun around. He had left his place on the bed and had silently made his way to her side. He was holding a sack in his hand, which he gave to Eeka.

"Here," he said quietly. "They aren't very good, but it was all the store would give me for one of my little baskets."

All was silent as Eeka opened the sack and looked inside. Slowly, unable to believe her eyes, she pulled out two of the most beautiful white fox skins she had ever seen. They must have been the ones her mother had spoken of at the store!

Immediately, everyone began talking about what fine skins they were—surely the best taken that year! They were passed from hand to hand, so much so that Eeka feared all the fur would be rubbed off. The women discussed how best to cut them to get the most trim and biggest ruff, while the men talked about their whiteness and who had trapped them.

Grandfather sat on the edge of his bed, holding a cup of tea and looking at the floor. The only sign that he heard the remarks about the skins

was his smile—a smile that showed how proud
he was.

And after being asked time and time again to
tell how he had gotten the skins into the house
without Eeka knowing, he related the story, quietly
in Eskimo. He told how he had gone to the store
the day before the party and how he had carefully
hidden the lovely, full furs under his bed so no
one would learn of his secret.

The rest of the evening was a blur to Eeka. She remembered holding the fox skins and rubbing the soft fur against her cheek.

On her way to bed, she stopped by where Grandfather lay. He seemed to be asleep, but Eeka knelt down beside him and whispered, "Thank you, Apah. Thank you very much." The old man put out a hand and touched Eeka gently on her head. He was smiling, his eyes closed, when she left him.

The last sound she heard, before drifting off to sleep, was her mother humming an old, old song as she swiftly cut up the skins and sewed them onto the new parka.

Questions

1. When trying to solve their problems, which characters in the story *might* have said the following:
   a. "I'll buy two white fox skins."
   b. "I'll keep busy so I won't be sad about something I won't receive."
   c. "If your father doesn't come back soon, we'll go and get him."

2. A story's *setting*—the time and place where the story happens—can cause problems. Tell two problems caused by this story's setting.

3. Find the words the author used to make the setting exciting.
   a. The wind ＿＿＿＿ the windows. (page 51)
   b. The lights from the houses ＿＿＿＿ in the swirls of snow. (page 51)

4. How does the author show you that Eeka's life is happy even though the setting is often cold and dangerous?

Activity   Make a Village Map

Make a map to show the village in the story. Draw pictures to show the school, Eeka's house, and the store. Label the places on your map.

CONNECTIONS

Meeting Nature's Challenges

People all around the world live in different *environments,* or surroundings, that affect their lives. Some people live in hot, dry deserts. Some people live in cold, snowy mountains. Some people live near hot, wet jungles. Some people live near cool, dry forests. In many environments, the weather changes with the seasons: warm in the summer, cold in the winter.

People have learned to *adapt,* or learn a way of life that suits their different environments. People can adapt to their environments with the houses they build, with the clothes they wear, and by the ways they live their day-to-day lives.

Here are two very different environments. Notice how the people in those environments have adapted.

72

The Frozen North

This is northern Alaska, a land of challenge. Northern Alaska is near the Arctic Circle and the North Pole. Life here is not easy. Winters are eight or nine months long. They are dark and bitterly cold. In the winter, the sun shines only an hour or two each day, and temperatures drop to about $-60°F$.

Temperatures rise above freezing ($32°F$) for only two or three months of the year. These two or three summer months are cool, even though the sun almost never sets. During these months, the top one or two feet of soil may thaw. Then mosses, shrubs, weeds, and wildflowers grow. The ground underneath, however, stays frozen all year round and cannot be plowed for farming.

Eskimos, or *Inuit* (IN·oo·it) as they call themselves, have lived in this harsh environment for thousands of years. They can live here because they have found ways to meet the problems of life in the Arctic.

Look at the Eskimo winter house on page 74. It has thick earth walls that keep in warm air and keep

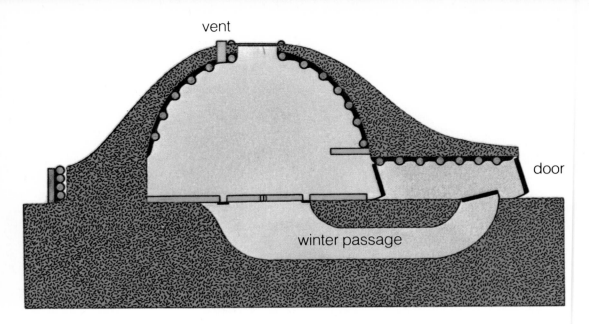

vent

door

winter passage

out cold air. The house has an opening, or *vent,* in the ceiling. The door is lower than the floor of the house and is separated from the house by a long, underground tunnel.

The Eskimos heat their houses with oil lamps. Two or three lamps can heat a house to 80° or 90°F. The door stays open, even in the coldest weather. Cold air collects in the underground tunnel. However, cold air is heavier than warm air, so the cold air in the tunnel cannot flow into the warm air in the house unless the Eskimos open the vent in the ceiling.

Once the vent in the ceiling is opened, the warm air in the room rises and flows outside. This leaves room for the cold air from the tunnel to come in and cool the house.

When the house has been cooled as much as the Eskimos want, they close the vent. The warm air settles back down into the house, stopping the cold air from the tunnel.

Eskimos also have learned to adapt their clothing to the weather. In winter they wear *two* suits made from the skins of the *caribou* (KAIR·ih·boo), the great deer that roam the Arctic. Eskimos wear the inner suit with the fur next to the body and the outer suit with the fur facing out. Body heat is trapped next to the body and between the two suits. Eskimo boots are sewn from caribou skins, too. The boots are so watertight that they can be blown up like balloons!

By adapting their homes and their clothing, Eskimos can live and thrive in one of nature's most challenging environments.

The Hot, Dry Desert

Far from Alaska lies the land of North Africa. The North African environment is quite different from northern Alaska, yet its climate is just as harsh. North Africa contains the world's largest desert—the *Sahara* (suh·HAR·uh), which is more than three million square miles in size.

The Sahara has mountains, rocky plateaus (pla·TOHZ), treeless plains, and sandy wasteland. The Sahara has less than eight inches of rain every year. Temperatures during the day are very hot, as high as 110°F. However, the desert sand does not hold the heat. When the sun sets, the desert becomes cool.

The problems faced by the North Africans living in the hot desert are different from those of the Eskimos living in the cold Arctic. Yet the desert people have adapted to their environment in ways much like the Arctic people have adapted to theirs.

Like the Eskimos, the people of the Sahara build houses with thick walls. In the desert, thick walls help keep heat *out* during the hot days and *in* during the cold nights. Mostly, though, their homes protect the North Africans from the scorching heat.

Desert people paint their homes white to reflect the sun's rays. They build houses close together to shade one another, and they plant trees for even more shade. Under their homes, they dig cool cellars in which they often stay during the hottest times of the year.

Desert people also use their clothing for protection from the heat. People of the Sahara wrap themselves up much like the Eskimos. However, the Eskimos wrap themselves up to stay warm, while the desert people wrap themselves up to stay cool. The desert people's robes, turbans, and veils keep the sun and wind from reaching their bodies. Because of the harsh desert heat and dryness, desert people must also protect themselves from *dehydration* (DEE·hy· DRAY·shuhn), or loss of water from the body. They must always be near water or carry it with them when they travel.

Nature's Challenge

The hot Sahara and the cold Arctic are only two of the many environments in which the people of the Earth live and make homes. Yet as different as one environment is from the other, people have found ways to adapt. A difficult environment is nature's challenge—to be met and overcome.

See pages T103–T104 in the front of this book for suggested postreading strategies.

Questions

1. Why can people live in places as different as the frozen north and the blazing desert?

2. What special problems does nature give to people who live in the frozen north? to people who live on a blazing desert?

3. In what kind of an environment do you live? How have you adapted to your environment?

Activities

1. **Locate Places on a Map**

   Look at a map or globe. Find these places:
   a. two countries as far north as Alaska
   b. the Sahara desert in North Africa
   c. the Alps mountains in Europe

   Talk about what kind of an environment each place may have. Then talk about ways that people may have adapted to these environments. Read an encyclopedia to learn if you are right.

2. **Plan a New Environment**

   Imagine that you have landed on a distant planet. Draw a picture of the new environment.

   Now write about how you will adapt to your environment. Think about what kind of clothes you will wear; where you will find food. water and shelter; and how you will travel around.

Problems

A poem by Calvin O'John

See page T105 in the front of this book for a suggested teaching plan for this selection.

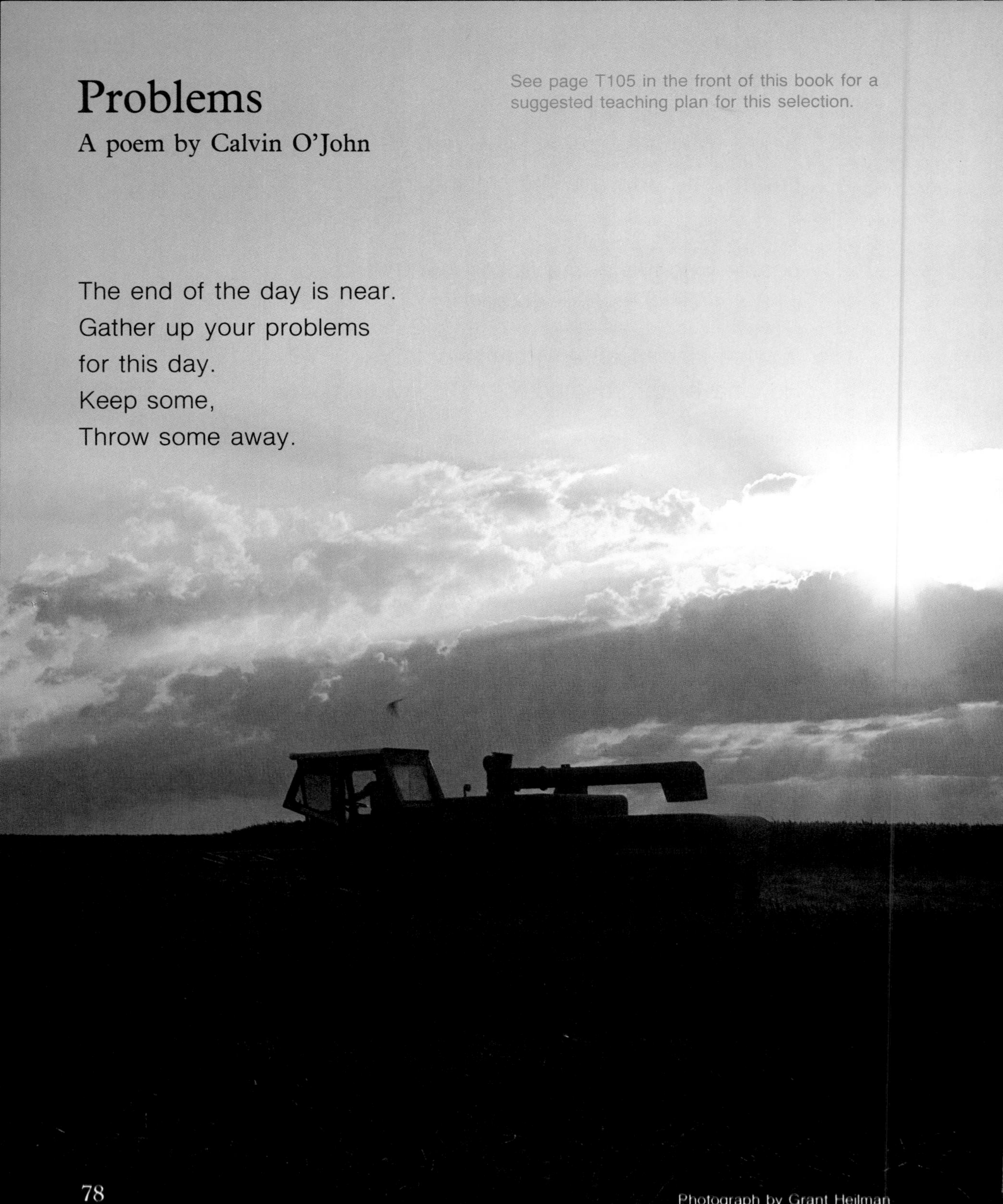

The end of the day is near.
Gather up your problems
for this day.
Keep some,
Throw some away.

78

Photograph by Grant Heilman

BOOKSHELF

Reading Level Easy

A Game of Catch by Helen Cresswell. Macmillan, 1977. During a game of tag in an empty castle gallery, Kate and Hugh hear children's laughter. Kate suspects it came from one of the paintings, but none of her friends or family believe her.

Reading Level Easy

Peter Pitseolak's Escape from Death by Peter Pitseolak. Delacorte Press, 1978. Peter, an Eskimo and an artist, tells his story of the great danger he and his son faced while stranded on a sheet of ice one night.

Reading Level Average

Sprout and the Magician by Jenifer Wayne. McGraw-Hill, 1977. The rabbit belonging to Tilly, Sprout's sister, disappears. A magician is Sprout's number one suspect.

Reading Level Average

Encyclopedia Brown Sets the Pace by Donald Sobol. Four Winds Press, 1982. This junior detective and his assistant Sally have their hands full looking for a stolen painting and exposing a "fixed" race.

Reading Level Challenging

The Frog Band and the Onion Seller by Jim Smith. Little, Brown, 1976. Dressed as an onion seller, Detective Le Flic, master of disguises, travels to England to find a hidden treasure.

2 When the Moon Shines

See pages T106–T107 in the front of this book for a suggested teaching plan.

See pages T107—T110 in the front of this book for a suggested teaching plan for this selection.

The Great Minu

A West African folk tale retold by Beth P. Wilson

Illustrated by Lyle Miller

Reading Level Challenging

82

Since ancient times storytelling has been important throughout the great continent of Africa. Long ago, people in villages would gather together in the evenings and tell stories. Often they would sit in a circle around an open fire. Sometimes one person would begin a story only to have others continue it until the story's end. The tales were both entertaining and clever, often with animals playing tricks on other animals or on people. Usually the wrongdoer was punished in some way.

Some storytellers journeyed from village to village, weaving a magic spell with tales of the tricky hare or the clever spider, and learning new stories as they moved along. Often the listeners would clap their hands, beat on drums, or dance during or after the storytelling.

Today African children are just as excited about telling and listening to folk tales as were their parents and grandparents before them. In West African villages, families often gather in the early evening after a meal of foo-foo (cooked yam balls dipped in vegetable-beef stew). Soon someone in the group, usually a grandmother, begins a story. Frequently the story is The Great Minu, which has long been a favorite of young and old.

Pronounced /a'·krə/.

A *thatched* roof is made of reeds and straw.

Across the ocean and far away, a poor African farmer prepared to make a journey to the big city of Accra. He walked around his small farm, taking note of the yams and corn growing in the garden. Then he fed his chickens and goats, latched his thatched-roof hut, and took off down the narrow, dusty road.

The farmer hummed happily to himself as the morning sun came into view. How exciting to be going to the big city! Nothing much happened in his tiny village, but since Accra was the largest city in Ghana, he would find much excitement there.

After walking for some time, he stopped to rest under a tulip tree. He leaned against the tree trunk and breathed in the morning air. Birds swooped and soared in the sunshine, but no man, woman, or child traveled the dusty road in either direction.

Soon he jumped to his feet and started down the road again. As he reached the first village along the way, he saw a woman on her knees, washing clothes in a stream of water. "Good day!" he called to the woman. "I'm on my way to the big city—I'm on my way to Accra!" The woman just smiled and went on washing her clothes.

Farther down the road he saw some men and boys making iron. They were too busy to look up when he passed, but he called out just the same. "Good day! I'm on my way to the big city—I'm on my way to Accra!" The men and boys stopped for a moment and nodded. Then they went on working as if he hadn't spoken.

Soon he saw a grandmother telling stories to her
little grandchildren. The traveler loved a story and
was tempted to stop. But he knew he must be on his
way. He waved his hand high and called out, "Good
day! I'm on my way to the big city—I'm on my way
to Accra!" The children turned to look, and the
grandmother smiled and waved. Then she went on
telling her story.

The traveler trudged along until he felt tired and
hungry. Finding a cool spot, he sat down by the side
of the road and opened his lunch bag. He ate a piece
of chicken and a big red banana. Then he took a
short nap under a cocoa tree.

As soon as the traveler woke up, he started off again because he still had quite a long way to go. At last he approached some farms on the <u>outskirts</u> of Accra. The first thing he noticed was a great herd of cows. He wondered who could own such a herd. Seeing a man with them, he asked, "To whom do these cows belong?"

The man did not know the language of the traveler. So he <u>shrugged</u> his shoulders and said, "Minu," meaning, "I do not understand."

The traveler thought Minu must be a person, and so he exclaimed, "Mr. Minu must be very rich!"

When the man *shrugged,* he raised his shoulders.

Entering the city, the traveler saw some large new buildings in the town square. He wondered who might own the fine buildings. But the man he asked could not understand his question, so he answered, "Minu."

"Good heavens!" cried the traveler. "What a rich fellow Mr. Minu must be to own all those cows and all these buildings, too!"

Soon he came to a great hotel surrounded by beautiful grounds and mahogany trees. A group of fashionably dressed ladies came down the front steps of the hotel. The traveler stepped up to them and asked who might be the owner of such a grand hotel.

The ladies smiled and said softly, "Minu."

"How wealthy Mr. Minu is!" exclaimed the astonished traveler.

He wandered from one neighborhood to another. Seeing a large house with many columns and porches, he stopped in surprise. "These homes in Accra are so grand—not a bit like the huts of my village," he said.

Just then a servant came out. The traveler stepped up hurriedly and asked, "Please tell me who owns this fine house."

The young woman <u>humped</u> her shoulders. "Minu," she mumbled. *Humped* means *shrugged.*

"How foolish of me to ask," the traveler said. "The Great Minu, of course." He stood for a moment, admiring the house and garden. Then he went on.

88

Finally he came to the harbor, where he saw men
loading bananas, cocoa beans, and mahogany onto a
huge ship. The blue sky above, the foamy green
ocean below, and the sailors rushing about on board
ship made quite a sight. Surprised at the great <u>cargo</u>,
the traveler <u>inquired</u> of a bystander, "To whom does
this fine vessel belong?"

"Minu," replied the puzzled man, who couldn't
understand a word the traveler said.

"To the Great Minu also?" the traveler asked.
"He is the richest man I ever heard of!"

Cargo refers to the
goods or freight
carried by a ship.

Inquired (line 6)
means *asked*.

Just as the traveler was setting out for home, he saw men carrying a coffin down the main street of Accra. A long <u>procession</u> of people, all dressed in black, followed the men. People on the sidelines shook their heads slowly. Sad faces looked up now and then. When the traveler asked one of the <u>mourners</u> the name of the dead person, he received the usual reply, "Minu."

"Mr. Minu is dead?" wailed the traveler. "Poor Mr. Minu! So he had to leave all his wealth—his herd of cows, his buildings, his grand hotel, and his fine ship—and die just like a poor person. Well, well, in the future I'll be content to live a simple life, to breathe the fresh air on my little farm, and to help the poor people in my little village."

The long dusty road back didn't seem as long as it had before. When the farmer arrived home, he unlatched the door of his hut and looked around inside. Then he climbed into his own snug bed and dreamed of the good *foo-foo* he would eat the next day.

See pages T108–T110 in the front of this book for suggested postreading strategies.

Questions

1. If you tell this story to an audience, you must be sure that they know the meaning of a certain word. What is the word? Why must your audience know it?

2. Do you think that the farmer would have enjoyed his trip to the city if he had understood what people where saying? Tell why or why not.

3. If the farmer told his neighbors about his exciting trip to the city, what would he describe as the lesson he learned?

4. Choose a word to complete each sentence.
   a. *Foo-foo* is a cooked (meat, vegetable).
   b. A thatched (door, roof) keeps out the rain.
   c. Men loaded the vessel in the (harbor, garden).

1. **Literal/Details** and **Interpretive/ Conclusion** "Minu," meaning "I don't understand" (page 86) The audience must know this word to recognize the humor of the story.
2. **Critical/Evaluation** Possible responses: yes, because he would have been able to talk with the people and would have understood the answers to his questions: no, because he would not have come home with such a feeling of having a good life.
3. **Interpretive/ Judgment** Possible responses: He might say that he learned it is better to live the simple life than to be rich; it is important to be content.
4. **Literal/Definitions** a. vegetable (page 83); b. roof (page 84); c. harbor (page 89)

Activity   Make a Story Plan

Suppose you are getting ready to tell the story "The Great Minu." Here is a plan to help you remember the first part of the story.

Farmer setting off for Accra	Woman washing clothes	Men and boys making iron	Grandmother telling stories

Finish this plan for the rest of the story. List, in order, the people or events the farmer saw.

The Ghost in the Attic

From the story *The Moffats* by Eleanor Estes

Illustrated by Susan Lexa

Reading Level Easy

See pages T110—T113 in the front of this book for a suggested teaching plan for this selection.

It's Halloween and the Moffat children have told Peter Frost that a ghost is in their attic. Since Peter Frost has played mean tricks on each of them, all of the Moffats want to scare him. Even Catherine-the-cat helps when she gets tangled in the rope attached to the ghost the Moffats have created. As they march to the attic with sheets, a carved pumpkin head, a scooter, and their mother's dressmaking form (Madame-the-bust), Joe, Sylvie, Jane, and Rufus don't realize how frightening their ghost will be.

Slowly the procession made its way out of the Grape Room, into the hall, up the stairs to the second floor. Joe led the way with his pocket flashlight. From the hall upstairs, a stepladder led to the attic which did not have a regular door but a hatch which Joe had to push up with his shoulders. It fell open with a groan and the strange musty smell of the attic greeted them. Joe set the head on the floor and flashed the light down the stepladder so the others could see to climb up.

93

Sylvie hoisted Madame up before her and climbed in. Then Rufus handed up his scooter and hoisted himself in. As Jane was making her way up, Catherine-the-cat leaped past her and disappeared into the dark recesses of the attic. Jane bit her tongue but managed to keep from screaming. That cat! She was always doing unexpected things behind you.

Here, *recesses* are the hidden corners of the attic.

The four Moffats stood around the entrance, the nearest point to the kitchen, to safety. Joe's tiny flashlight scarcely penetrated the darkness of the attic. But they knew what was up here all right without seeing. Dr. Witty had had many different hobbies. Collecting and stuffing wild animals and birds was one of them. He stored these in the attic in the yellow house. In one corner was a stuffed owl. In another, a stuffed wildcat. And all around were a great many little stuffed partridges and quail. The four children shivered, partly from cold, partly from excitement.

"Oh, let's hurry and get out of this place," said Jane.

They placed the scooter in the corner by the owl. Then they put Madame on the scooter, put the pumpkin head with its ominous, gaping mouth on her headless neck, and draped the sheets about her.

They tied one end of the rope to the scooter and made a loop in the other end in order to be able to pull the ghost around easily. The end of the rope with the loop they placed near the hatchway.

"All right," said Sylvie. "Now let's see how she looks."

They went to the head of the ladder. Joe flashed his light on Madame—Madame-the-bust no longer, or Mrs. Shoemaker or Miss Nippon either, but Madame-the-ghost!

"Phew!" he whistled.

"Boy, oh, boy!" said Rufus.

"Oh," shivered Jane, "come on."

As fast as they could, they pushed the hatch back in place and hurried helter-skelter to the kitchen where they warmed their hands over the kitchen fire.

"Boy, oh, boy!" said Rufus again, "what a ghost!"

Then they all put on the most fearful masks that Sylvie had made for them. And just in the nick of time too, for here was Peter Frost stamping on the back porch.

"Hey there, Moffats," he said witheringly. "Where's your old ghost then?"

Oh, his arrogance was insufferable.

"Don't worry," said Sylvie, "you'll see her all right. But you must be quiet."

"Haw-haw," jeered Peter Frost. But he stopped short, for out of the night came a long-drawn howl, a howl of reproach.

Sylvie, Joe, Jane, and Rufus had the same thought. Catherine-the-cat! They had forgotten her up there with the ghost. But Peter Frost! Why, he knew nothing of that of course, and although he was inclined to toss the matter lightly aside, still he blanched visibly when again from some mysterious dark recess of the house came the same wild howl.

The four Moffats knew when to be silent and they were silent now. So was Peter Frost. So was the whole house. It was so silent it began to speak with a thousand voices. When Mama's rocking-chair creaked, Peter Frost looked at it as though he expected to see the ghost sitting right in it. Somewhere a shutter came unfastened and banged against the house. The clock in the sitting-room ticked slowly, painfully, as though it had a lump in its throat, then stopped altogether. Even the Moffats began to feel scared, particularly Rufus. He began to think this whole business on a par with G–R–I–N–D your bones in "Jack and the Beanstalk."

Peter Frost swallowed his breath with a great gulp and said in a voice a trifle less jeering, "Well, what're we waitin' for? I want to see yer old ghost."

"Very well, then," said the four Moffats in solemn voices. "Follow us."

Here, *trifle* (line 4 from the foot of the text) means *a little bit.*

Jeering (line 4 from the foot of the text) means *taunting.*

Again they left the warm safety of the kitchen, mounted the inky black stairs to the second floor, each one holding to the belt of the one in front. When they reached the stepladder, they paused a moment to count heads.

Skin out is slang for leaving hurriedly.

"Aw, you don't think I'm gonna skin out without seeing your silly old ghost, do yer?" asked Peter Frost. However, blustering though his words were, there could be no doubt that his hand, the one that held onto Joe's belt, was shaking and shaking.

"Now we go up the stepladder," said Joe in a hoarse whisper. "I'll push open the hatch."

Cautiously the five mounted the stepladder. It seemed to lead to a never-ending pit of darkness.

"Why don't you light your flash?" asked Peter Frost, doing his best to sound carefree and easy.

"And scare away the ghost, I suppose," snorted Joe. "You know, a ghost isn't comin' out where there's a light and all this many people. That is, unless there's a certain one around it happens to be interested in."

Another howl interrupted Joe's words. This sounded so close to them now that the four Moffats were afraid Peter Frost would recognize the voice of Catherine-the-cat. But he didn't. He began to shake and shake more violently than ever, making the stepladder they were standing on shiver and creak.

Joe pushed the trap door up with his shoulders. It fell open with a groan just as it had done before. They all climbed in and stood on the attic floor. Except for a pale glow from the light below, the attic was in the thickest blackness. For a moment they stood there in silence. Then suddenly Joe gave a swift flash into the corner of the attic. It fell for a second on the stuffed wildcat.

Peter Frost started but said not a word.

Then swiftly Joe flashed the light in the other corner. The stuffed owl stared at them broodingly.

But Peter Frost said nothing.

And then Joe flashed his light on Madame-the-
ghost, herself. There she was, lurking in the corner,
her orange head gaping horribly. All the children
gasped, but still Peter Frost said nothing. All of a

sudden, without any warning whatsoever, Madame-the-ghost started careening madly toward them. And dragging heavy chains behind her too, from the sound.

Jane called out in a shrill voice:

"Peter Frost! Peter Frost!

E-e-e-e-e-e-e-e-e-e!"

Joe flashed his light on and off rapidly. Madame-the-ghost dashed wildly round and round the attic. The same howl rent the air! The shutters banged. Then Peter Frost let out a roar of terror. That THING was after HIM. He tore around the attic room, roaring like a bull. And the ghost, dragging its horrible chains, tore after him.

"Let me go," he bellowed. But he couldn't find the hatch. Around the attic and around the attic he stumbled, kicking over stuffed partridges and quail. Finally he tripped over the wildcat and sprawled on the floor. Joe flashed his light on them for a second and when Peter Frost saw that he was sitting on the wildcat, he let out another piercing yell and leaped to his feet. He had seen now where the hatch was and he meant to escape before that ghost could catch up with him. Again he tripped and was down once more, this time with the ghost right on top of him. She would smother him with those ghastly robes of hers.

"She's got me! She's got me!" he roared.

Frantically he shook himself free of the ghost, and in wild leaps he made again for the hatch.

See pages T111–T113 in the front of this
book for suggested postreading strategies.

But now Rufus and Jane too had stood all they
could of this nerve-racking business. They both
began howling with fright and screaming, "Mama,
Mama!" What with Peter Frost's yelling, Catherine-
the-cat's yowling, the screams of Rufus and Jane,
Sylvie herself began laughing hysterically and the
place sounded like bedlam. To make matters worse,
the battery of Joe's flashlight gave out, so there was
no way of turning on the light and showing
everyone there was no real ghost.

No, the ghost was real enough to Peter Frost, and
as he finally reached the hatch and clattered down
the stairs he thought he could still feel its cold
breath on his neck and cheeks. The four Moffats
followed after him, half tumbling, half sliding, until
they reached the kitchen. Peter Frost tore out the
back door with a bang and left the four of them
there in the kitchen, breathless and sobbing and
laughing all at once.

Questions

1. Why did the Moffats want to scare Peter Frost?

2. Why did the Moffats choose the attic as the place to scare Peter?

3. Should the Moffats tell Peter what really happened? Why or why not?

4. Match each group of words with the sentence that gives the meaning: **ominous and gaping, howl of reproach, insufferable arrogance.**
   a. "You can't scare me—ever!"
   b. "Then I saw the monster's wide-open jaws!"
   c. "Shame on you for forgetting me."

Activity   Describe the Strange Sounds

In the story, the Moffats' house "began to speak with a thousand voices" on Halloween night. Reread page 97 and make a list of the "voices" heard in the house. Then add other sounds you might hear in or around a house when it is dark. Use your list to help write a paragraph describing the sounds, or voices, in a strange dark house. Imagine that the house is speaking and you are listening.

1. Literal/Details Peter Frost had played mean tricks on all of the Moffats; he was an arrogant bully. (pages 93, 96)

2. Interpretive/Conclusion Possible response: The attic was dark and full of frightening stuffed animals. (pages 93–94)

3. Critical/Evaluation Possible responses: yes, because if they do not he will go on believing in ghosts; no, because Peter deserved a lesson—he had been mean

4. Literal/Definitions a. insufferable arrogance (page 96); b. ominous and gaping (page 94); c. howl of reproach (page 96)

What Night Would It Be?

A poem by John Ciardi

Pronounced /chär′·dē/.

See pages T113–T114 in the front of this book for a suggested teaching plan for this selection.

If the moon shines
On the black pines
And an owl flies
And a ghost cries
And the hairs rise
On the back
  on the back
    on the back of your neck—

If you look quick
At the moon-slick
On the black air
And what goes there
Rides a broom-stick
And if things pick
At the back
  at the back
    at the back of your neck—

Explain that the *moon-slick* is caused by the moon shimmering among dark clouds.

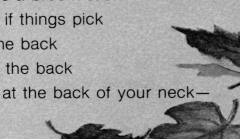

104

Would you know then
By the small men
With the lit grins
And with no chins,
By the owl's *hoo*,
And the ghost's *boo*,
By the Tom Cat,
And the Black Bat,
On the night air,
And the thing there,
By the thing,
  by the thing,
    by the dark thing there

(Yes, you do,
  yes, you do
    know the thing I mean)

That it's now,
  that it's now,
    that it's—Halloween!

Illustrated by Sharron O'Neil

Facts About Fiction

In the picture, each person is giving the answer *fiction*. That's because all three stories are made up. All such imaginary stories are fiction. Now if you asked what *kind* of fiction each person is reading, you would get three different answers. The first person would say *realistic fiction.* The second person would say *a folk tale.* The third person would answer *a fantasy.* Each story is an example of a different kind of fiction.

Although there are many kinds of fiction, the following chart tells you about these three.

See pages T114–T115 in the front of this book for a suggested teaching plan for this selection.

Three Kinds of Fiction

Realistic Fiction

The story usually takes place in the present.
The story is imaginary but could probably happen.
The main <u>characters</u> may remind you of people you know.
The story has an author.

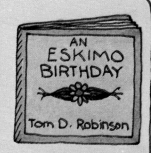

Folk Tale

Ordinary people often have their wishes granted.
Most of the characters act only one way—always good, always bad, silly, clever.
Some magic may happen—witches may cast spells or people may receive magic objects.
People made up the folk tale long ago.
The words *retold by* and the storyteller's name may appear with the tale.

Fantasy

Magical things happen—people fly or animals and toys talk.
The story has an author.

Here are six fiction books you might find in the library. Read the title and the description of each story. On a sheet of paper, write *realistic fiction, folk tale,* or *fantasy* to tell what kind of fiction is in each book.

1

Charlie is having a terrible time in first grade. He is very curious and is always getting into trouble. He never seems to behave well enough to have the honor of carrying the flag.

2

THE FOOL OF THE WORLD AND THE FLYING SHIP RETOLD BY Arthur Ransome

A poor young man, called the Fool of the World, finds a flying ship and meets seven people with magic powers. When the Fool must perform several difficult tasks to please the Czar, his new friends help him.

3

Pearl, a pig, meets a talking bone. They like each other immediately and start home together. On the way, a fox catches Pearl for his dinner, and the talking bone must try to save her.

See page T115 in the front of this book for suggested postreading strategies.

4

A dog and a cat are friends until a thief steals their master's good-luck ring. The two friends set off together to find it, but they return as enemies. (This story explains why dogs don't like cats.)

5

Jane finds a magic coin that can grant any wish. She and her brother and sisters wish for exciting adventures that take them to other countries and even through time!

6

Aunt Dew keeps one hundred pennies in an old wooden box—one penny for every year of her life. With these pennies, she tells Michael about her life—one event for each penny.

Have the students refer to the chart when deciding on categories for their books. Some children may choose, and want to explain, historical fiction or science fiction books.

Think of a favorite fiction story. Write the story's title, the author's name, and what *kind* of fiction it is. Be prepared to tell your classmates why you think your story is realistic fiction, a folk tale, or a fantasy.

See pages T116–T119 in the front of this book for a suggested teaching plan for this selection.

The Crane Maiden

A Japanese folk tale retold by Miyoko Matsutani Pronounced /mē·yō·kō   mä·tzoo·tä·nē/.

English version by Alvin Tresselt

Illustrated by Masami Miyamoto

Reading Level   Average

110

Long years ago, at the edge of a small mountain village in the snow country of Japan, there lived an old man and his wife. They had little in this world that they could call their own. But they were happy in their life together.

Now one winter morning the old man set out for the village with a bundle of firewood fastened to his back. It was <u>bitter</u> cold. He knew he would have little trouble selling the wood. Then with the money, he would buy some food so that he and his wife could have a good supper.

Explain that *bitter* usually refers to a taste; in this sentence it means *painful* or *stinging.*

As the old man trudged through the falling snow, he was suddenly aware of a fluttering sound, and a <u>pitiful</u> cry of *Koh, koh.* Turning from the path to investigate, he came upon a great crane frantically trying to free herself from a trap.

Pitiful means *worthy of sympathy.*

The old man's heart was touched with pity for the magnificent bird. While he tried to soothe the crane with tender words, his hands released the cruel spring of the trap. At once the crane flew up, joyfully calling *Koh, koh,* and disappeared into the snowy sky.

With a lighter step the old man went on through the snow. And when he had sold his wood, he returned once more to his humble house. While his old wife busied herself with preparing supper, he told her about rescuing the crane.

Humble means *simple*.

"That was a good deed," she said. "Surely the gods will one day reward you for your kind heart."

As she spoke these words, there came a tapping on the door. The old wife hurried to see who was there. Upon opening the door, she saw a beautiful young girl standing in the swirling snow. Her delicate face glowed like a peach beginning to ripen in the summer sun. And her dark eyes sparkled in the dancing firelight.

"Forgive my knocking at your door," she said in a soft voice, "but I have lost my way in the snow. May I share the warmth of your fire tonight?" Then bowing low before the two old people, she said, "My name is Tsuru (SOO•roo)."

Tsuru is the Japanese word for *crane*.

112

"Oh, you poor child!" cried the old wife. "Come in at once before you freeze in the bitter cold." They sat the girl down close to the <u>hearth</u>. Then the old wife piled more wood on the flames so that the girl would soon be warm.

The old couple shared their simple supper of hot porridge with Tsuru-<u>san</u>, all the time feasting their eyes on her great beauty. Then they gave her their bed with its warm <u>quilts</u> to sleep on, while they spent the night huddled on a pile of straw.

The term *san* is a polite way of addressing someone in Japanese.

Some students may know that *quilts* are cloth bed coverings filled with feathers or another soft material.

In the morning when they awoke, the old man and his wife were surprised to see a good fire already burning on the hearth. The water jar was filled with fresh clear water, the floors had been swept, and all the rooms were clean and tidy.

Tsuru-san, the sleeves of her <u>kimono</u> neatly tied back with a red cord, was busily stirring a pot over the fire. "Good morning," she said, bowing to the old couple. "If you will wash your hands we may eat breakfast, for the porridge is cooked and ready."

"In our old age we have a daughter!" said the old man, laughing.

"It is the gods smiling on us for your good deed of yesterday," replied his wife happily.

The snow and bitter cold continued for many days. And so Tsuru-san stayed in the shelter of the old couple's home. As she had neither mother nor father, it was at last decided that she would remain as a daughter to these people.

The children of the neighborhood were soon attracted to the house as Tsuru-san was such a delight to be with. The house rang with happy laughter. The hearts of the old man and his wife were filled with joy at the sound.

The illustration on the facing page shows the children in the story playing a traditional juggling game. Each child juggles bean-bags while singing a short nonsense song. If a child drops a beanbag, he or she is out of the game. The last child in the game is the winner.

114

115

And so the days of early winter passed. Soon it was time for the great New Year celebration. The old man spoke to his wife, saying, "Tsuru-san has been such a delight to us. If only I could give her a gift of a new kimono."

"Or if I could make her a rice cake for the New Year," his wife added.

But, alas, the winter had been hard. The old man had not been able to cut wood to sell. There was no money to buy even rice, much less a kimono.

Now Tsuru-san had heard them talking. It saddened her that these good people should be so poor. Coming before them she bowed low and said, "Dear parents, I know there has been no wood to sell. But perhaps I can help you and repay your great kindness to me. There is an old loom in the back room. I will weave cloth on it for you to sell in the village. Only you must promise that no one shall look at me while I am weaving."

Here, *odd* means strange.

The old man and his wife thought this was an <u>odd</u> request, but they quickly agreed. Tsuru-san locked herself in the room. Soon the old man and

116

his wife heard the sound of

Tin kola, kola, pon, pon,
Tin kola, kola, pon, pon

as the <u>shuttle</u> sped back and forth and the fabric grew in length.

For three days this continued. Tsuru-san stopped for neither food nor rest. Then at last the door opened and she stepped out, holding in her hands a <u>bolt</u> of cloth such as the old man and his wife had never seen in all their lives. They gasped at its beauty and marveled at its softness.

"Dear father," said the girl, "take this cloth into the village and sell it. It will be but small payment for the happy home you have given me."

Without wasting a moment, the old man hurried into the center of the village. When people saw the beautiful cloth he was carrying, a crowd soon gathered.

"I will pay ten gold pieces for your cloth," said one man.

"No, no!" cried another. "Sell it to me for twenty gold pieces!"

Each person who saw the cloth offered more money than the one before, until the old man finally sold the cloth for one hundred pieces of gold.

Stopping only long enough to buy rice for rice cakes, a kimono for Tsuru-san, and a few treats for New Year's Day, the man hurried home with his pockets jingling. "Tomorrow, tomorrow is the New Year's Day," he sang. "The New Year is the happy time, eating rice cakes whiter than snow."

Then such a hustle and bustle there was, as the old man and his wife prepared for the feast. As the old man pounded the rice, his wife made it into fine white cakes. And on New Year's Day all the children came in for a great party with their friend Tsuru-san.

Still the cold days of winter followed one after the other. At last one day Tsuru-san said to the old couple, "It is time for me to weave another bolt of cloth for you so that you will have money to live until the spring returns. But remember what I told you. No one is to look at me while I am working."

Again they promised. And the girl once more locked herself in the room and began weaving.

Tin kola, kola, pon, pon,
Tin kola, pon, pon

went the loom.

One day passed, and then the second. Still the sound of the loom filled the house. By now, the neighbors had grown curious.

"Is Tsuru-san weaving again?" asked one.

"Ah, soon you will have more gold pieces to hide under the floor," said another with a smile and a wink.

"The loom makes such an interesting sound," remarked the first one. "I would love to see what Tsuru-san is doing."

"We have promised not to watch her while she works," said the old man.

"What an odd request," cried one of the people. "I would not make such a promise to *my* daughter, you can believe me. What harm could there be in taking one look?"

Now in truth, the old woman had been most curious about Tsuru-san's weaving. Encouraged by her neighbor's remarks, she stepped up to a crack in the door.

"Stop, stop, old woman!" cried her husband when he saw what was happening. But it was too late. His wife had already peeked through the crack.

What a sight it was that met her eye! There, sitting at the loom, was a great white crane, pulling feathers from her body and weaving them into cloth.

See pages T117–T119 in the front of this
book for suggested postreading strategies.

The old woman stepped back. Before she
could tell what she had seen, the door opened.
Out stepped Tsuru-san, thin and pale, holding in
her hands a half-finished bolt of cloth.

"Dear parents," she said in a weak voice, "I
am the crane you rescued from the trap. I
wanted to repay your kindness by weaving you
another bolt of cloth." Then her eyes filled with
tears. "But now that you have seen me in my
true form I can no longer stay with you."

With this she kissed the man and his wife
tenderly, and walked out of the house. Instantly
she became a crane once more and, with a great
whish of her wings, flew up into the sky. Slowly
she circled overhead. Then with a single cry of
Koh as if to say good-bye, the crane maiden was
gone forever.

Questions

1. Literal/Details
Tsuru helps with housework and weaves cloth (pages 114–117); the old man frees the crane from the trap (page 111); the old couple give Tsuru a warm bed and food. (page 103)
2. Interpretive/Judgment a. old woman (pages 119–120); b. old man (pages 111–112); c. Crane Maiden (page 117)
3. Literal/Definitions a. a roll of cloth; b. a streak of lightning; c. locked the door; d. a pin or rod that fastens something in place.
4. Critical/Evaluation Possible responses: The old woman broke the promise so that the Crane Maiden had no choice; it would have been better if the Crane Maiden had stayed because she was needed and the old couple would have been kind to her.

1. The main characters in this story are kind to one another. List three kind things the characters did for one another.

2. Match the characters with the lessons they learned.

   Crane Maiden   old man   old woman

   a. "Do not break a promise."

   b. "A good deed will be rewarded."

   c. "Be kind to someone who is kind to you."

3. Draw or write what *bolt* means in each sentence.

   a. The Crane Maiden wove a *bolt* of cloth.

   b. The barn was struck by a *bolt* of lightning.

   c. The old woman *bolted* the door at night.

   d. The carpenter put a *bolt* through the wood.

4. Someone said, "I don't think the Crane Maiden should have gone away. She should have given the old couple one more chance." Do you agree? Why or why not?

Activity   Write Questions and Answers

Suppose you were able to ask Tsuru-san three questions. Write the three questions that you would most like to ask her. Then be Tsuru-san and answer them.

When my canary

A haiku by Shiki Pronounced /shē′·kē/.

Translated by Harry Behn

See page T119 in the front of this book for a suggested teaching plan for this selection.

When my canary
flew away, that was the end
of spring in my house.

In haiku, certain words stand for certain seasons. Here, the word *canary* stands for spring.

Illustrated by Carlos Marchiori

What the Gray Cat Sings

A poem by Arthur Guiterman

See pages T120–T121 in the front of this book for a suggested teaching plan for this selection.

The Cat was once a weaver,
   A weaver, a weaver,
An old and withered weaver
   Who labored late and long;
And while she made the <u>shuttle</u> hum
And wove the <u>weft</u> and clipped the <u>thrum</u>,
Beside the loom with <u>droning</u> drum
   She sang the weaving song:
     "Pr-rrum, pr-rrum,
Thr-ree thr-reads in the thr-rum,
     Pr-rrum!"

The Cat's no more a weaver,
   A weaver, a weaver,
An old and wrinkled weaver,
   For though she did no wrong,
A witch hath changed the shape of her
That dwindled down and clothed in fur
Beside the hearth with droning purr
   She thrums her weaving song:
     "Pr-rrum, pr-rrum,
Thr-ree thr-reads in the thr-rum,
     Pr-rrum!"

Illustrated by Marie-Louise Gay

CONNECTIONS

See pages T121–T122 in the front of this book for a suggested teaching plan for this selection.

Animals as Symbols

To the Japanese, the crane is special. Artists paint it. Poets write poems about it. Many people honor it in their folk tales. The crane is a *symbol* (SIM·buhl), or something that stands for something else. In Japan, the crane stands for good fortune or good luck. The crane brought luck to the old people in the Japanese tale "The Crane Maiden."

Symbols of Early Peoples

Using birds or animals as symbols is not a new idea. People did this long before there were towns or cities or nations. The early people lived close to nature. They knew and admired the animals and the way these animals seemed able to trick their enemies. Large family groups, called *clans,* often took an animal as their symbol. They carved their animal symbol over their doorways or on poles outside their houses.

When warriors of a clan went to battle, they placed a carving of their symbol on top of a pole. If the warriors got separated during a battle, they looked for their symbol and were able to find their leader.

126   Illustrated by Robert Masheris

Symbols of Ancient Nations

More than 5,000 years ago, soldiers in ancient Egypt used the falcon as their symbol. The falcon stood for the Egyptian king, or *pharaoh* (FAIR·oh). The people believed that the pharaoh really was a falcon in a human form.

In ancient Greece, cities had symbols. Soldiers from the city of Athens used an owl as their symbol. Soldiers from the city of Corinth fought under the symbol of a winged horse. The Roman army used the eagle as its symbol.

Symbols in the New World

Long before Europeans came to America, the American Indians were organized into clans, tribes, and even nations. The Iroquois Indians had eight clans. Each had an animal or bird as its symbol. The clans took the names of their symbols: Wolf, Deer, Bear, Beaver, Turtle, Snipe (a bird of the marshes), Heron, and Hawk. The clan's symbol was carved or painted above the doorway of every Iroquois house.

Members of the same clan thought of themselves as brothers and sisters. If a man of a Wolf clan visited a distant Iroquois village, he would go at once to a house with a wolf over the door. There he was sure to be welcomed as a brother, even though he was a total stranger.

About a thousand years ago, Vikings landed in
North America. It is possible that the first true flag
to fly over America had a raven on it. (A raven is
like a crow, but larger.) The raven was a symbol of
the Vikings. Their symbol was known as "Raven,
Terror of the Land."

In the 1700s, when America was being settled, many symbols were suggested for the new nation: a bucking horse, a beaver, a codfish, a deer, a wild turkey, and a pine tree. At that time, the symbol most widely used in America was the rattlesnake. In 1776, at the time of the American Revolution, rattlesnake flags were flown over many battlefields where Americans were fighting for independence from England. The words on the flag were a warning to England. (The word *tread* means "step.")

The American bald eagle was finally chosen as the symbol of America. On July 4, 1776, the day the Declaration of Independence was signed, Congress appointed three men to design a national seal, or symbol. Those men were Benjamin Franklin, John Adams, and Thomas Jefferson. It took them years to decide on what would be the best symbol for their new nation. Others joined with them to help. Benjamin Franklin was in France in 1782, when the final decision was made: the American bald eagle would be the national bird and symbol. Franklin was disappointed. He had wanted the wild turkey to be our national bird.

Here is the seal of the United States of America. At its center is the dignified and powerful American eagle. When Americans see this eagle, they know that it stands for, or *symbolizes,* America and its people.

See page T122 in the front of this book for suggested postreading strategies.

131

Questions

1. Literal / Details
A symbol is something that stands for something else. (page 126)
2. Literal / Detail
They used symbols for identification purposes. (pages 126–127)
3. Literal / Details
They carved animal symbols over their doorways or on top of a pole that served as clan identification. (page 126)
4. Critical / Evaluation Accept any answer that the student reasonably supports.

1. What is a symbol?

2. Why did early peoples use symbols?

3. How did early peoples use animals as symbols?

4. What bird or animal would you choose for your symbol? Why?

Activities

1. **Find Out About More Symbols**

    These animals are often used as symbols. Match each animal with the meaning of the symbol. Use a dictionary or an encyclopedia to help you.

1. a. peace
   b. cleverness
   c. busyness
   d. evil
   e. bad luck
   f. courage

   a. dove   bad luck
   b. fox   courage
   c. beaver   evil
   d. snake   busyness
   e. black cat   cleverness
   f. lion   peace

2. **Find Out About Your State**

    What is your state bird and your state flower? What does your state flag look like? Look in an encyclopedia or a book about the states. Find out why your state's bird and flower were chosen. If you like, draw a picture of your state's bird, flower, or flag.

BOOKSHELF

Reading Level Easy

The Ghost on Saturday Night by Sid Fleischman. Little, Brown, 1974. Opie guides a mean-looking stranger through the thick fog. His reward is two tickets to a ghost-raising. Opie doesn't know he has front-row seats to a bank robbery, too.

Reading Level Average

The Trouble with Jenny's Ear by Oliver Butterworth. Little, Brown, 1960. When Jenny hears thoughts before they are spoken, she begins to wonder what is wrong with her.

The Heavenly Zoo retold by Alison Lurie. Farrar, Straus & Giroux, 1979. A collection of tales from all over the world to explain the shapes people see in the star groups called the *constellations*.

Reading Level Challenging

A-Haunting We Will Go; Ghostly Stories and Poems collected by Lee Bennett Hopkins. Albert Whitman, 1977. Some of these ghost stories and poems will make you laugh. Some will make you shiver.

Reading Level Average

The Shrinking of Treehorn by Florence Parry Heide. Holiday House, 1971. Treehorn sees that shelves are getting higher and his clothes are getting looser. Can he really be shrinking?

Reading Level Challenging

3 Across the Land and Sea

See pages T123–T124 in the front of this book for a suggested teaching plan

135

Building the <u>Erie Canal</u>

An article

See pages T124–T126 in the front of this book for a suggested teaching plan for this selection.

In the 1800s Americans were trying to solve the problems of transportation to the west. One solution was to build a long canal across New York State to Lake Erie.

The Erie Canal was begun in 1817. Thousands of <u>*immigrants,*</u> *using shovels and pickaxes, had to dig the canal through a wilderness of swamps and forests.*

Explain that *immigrants* are people who have left their native country to settle in a new land.

Completed in 1825, the Erie Canal was 4 feet deep and 363 miles long. Horses, mules, and oxen were used to pull the boats and rafts that carried people, food, goods, and animals back and forth. A fast speed was eighty miles in twenty-four hours. Whenever a low bridge was approached, the cry went out, "Low bridge, everybody down!"

After eight years of work, the Erie Canal finally provided a route through the Appalachian Mountains and opened up the way west.

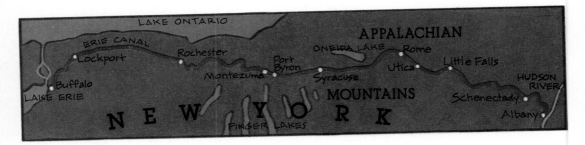

136

Illustrated by Dennis Ziemienski

The Erie Canal

A folk song

Illustrated by Peter Spier

1. I've got a mule, her name is Sal, Fif-teen miles on the
2. We better get on our way, old gal, Fif-teen miles on the

E-rie Ca-nal. She's a good old work-er and a good old pal,
E-rie Ca-nal. 'Cause you bet your life I'd nev-er part with Sal,

Fif-teen miles on the E-rie Ca-nal. We've hauled some barg-es in our day,
Fif-teen miles on the E-rie Ca-nal. Git up there, mule, here comes a lock,

Filled with lum-ber, coal, and hay, And we know ev-'ry
We'll make Rome 'bout six o'-clock, Just one more trip and

inch of the way From Al-ba-ny to Buf-fa-lo.
back we'll go Right back home to Buf-fa-lo.

Refrain

Low bridge, ev-'ry-bod-y down! Low bridge, for we're go-ing through a town, And you'll

al-ways know your neigh-bor, You'll al-ways know your pal, If you

ev-er nav-i-gat-ed on the E-rie Ca-nal.

I've got a mule, her name is Sal,
Fifteen miles on the Erie Canal.
She's a good old worker and a good old pal,
Fifteen miles on the Erie Canal.

We've hauled some <u>barges</u> in our day,
Filled with lumber, coal, and hay,
And we know ev'ry inch of the way
From Albany to Buffalo.

A *barge* is a flat-
bottomed boat used
for carrying cargo.

Low bridge, ev'rybody down!
Low bridge, for we're going through a town,

See pages T125–T126 in the front of this
book for suggested postreading strategies.

And you'll always know your neighbor,
You'll always know your pal,
If you ever navigated on the Erie Canal.

See pages T126–T129 in the front of this book for a suggested teaching plan for this selection.

Crossing the Creek

From the story *Little House on the Prairie*
by Laura Ingalls Wilder
Illustrated by Michel Allaire

Reading Level Challenging

Before leaving Wisconsin, the Ingalls family said farewell to their home, their friends, and most of their possessions. They were moving in a covered wagon to the prairie land of Kansas. Besides Pa and Ma Ingalls, there were three girls in the family—Mary, Laura, and Baby Carrie. There were no roads across the prairie, and days passed without the family seeing another person. At night the wolves howled. Laura and Mary were often frightened, but they felt safe when Ma, Pa, or Jack, their bulldog, was near.

In this part of their story, the Ingalls family comes to one of the many creeks they will have to cross on their journey west.

Laura was surprised because she did not see the creek. But the bottom lands were wide. Down here, below the prairie, there were gentle hills and open sunny places. The air was still and hot. Under the wagon wheels the ground was soft. In the sunny open spaces the grass grew thin, and deer had cropped it short.

For a while the high, bare cliffs of red earth stood up behind the wagon. But they were almost hidden behind hills and trees when Pet and Patty stopped to drink from the creek.

Bottom lands are land alongside a river.

143

The rushing sound of the water filled the still air. All along the creek banks the trees hung over it and made it dark with shadows. In the middle it ran swiftly, sparkling silver and blue.

"This creek's pretty high," Pa said. "But I guess we can make it all right. You can see this is a ford, by the old wheel ruts. What do you say, Caroline?"

"Whatever you say, Charles," Ma answered.

Pet and Patty lifted their wet noses. They pricked their ears forward, looking at the creek; then they pricked them backward to hear what Pa would say. They sighed and laid their soft noses together to whisper to each other. A little way upstream, Jack was lapping the water with his red tongue.

"I'll tie down the wagon-cover," Pa said. He climbed down from the seat, unrolled the canvas sides and tied them firmly to the wagon box. Then he pulled the rope at the back, so that the canvas puckered together in the middle, leaving only a tiny round hole, too small to see through.

Here, puckered means gathered together.

Mary huddled down on the bed. She did not like fords; she was afraid of the rushing water. But Laura was excited; she liked the splashing. Pa climbed to the seat, saying, "They may have to swim, out there in the middle. But we'll make it all right, Caroline."

To huddle means to crouch, curl up, or draw oneself together. Ask if someone can demonstrate crouching.

Laura thought of Jack and said, "I wish Jack could ride in the wagon, Pa."

Pa did not answer. He gathered the reins tightly in his hands. Ma said, "Jack can swim, Laura. He will be all right."

The wagon went forward softly in mud. Water began to splash against the wheels. The splashing grew louder. The wagon shook as the noisy water struck at it. Then all at once the wagon lifted and balanced and swayed. It was a lovely feeling.

The noise stopped, and Ma said, sharply, "Lie down, girls!"

Quick as a flash, Mary and Laura dropped flat on the bed. When Ma spoke like that, they did as they were told. Ma's arm pulled a smothering blanket over them, heads and all.

"Be still, just as you are. Don't move!" she said.

Mary did not move; she was trembling and still. But Laura could not help wriggling a little bit. She did so want to see what was happening. She could feel the wagon swaying and turning; the splashing was noisy again, and again it died away. Then Pa's voice frightened Laura. It said, "Take them, Caroline!"

The wagon lurched; there was a sudden heavy splash beside it. Laura sat straight up and clawed the blanket from her head.

Pa was gone. Ma sat alone, holding tight to the reins with both hands. Mary hid her face in the blanket again, but Laura rose up farther. She couldn't see the creek bank. She couldn't see anything in front of the wagon but water rushing at it. And in the water, three heads; Pet's head and Patty's head and Pa's small, wet head. Pa's fist in the water was holding tight to Pet's bridle.

Laura could faintly hear Pa's voice through the rushing of the water. It sounded calm and cheerful, but she couldn't hear what he said. He was talking to the horses. Ma's face was white and scared.

"Lie down, Laura," Ma said.

Laura lay down. She felt cold and sick. Her eyes were shut tight, but she could still see the terrible water and Pa's brown beard drowning in it.

For a long, long time the wagon swayed and swung, and Mary cried without making a sound, and Laura's stomach felt sicker and sicker. Then the front wheels struck and grated, and Pa shouted. The whole wagon jerked and jolted and tipped backward, but the wheels were turning on the ground. Laura was up again, holding to the seat; she saw Pet's and Patty's

scrambling wet backs climbing a steep bank, and Pa running beside them, shouting, "Hi, Patty! Hi, Pet! Get up! Get up! Whoopsy-daisy! Good girls!"

At the top of the bank they stood still, panting and dripping. And the wagon stood still, safely out of that creek.

Pa stood panting and dripping, too, and Ma said, "Oh, Charles!"

"There, there, Caroline," said Pa. "We're all safe, thanks to a good tight wagon-box well fastened to the <u>running-gear</u>. I never saw a creek rise so fast in my life. Pet and Patty are good swimmers, but I guess they wouldn't have made it if I hadn't helped them."

The *running gear* of a wagon consists of the wheels, axles, and other parts that help the wagon move.

If Pa had not known what to do, or if Ma had been too frightened to drive, or if Laura and Mary had been naughty and bothered her, then they would all have been lost. The river would have rolled them over and over and carried them away and drowned them, and nobody would ever have known what became of them. For weeks, perhaps, no other person would come along that road.

"Well," said Pa, "all's well that ends well," and Ma said, "Charles, you're wet to the skin."

Before Pa could answer, Laura cried, "Oh, where's Jack?"

They had forgotten Jack. They had left him on the other side of that dreadful water and now they could not see him anywhere. He must have tried to swim after them, but they could not see him struggling in the water now.

Laura swallowed hard, to keep from crying. She knew it was shameful to cry, but there was crying inside her. All the long way from Wisconsin poor Jack had followed them so patiently and faithfully, and now they had left him to drown. He was so tired, and they might have taken him into the wagon. He had stood on the bank and seen the wagon going away from him, as if they didn't care for him at all. And he would never know how much they wanted him.

Pa said he wouldn't have done such a thing to Jack, not for a million dollars. If he'd known how that creek would rise when they were in midstream, he would never have let Jack try to swim it. "But that can't be helped now," he said.

He went far up and down the creek bank, looking for Jack, calling him and whistling for him.

It was no use. Jack was gone.

At last there was nothing to do but to go on. Pet and Patty were rested. Pa's clothes had dried on him while he searched for Jack. He took the reins again, and drove uphill, out of the river bottoms.

Laura looked back all the way. She knew she wouldn't see Jack again, but she wanted to. She didn't see anything but low curves of land coming between the wagon and the creek, and beyond the creek those strange cliffs of red earth rose up again.

Then other <u>bluffs</u> just like them stood up in front of the wagon. Faint wheel tracks went into a crack between those earthen walls. Pet and Patty climbed till

Bluffs are cliffs.

the crack became a small grassy valley. And the valley widened out to the High Prairie once more.

No road, not even the faintest trace of wheels or of a rider's passing, could be seen anywhere. That prairie looked as if no human eye had ever seen it before. Only the tall wild grass covered the endless empty land and a great empty sky arched over it. Far away the sun's edge touched the rim of the earth. The sun was enormous and it was throbbing and pulsing with light. All around the sky's edge ran a pale pink glow, and above the pink was yellow, and above that blue. Above the blue the sky was no color at all. Purple shadows were gathering over the land, and the wind was mourning.

Pa stopped the mustangs. He and Ma got out of the wagon to make camp, and Mary and Laura climbed down to the ground, too.

"Oh, Ma," Laura begged, "Jack has gone to heaven, hasn't he? He was such a good dog, can't he go to heaven?"

Ma did not know what to answer, but Pa said: "Yes, Laura, he can. God that doesn't forget the sparrows won't leave a good dog like Jack out in the cold."

Laura felt only a little better. She was not happy. Pa did not whistle about his work as usual, and after a while he said, "And what we'll do in a wild country without a good watchdog I don't know."

Mustangs are small wild horses that live in the southwestern plains.

150

151

Camp on the High Prairie

Pa made camp as usual. First, he <u>unhitched</u> and <u>unharnessed</u> Pet and Patty, and he put them on their picket-lines. Picket-lines were long ropes fastened to iron pegs driven into the ground. The pegs were called picket-pins. When horses were on picket-lines they could eat all the grass that the long ropes would let them reach. But when Pet and Patty were put on them, the first thing they did was to lie down and roll back and forth and over. They rolled till the feeling of the harness was all gone from their backs.

While Pet and Patty were rolling, Pa pulled all the grass from a large, round space of ground. There was old, dead grass at the roots of the green grass, and Pa would take no chance of setting the prairie on fire. If fire once started in that dry under-grass, it would sweep that whole country bare and black. Pa said, "Best be on the safe side, it saves trouble in the end."

This means that Pa released the horses from the wagon and took off their harnesses.

152

When the space was clear of grass, Pa laid a handful of dry grass in its center. From the creek bottoms he brought an armful of twigs and dead wood. He laid small twigs and larger twigs and then the wood on the handful of dry grass, and he lighted the grass. The fire crackled merrily inside the ring of bare ground that it couldn't get out of.

Then Pa brought water from the creek, while Mary and Laura helped Ma get supper. Ma measured coffee beans into the coffee-mill and Mary ground them. Laura filled the coffee-pot with the water Pa brought, and Ma set the pot in the coals. She set the iron bake-oven in the coals, too.

While it heated, she mixed cornmeal and salt with water and patted it into little cakes. She greased the bake-oven with a pork-rind, laid the cornmeal cakes in it, and put on its iron cover. Then Pa raked more coals over the cover, while Ma sliced fat salt pork. She fried the slices in the iron spider. The spider had short legs to stand on in the coals, and that was why it was called a spider. If it had had no legs, it would have been only a frying pan.

The coffee boiled, the cakes baked, the meat fried, and they all smelled so good that Laura grew hungrier and hungrier.

Pa set the wagon-seat near the fire. He and Ma sat on it. Mary and Laura sat on the wagon tongue. Each of them had a tin plate, and a steel knife and a steel fork with white bone handles. Ma had a tin cup and Pa had a tin cup, and Baby Carrie had a little one all her own, but Mary and Laura had to share their tin cup. They drank water. They could not drink coffee until they grew up.

While they were eating supper the purple shadows closed around the camp fire. The vast prairie was dark and still. Only the wind moved stealthily through the grass, and the large, low stars hung glittering from the great sky.

The camp fire was cozy in the big, chill darkness. The slices of pork were crisp and fat, the corncakes were good. In the dark beyond the wagon, Pet and Patty were eating, too. They bit off bites of grass with sharply crunching sounds.

"We'll camp here a day or two," said Pa. "Maybe we'll stay here. There's good land, timber in the bottoms, plenty of game—everything a man could want. What do you say, Caroline?"

"We might go farther and fare worse," Ma replied.

"Anyway, I'll look around tomorrow," Pa said. "I'll take my gun and get us some good fresh meat."

He lighted his pipe with a hot coal, and stretched out his legs comfortably. The warm, brown smell of tobacco smoke mixed with the warmth of the fire. Mary yawned, and slid off the wagon tongue to sit on the grass. Laura yawned, too. Ma quickly washed the tin plates, the tin cups, the knives and forks. She washed the bake-oven and the spider, and rinsed the dish-cloth.

For an instant she was still, listening to the long, wailing howl from the dark prairie. They all knew what it was. But that sound always ran cold up Laura's backbone and crinkled over the back of her head.

Ma shook the dish-cloth, and then she walked into the dark and spread the cloth on the tall grass to dry. When she came back Pa said: "Wolves. Half a mile away, I'd judge. Well, where there's deer there will be wolves. I wish——"

He didn't say what he wished, but Laura knew. He wished Jack were there. When wolves howled in the Big Woods, Laura had always known that Jack would not let them hurt her. A lump swelled hard in her throat and her nose smarted. She winked fast and did not cry. That wolf, or perhaps another wolf, howled again.

"Bedtime for little girls!" Ma said, cheerfully. Mary got up and turned around so that Ma could unbutton her. But Laura jumped up and stood still. She saw something. Deep in the dark beyond the firelight, two green lights were shining near the ground. They were eyes.

Cold ran up Laura's backbone, her scalp crinkled, her hair stood up. The green lights moved; one winked out, then the other winked out, then both shone steadily, coming nearer. Very rapidly they were coming nearer.

"Look, Pa, look!" Laura said. "A wolf!"

Pa did not seem to move quickly, but he did. In an instant he took his gun out of the wagon and was ready to fire at those green eyes. The eyes stopped coming. They were still in the dark, looking at him.

"It can't be a wolf. Unless it's a mad wolf," Pa said. Ma lifted Mary into the wagon. "And it's not that," said Pa. "Listen to the horses." Pet and Patty were still biting off bits of grass.

A *lynx* is a wild cat of northern North America.

Tawny is brownish orange.

A *brindled* animal is light colored with darker-colored streaks.

"A lynx?" said Ma.

"Or a coyote?" Pa picked up a stick of wood; he shouted, and threw it. The green eyes went close to the ground, as if the animal crouched to spring. Pa held the gun ready. The creature did not move.

"Don't, Charles," Ma said. But Pa slowly walked toward those eyes. And slowly along the ground the eyes crawled toward him. Laura could see the animal in the edge of the dark. It was a tawny animal and brindled. Then Pa shouted and Laura screamed.

The next thing she knew she was trying to hug a jumping, panting, wriggling Jack, who lapped her face and hands with his warm wet tongue. She couldn't hold him. He leaped and wriggled from her to Pa to Ma and back to her again.

"Well, I'm beat!" Pa said.

"So am I," said Ma. "But did you have to wake the baby?" She rocked Carrie in her arms, hushing her.

Jack was perfectly well. But soon he lay down close to Laura and sighed a long sigh. His eyes were red with tiredness, and all the under part of him was caked with mud. Ma gave him a cornmeal cake and he licked it and wagged politely, but he could not eat. He was too tired.

"No telling how long he kept swimming," Pa said. "Nor how far he was carried downstream before he landed." And when at last he reached them, Laura called him a wolf, and Pa threatened to shoot him.

See pages T128—T129 in the front of this
book for suggested postreading strategies.

But Jack knew they didn't mean it. Laura asked
him, "You knew we didn't mean it, didn't you, Jack?"
Jack wagged his stump of a tail; he knew.

Questions

1. The author used colors to help you see the scene at the creek. What colors did she use to describe the following:
   a. The water in the creek was _____ and _____.
   b. The cliffs beyond the creek were _____.
   c. The shadows on the land were _____.
   d. The sky was _____, _____, and _____.

2. What was one way that Laura showed she was brave?

3. Imagine that you are Jack. Tell what happened to you from the time you watched the Ingalls family start across the creek until the time you found them again.

4. What do you think Pa would do differently if the family had to cross another creek? Give reasons for your answer.

Activity   Retell an Event

In this story, the Ingalls family tried to be cheerful, brave, and kind even when they were in danger. Think about how the family acted in those ways. Then think of another story in which the characters showed those traits. Write the title of the story and the author's name. Tell about one event in the story when the characters face a challenge the same way the Ingalls family did.

About LAURA INGALLS WILDER

Laura Ingalls Wilder's books make the past come alive for readers of today. Her books begin with the Ingalls family living in a cabin in Wisconsin in the 1860s. They follow Laura and her family across the prairie by covered wagon to Kansas, Minnesota, and the Dakotas. All these adventures are seen through the eyes of the young Laura Ingalls as she grows up on the frontier.

Laura Ingalls Wilder did not begin writing her books until she was more than sixty years old. Her daughter Rose encouraged her to write about her early life. Every day Mrs. Wilder recalled her past and wrote about it in pencil on orange-colored tablets. Mrs. Wilder's first book was *The Little House in the Big Woods*. By the time she died at the age of ninety, she had written eight more.

More Books by Laura Ingalls Wilder

On the Banks of Plum Creek   (Harper & Row, 1937)

By the Shores of Silver Lake   (Harper & Row, 1939)

Little Town on the Prairie   (Harper & Row, 1953)

CONNECTIONS

See pages T129–T131 in the front of this book for a suggested teaching plan for this selection.

From Sea to Shining Sea

The new land of the United States seemed a land of promise to many people. People came from many places, across great oceans, north from Mexico, and south from Canada, to settle in the new country. Still other people moved from one part of the United States to another. This is the land these people traveled in their search for land or riches or a new home.

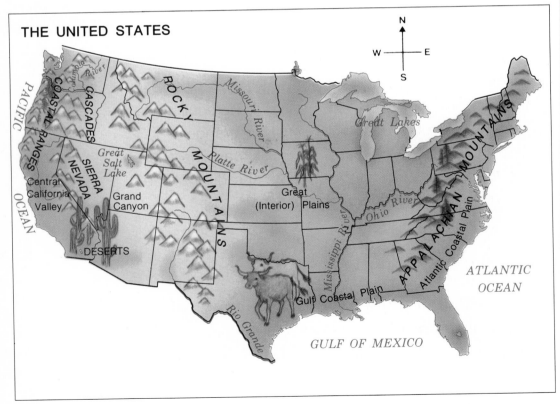

THE UNITED STATES

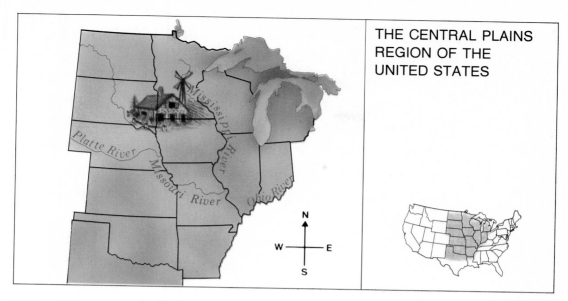

THE CENTRAL PLAINS REGION OF THE UNITED STATES

The Central Plains

Many thousands of people came to settle in the huge middle part of the United States called the **Central Plains.** This area had been explored and claimed by the French and Spanish during the 1500s and 1600s. Two hundred years later, all of this land was part of the United States.

The pioneers who came to this section wanted the land for farming and ranching. Some of the richest farm and grazing land in the world lies in the Central Plains of the United States.

The Plains are watered by one of the world's largest river systems: the Mississippi River and its *tributaries* (TRIB·yoo·tehr·eez), or branch rivers. The Mississippi begins high up in northern Minnesota and flows all the way down to the Gulf of Mexico. In an old folk song, people sang, "Mighty Mississippi, roll along."

The Mississippi did roll along. It carried the earliest French and Spanish explorers. It carried water to farms and ranches all over the Central Plains. It carried boats full of goods from United States factories as well as goods from Europe. People moving north or south, east or west, used the Mississippi and its tributaries to carry their belongings.

Many of the people who crossed the Mississippi settled in the Central Plains. Others moved on. Moving east or moving west, settlers found they had to cross mountains: the Appalachians (AP·uh·LAY·shunz) in the east and the Rockies in the west.

The Mountains

The **Appalachian Highlands** stand between the Central Plains and the East Coast of the United States. The Appalachian Highlands are made up of mountains, steep forested valleys, and low, level lands. Some of the valleys and lowlands have rich farmlands. Other parts of the Appalachian Highlands are rich in coal and petroleum. Some settlers to this area became farmers. Others became miners.

The **Rocky Mountains** stand between the Central Plains and the West Coast of the United States. These mountains are very different from the Appalachian Highlands. The Rocky Mountains, jagged and snow-capped, are among the world's highest mountains.

People who crossed the Rockies told of danger and hardships. Many others died crossing the mountains. They died from the cold, from exhaustion, and

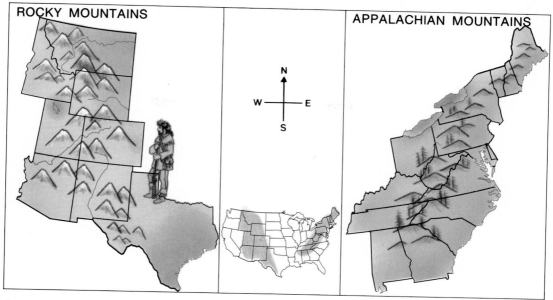

from hunger. Yet people had to cross the Rockies going west. There was no way around the mountains. The Rocky Mountains stretch all the way from northern New Mexico through Canada and into Alaska.

The Deserts

Many people crossed the desert regions of the United States in their search for land or riches. The desert regions lie west of the Rocky Mountains. The land in this area is very dry and hot with few plants. The **Great Basin** is the largest desert, 200,000 square miles of barren land in California, Idaho, Nevada, Oregon, Utah, and Wyoming.

The **Painted Desert** in Arizona, the **Mojave** (moh·HAH·vee) **Desert** in California, and the **Sonoran** (saw·NAW·rahn) **Desert** in New Mexico

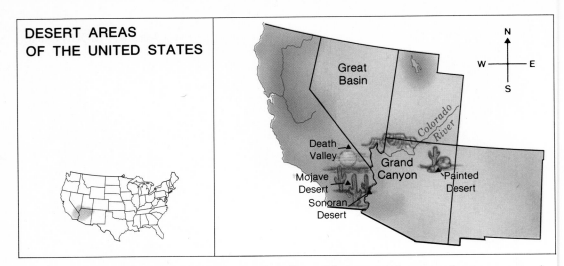

DESERT AREAS OF THE UNITED STATES

Great Basin

Colorado River

Death Valley

Grand Canyon

Mojave Desert

Painted Desert

Sonoran Desert

N W E S

are other desert regions that people may have crossed on their journeys from Mexico or parts of the United States. Just as some people were not prepared for the ruggedness of the Rockies, so others were not prepared for the harshness of the deserts. Many died from the heat or from thirst.

The Coasts

Some of the earliest people to come to the United States sailed from Europe across the Atlantic Ocean. The English and French settled along the Atlantic Coast. The Spanish settled in what is now Florida and along the coast of the Gulf of Mexico. The Spanish then moved across the desert regions to settle in what is now New Mexico, Arizona, and California.

People who came to the Atlantic Coast found flat lands that run along the Atlantic Sea Coast and the Gulf of Mexico. Along the Atlantic Coast, the plains are called the **Atlantic Coastal Plains.**

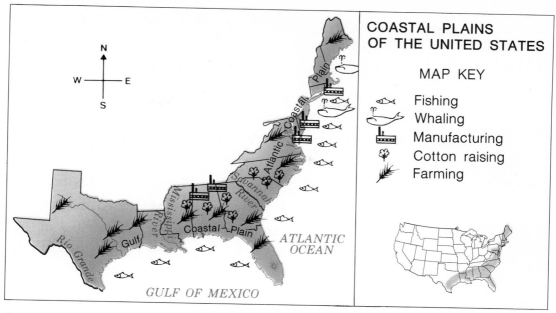

COASTAL PLAINS OF THE UNITED STATES

MAP KEY

- Fishing
- Whaling
- Manufacturing
- Cotton raising
- Farming

Around the Gulf of Mexico, the plains are called the **Gulf Coastal Plains.**

English colonists who first came to the upper Atlantic Coastal Plains started small farms. The land was not very good for farming, however. The Atlantic Coast had many good *harbors,* places where ships can dock safely. Later colonists turned to fishing, whaling, and shipping.

Many rivers cross the Atlantic Coastal Plains. The rushing waters from the rivers provided power for manufacturing, which started to grow in the middle of the 1880s.

Colonists from France and England settled the lower Atlantic Coastal Plains. The climate there and across the Gulf Coastal Plains ranges from warm to hot, ideal for growing cotton. Great cotton plantations were built where the coastal plain widens in Virginia.

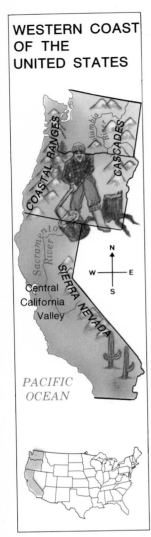

WESTERN COAST OF THE UNITED STATES

The same Mississippi River that waters the Central Plains flows through the Gulf Coastal Plains. Another important river in this region is the Rio Grande (REE•oh GRANDE), or Big River, as it was named by the Spanish settlers. The Rio Grande is the boundary between the United States and Mexico.

The far western coast of the United States looks out over the Pacific Ocean. Mountain ranges lie along the edge of the coast and plunge to the sea. Beyond these mountains lie the Central Valley of California and two more mountain ranges, the Sierra Nevada and the Cascade Mountains.

The Central Valley of California has very rich farmland that is good for growing fruits and vegetables. During the 1840s and 1850s, the discovery of gold led many people to California. It was the rich farmland, however, that made many stay and trade their miners' picks and axes for plows and hoes.

The Sierra Nevada range and the Cascade range extend almost the length of the Pacific Coast from Canada to Mexico. The Cascade Mountains are heavily forested. Settlers to the area now called Washington and Oregon turned to logging. These loggers supplied much of the United States with lumber for homes, furniture, and paper goods.

From east to west, north to south, across mountains and rivers and deserts, people pioneered and settled and built in the United States. By the end of the 1800s, people from all over the world had become Americans living in a proud, young nation that stretched "from sea to shining sea."

See pages T130–T131 in the front of this book for suggested postreading strategies.

Questions

1. Look at the map on page 162. Find your state. In what region do you live? What is the land like in your region?

2. If you were a pioneer moving west, where would you choose to stop and build your home? Why?

1. Critical/Evaluation Accept any answer that the student reasonably supports.
2. Critical/Evaluation Accept any answer that the student reasonably supports.

Activities

1. **Plan a Trip**

   Suppose you were a pioneer traveling from the East Coast of the United States to the West Coast. You want to travel across the middle of the United States in a straight line. List the land regions you will travel through as you go. Then make a list of supplies you will need to make your trip. Use the map on page 162 to help you.

2. **Be a Settler**

   Look back over this selection and decide where you would like to settle and build a home. Then tell about or draw the kind of house you would build; how you would get food and water; what kinds of clothing you would need; and what problems you might face. If you need more information about pioneers, look in books about the history of the West or in an encyclopedia.

Kansas Boy

A poem by Ruth Lechlitner

See pages T132–T133 in the front of this book for a suggested teaching plan for this selection.

Here, salty (line 7)
means *having to do
with the sea.*

This Kansas boy who never saw the sea
Walks through the young corn rippling at his knee
As sailors walk; and when the grain grows higher
Watches the dark waves leap with greener fire
Than ever oceans hold. He follows ships,
Tasting the bitter spray upon his lips,
For in his blood up-stirs the salty ghost
Of one who sailed a storm-bound English coast.
Across wide fields he hears the sea winds crying,
Shouts at the crows—and dreams of white gulls flying.

Illustrated by Craig Marshall

171

The Jumblies

From the poem

by Edward Lear

See pages T133—T135 in the front of this book for a suggested teaching plan for this selection.

They went to sea in a sieve, they did;
    In a sieve they went to sea:
In spite of all their friends could say,
On a winter's morn, on a stormy day,
    In a sieve they went to sea.
And when the sieve turned round and round,
And every one cried, "You'll all be drowned!"
They called aloud, "Our sieve ain't big;
But we don't care a button, we don't care a fig:
    In a sieve we'll go to sea!"
      Far and few, far and few,
        Are the lands where the Jumblies live:
      Their heads are green, and their hands are blue;
        And they went to sea in a sieve.

172

They sailed away in a sieve, they did,
   In a sieve they sailed so fast,
With only a beautiful pea-green veil
Tied with a ribbon, by way of a sail,
   To a small tobacco-pipe mast.
And every one said who saw them go,
"Oh! won't they be soon upset, you know?
For the sky is dark, and the voyage is long;
And, happen what may, it's extremely wrong
   In a sieve to sail so fast."
     Far and few, far and few,
       Are the lands where the Jumblies live:
      Their heads are green, and their hands are blue;
       And they went to sea in a sieve.

Illustrated by Jane Teiko Oka

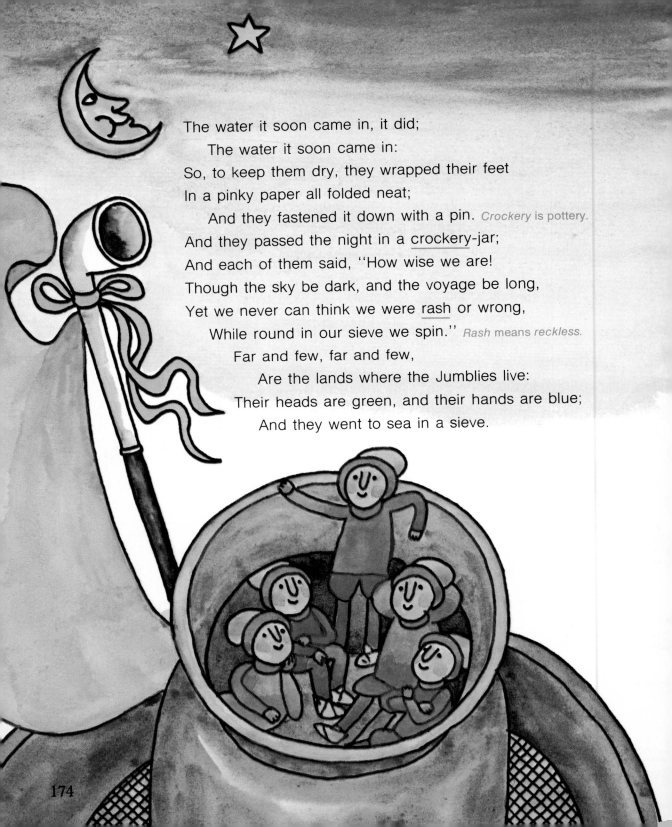

The water it soon came in, it did;
   The water it soon came in:
So, to keep them dry, they wrapped their feet
In a pinky paper all folded neat;
   And they fastened it down with a pin. *Crockery* is pottery.
And they passed the night in a crockery-jar;
And each of them said, "How wise we are!
Though the sky be dark, and the voyage be long,
Yet we never can think we were rash or wrong,
   While round in our sieve we spin." *Rash* means *reckless.*
   Far and few, far and few,
     Are the lands where the Jumblies live:
Their heads are green, and their hands are blue;
   And they went to sea in a sieve.

174

See pages T134–T135 in the front of this
book for suggested postreading strategies.

And in twenty years they all came back,—

    In twenty years or more;

And every one said, "How tall they've grown!"

For they've been to the Lakes, and the Torrible Zone,

    And the hills of the Chankly Bore."

And they drank their health, and gave them a feast

Of dumplings made of beautiful yeast;

And every one said, "If we only live,

We, too, will go to sea in a sieve,

    To the hills of the Chankly Bore."

      Far and few, far and few,

        Are the lands where the Jumblies live:

        Their heads are green, and their hands are blue;

        And they went to sea in a sieve.

Remind students that the hot, humid climate zone around the middle of the earth is called the *Torrid Zone*. Lear is making a play on the words *torrid* and *horrible*.

175

See pages T135—T138 in the front of this book for a suggested teaching plan for this selection.

176

Half a Kingdom

Reading Level Average

An Icelandic folk tale retold by Ann McGovern
Illustrated by Jane Teiko Oka

When you wake up in the morning, you never can tell what might happen to you during the day.

One fine morning, Prince Lini woke up in his castle on the hill. He didn't have the slightest idea what was going to happen to him that day.

Pronounced /lĭ'·nē/.

He rode into the forest with his friends. Suddenly, from nowhere, a thick cold fog blew into the woods. The cloud of fog covered the prince from head to toe. A minute later the fog drifted away and was gone. Gone, too, was Prince Lini.

His friends searched for him all that day and all that night. And in the morning they rode to the castle to tell the king the strange story of the fog that rolled in from the sky and took away his son.

Now the king loved his son more than anything, even more than the riches of his kingdom, which he loved very much. He sent for his strongest men and his wisest men. "Whoever finds Prince Lini," he said, "and brings him back to me, will win half of my kingdom."

The strongest men (and those not so strong) searched far and wide. The wisest men (and those not so wise) searched wide and far. All over the kingdom people heard the news that the prince had disappeared in a cloud of fog. Anyone who had ever wanted half a kingdom set out to search for the prince.

One fine morning, Signy, a poor peasant girl, Pronounced /sĭg′·nē/. woke up in her cottage at the edge of the forest. She didn't have the slightest idea what was going to happen to her that day.

But she had heard about the missing prince and about the king's reward of half the kingdom. She knew that the strongest and the wisest men had looked far and wide.

I'll look near and narrow, she thought.

Signy knew the secret places of the forest better than anyone else. She put on a pair of sturdy shoes for walking and took along some food. And she set out to search for Prince Lini.

All that day she looked. She saw nothing but tree shapes in the snow. All that day she called. She heard nothing but the song of the icy wind.

The sun began to set and the sky turned rosy. Soon it would be dark. Signy walked through a narrow place between the rocks to her favorite warm cave and peered inside. There, stretched out on a golden bed, was Prince Lini, fast asleep.

She ran into the cave and tried to wake him. But he slept on, in a deep, deep sleep.

All of a sudden she heard a clattering, a chattering. She ran to hide in the darkest corner of the cave.

Two troll girls—a tall troll and a shorter troll—entered the cave. "Fee, Foo, Fum, Firl. I smell the flesh of a human girl," sang the short troll.

"No," said the tall troll, "it's only Prince Lini."

Then the trolls whistled. Signy listened carefully to the notes of the whistle. Two swans flew into the cave. The short troll said:

Sing O sing O swans of mine,
Sing Prince Lini awake.

181

The swans sang. Prince Lini stirred, rubbed his eyes, and sat up.

"Now," said the short troll, "for the ninety-seventh time, will you marry one of us?"

"Never," said the prince. "Never, never, never."

"You'll be sorry," the tall troll said. Then she commanded the swans:

> *Sing O sing O swans of mine,*
> *Sing Prince Lini asleep.*

The swans sang and Prince Lini fell fast asleep again. The swans flew out of the cave.

From her hiding place, Signy could see and hear everything. The next morning the trolls left the cave with a clattering and a chattering. Signy crept from her hiding place. She remembered how the trolls whistled, and she whistled the same notes.

The swans flew into the cave. Signy said:

> *Sing O sing O swans of mine,*
> *Sing Prince Lini awake.*

The swans sang.

Prince Lini stirred, rubbed his eyes, sat up, and rubbed his eyes again. "Troll!" he said. "What has happened to you? You look very different."

"I'm not a troll," said Signy, "and nothing has happened to me except that I found you. I'm Signy."

"I'm very pleased to meet you," said the prince.

The prince told Signy how the trolls had cast a spell upon him with their magic fog and how they were holding him a prisoner until he agreed to marry one of them.

Then Signy told the prince how sad the king was, and how he had even offered half the kingdom to anyone who found his son and brought him home.

"No one has found me yet except you," said the prince. "But I don't know whether I *want* to be found. It's nice and warm in this cave. It's nice to have the trolls asking me to marry them every day."

Signy gave the prince a funny look.

"That wasn't true," said the prince. "The real reason is that I don't want to go home. It makes me sad to see how the kingdom is run. And the king will listen to no one. The rich are too rich and hardly work. The poor are too poor and work too hard."

"Yes," said Signy sadly.

The prince looked at Signy and began to laugh. He jumped up and down on the golden bed, laughing and laughing.

"What's so funny about being poor?" Signy asked.

"That's just it!" cried the prince. "You won't be poor if you get half the kingdom and you can share it with everyone! Please, Signy, take me back to the king and take half the kingdom. Please!"

"First things first," said Signy. "The first thing is to get you out of here."

"Why can't we run away right now while I'm awake?" said the prince.

"No," said Signy. "The trolls would surely send down their magic fog before we got out of the woods. They would make me a prisoner, too, along with you. You must find out from the trolls where they go and what they do during the day. It's the only way."

The prince agreed.

The sun began to set and the sky turned rosy. Then Signy whistled. The swans flew into the cave and sang Prince Lini asleep.

Again Signy hid in the dark corner. Soon the trolls came in with a clattering, a chattering. They woke Prince Lini in their usual way. And in their usual way they asked him their usual question.

"Now," said the tall troll, "for the ninety-eighth time, will you marry one of us?"

The prince pretended to think about it. "Tell me," he said, "where do you go and what do you do during the day?"

"We go to the big oak tree in the middle of the forest," the tall troll said.

"And we take out our giant golden egg," the short troll said.

"And we toss it back and forth, and back and forth," the tall troll said.

"What happens if you drop it?" Prince Lini asked.

"Oh, we never drop it," the short troll said. "If we drop it and it breaks, we would disappear forever."

"Enough of this chatter," said the tall troll. "Now for the ninety-ninth time, will you marry one of us?"

"Never, never, never, never, NEVER!" said the prince.

"Oh," said the tall troll, shaking with rage. "Tomorrow you will see how sorry you will be!"

"The end is near for you," said the short troll.

The trolls whistled. The swans sang and Prince Lini slept.

The next morning when the trolls left the cave, Signy whistled for the swans. The swans sang and Prince Lini awoke.

"You were wonderful," Signy said. "Now we will go to the middle of the forest to the big oak tree. You must do exactly what I tell you." And she whispered her plan to the prince.

They left the cave and walked to the middle of the forest. There they saw the two trolls under the big oak tree. The trolls were throwing the giant golden egg to and fro, to and fro.

Signy whispered to the prince, "Be careful. Your life is in danger."

Prince Lini picked up a stone. He aimed carefully and threw it. The stone hit the giant golden egg. It fell to the ground, broken to bits.

Suddenly from nowhere a thick cold fog blew into the woods. The cloud of fog covered the two trolls. A minute later the fog drifted away and was gone. And gone, too, were the trolls. Gone forever, to the place where trolls live.

Signy and Prince Lini ran all the way to the palace. "Wait outside," Signy told the prince. "It's better if I see your father alone."

"Who are you?" the king asked when he saw Signy. "And what do you want?"

"I am Signy, a peasant girl," she said, "and I want half of your kingdom, for I found your son."

"Don't be silly," said the king. "How can a girl find my son when my strongest and my wisest men could not find him!"

"That's too bad for them," Signy said. "If what I say is true, will you keep your promise and give me half of your kingdom?"

"Go away," said the king. "It can't be true."

Signy ran to the door and flung it open. The king was beside himself with joy to see his lost

son. After the two hugged and cried tears of
happiness, Prince Lini told his father about the
trolls and the magic spell and how Signy found
him and freed him.

"Now will you give up half your kingdom?"
Signy asked the king.

"Oh, my precious kingdom!" the king sighed.

"What about your precious son and your
promise!" said the prince.

The king looked at Signy carefully. "A girl
like you found my son? A peasant girl—not even
a princess! But my precious son is right. And a
promise is a promise. I give you half my kingdom."

Prince Lini turned to Signy. "I love you," he said. "Will you marry me? I'll help you rule your half of the kingdom, if you like."

Signy said, "Let's play checkers while I think it over."

They played checkers and Signy thought it over. She thought it would be wonderful to marry Prince Lini. "We can share half the kingdom and share adventures, too, for the rest of our lives," she told him.

And that is exactly what they did, happily and forever after.

See pages T136–T138 in the front of this book for suggested postreading strategies.

Questions

1. Who might have said the following:
   a. "We can't find Prince Lini."
   b. "Prince Lini won't marry either of us."
   c. "I don't want to share my kingdom."

2. Tell two problems Signy had to solve before she could return Prince Lini to the king.

3. Which word best describes the story? Give reasons for your answer.
   a. serious   b. fanciful   c. sad

4. Will Signy be a good queen? What did you learn about her in the story that makes you think the way you do?

5. Folk tales often describe settings and happenings that make you "see" exciting pictures in your mind. Which part of the story causes you to "see" the most exciting picture in your mind? Describe it.

Activity   Write the Beginning of a Story

"Half a Kingdom" has a bright, happy beginning. Read the first three paragraphs of the beginning again. Then write a lively beginning that might start a story about the further adventures of Signy and Lini.

1. **Interpretive/Details** a. the men who searched for Prince Lini (pages 178–179, 188); b. the trolls (pages 182, 185–186); c. the King (page 189)

2. **Literal/Details** Possible responses: She had to awaken the Prince (pages 180–182); she had to get rid of the trolls (pages 185–188).

3. **Interpretive/Judgment** Possible response: b. because it is humorous and pokes fun at the way things usually occur in folk tales

4. **Critical/Synthesis** Possible responses: She will be a good queen because she was clever enough to find the Prince and get him home; a bad queen because she was bossy and she had to play checkers before she made a decision.

5. **Critical/Appreciation** Possible responses: the golden egg scene (page 186); Signy walking through the forest looking for the prince (page 179); the cave itself with the Prince asleep and Signy finding him (page 180)

At Night May I Roam

A Sioux chant

at night may I roam
against the winds may I roam
at night may I roam
when the owl is hooting
may I roam

at dawn may I roam
against the winds may I roam
at dawn may I roam
when the crow is calling
may I roam

See pages T138—T139 in the front of this
book for a suggested teaching plan for this
selection.

192

Illustrated by Sarn Suvityasiri

BOOKSHELF

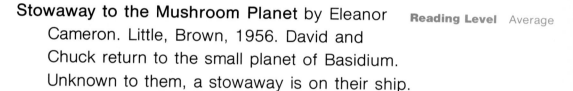

Pioneers on Early Waterways by Edith McCall. **Reading Level** Average
Children's Press, 1980. With a great deal of
determination, early settlers made their way to
the lands out West by raft, flatboat, barge, and
even steamboat.

The Prairie Community by Kathleen Vyn. Julian **Reading Level** Challenging
Messner, 1978. Plant and animal life on the
prairie changed when people began to live
there. Read about what it was like before the
settlers came.

Stowaway to the Mushroom Planet by Eleanor **Reading Level** Average
Cameron. Little, Brown, 1956. David and
Chuck return to the small planet of Basidium.
Unknown to them, a stowaway is on their ship.

Letters to Horseface: Wolfgang Amadeus **Reading Level** Challenging
Mozart's Journey to Italy 1769–1770 When
He Was a Boy of Fourteen by F. N. Monjo.
Viking Press, 1975. A young composer writes
humorous letters to his sister, whom he calls
Horseface.

Explorers in a New World by Edith McCall. **Reading Level** Challenging
Children's Press, 1980. Imagine yourself
discovering a new area. Take a look at how
some of the people felt who first explored our
land.

See pages T140–T141 in the front of this book for a suggested teaching plan for this selection.

4 When Paths Cross

See pages T141–T143 in the front of this book for a suggested teaching plan for this selection.

The Lion and the Mouse

An Aesop fable retold by Anne Terry White

Illustrated by Masami Sam Daijogo

Reading Level Average

In the heat of the day a Lion lay asleep at the edge of a wood. He lay so still that a Mouse ran right across his nose without knowing it was a nose, and a Lion's at that.

Bang! The Lion clapped his paw to his face and felt something caught. It was furry. Lazily he opened his eyes. He lifted up one side of his huge paw just a little bit to see what was under it and was amused to find a Mouse.

"Spare me, Great King!" he heard the little creature squeak in its tiny voice. "I didn't mean to do it! Let me go, and someday I will repay you."

"That's very funny," said the Lion, and he laughed. "How can a little thing like you help me, the great King of Beasts?"

197

"I don't know," the Mouse replied, "but a little creature *can* sometimes help a big one."

"Well, you have made me laugh," the Lion said, "which is something I seldom do. And anyway, you would hardly make half a mouthful. So—" He raised his paw and let the Mouse go.

A few days later the Lion was caught in a hunter's net. The woods rang with his angry roaring and the little Mouse heard him.

"That is my kind Lion!" she cried. "He is in trouble!" As fast as she could, she ran toward the spot from which the roaring came, and there he was. The Lion was thrashing around so in the net that the Mouse didn't dare to come near for fear of being crushed.

"O King, be patient!" she cried. "I will gnaw through the ropes and set you free."

So the Lion lay still while the Mouse worked away with her sharp teeth. And in a short time he was able to creep out of the net.

"You see? I told you I would repay you," the Mouse said happily. "A little creature sometimes really can help a big one."

And the Lion had to admit it was true.

Little friends may prove to be great friends.

See pages T142–T143 in the front of this book for suggested postreading strategies.

199

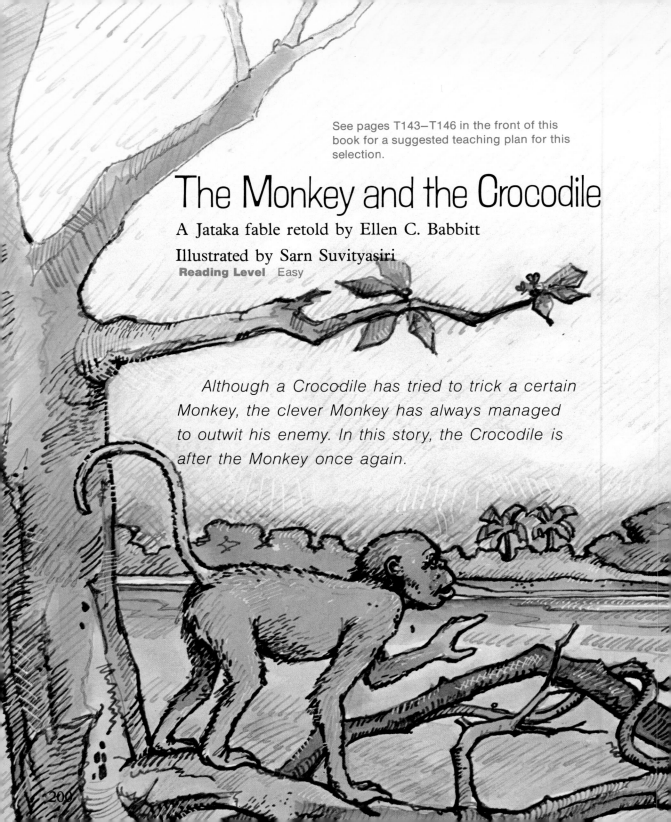

See pages T143–T146 in the front of this book for a suggested teaching plan for this selection.

The Monkey and the Crocodile

A Jataka fable retold by Ellen C. Babbitt

Illustrated by Sarn Suvityasiri

Reading Level Easy

Although a Crocodile has tried to trick a certain Monkey, the clever Monkey has always managed to outwit his enemy. In this story, the Crocodile is after the Monkey once again.

The Monkey lived in a great tree on a river-bank. The Monkey soon moved away from that tree. He wanted to get away from the Crocodile, so that he might live in peace.

But the Crocodile found him, far down the river, living in another tree.

In the middle of the river was an island covered with fruit trees. Halfway between the bank of the river and the island, a large rock rose out of the water. The Monkey could jump to the rock, and then to the island. The Crocodile watched the Monkey crossing from the bank of the river to the rock, and then to the island.

He thought to himself, "The Monkey will stay on the island all day, and I'll catch him on his way home at night."

The Monkey had a fine feast, while the Crocodile swam about, watching him all day.

Toward night the Crocodile crawled out of the water and lay on the rock, perfectly still.

When it grew dark among the trees, the Monkey started for home. He ran down to the river bank, and there he stopped.

"What is the matter with the rock?" the Monkey thought to himself. "I never saw it so high before. The Crocodile is lying on it!"

But he went to the edge of the water and called, "Hello, Rock!"

No answer.

Then he called again, "Hello, Rock!"

Three times the Monkey called, and then he said, "Why is it, Friend Rock, that you do not answer me tonight?"

"Oh," said the stupid Crocodile to himself. "The rock answers the Monkey at night. I'll have to answer for the rock this time."

So he answered: "Yes, Monkey! What is it?"

The Monkey laughed, and said, "Oh, it's you, Crocodile, is it?"

"Yes," said the Crocodile. "I am waiting here for you. I am going to eat you."

"You have caught me in a trap this time," said the Monkey. "There is no other way for me to go home. Open your mouth wide so I can jump right into it."

Now the Monkey well knew that, when Crocodiles open their mouths wide, they shut their eyes.

203

While the Crocodile lay on the rock with his mouth wide open and his eyes shut, the Monkey jumped.

But not into his mouth! Oh, no! He landed on the top of the Crocodile's head, and then sprang quickly to the bank. Up he whisked into his tree.

When the Crocodile saw the trick the Monkey had played on him, he said, "Monkey, you have great cunning. You know no fear. I'll let you alone after this."

"Thank you, Crocodile," said the Monkey. "But I shall be on the watch for you just the same."

See pages T144–T146 in the front of this book for suggested postreading strategies.

Questions

1. "I was smart to lie on the rock, but I made a mistake." Who in the story might say that? What was his mistake?

2. Why didn't the Monkey trust the Crocodile at the end of the fable?

3. If the Monkey told this fable to his friends, which lesson might he give at the end?
   a. "Don't go near the water."
   b. "Jump now and ask questions later."
   c. "Look before you leap."

4. Why would a storyteller like to tell this story? Why would people like to hear it?

5. The Monkey said, "You have caught me in a trap." What does he mean?
   a. You have outwitted me.
   b. You have frightened me.
   c. You have put me in a cage.

1. Interpretive/ Judgment the Crocodile; his mistake was to answer the Monkey's question. (page 202)
2. Interpretive/ Judgment The Monkey knew the Crocodile might try to trick him again. (page 204)
4. Critical/Evaluation Possible responses: The storyteller would have a chance to imitate a monkey and crocodile talking; the story-teller would be sure to get a laugh at the monkey's cleverness. People would like it because of its moral or because it is funny to hear about a small animal tricking a larger one.
3. Critical/Analysis c.
5. Interpretive/Figurative Language a.

Activity   Finish a Fable

One day the Monkey climbed a tree to get a coconut. Meanwhile, the Crocodile pretended to be a log beneath the tree. "This time," he said, "I won't say a word, and I'll keep my eyes open."

Finish the fable. End with a *moral,* or lesson.

See pages T146–T148 in the front of this book for a suggested teaching plan for this selection.

From

Guess Who
Reading Level Easy
My Favorite Person Is

A story by Byrd Baylor
Illustrated by Christa Kieffer

I happened to be in an alfalfa field,
barefoot, sort of lying down
watching ladybugs climb yellow flowers
when I saw this little kid
who was also barefoot,
sort of lying down
watching ladybugs climb yellow flowers,
helping them up again when they fell off.

"Want to see my favorite one?"
she called to me.

So I went over to where she was.

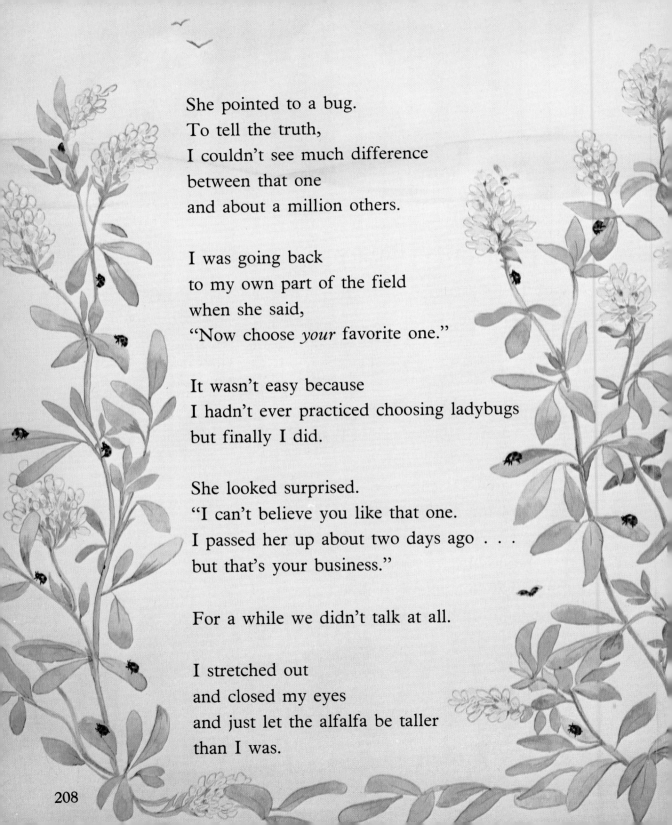

She pointed to a bug.
To tell the truth,
I couldn't see much difference
between that one
and about a million others.

I was going back
to my own part of the field
when she said,
"Now choose *your* favorite one."

It wasn't easy because
I hadn't ever practiced choosing ladybugs
but finally I did.

She looked surprised.
"I can't believe you like that one.
I passed her up about two days ago . . .
but that's your business."

For a while we didn't talk at all.

I stretched out
and closed my eyes
and just let the alfalfa be taller
than I was.

But she said,
"What's your favorite thing—
sleeping or being awake?"

"Awake," I said.

"Then wake up and we can play
the tell-what-your-favorite-thing-is game."

"I think we are already playing it,"
I said.

She said,
"We are, and it's my turn.
My favorite turn is FIRST."

So I said, "Go ahead."

She said,
"Tell me your favorite color."

I said, "Blue."

But she said,
"See, you've already done it wrong.
In this game you can't just say it's blue.
You have to say what *kind* of blue."

Point out that
". . . the blue on a
lizard's belly . . ." is
a *word picture*. After
they read the story,
ask the students to
find other examples
of word pictures.

So I said,
"All right. You know the blue
on a lizard's belly?
That sudden kind of blue
you see just for a second sometimes—
so blue that afterwards
you always think you made it up?"

"Sure," she said.
"I know that kind of blue."

Then she told me *hers*
and it was brown.
She said, "And the brown I like the best
is a dark reddish brown
that's good for mountains and for rocks.
You see it in steep cliffs a lot."

I said,
"I know that kind of brown."

210

Then we chose our favorite sounds.

She said hers was *bees*
but not just one or two.
She said it takes about a thousand bees
buzzing in all the fields around
to make the kind of loud bee sound
she likes.

For mine, I chose a bird I'd heard
one morning in the mountains in New Mexico
and never saw and never heard again
and couldn't even say why
I still remembered it.

She said it was all right
that I didn't know its name.

We must have named
a hundred favorite things
that afternoon.

Her favorite thing to taste
is snow and honey mixed . . .
a little more honey than snow.

Mine is bread just baked at home,
still warm.

Her favorite smell is the alfalfa
growing in this field.

Mine is *desert* rain—
not rain anywhere else.

Finally I said,
"What's your favorite time of day?"

And she said,
"Now, just about now
when I've been running in the field
and getting out of breath
and falling down
and watching ladybugs
and finding someone to play
the tell-what-your-favorite-thing-is game
and playing it and then maybe
walking back as far as the road together."

I was going to say
that sunrise is my favorite time of day

but when I thought about it
I wanted to choose *now* too.

I wasn't sure she'd let us both
choose the same thing
but she was nice about it.

She said, "We can.
That's my favorite way
to end the game."

See pages T147–T148
in the front of this
book for suggested
postreading strategies.

By then it was getting late
so we walked back as far as the road
together.

Questions

1. In this story two girls talked about their favorite ladybugs and their favorite colors. What other favorite things did they describe?

2. Look at the pictures on pages 212 and 213. What favorite things from the story do these pictures show you? Which two senses (sight, hearing, touch, taste, smell) do they describe?

3. Why did one girl claim it was wrong to say that blue is someone's favorite color?

4. If *you* were describing your favorite color, what would you say?

5. Choose the correct word for each sentence.
   a. Ice cream is my favorite (desert, dessert).
   b. My cactus was found in the (desert, dessert).

Activity   Write Word Pictures

The two girls in this story used *word pictures* to describe their favorite things. A favorite color was described as "a dark reddish brown that's good for mountains and for rocks." The word pictures helped you see, hear, taste, touch, or smell each favorite thing.

Think of three of your favorite things. Write word pictures to describe them.

Some People

A poem by Rachel Field

See pages T148–T149 in the front of this book for a suggested teaching plan for this selection.

Isn't it strange some people make
    You feel so tired inside,
Your thoughts begin to shrivel up
    Like leaves all brown and dried!

But when you're with some other ones,
    It's stranger still to find
Your thoughts as thick as fireflies
    All shiny in your mind!

Illustrated by Francis Livingston

Hope

A poem by Langston Hughes

See pages T150–T151 in the front of this book for a suggested teaching plan for this selection.

Sometimes when I'm lonely,
Don't know why,
Keep thinkin' I won't be lonely
By and by.

Illustrated by Francis Livingston

Dreams

A poem by Langston Hughes

Hold fast to dreams
For if dreams die
Life is a broken-winged bird
That cannot fly.

Hold fast to dreams
For when dreams go
Life is a barren field   *Barren means without*
Frozen with snow.   *growth; empty.*

See pages T150–T151 in the front of this book for suggested postreading strategies.

Illustrated by Francis Livingston

About LANGSTON HUGHES

Langston Hughes, one of America's great poets, came to national attention almost by accident. He was working as a busboy in a hotel restaurant in Washington, D.C. One night he saw Vachel Lindsay, a famous poet, eating in the restaurant. Too shy to speak, Langston Hughes instead dropped three of his poems at Vachel Lindsay's plate. That evening Mr. Lindsay praised these poems and read them to a large group of people. The next morning newspaper reporters interviewed Langston Hughes and took his picture in his busboy's uniform. His poems appeared in the newspaper. Soon he was publishing his work in books and newspapers.

In addition to poetry, Langston Hughes wrote stories, plays, books, and operas. Much of his writing is about his experiences as a member of the Black community. His writing has helped others to understand and appreciate this experience.

Books of Poetry by Langston Hughes

The Dream Keeper   (Alfred A. Knopf, 1945)
Selected Poems of Langston Hughes   (Alfred A. Knopf, 1959)

See pages T151–T153 in the front of this book for a suggested teaching plan for this selection.

Reading Level Challenging

The Escape

From the story *Charlotte's Web* by E. B. White

Illustrated by Garth Williams

Ever since Wilbur, the <u>runt of the pig litter</u>, was given to Fern to raise, he has had constant love and care. He was fed from a bottle, played with, and allowed to follow Fern around like a puppy. The day came, though, when Wilbur had to be sold. Parting from Fern was made a little easier when her uncle Homer Zuckerman agreed to buy him. Wilbur would then be close by, and Fern could walk down the road to visit him in the Zuckerman barn.

The *runt of the litter* is the smallest of the animals produced in one birth.

One afternoon in June, when Wilbur was almost two months old, he wandered out into his small yard outside the barn. Fern had not arrived for her usual visit. Wilbur stood in the sun feeling lonely and bored.

"There's never anything to do around here," he thought. He walked slowly to his food <u>trough</u> and sniffed to see if anything had been overlooked at lunch. He found a small strip of potato skin and ate it. His back itched, so he leaned against the fence and rubbed against the boards. When he tired of this, he walked indoors, climbed to the top of the <u>manure</u> pile, and sat down. He didn't feel like going to sleep, he didn't feel like digging, he was tired of standing still, tired of lying down. "I'm less than two months old and I'm tired of living," he said. He walked out to the yard again.

Pronounced /troff/.

Manure is waste material used for fertilizer.

"When I'm out here," he said, "there's no place to go but in. When I'm indoors, there's no place to go but out in the yard."

"That's where you're wrong, my friend, my friend," said a voice.

Wilbur looked through the fence and saw the goose standing there.

"You don't have to stay in that dirty-little dirty-little dirty-little yard," said the goose, who talked rather fast. "One of the boards is loose. Push on it, push-push-push on it, and come on out!"

"What?" said Wilbur. "Say it slower!"

"At-at-at, at the risk of repeating myself," said the goose, "I suggest that you come on out. It's wonderful out here."

"Did you say a board was loose?"

"That I did, that I did," said the goose.

Wilbur walked up to the fence and saw that the goose was right—one board was loose. He put his head down, shut his eyes, and pushed. The board gave way. In a minute he had squeezed through the fence and was standing in the long grass outside his yard. The goose chuckled.

"How does it feel to be free?" she asked.

"I like it," said Wilbur. "That is, I *guess* I like it." Actually, Wilbur felt queer to be outside his fence, with nothing between him and the big world.

"Where do you think I'd better go?"

Queer is another word for *strange*.

222

"Anywhere you like, anywhere you like," said the goose. "Go down through the orchard, root up the sod! Go down through the garden, dig up the radishes! Root up everything! Eat grass! Look for corn! Look for oats! Run all over! Skip and dance, jump and prance! Go down through the orchard and stroll in the woods! The world is a wonderful place when you're young."

Sod is ground covered with grass.

"I can see that," replied Wilbur. He gave a jump in the air, twirled, ran a few steps, stopped, looked all around, sniffed the smells of afternoon, and then set off walking down through the orchard. Pausing in the shade of an apple tree, he put his strong snout into the ground and began pushing, digging, and rooting. He felt very happy. He had plowed up quite a piece of ground before anyone noticed him. Mrs. Zuckerman was the first to see him. She saw him from the kitchen window, and she immediately shouted for the men.

"Ho-*mer!*" she cried. "Pig's out! Lurvy! Pig's out! Homer! Lurvy! Pig's out. He's down there under that apple tree."

"Now the trouble starts," thought Wilbur. "Now I'll catch it."

The goose heard the racket and she, too, started hollering. "Run-run-run downhill, make for the woods, the woods!" she shouted to Wilbur. "They'll never-never-never catch you in the woods."

223

A *commotion* is a noisy disturbance.

The cocker spaniel heard the <u>commotion</u> and he ran out from the barn to join the chase. Mr. Zuckerman heard, and he came out of the machine shed where he was mending a tool. Lurvy, the hired man, heard the noise and came up from the asparagus patch where he was pulling weeds. Everybody walked toward Wilbur and Wilbur didn't know what to do. The woods seemed a long way off, and anyway, he had never been down there in the woods and wasn't sure he would like it.

"Get around behind him, Lurvy," said Mr. Zuckerman, "and drive him toward the barn! And take it easy—don't rush him! I'll go and get a bucket of <u>slops</u>."

Slops are leftover food fed to pigs.

The news of Wilbur's escape spread rapidly among the animals on the place. Whenever any creature broke loose on the Zuckerman's farm, the event was of great interest to the others. The goose shouted to the nearest cow that Wilbur was free, and soon all the cows knew. Then one of the cows told one of the sheep, and soon all the sheep knew. The lambs learned about it from their mothers. The horses, in their stalls in the barn, pricked up their ears when they heard the goose hollering; and soon the horses had caught on to what was happening. "Wilbur's out," they said. Every animal stirred and lifted its head and became excited to know that one of his friends had got free and was no longer penned up or tied fast.

Wilbur didn't know what to do or which way to run. It seemed as though everybody was after him. "If this is what it's like to be free," he thought, "I believe I'd rather be penned up in my own yard."

The cocker spaniel was sneaking up on him from one side, Lurvy the hired man was sneaking up on him from the other side. Mrs. Zuckerman stood ready to head him off if he started for the garden, and now Mr. Zuckerman was coming down toward him carrying a pail. "This is really awful," thought Wilbur. "Why doesn't Fern come?" He began to cry.

The goose took command and began to give orders.

"Don't just stand there, Wilbur! Dodge about, dodge about!" cried the goose. "Skip around, run toward me, slip in and out, in and out, in and out! Make for the woods! Twist and turn!"

The cocker spaniel sprang for Wilbur's hind leg. Wilbur jumped and ran. Lurvy reached out and grabbed. Mrs. Zuckerman screamed at Lurvy. The goose cheered for Wilbur. Wilbur dodged between Lurvy's legs. Lurvy missed Wilbur and grabbed the spaniel instead. "Nicely done, nicely done!" cried the goose. "Try it again, try it again!"

"Run downhill!" suggested the cows.

"Run toward me!" yelled the gander.

"Run uphill!" cried the sheep.

"Turn and twist!" honked the goose.

"Jump and dance!" said the rooster.

"Look out for Lurvy!" called the cows.

"Look out for Zuckerman!" yelled the gander.

"Watch out for the dog!" cried the sheep.

"Listen to me, listen to me!" screamed the goose.

Poor Wilbur was <u>dazed</u> and frightened by this hullabaloo. He didn't like being the center of all this fuss. He tried to follow the instructions his friends were giving him, but he couldn't run downhill and uphill at the same time, and he couldn't turn and twist when he was jumping and dancing, and he was crying so hard he could barely see anything that was happening. After all, Wilbur was a very young pig— not much more than a baby, really. He wished Fern were there to take him in her arms and comfort him. When he looked up and saw Mr. Zuckerman standing quite close to him, holding a pail of warm slops,

Dazed means confused.

226

he felt relieved. He lifted his nose and sniffed. The smell was delicious—warm milk, potato skins, wheat middlings, Kellogg's Corn Flakes, and a popover left from the Zuckerman's breakfast.

Middlings are coarsely ground wheat mixed with bran.

"Come, pig!" said Mr. Zuckerman, tapping the pail. "Come pig!"

Wilbur took a step toward the pail.

"No-no-no!" said the goose. "It's the old pail trick, Wilbur. Don't fall for it, don't fall for it! He's trying to lure you back into captivity-ivity. He's appealing to your stomach."

Captivity is the state of being controlled or held prisoner.

227

Appetizing means appealing to the sense of taste.

Wilbur didn't care. The food smelled <u>appetizing</u>. He took another step toward the pail.

"Pig, pig!" said Mr. Zuckerman in a kind voice, and began walking slowly toward the barnyard, looking all about him innocently, as if he didn't know that a little white pig was following along behind him.

"You'll be sorry-sorry-sorry," called the goose.

Wilbur didn't care. He kept walking toward the pail of slops.

"You'll miss your freedom," honked the goose. "An hour of freedom is worth a barrel of slops."

Wilbur didn't care.

When Mr. Zuckerman reached the pigpen, he climbed over the fence and poured the slops into the trough. Then he pulled the loose board away from the fence, so that there was a wide hole for Wilbur to walk through.

"Reconsider, reconsider!" cried the goose.

Wilbur paid no attention. He stepped through the fence into his yard. He walked to the trough and took a long drink of slops, sucking in the milk hungrily and chewing the popover. It was good to be home again.

While Wilbur ate, Lurvy fetched a hammer and some 8-penny nails and nailed the board in place. Then he and Mr. Zuckerman leaned lazily on the fence and Mr. Zuckerman scratched Wilbur's back with a stick.

"He's quite a pig," said Lurvy.

228

Questions

1. Wilbur was bored at the beginning of the story. How did he feel when he escaped? How did he feel when he was discovered? How did he feel at the end of the story?

2. Did Wilbur fail in his escape? What might Wilbur say that he gained from his attempt to escape?

3. At the end of the story the goose said to Wilbur, "An hour of freedom is worth a barrel of slops." How might Wilbur have answered?

4. The goose said the same words over and over: "run-run-run" and "push-push-push" and "no-no-no." Why did the goose do that?

5. What words in the story are the *opposites* of these words?

   outdoors   captivity   contented

6. Wilbur acts the way a real pig would act, except for one thing. What is it? Do you think it helps make the story more fun to read? Tell why or why not.

Activity   Write a Letter to Wilbur

Write Wilbur a letter that will help him when he is bored. In your letter, suggest at least three things that Wilbur can do to end his boredom.

1. Literal/Details and **Interpretive/Judgment** He was bored in his pen (page 221), happy when he escaped (page 223), frightened when he was discovered (page 223), relieved when he returned to his pen. (page 227)

2. Critical/Evaluation Possible responses: that he was no longer bored; that he got some good food; that now he knows what it is like outside

3. Interpretive/Judgment Possible response: He might have said, "That's all very well for you, but I don't like it out there with everybody shouting at me."

4. Interpretive/Conclusion Possible response: The repeated words resembled goose sounds.

5. Literal/Definitions indoors (page 222); freedom (page 227); bored (page 221)

6. Interpretive/Reality and Fantasy Possible responses: Wilbur can talk. It helps the story because it makes the story funnier and helps the reader know more about him.

See pages T154–T157 in the front of this book for a suggested teaching plan for this selection.

Reading Level Average

Sound of Sunshine, Sound of Rain

A story by Florence Parry Heide

Illustrated by Kenneth Longtemps

Morning Voices

It must be morning, for I hear the morning voices.

I have been dreaming of a sound that whispers *Follow me, Follow me,* but not in words. I follow the sound up and up until I feel I am floating in the air.

Now I am awake, and I listen to the voices.

My mother's voice is warm and soft as a pillow.

My sister's voice is little and sharp and high, like needles flying in the air.

I do not listen to the words but to the sound. Low, high, low, high, soft, hard, soft, hard, and then the sounds coming together at the same time and making a new sound. And with it all, the sharp sounds of my sister's heels putting holes in what I hear.

Then I hear the slamming of kitchen drawers and the banging of pans and there is no more talking.

My bed is in the living room. I reach out to feel whether my mother has laid my clothes on the chair beside my bed. They are there, and I feel the smoothness and the roughness of them.

I reach under the chair to find which shoes my mother has put there. They are my outside shoes, not my slippers, so today must be a warm day. Maybe I can go to the park.

I tap my good luck song on the wall beside my bed.

I put my feet on the floor and feel the cool wood and curl my toes against it. Then it is four steps to the table, then around the table, touching the chairs, and then seven steps to the window. I put my cheek against the window, and I can feel the warm sun. Now I am sure I can go to the park, if my sister has time to take me on her way to study.

I take my clothes into the bathroom, and I wash and dress there. Hot water, cold water, soapy water, plain water, loud water, still water. Then I make sure I have turned the faucets tight. I make sure I have buttoned all of my buttons the right way, or my sister will be cross, and maybe not have time to take me to the park.

I tap my good luck song against the door before I open it.

When I open the door, I hear the voices again. My sister's voice is like scissors cutting away at my mother's voice.

I sit at the table, and my mother gives me my breakfast. I breathe on the hot chocolate so I can feel it on my face coming back warm. I drink just a little at a time so I can keep holding the warm cup.

"Eat while it's hot," says my sister to me, loudly.

"Does he have to be so slow?" says my sister to my mother in her quiet voice. My sister thinks because I cannot see that maybe I cannot hear very well, and she talks loudly to me, and softly when she does not want me to hear, but I hear.

"You spilled," says my sister, loudly.

"I can't be late," she says in her quiet voice to my mother. "Everybody's always late but me, and I won't be late."

After breakfast I go over to the window again. When I put my cheek against the glass it is warmer than before, so today will be a good day. I tap my good luck song against the window.

My sister says she will take me to the park on her way to study. She gives me my jacket and tells me to wait for her outside on the steps.

I go down the outside steps. There are seven steps. Seven is my most magic number. Seven up, seven down, seven up, seven down. I go up and down, waiting for my sister.

My sister comes out. She takes my hand. She walks very fast, but I can still count the steps to the park, and I can still remember the turns. Someday I can go there by myself. I listen to the street noises and try to sort them out.

My sister's hand is not soft. I can feel her nails, little and sharp, like her voice, and I listen to her heels making holes in all the other sounds.

The park seems a long way off.

When we get to the park we go first to the bench. My sister waits to make sure I remember my way in the park. Fourteen steps to the <u>bubbler</u>. Around the bubbler, twenty steps to the curb.

A bubbler is a drinking fountain with a vertical nozzle.

I go back to the bench. I try to hurry so my sister won't have to wait long and be cross. Now seventeen steps to the phone booth, four benches on the way and I touch them all. Then I come back to my bench. My sister puts money in my pocket so I can telephone.

She talks to me and to herself.

"Filthy park," she says, and it is as if she were stepping on the words. "No grass. Trees in cages. Since when do benches and old newspapers make a park?" She pulls my jacket to straighten it.

Now she is gone and I have my morning in the sun.

I try each bench, but mine is still the best one.

I go to the bubbler and press my mouth against the water and feel it on my tongue, soft and warm. I put my finger on the place where the water comes out. I walk around and around the bubbler, and then I try to find my bench. It is one of my games. I have many games.

I walk over to the telephone booth, touching the four benches on the way. I stand inside the booth. I feel in my pocket to see if the money my sister gave me is still there. It is.

I practice dialing our number so I will be sure I have it right. Then I put my dime in and call. I let it ring two times and then I hang up and get my dime back. My sister says that way my mother will know I am all right.

I blow on the glass and it blows back to me. I tap my good luck song on it and go back to my bench.

I play one of my games. I listen to every sound and think if that sound would be able to do something to me, what it would do. Some sounds would scratch me, some would pinch me, some would push me. Some would carry me, some would crush me, and some would rock me.

A New Voice

I am sitting on my bench tapping my good luck song with my shoes when I hear the bells of an ice cream truck. I feel the money in my pocket. I have

the dime and I also have a bigger one. I know I have
enough for an ice cream bar.

I walk out to the curb, touching the cages around
the trees. I wait until the bells sound near, and I
wave.

The ice cream man stops. He is near enough for
me to touch his cart. I hold out my money.

Now I feel him seeing me, but he does not take
my money.

"Here," I say, but he does not take the money from me.

"Guess what?" he says, and his voice is soft and kind as fur. "Every tenth kid wins a free ice cream bar, and you're the lucky one today."

I can feel him getting off his cart and going around to open the place where he keeps his ice cream bars. I can feel him putting one near my hand and I take it. I start back to my bench.

"You gonna be okay by yourself now?" the ice cream man calls, so I know he is seeing me.

I sit on the bench. I listen for the sound of his cart starting up and his bells ringing, but I can only hear the other sounds, the regular ones. Then I hear him walking over to my bench.

I am sorry, because I only want to feel the ice cream and see how long I can make it last. I do not want anyone to sit with me, but he is sitting with me now. I am afraid I will spill and he will see me.

He starts to talk, and his voice is soft as a sweater. His name is <u>Abram</u>. He tells me about the park.

Pronounced /ā′·brəm/.

My sister says the trees are in cages because if they weren't in cages they wouldn't stay in such a terrible park. They'd just get up and go somewhere pretty.

Abram says the trees are in cages to keep them safe so they can grow up to be big and tall. "Like

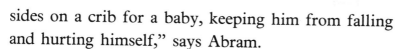

sides on a crib for a baby, keeping him from falling and hurting himself," says Abram.

My sister says the park is ugly and dirty.

Abram says there are a few little bits of paper, and a couple of cans and some bottles, but he says he can squint up his eyes and all those things lying around shine like flowers. Abram says you see what you want to see.

My sister says the park is just for poor folks, and that no one would ever come here if they had a chance to go anywhere else.

Abram says the park is just for lucky people, like him and me. He says the people who come to this park can see things inside themselves, instead of just what their eyes tell them.

After a while Abram goes away. He says he will come back and look for me tomorrow. I hear his ice cream bells go farther and farther away until I do not hear them anymore.

While I am waiting for my sister to come for me, I fall asleep on the bench. I have a good dream. I dream that Abram lifts me so I can touch the leaves of a tree. All of the leaves are songs, and they fall around me and cover me. I am warm and soft under the songs.

My sister shakes me awake. "You'll catch cold lying here," she says.

The next day while I am sitting on my bench, I hear the ice cream bells and I walk out to the curb, touching the cages of the trees as I go. Abram gives me an ice cream bar and we walk together back to the bench. I do not have to touch the cages because I am with him.

After I finish my ice cream bar, Abram gives me some paper clips so I can feel them in my pocket. He shows me how I can twist them to make little shapes.

After he leaves, I feel them. There are seven paper clips.

You may wish to discuss this passage after the students read the story.

That night I dream that someone is gathering in a big net everything in the world that makes a sound, and I am tumbled in the net with dogs and cars and whistles and busses. I try to get out of the net and my sister shakes me awake.

"Stop thrashing around," she says. "You're all tangled up in the blanket."

Something Special

The next day Abram brings me a balloon. I can feel it round and tight. It tugs at the string.

Abram says some balloons are filled with something special that makes them want to fly away, up to the sun, and this balloon is filled with that something special.

He says some people are filled with something special that makes them pull and tug, too, trying to get up and away from where they are.

240

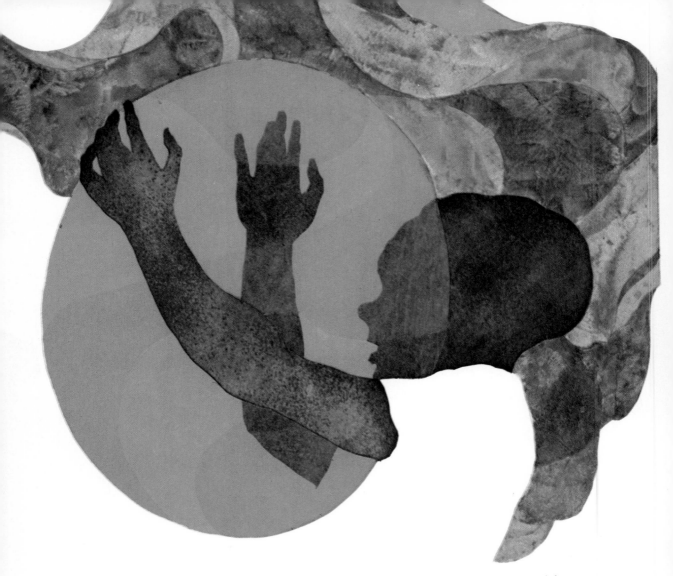

His voice is like a kitten curled on my shoulder.

He tells me my balloon is red, and then he tells me about colors.

He says colors are just like sounds. Some colors are loud, and some colors are soft, and some are big and some are little, and some are sharp and some are tender, just like sounds, just like music.

What is the best color, I wonder?

He says all colors are the same, as far as that goes. There isn't a best color, says Abram. There isn't a good color or a bad color.

Colors are just on the outside. They aren't important at all. They're just covers for things, like a blanket.

Color doesn't mean a thing, says Abram.

When my sister comes, she asks me where I got my balloon. I tell her about my friend. I hold on to the string of my balloon while we walk.

When we get home, I tie the string of my balloon to my chair.

I have a bad dream in the night. I dream that my ears are sucking in every sound in the world, so many sounds I cannot breathe. I am choking with the sounds that are pulled into me and I have to keep coughing the sounds away as they come in or I will smother.

"Here's some stuff for your cold," says my sister.

When I am awake again, I cannot tell if it is morning. I hear noises but they are not the morning noises. My sister has her quiet voice, and I do not hear the little hard sounds of her heels making holes in the morning.

She is wearing slippers. She tells my mother she is not going to go to study today.

There is no hurry about today. I reach for my balloon. The string lies on the chair, and I find the balloon on the floor, small and soft and limp. It does not float. It lies in my hand, tired and sad.

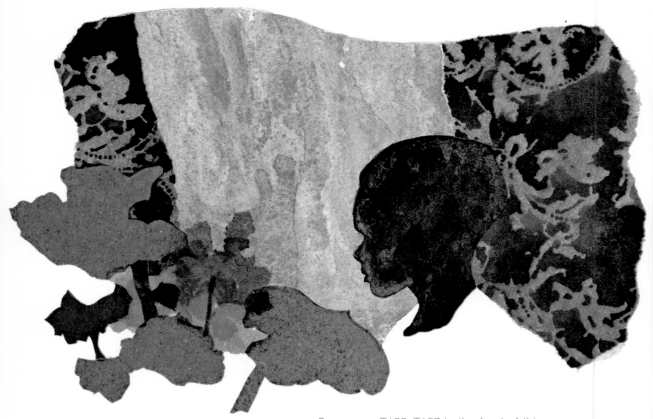

See pages T155–T157 in the front of this
book for suggested postreading strategies.

I lie there and listen to the sound of slippers on
the kitchen floor.

I tap my good luck song against the wall over and
over, but I hear the rain and know I will not go to
the park today.

Tomorrow it will be a nice day. Tomorrow my
sister will feel better, and I will go to the park and
find Abram. He will make my balloon as good as
new.

Now I walk over to the window and lean my
head against it. The rain taps its song to me against
the glass, and I tap back.

Questions

1. In this story, whose voice was like scissors cutting? Whose voice was like a kitten? Whose voice was like a pillow?

2. Abram said that you can see what you want to see. What did he mean?

3. What do you think happened to the boy on the day after the story ended?

4. The pictures do not show exactly how the boy's home looked, or how the park looked, or how the balloon looked. Why? How has the artist helped you feel as the boy felt by making the pictures as they are?

5. The boy in the story imagined that different sounds might scratch, pinch, push, crush, or rock him. He did not say what might cause each sound. For example, a tree branch *scratching* a moving car might cause a certain sound. Describe what you think might cause sounds that would pinch, push, crush, or rock.

1. **Literal/Details** sister (page 233); Abram (page 242); mother (page 231)

2. **Interpretive/Character Traits (Inferred)** that you could see either beauty or ugliness in something, depending on your attitude toward it (page 239)

3. **Critical/Evaluation** Accept any answer that the student reasonably supports.

4. **Critical/Appreciation** the pictures attempt to show how things "felt" to him

5. **Interpretive/Details (Inferred)** Possible responses: A pinching sound might be made by a tight-fitting door as it is being closed; a pushing sound, by a bus as it speeds by; a crushing sound, by bottles and cans being dumped into a trash barrel; a rocking sound, by water lapping against the side of a boat.

Activity Draw a Picture of the Park

Draw a picture of the park as Abram described it. Add things that you think Abram might see in the park, but that he did not talk about.

See pages T157–T158 in the front of this book for a suggested teaching plan for this selection.

CONNECTIONS

The Turkey or the Eagle?

I'm a true native of America.

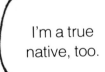

I'm a true native, too.

When the United States first declared itself a free country, its leaders felt that the new nation needed a symbol. The leaders wanted a symbol that would stand for the ideals that their new country was fighting for. From July 1776 until June 1782, many ideas were suggested.

One idea was the Greek hero Hercules, who is thought to be very strong and brave. Another idea was Moses, who is said to have led the people of Israel out of Egypt and into the Promised Land. A third idea was Liberty and Justice drawn as strong women overcoming the English king, George.

The United States Congress did not like any of these ideas. Then, in 1782, a Philadelphian named William Barton drew a picture that showed a golden eagle as the symbol of the new country. Secretary of Congress Charles Thompson changed the golden eagle to the American bald eagle.

After making a few more changes to Mr. Barton's design, Secretary Thompson presented the design to Congress. Congress liked it. On June 20, 1782, the American bald eagle became the official symbol of the new United States of America.

Right away, many people disagreed with the choice of the bald eagle. These people thought that

246

Illustrated by Ed Parker

the American wild turkey would have been a more fitting choice. The argument between these two groups has continued to this very day. Read why each side believes its choice to be the right one. Then decide for yourself.

Wild Turkey

People who wanted the wild turkey pointed out that it was a true American. The bird had always been admired by the Indians. When colonists came to the eastern shores, the wild turkey quickly became a favorite. The colonists thought that it was one of the most beautiful birds in the New World. The wild turkey's bronze-green feathers were prized as decorations for the colonists' hats or blankets.

People also thought that the wild turkey was a proud bird. Its great size and weight seemed to give it a stately appearance. A full-grown wild turkey weighs between ten and thirty pounds. It is four feet long from the tip of its beak to its tail feathers and stands three feet tall. The bird's broad wings can open to a length of five feet from one wing tip to the other.

Wild turkeys are also known for their swiftness and sharp senses. Wild turkeys do not fly very often, but they *do* run—up to 20 miles an hour. They also have very sharp eyesight and hearing. Hunters say that a wild turkey can easily lead them into wild forest country and then get away.

Ben Franklin summed up the argument for the wild turkey by pointing out that it was not only a handsome and useful bird, but also a "respectable" one. The wild turkey gathers its own food supply of small nuts, seeds, and insects. The bald eagle has been known to take prey caught by another bird.

Bald Eagle

Many people agreed with the choice of the bald eagle as the symbol of the United States. They said that it, too, was a true American, for the bald eagle can be found only in North America. With its shining white head feathers and its deep brown wings, many people believe it to be a very handsome bird.

An American bald eagle stands three feet tall from beak tip to *talons,* or claws. Those same talons and hooked beak, along with the bird's large pale eyes, make the American bald eagle look fierce and brave. With outspread wings, the American bald eagle measures seven feet long and seems to fly effortlessly. Many people say that the bald eagle flies so high that it disappears from sight.

Those people who favor the eagle point out that it feeds mostly on fish and other small animals. They say that the eagle takes prey from other birds only when the food supplies are short. President Kennedy said this about the bald eagle, "The fierce beauty and proud independence of this great bird aptly symbolize the strength and freedom of America."

See page T158 in the front of this book for suggested postreading strategies.

Questions

1. If you were voting for our national symbol, which would you choose, the turkey or the eagle? Why?

2. If you were choosing another animal to represent the United States, which animal would you choose? Why?

1. Critical / Evaluation Accept any answer that the student reasonably supports.

2. Critical / Evaluation Accept any answer that the student reasonably supports.

Activities

1. **Make a Poster**

   Design and draw a poster to support your candidate for the symbol of the United States. Your poster should contain a picture of your animal and a *slogan,* or catchy phrase, that will make people want to support your choice.

2. **Write a Summary**

   Write a one-paragraph summary of your argument for the bald eagle or the wild turkey. The summary should state the main reasons for your choice. Try to give at least three reasons in your paragraph.

See pages T158–T161 in the front of this book for a suggested teaching plan for this selection.

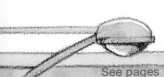

Mexicali /mĕk′•sĭ•kăl′•ē/ is the capital of Baja /bä′•hä/ California, Mexico, near the United States-Mexico border.

Mexicali Soup

A story by Kathryn Hitte and William D. Hayes
Illustrated by Bill and Judy Anderson   **Reading Level**   Average

Juanita /wä•nē′•tä/.

All the way across town Mama sang to herself—to herself and the little one, little Juanita. Here on the streets of the great fine city, she sang an old tune from the old home in the mountains. And she thought of what she would buy in the markets.

Only the best of everything. Potatoes and peppers—the best! Tomatoes and onions—the best! The best garlic. The best celery. And then, cooked all together, ah! The best soup in the world! Mama's Special Mexicali Soup. The soup that always made everyone say, "Mama makes the best soup in the world."

Sí is the Spanish word for *yes.*

"Ah, *sí!*" Mama thought with a smile. "Yes! Our supper tonight will be a very special supper for my Rosie and Antonio and Juan and Manuel and Maria, and for the little one—and for Papa, too. A very special supper of my Mexicali Soup."

Antonio /än•tōn′•yō; *Juan* /wän/; *Manuel* /män•wel′/.

"Mama! Yoo-hoo, Mama!"

There was the fine new school building where Juan and Manuel and Maria went to school, and there was Maria with her new city friend, waving and calling.

"Wait a minute, Mama!" Maria came running to put her schoolbooks in the stroller with Juanita. "Mama, may I play a while at Marjorie's house? Please?"

"Very well," Mama said. "A while. But do not be late for supper, Maria. I am making my special soup tonight."

"Mmmm-mmm, Mexicali Soup!" Maria said. Then she looked thoughtful. Then she frowned. "But—Mama?"

"Yes, Maria?"

"Mama, there are such a lot of potatoes in your Mexicali Soup."

"Of course," Mama said, smiling.

"Marjorie doesn't eat potatoes. Her mother doesn't eat them. Her sister doesn't eat them. Potatoes are too fattening, Mama. They are too fattening for many people in the city. I think we should do what others do here. We are no longer in the mountains of the West, Mama, where everyone eats potatoes. We are in the city now. So would you—Mama, would you please leave out the potatoes?"

"No potatoes," Mama said thoughtfully. She looked at Maria's <u>anxious</u> face. She <u>shrugged</u>. "Well, there are plenty of good things in the Mexicali Soup without potatoes. I will add more of everything else. It will still make good soup."

Anxious means *worried.*

Shrugged (line 25) means *raised the shoulders.*

Maria kissed Mama's cheek. "Of course it will, Mama. You make the best soup in the world."

Mama went on with Juanita to the markets, to the street of little markets, thinking aloud as she went. "Tomatoes, onions, celery. Red peppers, chili peppers, good and hot. And garlic. But no potatoes."

Santini /san·tē′·nē/.

Vierra /vâr′·rä/.

Mama went to Mr. Santini's little market for the best tomatoes and celery. She went to Mr. Vierra's little market for the best onions and garlic. "And the peppers," she said to Juanita. "We will buy the peppers from Antonio. Our own Antonio, at the market of Mr. Fernandez. Here is the place. Ah! What beautiful peppers!"

Fernandez /fâr·nän′·dās/.

Antonio came hurrying out of the store to the little stand on the sidewalk. "Let me help you, Mama! I hope you want something very good for our supper tonight. I get very hungry working here," Antonio said.

"Ah, *sí!*" Mama said. "Yes, Antonio. For tonight—something special!" She reached for the hot red peppers strung above her head. "Mexicali Soup."

"Hey! That's great," Antonio exclaimed. Then he looked thoughtful. Then he frowned. "But—Mama—"

"Yes?" Mama said, putting some peppers on the scale.

"Well—Mama, you use a lot of hot peppers in your soup."

"Of course," Mama said, smiling.

"A lot," Antonio repeated. "Too many, Mama. People here don't do that. They don't cook that way. They don't eat the way we did in the mountains of the West. I know, Mama. I have worked here for weeks now, after school and Saturdays. And in all that time, Mama, I have not sold as many hot peppers to other ladies as you use in a week."

Mamacita
/mä·mä·sē′·tä/ is a
Spanish word for
mother.

"*Mamacita*," Antonio said. "Please don't put hot peppers in the soup."

"No peppers," Mama said thoughtfully. She looked at Antonio's anxious face. "Well—" Mama shrugged. "There are plenty of good things in the soup without peppers. I will add more of something else. It will still make good soup."

Antonio took the peppers out of the scale and put them back on the stand. "Of course it will, Mama." He kissed her cheek. "Everyone knows you make the best soup in the world."

Mama went on with Juanita toward home. "Tomatoes, onions, garlic, celery," she said to herself. "Yes. I can still make a good soup with those." She hummed softly to herself as she crossed a

street blocked off from traffic, a street that was only for play.

"Hey, Mama! *Mamacita*!"

Juan and Manuel left the game of stickball in the play street. They raced each other to the spot where Mama stood.

"Oh, boy! Food!" said Juan when he saw the bags in the stroller. He opened one of the bags. "Tomatoes and celery—I know what that means."

"Me, too," said Manuel. He peeked into the other bag. "Onions and garlic. Mexicali Soup! Right, Mama?" Manuel rubbed his stomach and grinned. Then he looked thoughtful. Then he frowned. "But, Mama—listen, Mama."

"I am listening," Mama said.

"Well, I think we use an awful lot of onions," Manuel said. "They don't use so many onions in the lunchroom at school, or at the Boy's Club picnics. You know, Mama, they have different ways of doing things here, different from the ways of our town on the side of the mountain. I think we should try new ways. I think we shouldn't use so many onions. *Mamacita*, please make the Mexicali Soup without onions."

"Manuel is right!" Juan said. "My teacher said only today there is nothing that cannot be changed, and there is nothing so good that it cannot be made better, if we will only try. I think there may be better ways of making soup than our old way. Make the soup tonight without tomatoes, Mama!"

"No tomatoes?" Mama said. "And no onions? In Mexicali Soup?" Mama looked at the anxious faces of Juan and Manuel. Then she shrugged. She closed the two bags of groceries carefully. She pushed the stroller away from the play street. She shrugged again.

Voices came after her. Juan's voice said, "We will be hungry for your soup tonight, Mama!" Manuel's voice called, "*Mamacita*! You make the best soup in the world!"

In the big kitchen at home, Mama put the
groceries on the table by the stove. She hummed
a little soft tune that only Mama could hear. She
stood looking at the groceries. No potatoes. No
peppers. Tomatoes—Mama pushed the tomatoes
aside. Onions—she pushed the onions aside.

Mama sat down and looked at what was left.

The front door clicked open and shut. Rosie
came into the kitchen. <u>Rosita</u>, the young lady of
the family.

Rosita /rō·sē′·tä/.

"Hi, Mama. Oh, Mama—I hope I'm in time! I heard you were making—" Rosie stopped to catch her breath. She frowned at the groceries on the table. "All the way home I heard it. The boys and Maria—they all told me—and Mama! I want to ask you—please! No garlic."

Mama stopped humming.

Rosie turned up her nose and spread out her hands. "No garlic. Please. Listen, Mama. Last night, when my friend took me to dinner, I had such a fine soup! Delicious! The place was so elegant, Mama—so refined. So expensive. And no garlic at all in the soup!"

Rosie bent over and kissed Mama's cheek. "Just leave out the garlic, *Mamacita*. You make the best soup in the world."

Elegant and *refined* mean the same as *tasteful*.

A deep voice and many other voices called all at once, and the front door shut with a bang. "Mama! We are home, Mama!" Then all of them, Juan and Manuel and Antonio, with Maria pulling Papa by the hand—all of them came to stand in the kitchen doorway.

Papa reached for the baby, the little Juanita, and swung her onto his shoulders. "I have heard of something special," Papa said. "I have heard we are having Mexicali Soup tonight."

Mama said nothing. But Mama's eyes <u>flashed fire</u>. She waited.

"Your soup, Mama—" Papa said. "It is simply the best soup in the world!"

Discuss the meaning of the phrase *flashed fire.*

261

"Ah, *sí!* But you want me to leave out something?" Mama's voice rose high. "The celery,
perhaps? You want me to make my Mexicali Soup
without the celery?"

Papa raised his eyebrows. "Celery?" Papa
opened his hands wide and shrugged. "What is
celery? It is a little nothing! Put it in or leave it out,
Mamacita—it does not matter. The soup will be
just as—"

"Enough!" Mama said. "Out of my kitchen—all
of you!" Mama waved her arms wide in the air.
The fire in Mama's eyes flashed again. "I am
busy! I am busy getting your supper. I will call
you. Go."

"But, Mama," said Rosie, "we always help you with—"

"No!" Mama said. "Out!"

Rosie and Juan and Manuel, Antonio and Maria, and Papa with the baby, tiptoed away to the living room.

There was only silence coming from the kitchen. Then, the sound of a quiet humming. Soon the humming mixed with the clatter of plates and spoons, the good sounds of the table being set for supper.

The humming turned into singing. Mama was singing a happy song from the old home in the mountains. Juan and Manuel, Antonio and Maria, Rosie and Papa, looked at one another and smiled and nodded. Mama was singing.

Then from the kitchen Mama's voice called to them. "The soup is finished. Your supper is ready. Come and eat now."

"Ah! That is what I like to hear," said Papa, jumping up with Juanita. "The soup is ready before I have even begun to smell it cooking."

"Mmm-mmm!" said Juan and Manuel, racing for the big kitchen table.

"Mmm-mmm!" said Maria and Antonio and Rosie when they saw the steaming bowls on the table. "Mama makes the best soup in the world."

But what was the matter?

"This doesn't look like Mexicali Soup," said Maria, staring at the bowl before her.

"It doesn't smell like Mexicali Soup," said Antonio, sniffing the steam that rose from his bowl.

"It doesn't taste like Mexicali Soup," said Juan and Manuel, sipping a sip from their spoons.

"This is not Mexicali Soup," said Rosie, setting her spoon down hard with a clang. "This is nothing but hot water!"

Everyone looked at Mama.

Mama smiled and hummed the old tune from the mountains.

"You have forgotten to bring the soup, *Mamacita*?" suggested Papa.

"No," Mama said, still smiling. "The soup is in your bowls. And it is just what you wanted. I made the soup the way my family asked me to make it.

"I left out the potatoes that Maria does not want. I left out the peppers that Antonio does not want. I left out the tomatoes that Juan does not want. I left out the onions that Manuel does not want. For Rosita, I left out the garlic. And for Papa, I left out the celery, the little nothing that does not matter.

"The *new* Mexicali Soup! It is so simple! So quick! So easy to make," Mama said. "You just leave everything out of it."

See pages T159–T161 in the front of this book for suggested postreading strategies.

Questions

1. Literal / Details
old recipe: potatoes, chili peppers, tomatoes, onions, garlic, celery (page 250); new recipe: hot water (page 264)
2. Inference / Conclusion Possible responses: a. "Just because we came to the city doesn't mean that they can put on airs and try to imitate people here!: b. "Now we'll see what they think of their new soup!"
3. Critical / Evaluation Accept any answer that the student reasonably supports.
4. Literal / Details a. anxious (page 256); b. refined, elegant (page 260)

1. What are the two recipes for Mama's Special Mexicali Soup? Write the old recipe and the new recipe.

2. Tell what Mama was thinking when:
   a. Mama's eyes flashed fire.
   b. Mama smiled and hummed the old tune from the mountains.

3. What lesson do you think the family learned from Mama's new Mexicali Soup? Do you think it is a useful lesson? Tell why or why not.

4. Complete the sentences with words from the story.
   a. When Antonio was worried, his face was _____ .
   b. When Rosita told about an expensive place to eat, she said it was _____ and _____ .

Activity   Write a Cast of Characters

Cast of
Characters

Mama
Juanita

If you were making *Mexicali Soup* into a play, you would need a *cast of characters,* which is a list of all the actors in the play. Finish the cast of characters started here. List all the characters in the order in which they appear in the story.

BOOKSHELF

Reading Level Challenging

The Great Bamboozlement by Jane Flory.
Houghton Mifflin, 1982. Set in pioneer days,
a family trades their Pennsylvania farm for a
floating store and sets off down the Mononga-
hela River only to find themselves in the
middle of trouble.

Reading Level Average

A Dog on Barkham Street by Mary Stolz. Harper
& Row, 1960. Edward has two problems—not
having a dog and being hounded by Martin,
the bully of Barkham Street. Martin's side of
the story is told in another book, *The Bully of
Barkham Street.*

Reading Level Average

Do You Have the Time, Lydia? by Evaline Ness.
E. P. Dutton, 1971. Lydia starts many projects,
but she never finishes what she begins. When
her brother asks her to build a box car with
him, Lydia never seems to have the time to
help.

Reading Level Average

Sadako and the Thousand Paper Cranes by
Eleanor Coerr. G. P. Putnam's, 1977. While in
a hospital, Sadako begins to fold paper
cranes. She hopes her wish for health will be
granted if she can fold a thousand cranes.

Reading Level Easy

Three Wishes by Lucille Clifton. Viking Press,
1976. When Zenobia finds a penny with her
birth year on it, her friend Victor tells her she
will be granted three wishes.

See pages T162–T163 in the front of this book for a suggested teaching plan.

5 What a Character!

See pages T163–T166 in the front of this
book for a suggested teaching plan for this
selection.

Reading Level Average

Spunky Ramona

From the story *Ramona the Brave* by Beverly Cleary
Illustrated by Jennie Williams

*Ramona Geraldine Quimby is convinced nobody
loves her. Even the family cat, Picky-picky, keeps away
from her. Ramona likes being a little different though.
She signs her last name with a special Q: ⌇, and
she can draw better than anyone in her first grade
class. Then one day a girl named Susan copies an owl
Ramona is drawing, and the teacher, Mrs. Griggs,
picks up Susan's owl to praise. Terribly angry, Ramona
scrunches up Susan's owl. Later she has to apologize
in front of the class. Ramona begins to hate school. If
only her older sister Beezus felt the same way!*

One afternoon Mrs. Griggs handed each member of
Room One a long sealed envelope. "These are your
progress reports for you to take home to your parents,"
she said.

Ramona made up her mind then and there that she
was not going to show any progress report to her
mother and father if she could get out of it. As soon as

270

she reached home, she hid her envelope at the bottom
of a drawer under her summer playclothes. Then she
got out paper and crayons and went to work on the
kitchen table. On each sheet of paper she drew in
black crayon a careful outline of an animal: a mouse
on one sheet, a bear on another, a turtle on a third.
Ramona loved to crayon and crayoning made her
troubles fade away. When she had filled ten pages with
outlines of animals, she found her father's stapler and
fastened the paper together to make a book. Ramona

could make an amazing number of things with paper, crayons, staples, and Scotch tape. Bee's wings to wear on her wrists, a crown to wear on her head, a paper catcher's mask to cover her face.

"What are you making?" asked her mother.

"A coloring book," said Ramona. "You won't buy me one."

"That's because the art teacher who talked to the P.T.A. said coloring books were not creative. She said children needed to be free and creative and draw their own pictures."

"I am," said Ramona. "I am drawing a coloring book. Howie has a coloring book, and I want one too."

"I guess Howie's mother missed that meeting." Mrs. Quimby picked up Ramona's coloring book and studied it. "Why, Ramona," she said, sounding pleased, "you must take after your father. You draw unusually well for a girl your age."

"I know." Ramona was not bragging. She was being honest. She knew her drawing was better than most of the baby work done in Room One. So was her printing. She went to work coloring her turtle green, her mouse brown. Filling in outlines was not very interesting, but it was <u>soothing</u>. Ramona was so busy that by dinnertime she had forgotten her hidden progress report.

Soothing means *calming.*

Ramona forgot until Beezus laid her long white envelope on the table after the dessert of canned peaches and store macaroons. "Mr. Cardoza gave us our progress reports," she announced.

Mr. Quimby tore open the envelope and pulled out the yellow sheet of paper. "M-m-m. Very good, Beezus. I'm proud of you."

"What did he say?" Beezus asked. Ramona could tell that Beezus was eager to have the family hear the nice things Mr. Cardoza had to say about her.

"He said, 'Beatrice has shown marked improvement in math. She is willing and a <u>conscientious</u> pupil, who gets along well with her <u>peers</u>. She is a pleasure to have in the classroom.'"

Beezus is *conscientious* because she always does her work carefully.

Peers are people who are the same age.

"May I please be excused?" asked Ramona and did not wait for an answer.

"Just a minute, young lady," said Mr. Quimby.

"Yes, what about your progress report?" asked Mrs. Quimby.

"Oh . . . that old thing," said Ramona.

"Yes, that old thing." Mr. Quimby looked amused, which annoyed Ramona. "Bring it here," he said.

Ramona faced her father. "I don't want to."

Mr. Quimby was silent. The whole family was silent, waiting. Even Picky-picky, who had been washing his face, paused, one paw in the air, and waited. Ramona turned and walked slowly to her room and slowly returned with the envelope. <u>Scowling</u>, she thrust it at her father who tore it open.

To *scowl* is to frown angrily.

"Does Beezus have to hear?" she asked.

"Beezus, you may be excused," said Mrs. Quimby. "Run along and do your homework."

Ramona knew that Beezus was in no hurry to run along and do her homework. Beezus was going to listen, that's what Beezus was going to do. Ramona scowled more ferociously as her father pulled out the sheet of yellow paper.

"If you don't look out, your face might freeze that way," said Mr. Quimby, which did not help. He studied the yellow paper and frowned. He handed it to Mrs. Quimby, who read it and frowned.

"Well," said Ramona, unable to stand the suspense, "what does it say?" She would have grabbed it and tried to read it herself, but she knew it was written in cursive.

Mrs. Quimby read, "'Ramona's <u>letter formation</u> is excellent, and she is developing good <u>word-attacking skills</u>.'"

Letter formation is the way you shape your letters.

When you try to sound out words, you are using word-attacking skills.

Ramona relaxed. This did not sound so bad, even though she had never thought of reading as attacking words. She rather liked the idea.

Mrs. Quimby read on. "'She is learning her numbers readily.'"

That mitten counting, thought Ramona with <u>scorn</u>.

"'However, Ramona sometimes shows more interest in the seatwork of others than in her own. She needs to learn to keep her hands to herself. She also needs to work on self-control in the classroom.'"

Scorn is disrespect. Ramona thought that her counting exercises were too simple.

"I do not!" Ramona was angry at the unfairness of her teacher's report. What did Mrs. Griggs think she had been working on? She hardly ever raised her hand anymore, and she never spoke out the way she used to. And she wasn't really interested in Davy's seatwork. She was trying to help him because he was having such a hard time.

"Now, Ramona." Mrs. Quimby's voice was gentle. "You must try to grow up."

Ramona raised her voice. "What do you think I'm doing?"

"You don't have to be so noisy about it," said Mr. Quimby.

Of course, Beezus had to come butting in to see what all the fuss was about. "What did Mrs. Griggs say?" she wanted to know, and it was easy to see she knew that what Mr. Cardoza had said was better.

"You mind your own business," said Ramona.

"Ramona, don't talk that way." Mr. Quimby's voice was mild.

"I will *too* talk that way," said Ramona. "I'll talk any way I want!"

"Ramona!" Mr. Quimby's voice held a warning.

To be *defiant* is to boldly resist authority or refuse to obey it.

Ramona was <u>defiant</u>. "Well, I will!" Nothing could possibly get any worse. She might as well say anything she pleased.

"Now see here, young lady—" began Mr. Quimby.

Ramona had had enough. She had been miserable the whole first grade, and she no longer cared what happened. She wanted to do something bad. She wanted to do something terrible that would shock her whole family, something that would make them sit up and take notice. "I'm going to say a bad word!" she shouted with a stamp of her foot.

That silenced her family. Picky-picky stopped washing and left the room. Mr. Quimby looked surprised and—how could he be so disloyal?—a little amused. This made Ramona even angrier. Beezus looked interested and curious. After a moment Mrs. Quimby said quietly, "Go ahead, Ramona, and say the bad word if it will make you feel any better."

Ramona clenched her fists and took a deep breath. "Guts!" she yelled. "*Guts! Guts! Guts!*" There. That should show them.

Ramona's father seemed *disloyal* because he did not take her side.

277

Unfortunately, Ramona's family was not shocked and horrified as Ramona had expected. They laughed. All three of them laughed. They tried to hide it, but they laughed.

"It isn't funny!" shouted Ramona. "Don't you dare laugh at me!" Bursting into tears, she threw herself face down on the couch. She kicked and she pounded the cushions with her fists. Everyone was against her. Nobody liked her. Even the cat did not like her. The room was silent, and Ramona had the satisfaction of knowing she had stopped their laughing. She heard responsible old Beezus go to her room to do her responsible old homework. Her parents continued to sit in silence, but Ramona was past caring what anyone did. She cried harder than she ever had cried in her life. She cried until she was limp and exhausted.

Then Ramona felt her mother's hand on her back. "Ramona," she said gently, "what are we going to do with you?"

With red eyes, a swollen face, and a streaming nose, Ramona sat up and <u>glared</u> at her mother. "Love me!" Her voice was fierce with hurt. Shocked at her own words, she buried her face in the pillow. She had no tears left.

"Dear heart," said Mrs. Quimby. "We *do* love you."

Ramona sat up and faced her mother, who looked tired, as if she had been through many scenes with Ramona and knew many more lay ahead. "You do

Glared means *stared angrily.*

278

not. You love Beezus." There. She had said it right out loud. For years she had wanted to tell her parents how she felt.

Mr. Quimby wiped Ramona's nose on a Kleenex, which he then handed to her. She clenched it in her fist and <u>glowered</u> at her parents.

"Of course we love Beezus," said Mrs. Quimby. "We love you both."

"You love her more," said Ramona. "A whole lot more." She felt better for having said the words, getting them off her chest, as grown-ups would say.

"Love isn't like a cup of sugar that gets used up," said Mrs. Quimby. "There is enough to go around. Loving Beezus doesn't mean we don't have enough love left for you."

Glowered is another way to say *glared.*

"You don't laugh at Beezus all the time," said Ramona.

"They used to," said Beezus, who was unable to stay away from this family discussion. "They always laughed at the funny things I did, and it used to make me mad."

Ramona sniffed and waited for Beezus to continue.

Beezus was serious. "Like the time when I was about your age and thought frankincense and myrrh were something the three Wise Men were bringing to the baby Jesus to put on his rash like that stuff Mom used on you when you were a baby. Mom and Dad laughed, and Mom told all her friends, and they laughed too."

"Oh, dear," said Mrs. Quimby. "I had no idea I upset you that much."

Toilet water is a kind of mild perfume.

"Well, you did," said Beezus, still grumpy over the memory. "And there was the time I thought toilet water was water out of the toilet. You practically had hysterics."

Hysterics are a fit of uncontrollable laughing or crying.

"Now you're exaggerating," said Mrs. Quimby.

Comforted by this unexpected support from her sister, Ramona scrubbed her face with her soggy Kleenex. "Mama, if you really do love me, why do I have to go to school?" At the same time she wondered how she could find out what frankincense and myrrh were without letting anyone know of her ignorance. She had always thought in a vague sort of way that they were something expensive like perfume done up in an extra-fancy Christmas wrapping.

"Ramona, everyone has to go to school," Mrs. Quimby answered. "Loving you has nothing to do with it."

"Then why can't I be in the other first grade, the one in Room Two?" Ramona asked. "Mrs. Griggs doesn't like me."

"Of course she likes you," contradicted Mrs. Quimby.

"No, she doesn't," said Ramona. "If she liked me, she wouldn't make me tell Susan in front of the whole class that I was sorry I scrunched her owl, and she would ask me to lead the Pledge Allegiance. And she wouldn't say bad things about me on my progress report."

Scrunched means *crushed* or *crunched*. The word sounds like something is being crushed.

"I told you Mrs. Griggs was great on apologies," Beezus reminded her family. "And she will get around to asking Ramona to lead the flag salute. She asks everybody."

"But Beezus, you got along with Mrs. Griggs when you had her," said Mrs. Quimby.

"I guess so," said Beezus. "She wasn't my favorite teacher, though."

"What was wrong with her?" asked Mrs. Quimby.

"There wasn't anything really wrong with her, I guess," answered Beezus. "She just wasn't very exciting is all. She wasn't mean or anything like that. We just seemed to go along doing our work, and that was it."

"Was she unfair?" asked Mrs. Quimby.

Beezus considered the question. "No, but I was the kind of child she liked. You know . . . neat and dependable."

"I bet you never wasted paste," said Ramona, who was not a paste waster herself. Too much paste was likely to spoil a piece of artwork.

"No," admitted Beezus. "I wasn't that type."

Ramona <u>persisted</u>. "*Why* can't I change to Room Two?"

Mr. Quimby took over. "Because Mrs. Griggs is teaching you to read and do arithmetic, and because the things she said about you are fair. You do need to learn self-control and to keep your hands to yourself. There are all kinds of teachers in the world just as there are all kinds of other people, and you must learn to get along with them. Maybe Mrs. Griggs doesn't understand how you feel, but you aren't always easy to understand. Did you ever think of that?"

"Please, Daddy," begged Ramona. "Please don't make me go back to Room One."

"Buck up, Ramona," said Mr. Quimby. "Show us your spunk."

Ramona felt too exhausted to show anyone her spunk, but for some reason her father's order made her feel better. If her mother had said, Poor baby, she would have felt like crying again. Mrs. Quimby led her from the room and, skipping her bath, helped her into bed. Before the light was turned out, Ramona noticed that *Wild Animals of Africa* had been returned to her bookcase.

See pages T164–T166 in the front of this
book for suggested postreading strategies.

"Stay with me, Mama," <u>coaxed</u> Ramona, dreading
<u>solitude</u>, darkness, and the gorilla in the book. Mrs.
Quimby turned off the light and sat down on the bed.

"Mama?"

"Yes, Ramona?"

"Isn't *guts* a bad word?"

Mrs. Quimby thought for a moment. "I wouldn't say
it's exactly a bad word. It isn't the nicest word in the
world, but there are much worse words. Now go to
sleep."

Ramona wondered what could be worse than guts.

Coaxed means *tried to
persuade.*

Ramona is *dreading
solitude,* or is afraid
of being alone.

283

Questions

1. Tell two things that made Ramona unhappy.

2. List at least two things Ramona did to try to make herself feel better.

3. Why did Ramona feel better at the end of the story?

4. These words describe Ramona: **creative, defiant, conscientious, miserable.** Match a word with the sentence that gives its meaning.
   a. Ramona always worked carefully on her drawings.
   b. Ramona refused to obey her father.
   c. After supper, Ramona felt very unhappy.
   d. Ramona made up a new way to sign her name.

5. The title of this story, "Spunky Ramona," tells that Ramona is fearless and brave. What was one thing Ramona did because she was spunky?

6. Do you think that Ramona's progress report was fair? Why or why not?

Activity   Tell About a Terrible, Funny Time

"It seems funny now, but it didn't seem funny when it happened." Suppose *you* said that several years from now. Write or draw what you might be talking about.

About BEVERLY CLEARY

Though known for her humorous stories, Beverly Cleary says, "I don't try to be funny. Because of some lucky quirk . . . my stories turn out to be humorous."

Beverly Cleary has written several books about Ramona Quimby and her family. She has also written a series of books about Henry Huggins. Henry, Ramona, and their friends all live in the same imaginary neighborhood. It is much the same as the neighborhood in which Beverly Cleary grew up. The characters in her stories are similar to children she knew, and ideas for her stories often come from events in her own life.

Beverly Cleary didn't enjoy reading until she was eight. Then she went to the library often. After college, she became a librarian. Later, as an author, she wrote the books she had longed to read as a child.

More Books by Beverly Cleary

Ramona Quimby, Age 8   (Morrow, 1981)

Runaway Ralph   (Morrow, 1970)

Ralph S. Mouse   (Morrow, 1982)

Dear Mr. Henshaw   (Morrow, 1983)

My Sister Jane

A poem by Ted Hughes

See pages T166–T167 in the front of this book for a suggested teaching plan for this selection.

And I say nothing—no, not a word
About our Jane. Haven't you heard?
She's a bird, a bird, a bird, a bird.
Oh it never would do to let folks know
My sister's nothing but a great big crow.

Each day (we daren't send her to school)
She pulls on stockings of thick blue wool
To make her pin crow legs look right,
Then fits a wig of curls on tight,
And dark spectacles—a huge pair
To cover her very crowy stare.
Oh it never would do to let folks know
My sister's nothing but a great big crow.

When visitors come she sits upright
(With her wings and her tail tucked out of sight).
They think her queer but <u>extremely</u> polite.   *Extremely* means *very.*
Then when the visitors have gone
She whips out her wings and with her wig on
Whirls through the house at the height of your
    head—
Duck, duck, or she'll knock you dead.
Oh it never would do to let folks know
My sister's nothing but a great big crow.

286   Illustrated by Mila Lazarevich

At meals whatever she sees she'll stab it—
Because she's a crow and that's a crow habit.
My mother says, "Jane! Your manners! Please!"
Then she'll sit quietly on the cheese,
Or play the piano nicely by dancing on the keys—
Oh it never would do to let folks know
My sister's nothing but a great big crow.

CONNECTIONS

Folk Heroes of the United States

Back in the days when the United States was young, workers amused themselves by swapping tall tales about their favorite heroes. A *tall tale* is a story that may have a *little* bit of truth in it. Then the truth is s-t-r-e-t-c-h-e-d beyond belief to make a story that is just plain fun. Every region of the United States has its own tall tales and its own heroes. Here are some tall tales and the regions from which they came.

Illustrated by Betsy Day

THE NORTH: Tales of Paul Bunyan

Across the top of Minnesota, Wisconsin, and Michigan is a huge evergreen forest called the North Woods. Cutting down trees for lumber, or *logging,* is an important industry here. In the past, loggers cut down trees with axes and handsaws—a hard, dangerous job. Stories grew up about the great strength and daring of loggers, especially that greatest logger of them all—Paul Bunyan!

Paul Bunyan was the biggest, strongest, toughest logger who ever lived. At birth, Paul weighed 86 pounds. When he was full grown, he was taller than the tallest pine tree.

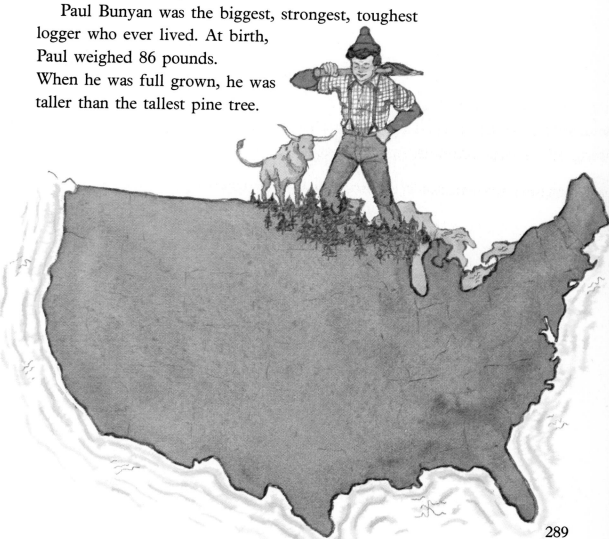

Paul began logging in Maine. He was so fast at cutting down trees that he soon ran out of woods in that state. So he hired a crew and headed west. Paul and his crew set up camp along the Onion River. Paul's crew, of course, was a *big* crew. It had many men, and the men were *big* (though not as big as Paul). Paul's camp was huge. The tables where the loggers ate were so long that the waiters wore roller skates when they served meals. Paul had to dig the Great Lakes so his men would have plenty of water to drink!

Paul didn't remain at the Onion River camp, however. After logging the North Woods, Paul turned to North Dakota. "Aha!" he thought. "A nice flat state—perfect for growing wheat!" In those days, however, North Dakota was covered with trees so tall that it took a week to see up to their tops. In no time at all, Paul Bunyan had cut down those trees and pounded their stumps right into the ground!

THE SOUTH: Tales of John Henry

While loggers in the North swapped tales about Paul Bunyan and his mighty axe, "steel-drivin' men" in the South boasted of John Henry and his mighty hammer. "Steel-drivin' men" were railroad workers who had the most dangerous job of all—blasting through mountains to make railroad tunnels. To do this job, they drove long steel rods deep into solid rock to make holes for dynamite. Those holes had to be about seven feet deep!

Some people say there really *was* a John Henry.
They say he was a "steel-drivin' man" of great size
and strength. John Henry worked for the Chesapeake
and Ohio Railroad in West Virginia during the
1870s. Through the years the tales that were told
about him grew taller and taller.

People in the South say that when John Henry
was born, lightning split the air. The earth shook,
and the Mississippi River ran upstream 1,000 miles.
John Henry weighed 44 pounds when he was born.
After his first meal, he went looking for work. He
got a job with the C&O Railroad, laying track and
blasting tunnels.

People say that John Henry died a hero's death. His crew had put him against a steam drill in a steel-driving race. John Henry won—but he died that night of a burst blood vessel.

THE EAST: Tales of Stormalong

In the late 1700s, New England's seaports were busy places. At about this time New England sailors began telling tales about a sailor named Alfred Bulltop Stormalong. Old Stormalong, or Stormy as he was called, was a daring and skillful sailor. It was

even said that he was born with ocean water flowing through his veins.

Like Paul Bunyan and John Henry, Old Stormalong was a huge man. Old Stormy was as tall as a whale standing on end. Only one ship was big enough for him. That was the *Courser*. The *Courser* was so big that it took a person 24 hours to make the trip from front to back on horseback. The ship's masts were so tall that they were hinged to let the sun and moon pass by.

One day, Stormalong and his crew were fishing in the Atlantic Ocean. The captain decided it was time to move on. He ordered them to pull up the anchor and set sail. The crew could not make the anchor move. Old Stormy jumped overboard to take a look. He found a giant squid holding the anchor in fifty of its slimy arms. The squid's other fifty arms grabbed the sea bottom. A huge fight took place. When the water cleared, the anchor was free. Stormalong had tied every one of the squid's hundred arms into a double knot.

THE WEST: Tales of Pecos Bill and Slue-Foot Sue

In the days of the Old West, cowhands drove cattle a long way to market. At night they would gather around the campfire and tell stories about Pecos Bill and his bride Slue-Foot Sue. Pecos Bill was raised by a coyote and taught by a grizzly bear.

See pages T168–T169 in the front of this book for suggested postreading strategies.

Pecos Bill went on to teach ranchers a thing or two. It was Pecos Bill who invented the lasso, cattle branding, the cattle roundup, and the rodeo. He was perhaps the most remarkable man who ever rode the range.

Slue-Foot Sue, Bill's bride, was remarkable, too. It was love at first sight when Bill saw Sue riding a catfish the size of a whale down the Rio Grande. Sue and Bill raised a large family. They even adopted a litter of coyote pups. People said the pups were so smart that two of them were elected to Congress!

294

Questions

1. Think about the tall-tale heroes of the North, South, East, and West. How are they alike? Give at least two examples.

2. Who is your favorite tall-tale hero? Why did you choose that hero?

Activities

1. **Retell a Story**

   Choose one of your favorite American folk songs. Write the story the song tells.

2. **Make a Bulletin Board**

   Choose a tall-tale hero from the stories here or from library books. Cut pictures from magazines, or draw your own, that show the region of your hero's "birth." With your classmates make a bulletin board of the regions of the United States and their tall-tale heroes.

1. Interpretive/Comparison Possible responses: They are all bigger, better, and smarter than an ordinary person and are able to do superhuman things. Examples: Bunyan—taller than a pine tree and able to cut down all the trees in Maine; Henry—weighed 44 pounds at birth and won a race against a steam drill; Stormalong—tall as a whale standing on end and wrestled a giant squid; Slue-Foot Sue—rode a catfish the size of a whale.
2. Critical/Evaluation Accept any answer that the student reasonably supports.

Four Fearsome Critters

Folklore collected by Alvin Schwartz

Illustrated by Ed Taber

See pages T170–T172 in the front of this book for a suggested teaching plan for this selection.

Reading Level Challenging

It is said that there are strange creatures
all around us—
    in the woods,
        in the mountains,
          in the lakes,
            everywhere.
Ranchers, woodcutters, hunters, and other people
see these creatures again and again.
Or so they say.
Here is what they tell of them.

hide-behind

When a hunter enters the deepest woods
and does not come back,
most people say the hunter got lost.
But some say the hunter was grabbed
by a hide-behind
that hid behind a tree.

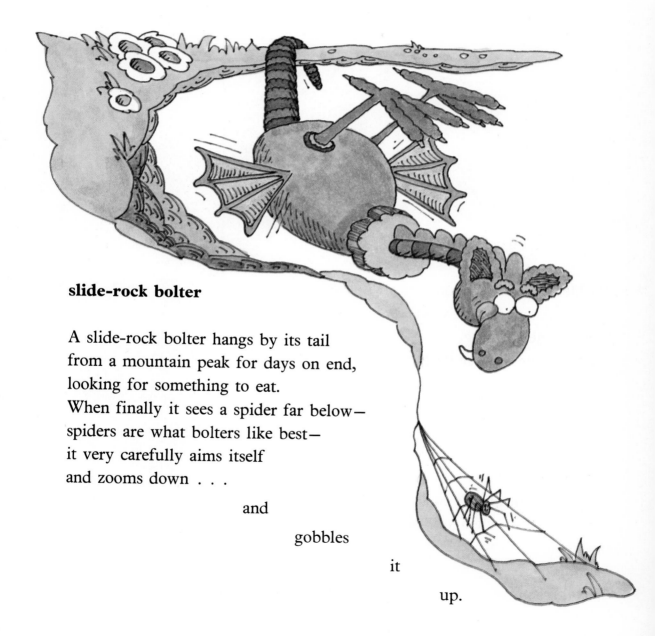

slide-rock bolter

A slide-rock bolter hangs by its tail
from a mountain peak for days on end,
looking for something to eat.
When finally it sees a spider far below—
spiders are what bolters like best—
it very carefully aims itself
and zooms down . . .

           and

                gobbles

                        it

                            up.

kickle snifters

Kickle snifters are about the size of your thumb.
They live inside men's beards.
But this gets boring,
and they are forever peeking out.
They also are forever laughing,
because beard hair tickles.

You are most likely to see kickle snifters
at your grandfather's house,
or your great-uncle's house.
You see them when you have eaten too much supper,
and you begin to feel sleepy,
and your eyes try to close,
and things don't look the way they usually do.

whing-whang

On nights when the moon
is a giant orange in the sky,
the whing-whang leaps about the beach
and with its tail writes
whing-whang, whing-whang, whing-whang
in the sand.
But when the moon goes down
and the sun comes up,
it rubs out what it has written
and disappears.

A Note from the Author

The creatures in this bestiary live only in our imaginations. Folklorists classify our folk animals as "fearsome critters," although most are funny, not fearsome. One folklorist has said that eighty-one different kinds of "critters" have been identified. But clearly there are more.

The next time you are in the woods or anywhere, look closely and listen carefully. You, too, may see a fearsome critter.

There Was an Old Man with a Beard

A <u>limerick</u> by Edward Lear

See pages T172–T174 in the front of this book for a suggested teaching plan for this selection.

There was an Old Man with a beard,

Who said, "It is just as I feared!—

    Two Owls and a Hen,

    Four larks and a <u>Wren</u>, A *wren* /ren/ is a small bird.

Have all built their nests in my beard."

Illustrated by Marie-Louise Gay

A Young Lady of Ealing

A limerick

There was a young lady of Ealing,
Who had a <u>peculiar</u> feeling
   That she was a fly,
   And wanted to try
To walk upside down on the ceiling.

Peculiar means *strange.*

Illustrated by Marie-Louise Gay

See pages T174—T178 in the front of this book for a suggested teaching plan for this selection.

Paddington Goes to the Hospital

A play by Michael Bond and Alfred Bradley

Illustrated by Tony Kenyon

Reading Level Challenging

Paddington, a small brown bear from Peru, is always willing to help people. Sometimes this gets him into trouble with the Browns, the kind people who have given him a home. More often, however, Paddington's problems are with the Browns' neighbor Mr. Curry. No matter what happens, if Mr. Curry is involved, Paddington is sure to get the worst of it—until now. For Mr. Curry is in the hospital pretending he hurt his leg, and Paddington finally has a chance to get even.

Characters		
Mrs. Brown	Nurse	Mr. Curry
Mrs. Bird	Mr. Heinz Pronounced /hīnz/.	
Paddington	Sir Archibald	

302

SCENE ONE

The Browns' *sitting room.* Mrs. Brown *is making up a basket of food when* Mrs. Bird *comes in.*

Mrs. Brown: If I see another bunch of grapes, I shall scream. That's the third this week. Not to mention four <u>pots</u> of jam, two dozen eggs, and a jar of <u>calves-foot jelly</u>.

Mrs. Bird: I thought Mr. Curry was supposed to be ill. He seems to have a very healthy appetite.

Pots are jars.

Calves-foot jelly is a gelatinous English delicacy made from meat and meant to be spread on bread. It is not sweet like other jellies.

Mrs. Brown: He says he hurt his leg in the launderette the other day. I don't know how long he'll be in hospital.

Mrs. Bird: If you ask me, Mr. Curry will be coming out of hospital <u>when it suits *him*</u> and not a minute before. He knows when he is on to a good thing. <u>Free board and lodging</u>.

Mrs. Brown: And everybody at his beck and call.

Mrs. Bird: He has a <u>relapse</u> every time the doctor says he is getting better. The ward nurse has given him some strong hints that they're short of beds, but he takes no notice. And I'm certainly not having him staying here.

(Paddington *comes in carrying a letter.*)

Paddington: There's a letter for you, Mrs. Brown. It looks like Mr. Curry's writing.

Mrs. Brown: Yes, I'm afraid you're right. (*She opens the envelope.*)

Mrs. Bird: What does he say?

Mrs. Brown (*Reading*): "Dear Mrs. Brown, My leg is still troubling me. Will you please send some more apples? I didn't like the last lot—they were too sour. Also another cherry cake. P.S. Two cherries were missing from the one you sent last week."

Paddington (*Guiltily*): Perhaps they were a bit loose?

Mrs. Bird (*With meaning*): Perhaps!

Mrs. Brown: "P.P.S. I would like them as soon as possible. Paddington could bring them round to the hospital. . . ." Do you mind taking this parcel to him, Paddington?

Paddington (*Cheerfully*): No. I don't think I've ever been to a hospital before. I wonder if it's like the Daredevil Doctor series on television?

Mrs. Bird: I shouldn't think so for one moment.

Mrs. Brown: There now. It's packed. And I've fixed the cherries *firmly* in the cake this time, so let's hope they don't fall out.

Mrs. Bird: I've packed you some sandwiches and a thermos flask of cocoa. But be careful. It's very hot.

Paddington: Thank you, Mrs. Bird. I won't be long. (*He puts on his hat as he goes out.*)

Mrs. Brown: I do hope we're doing the right thing, letting him go by himself.

Mrs. Bird: I shouldn't worry about that bear. He knows how to look after <u>number one</u>.

Here, Mrs. Bird is saying that Paddington can take care of himself, or *number one.*

Mrs. Brown: It wasn't Paddington I was thinking of. It's the hospital. . . .

SCENE TWO

A small room in the hospital. A Nurse *sits at the desk with a telephone. She is finishing a conversation.*

Nurse: Yes, Sir Archibald. Very good, Sir Archibald.

(*She replaces the phone as* Paddington *knocks at the door.*)

Nurse: Come in.

Paddington: Good morning.

Nurse: Good morning. Can I help you?

Paddington: I've come to see Mr. Curry.

Nurse (*Looking through a list*): Mr. Curry. . . . Have you any idea what he does?

Paddington: He grumbles a lot.

Nurse: That doesn't help. I think I'd better pass you on to the person who deals with inquiries.

Paddington: Thank you very much. Is he the head man?

Nurse: The *head* man. Bless me! Why didn't you say so before? You want the doctor who looks after things up here. (*She taps her head.*)

Paddington: Up here? (*He taps his own head.*)

Head shrinker is slang for *psychiatrist,* a doctor for people with emotional problems.

Nurse: He's what we call the head shrinker.

Paddington: My hat *is* a bit tight. But I don't think I want my head shrunk. Couldn't you stretch my hat instead?

Nurse: Stretch your hat?

Paddington: Yes. If it was a bit bigger, I could carry more sandwiches in it.

Nurse (*Leaning across the desk*): Sandwiches?

Paddington (*Leaning across the desk so that they are nose-to-nose*): Yes, but I would still have to find somewhere for my cocoa.

Alarmed means frightened.

Nurse (*Alarmed*): There, there. There's nothing to worry about. (*Picks up the phone quickly and dials a number.*) Mr. Heinz, could you come quickly, please? There's a patient who needs you urgently. Thank you. (*Replaces the phone*)

Paddington: Mr. Heinz! I don't want to see Mr. Heinz. I want to see Mr. Curry. I've brought him one of Mrs. Bird's cherry cakes.

Nurse (*Soothingly*): I think you'll find Mr. Heinz much nicer. He'll soon take your worries away. (Mr. Heinz *enters*.) Oh, Mr. Heinz, I'm so glad to see you. (*She looks at* Paddington.) There's the patient. (*She hurries out.*)

Paddington: Patient? Have I got long to wait?

Mr. Heinz: Oh, no, in fact I'll start right away. Just open your coat, please.

Paddington: I'm sorry about the cherry cake.

Mr. Heinz (*Taking off his glasses and staring at* Paddington): You are sorry about the *cherry cake*?

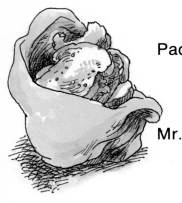

Paddington: Yes. I wish I could give you a slice, but Mr. Curry would only complain. I can give you one of my marmalade sandwiches.

Mr. Heinz (*A slight shudder*): No, thank you. Now, I'd like to play a little game. It's really to test your reactions. (*He sits down in a chair by his desk.*)

When Mr. Heinz tests *reactions,* he is testing to see how quickly someone answers.

Paddington: A game to test my <u>reactions</u>? I didn't know I had any.

Mr. Heinz: Oh, yes. (*He puts his feet up on another chair.*) Everybody has reactions. Some have fast ones and some have slow. (Paddington *sits on his feet.*) Oooh!

Paddington: I'm sorry, Mr. Heinz.

Mr. Heinz: Now I'm going to call out some words—quite quickly—and each time I call one out, I want you to give me another word which has the opposite meaning . . . right?

Paddington (*Promptly, as he settles down in the other chair*): Wrong.

Mr. Heinz: What's the matter? Aren't you comfortable?

Paddington: Oh, yes, but you told me to say the opposite every time you gave me a word.

Mr. Heinz: That wasn't the word, bear! Wait until I give you the go ahead. Once you start I don't want to hear anything else. Ready. . . . Three . . . two . . . one . . . go!

Paddington: Stop!

Mr. Heinz: What's the matter?

Paddington: You said ''go'' so I said ''stop.''

Mr. Heinz: Oh. Very good.

Paddington: Very bad.

Mr. Heinz: Look here!

Paddington: Look there! (*A pause*) Can't you think of any more words, Mr. Heinz?

Mr. Heinz (*Drums his fingers on the desk for a moment, then decides to try again*): White.

Paddington: Black.

Mr. Heinz: Big.

Paddington: Small.

Mr. Heinz: Fast.

Paddington: Slow.

Mr. Heinz: Dark.

Paddington: Light.

In England, the word *fine* can mean *fine weather*—that is, *dry weather*.

Mr. Heinz: <u>Fine.</u>

Paddington: Wet.

Mr. Heinz: That's good. We've finished.

Paddington: That's bad. We've started.

Mr. Heinz: No, we haven't!

Paddington: Yes, we have!

Mr. Heinz (*Thumping the table*): No . . . no . . . no!

Paddington (*Thumps the table too, in his excitement*): Yes . . . yes . . . yes!

Mr. Heinz (*Yelling*): Will you stop!

Paddington: Will you go!

Mr. Heinz (*His head in his hands*): Why did I ever take this up? I should have my head examined.

Paddington (*Sitting up*): Perhaps it needs shrinking. I should go and talk to the nurse who was here a few minutes ago. She might be able to help you. She knows all about those things.

(*As Paddington gets up, Mr. Heinz makes a dash for the door.*)

Mr. Heinz: I shall be gone for five minutes. Five minutes! And if you're still here when I get back, I'll I'll . . . (*He hurries out, at a loss for words.*)

Paddington (*Looking round the room*): What a funny hospital. It's not at all like the one in Daredevil Doctor. Hmm. It must be time for lunch. (*He takes a sandwich out.*) I'm glad Mrs. Brown remembered to give me some cocoa. (*He fills the thermos cup and takes a mouthful.*) Ow! (*He hops round the room in agony.*) Ooh! (*He picks up a doctor's bag from the corner of the room, opens it, and examines his tongue in a mirror.*) I knew it. I've blistered my tongue . . . (*He becomes interested in the contents of the bag.*) What's this? (*He puts on a stethoscope and listens to his own heart.*) Hmm. I wonder what it's like to be a doctor.

(*He slips on a white gown and hangs the stethoscope round his neck.*)

A *surgeon* is a doctor who performs operations in a hospital.

Paddington (*Pretending to be a television <u>surgeon</u>*): Nurse! Instruments ready? All right, bring in the patient. (*He puts on his operating mask and paces up and down.*) Now this is serious . . .

(*The* Nurse *comes in suddenly.*)

Nurse: It certainly is serious. Sir Archibald is coming.

Paddington: Is he?

Nurse: And he's in a terrible mood. You know he doesn't like students who aren't <u>punctual</u>.

Punctual means on time.

Paddington: Student? But I'm not . . .

Nurse: He's here now. I'd say I'm sorry <u>straight away</u>, if I were you.

Straight away means right away.

Sir Archibald (*Storming in*): Ah, there you are.

Paddington: Good morning, Sir Archibald. I'm sorry, Sir Archibald!

Sir Archibald: Sorry? I should think so! Good afternoon's more like it! Now that you *are* here, perhaps you can give us the benefit of your advice. I'd like to have your <u>diagnosis</u>.

A diagnosis is a doctor's determination of the nature of an illness.

Paddington: My diagnosis! (*He begins to unload his basket.*) There's a cherry cake, some eggs, some calves-foot jelly, but I don't think Mrs. Brown packed a diagnosis.

Sir Archibald: Calves-foot jelly. Did you say *calves-foot jelly*?

Paddington: Yes. Grant Dexter says it's very good if you're ill.

Sir Archibald: Grant Dexter! And who might he be?

Paddington: You don't know Grant Dexter? He's the Daredevil Doctor. He's very good at curing people. All his patients get better.

Sir Archibald: Are you suggesting mine don't, Doctor . . . whatever your name is?

Paddington: Doctor? I'm not a doctor, Sir Archibald. (*He pulls off his mask.*) I'm a bear. I've come to visit Mr. Curry.

Sir Archibald (*On the point of exploding*): Curry? Did you say Curry?

Paddington: That's right.

Sir Archibald: Are you a friend of his?

Paddington: Well, I'm not really a friend. He lives next door and I've brought him some food.

Sir Archibald: Food! That's the last thing he needs. It will only make him stay longer. That man's entirely without scruples.

Paddington: Mr. Curry's without scruples! I thought he'd only hurt his leg!

Sir Archibald: Scruples, bear, are things that stop some people taking advantage of others.

Paddington: Oh. I don't think Mr. Curry's got any of those, Sir Archibald. Mrs. Bird's always grumbling because he takes advantage of others.

Sir Archibald: I see. (*Thoughtfully*) Are you any good at tricks, bear?

Paddington: Oh, yes, Sir Archibald. Bears are very good at tricks.

Sir Archibald: I thought you might be. Nurse, wheel Mr. Curry in here. We'll see him privately.

(*The* Nurse *goes and* Sir Archibald *turns to* Paddington.)

Sir Archibald: I think it's time we gave Mr. Curry a surprise—and I think you're the one to give it. Now, if you'll just put your mask back on, bear . . .

Paddington: Yes, Sir Archibald. (*He does.*)

Sir Archibald: I'll give you a chance to see what it's like to be—what did you say his name was?

Paddington: Grant Dexter. The Daredevil Doctor.

Sir Archibald: Now I've an idea. (*He goes to the door and returns with a tool box.*) The workmen left these when they were doing some repairs. When I tell you to get your instruments ready, this is the box I want you to take them from.

Paddington: Right, Sir Archibald.

(Mr. Curry *arrives in a wheelchair pushed by the* Nurse.)

Sir Archibald: Good morning, Mr. Curry. How's the patient today?

Mr. Curry: Ooooooooh! Worse, much worse.

Sir Archibald (*Cheerfully*): I thought you might be. That's why we have decided to operate.

Mr. Curry (*Sitting up quickly*): Operate? Did you say operate?

Sir Archibald: Yes, that's right. No good playing around with these things. I'd like to introduce you to . . . a <u>colleague from overseas</u>. He specializes in legs. Does something or other to the knee. Nobody quite knows what, but it seems to work very well in the jungle. Quite a few of his patients still manage to get about more or less. (*To Paddington*) Perhaps you'd like to listen to the patient's heart?

Here, a *colleague from overseas* is a doctor from the other side of the ocean. Ask where "overseas" would be in relation to England.

Paddington: Of course, Sir Archibald. (*He sticks the stethoscope under the blanket.*)

Sir Archibald: What can you hear?

Paddington: It's got a very strong beat. (*He jumps up and down to the rhythm.*) I think it's Pick of the Pops.

Mr. Curry: <u>Pick of the Pops</u>! You've got your stethoscope on my transistor radio!

Pick of the Pops is a radio program of popular music.

Paddington: I'm sorry, Mr. Curry. (*In his confusion he reverses the stethoscope and puts the headpiece on* Mr. Curry. *He shouts in the other end.*) Are you there?

(Mr. Curry *jumps.*)

Mr. Curry: Of course I am! (*He turns to* Sir Archibald.) Is this . . . this *person* going to be allowed to operate on me? He's not big enough for a start.

Sir Archibald (*Calmly*): Oh, don't worry about his size. We'll give him a box to stand on.

Mr. Curry: A box to stand on!

Sir Archibald: Yes. It may make him a bit wobbly, but it'll be all right.

Mr. Curry: What!

Sir Archibald (*He turns to* Paddington *with a wink.*): Now, if you would just like to get your instruments ready.

Paddington: Certainly, Sir Archibald. (*He opens the carpenter's tool box.*) One hammer . . . (*He puts it on the desk.*)

Mr. Curry: A hammer!

Paddington: One chisel. (*He puts it next to the hammer.*)

Mr. Curry: A chisel!

Paddington: And one saw. (*He brings out a large carpenter's saw.*)

Mr. Curry: A saw!

Sir Archibald: How about something to put him to sleep with, nurse?

(*The* Nurse *hands* Paddington *an enormous mallet.*)

A *mallet* is a kind of hammer.

"I'm off" means *"I'm going."*

Mr. Curry: <u>I'm off</u>. (*He leaps out of the chair.*)

Sir Archibald: Ah, Mr. Curry, I'm glad you're feeling better. You can leave the hospital today.

Mr. Curry: Leave? I don't know what you're talking about.

Sir Archibald: You aren't limping any more, Mr. Curry. In fact, I would say you are completely cured.

Mr. Curry (*Realizes he's been beaten*): Bah! (*He storms out.*)

Subsided is another word for *dwindled* or *decreased.*

Sir Archibald (*After his laughter has <u>subsided</u>*): It seems we have another free bed in the ward after all, nurse. (*He removes* Paddington's *mask and shakes his paw warmly.*) Congratulations, bear. I've never in all my life seen a patient recover so quickly. Perhaps you would like to keep your stethoscope as a souvenir?

Paddington: Thank you very much, Sir Archibald. (*He picks up his basket.*) Would you like some of this cake? I don't suppose Mr. Curry will be needing it now.

Sir Archibald: Mmm. It does seem rather a pity to waste it. (*He looks over his shoulder to make sure the nurse can't hear and then lowers his voice.*) Do you like the cherries?

Paddington (*Lowers his voice too*): I think they're the best part. Except Mrs. Bird's put them on extra tightly this time.

Sir Archibald (*Reaches for the tool box*): I don't doubt we'll find something to lever them off with. (*He hands* Paddington *a suitable tool.*) After you . . .

Lever them off means *pry them off.*

Suitable means *useful for the job.*

Paddington: No, after you, Sir Archibald. (*Together, they dig into the basket.*)

(*Curtain*)

See pages T175–T178 in the front of this book for suggested postreading strategies.

Questions

1. Why does Mrs. Brown worry about the hospital when Paddington goes there?

2. Why don't people act surprised when Paddington—a bear—walks up to them and starts talking?

3. Paddington makes friends easily. Who becomes his friend in this play? Why is it easy to become friends with Paddington?

4. Suppose you asked Paddington what he learned from his visit to the hospital. Which of these would be his best reply?
   a. "Never do what people tell you to do."
   b. "Things usually turn out all right."
   c. "If you work hard, you will be rewarded."

5. Paddington had trouble understanding some of the words people used. One of the words was *scruples*. Tell what the doctor meant by *scruples*. Then tell what Paddington thought he meant.

Activity   Draw Mixed-Up Pictures

Suppose that Paddington got mixed up when he drew pictures of these sentences. Show what he might draw.

The baseball player hit a *fly* into the backfield.
On our hike we came to a *fork* in the road.

About MICHAEL BOND

Michael Bond, creator of Paddington the bear, is an English writer. He lives with his wife and his daughter in a small town near London, England.

At first Mr. Bond wrote stories, articles, and plays for adults. Then one Christmas Eve he bought a small toy bear. "I saw it left on a shelf of a London store, felt sorry for it, and named it Paddington," he said. As a result, he wrote his first children's book, *A Bear Called Paddington.*

Michael Bond has created other animal characters, too—a mouse called Thursday, and a guinea pig called Olga da Polga. "I like writing about animals," Mr. Bond says. "They sometimes seem more real to me than people. They can also get away with things people never could."

More Books by Michael Bond

Paddington Takes to TV   (Houghton Mifflin, 1974)

Paddington Takes the Test   (Houghton Mifflin, 1980)

Paddington On Screen   (Houghton Mifflin, 1982)

The Complete Adventures of Olga da Polga   (Delacorte, 1983)

The theater lights dim. The curtain goes up. You are about to see a play. As the actors move and speak, you find out what is happening. With the costumes and scenery, you picture the time and place.

A play is meant to be performed. That is the main difference between a play and a story. When it is written, a play *looks* different, too. It has

a cast of characters

Characters	Mrs. Brown	Paddington
	Mrs. Bird	Nurse

stage directions

(Paddington *comes in carrying a letter.*)

dialogue

Paddington: There's a letter for you, Mrs. Brown. It looks like Mr. Curry's writing.

Mrs. Brown: Yes, I'm afraid you're right.

326

See pages T178–T179 in the front of this book for a suggested teaching plan for this selection.

How does a story look different from a play?

1 Does it have characters?

2 Does it have stage directions?

3 Does it have dialogue?

You will find this bear's answers below.

1. A story *does* have characters, but they are not listed at the beginning in a cast of characters.

2. A story *does not* have stage directions, but it *does* tell what the characters do and how they feel. This information is not in parentheses.

3. A story *does* have dialogue, but the dialogue is usually in quotation marks.

REMEMBER!

The <u>cast of characters</u> lists the names of the characters in the play.

The <u>stage directions</u> tell what the characters do and how they speak.

The <u>dialogue</u> is what the characters say.

Read the fable of "The North Wind and the Sun." Be ready to change some of this fable into a play.

The North Wind and the Sun

One day the North Wind boasted to the Sun, "I am much stronger than you." The Sun smiled and replied, "Don't be so sure. *I* may be stronger than *you*." Just then a traveler wrapped in a cloak came walking down the road. "Let's have a contest," said the Sun. "Whoever can make that traveler take off her cloak is the stronger. You may try first."

The North Wind blew as hard as he could upon the traveler. "Who-o-o-o," he howled. The traveler only wrapped the cloak more tightly than ever around her

328

See pages T178–T179 in the front of this book for suggested postreading strategies.

shoulders, and said, "I'm glad I wore my cloak. That north wind is *cold!*"

Then the Sun said, "Now it's my turn." She shone so brightly that the traveler began to feel warm. The traveler smiled and said, "Thank you, Sun," and she took off her cloak as she sat down to rest. "Kindness works better than force," explained the Sun to the North Wind.

On a piece of paper, write the cast of characters for the play of "The North Wind and the Sun." Then read the beginning of the play below and write the next line of dialogue for the Sun. Change the rest of the fable into a play if you wish.

Characters

North Wind *(Boasting)*: I am much stronger than you.

Sun *(Smiling)*: Don't be so sure. I may be stronger than you.

(A traveler wrapped in a cloak comes walking down the road.)

Sun:

Digging into the Past

Reading Level Challenging

From the story *Miss Pickerell Goes on a Dig*

by Ellen MacGregor and Dora Pantell

Illustrated by Lydia Halverson

Miss Lavinia Pickerell is heading an archaeological dig on a hillside near her home town of Square Toe City. It all started when Miss Pickerell's nephew Euphus was digging for rocks on the hillside and found an odd-shaped piece of very old glass. Now Miss Pickerell is looking for more evidence of the inhabitants who might have lived in the area hundreds of years ago. Miss Pickerell is racing against time, however. In just two days, the hillside will be leveled by the county to make way for a new road.

Miss Pickerell is aided in her dig by world-famous archaeologist Professor Tuttle and her friends Mr. Humwhistel, Mr. Rugby, and Mr. Esticott. On the second day of the dig, Miss Pickerell arrives at the site to find that Mr. Humwhistel has organized the town's Boy and Girl Scouts to help. Miss Pickerell follows Mr. Esticott down into the dig, little realizing what awaits her at the bottom.

Down to the Indians

Miss Pickerell saw Mr. Humwhistel first. He was directing three teams of workers. The first consisted of Mr. Rugby, Mr. Esticott, and the bigger Boy Scouts. They were busy digging. The second team, made up of all the smaller boys, was removing the earth from the finds. The third team was all girls. They were sifting the earth to make sure the second team had not missed anything.

"We're up to the Indians," Mr. Rugby said, emerging from the pit to announce the news.

"Down to the Indians, you mean," argued Mr. Esticott, who followed.

"Has anyone shown Miss Pickerell our discoveries?" Professor Tuttle asked.

"Euphus is standing guard over them," Mr. Humwhistel said. "He's been our official record keeper this morning."

Euphus showed Miss Pickerell some cups of buffalo horn, several copper bowls, ladles, and spoons, two cradle boards, a pile of arrowheads, another pile of blunt-tipped arrows, and what looked like a doll. Professor Tuttle blew some of the dirt off the doll by puffing on it softly, and showed Miss Pickerell that it had movable arms and legs.

"And these blunt-tipped arrows," he said, "were also toys. The Indian boys played with them. The blunt tips were to keep the boys from getting hurt."

"Forevermore!" Miss Pickerell gasped.

"Yes, indeed," Professor Tuttle said. "Our first finds, the purple glass, the snuffbox, the rusty hinge, the toothpick—all of those were from the colonial period. We're digging into the Indian times, now. Mr. Esticott, why don't you take Miss Pickerell into the test pit and show her where we made our discoveries? In the meantime, I'll sort out some of these finds for possible dating."

Mr. Esticott turned to Miss Pickerell. "You'll have to climb down a ladder to get inside now," he told her. "We've dug pretty deep."

Explain that on an archeological dig, workers dig away layers of earth which have piled up over time. The remains of people who lived on the area long ago would be deepest. Mr. Rugby is saying they have found things used by Indians who once lived in the area.

The *colonial period* is the time when Europeans settled in America and formed colonies ruled by European countries.

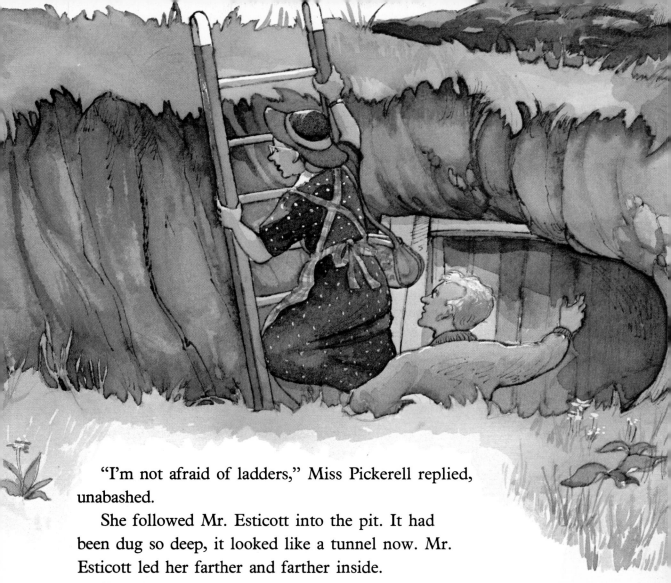

"I'm not afraid of ladders," Miss Pickerell replied, unabashed.

She followed Mr. Esticott into the pit. It had been dug so deep, it looked like a tunnel now. Mr. Esticott led her farther and farther inside.

"It's like a house with different rooms in it," Mr. Esticott said. "This is the part where we found the doll and the cradle board and the blunt-tipped arrows."

"Mercy!" Miss Pickerell breathed.

Mr. Esticott walked on a little farther.

"And this is the place where we unearthed the bowls and the spoons and the ladles," he told her.

"Maybe it was a kitchen," Miss Pickerell said. "Or even a dining room. That is, if they had dining rooms in those days."

"And here," Mr. Esticott said, moving on quickly and motioning for her to join him, "here is where . . ."

The sound of stones falling and the sudden, choking smell of heavy dust, rapidly accumulating, came before Mr. Esticott had a chance to finish.

Miss Pickerell staggered forward. "What . . . what . . ." she asked, trying hard to talk through the dust that was sweeping around her.

"The shoring." Mr. Esticott's voice spoke from sudden darkness beside her. "I think it has caved in."

Miss Pickerell groped blindly. Right in front of her was what seemed to be a short wall, extending up only to her chin. It felt solid. She got down on her hands and knees next to it, and reached out a hand toward Mr. Esticott, pulling him down with her.

Suddenly all was quiet. Miss Pickerell could hear the sound of her own heart beating, and Mr. Esticott's quick, heavy breathing.

"Mr. Esticott!" she whispered. "Are you all right?"

"Yes," he replied, "except for this dust which has gotten up into my nose. I can't . . ."

"Do you have a flashlight?" Miss Pickerell interrupted.

"In my back pocket," Mr. Esticott said. "I'll get it."

The flashlight was small. When Mr. Esticott held
it out, Miss Pickerell could just barely see what had
happened. The wooden boards used as shoring on the
right side of the pit had completely collapsed. With
them had fallen stones and hard-packed clumps of
earth. The ladder, which had been pushed by the
impact into an uncertain horizontal position, was
covered with rocks and boards. The opening out of
the pit was solidly blocked.

In the flashlight's beam, Miss Pickerell caught a glimpse of Mr. Esticott's face. His eyes were full of fear.

"We're trapped," he said shakily. "Sealed in!"

"Stop talking that way," Miss Pickerell said, hoping she sounded firm enough. "There must be a way out."

"Where?" Mr. Esticott asked.

"I don't know yet," Miss Pickerell said. "But I plan to find out. Let me have that flashlight, please."

Mr. Esticott handed over the flashlight reluctantly. "I don't think you ought to poke around too much, Miss Pickerell," he cautioned. "It might be dangerous. You could be upsetting something that would start another avalanche."

Miss Pickerell thought about this.

"You may be right," she said, sighing.

"They know outside the pit that the shoring has caved in," Mr. Esticott went on, talking more confidently now. "They're bound to come and rescue us."

"Yes," Miss Pickerell said. She tried hard to be patient and wait. It was very difficult. Minutes passed. There was no sign of movement from outside. And the air inside was getting more suffocating by the second.

"I can't bear it," Miss Pickerell said finally. "I can't bear just sitting here and doing nothing. There must be *something* we can do to help ourselves."

"What?" Mr. Esticott asked, sounding desperate.

"Look for another way out," Miss Pickerell said, resolutely holding the flashlight out in front of her.

Both Miss Pickerell and Mr. Esticott saw the opening at the same instant. It was at the right, not too far from where the lower part of the wall ended. The crash of timber and stones had rolled away some of the earth there, revealing a hole just large enough to crawl through.

"Where do you suppose it leads?" Mr. Esticott asked breathlessly.

"We'll soon know," Miss Pickerell said.

Clutching the flashlight in one hand and Mr. Esticott's arm with the other, she began moving in the direction of the opening. It was hard to move quickly. The ground was rough and rocky and every once in a while she or Mr. Esticott came close to falling.

When they reached the hole, Miss Pickerell crawled through first. Mr. Esticott followed immediately.

What they saw made them both gasp. They were in what seemed to be a small room, shaped like an upside-down cup. And lying so near to the entrance that they almost stumbled over it, was a pile of what looked very much like weapons. Miss Pickerell turned the flashlight full on them.

"Spearheads!" Mr. Esticott exclaimed, pointing to those first.

"Arrowheads!" Miss Pickerell said, noticing these next. "Stone-tipped arrowheads."

"I've seen pictures of them in the new dictionary my cousin sent me last year," Mr. Esticott said. "In the A section."

"They're also likely to be in the F section," Miss Pickerell added. "Under FLINT. Both spearpoints and arrowheads were often made of hard flint stone. Professor Tuttle will be most interested in what we've found."

"Yes, *when* we're able to get out and tell him about it," Mr. Esticott replied.

"We'll get out soon," Miss Pickerell said, trying to feel optimistic. "We might even find an exit leading out from this room. Let's walk all around it."

Once again, holding the flashlight in front of her, she began to creep carefully forward. Mr. Esticott followed, almost in her footsteps. When she had gone far enough to be able to touch a wall of the vaultlike chamber, she stopped and deliberately dropped her bright white handkerchief. "So that we'll know where we started from," she said.

They continued to grope their way around the curve of the room. Miss Pickerell kept swinging the flashlight upward and downward in a series of slow arcs. Mr. Esticott fumbled all along the clay-packed walls for an opening. There was none.

"Let's try the ground," Mr. Esticott suggested when they were back at the spot marked by the handkerchief. "Perhaps there's a tunnel leading out from underneath."

Miss Pickerell did not answer. She was staring at something on the wall. "Here's a spot we must have missed," she said.

Mr. Esticott moved over to where she stood and stared too.

Built into the wall quite near the ground was what seemed to be a crude fireplace. And in and around this hearth were set a number of interestingly shaped stones, each bearing a pattern of regular ridges, and with a slightly hollowed-out center. The rocks were black with soot.

"Why, it looks like a fireplace—doesn't it?" exclaimed Mr. Esticott.

"It most certainly does, Mr. Esticott," Miss Pickerell replied. "But there's something about those rocks! Something strange. I'm taking one of them back with me!"

She leaned down and pulled until she had loosened one of the rocks. She examined it thoughtfully. Then she put it in her apron pocket. "I know what these rocks remind me of!" she said at last. "I know, but I don't understand it at all."

Miss Pickerell and Mr. Esticott stood now in almost total blackness. The flashlight was flickering badly.

"We'd better put it out," Miss Pickerell suggested. "Unless you have an extra battery with you."

"I haven't," Mr. Esticott sighed. "What do we do now?"

"First we'll go back and wait," Miss Pickerell said. "We'd better get back to where we started from, before your flashlight goes dead. It's certainly time the rescuers were getting down to us!"

A Sign from the Rescuers

When Miss Pickerell and Mr. Esticott had crawled back through the hole and were once more seated on the uneven ground near the low wall, Miss Pickerell took one last look around. "Let's get our bearings," she said firmly. "We're between the wall and the left-hand side of the pit. The rescuers will most probably come from the left side because that's the part where the shoring is still fairly intact. What do you think, Mr. Esticott?"

"I think so, too," he said.

"We'll listen for sounds from that direction," Miss Pickerell said, accompanying her words with a brisk snap of the "off" switch. "We'll turn the flash-light on every fifteen minutes or so to look for signs of movement."

Mr. Esticott had nothing to say.

Miss Pickerell tried to think of something to talk about that might make them feel better. "Just imagine, Mr. Esticott," she said, "hundreds and hundreds of years ago a family lived in that strange-shaped room, and a mother cooked dinner in that very fireplace."

"Is there any way we can tell exactly when that was?" Mr. Esticott asked.

Miss Pickerell reached into her pocket and pulled out the rock. She turned the flashlight on it briefly.

"The answer is in the carbon soot on this rock, Mr. Esticott," she said. "The soot is all that's left of a piece of wood that was burned in that fireplace. If we can tell how old the soot is, we'll know when people used the fireplace!"

"But how can we tell how old the soot is?" Mr. Esticott asked bewildered.

"Wait! Sh!" Miss Pickerell hissed sharply.

A tiny scratching noise seemed to be coming from somewhere up above. Miss Pickerell turned on the flashlight immediately. But she saw nothing. And the sound was not repeated.

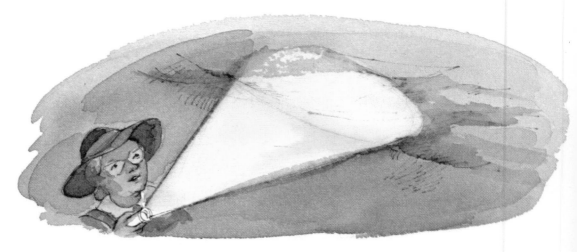

Mr. Esticott sighed. "What were you saying about dating soot?" he asked.

"I was going to tell you about the carbon-14 test," Miss Pickerell answered. "I learned about it once when I was helping someone look for uranium. It's a scientific way of dating things that were once alive."

"I don't see how that has anything to do with soot," Mr. Esticott said, sounding doubtful.

"It's really very simple," Miss Pickerell told him. "The soot on this rock was formed when wood was burned in that fireplace. And the wood came from a living tree. Of course, every living thing contains radioactive carbon-14, because carbon-14 is in the air. For example, plants take it in."

Miss Pickerell stopped suddenly. Again, it seemed to her that she heard small sounds above her. Again, there was nothing when she strained her ears to listen and when she turned the flashlight on to look. She sighed heavily.

"After a plant dies," she resumed, "the carbon-14 disintegrates at a *known* rate, a certain amount every year. If we can get a scientist to measure how much carbon-14 is left in this soot, we'll have a very good idea of its age."

"Oh!" Mr. Esticott said.

Miss Pickerell said nothing more. She felt tired after her long speech. It was becoming harder and harder to breathe in the close atmosphere. She was also very thirsty. She searched in her knitting bag for the peppermint candy drops she usually carried there.

You might ask some students to use an encyclopedia to research radioactive dating and to present their findings to the class in a short oral report.

The air was hot and stuffy because no fresh air was getting in.

She found two. Mr. Esticott gladly accepted one when she offered it to him.

She was just taking the wrapper off her own piece when she thought she heard noises again. This time, they sounded louder and seemed definitely to come from the left side of the pit. Miss Pickerell turned the flashlight on.

"Maybe they're tapping," she said. "I'm going to tap back."

"Why not shout?" Mr. Esticott asked and began immediately, "Hello! We're here!"

Miss Pickerell joined him. "Hello! Right here!"

No one answered.

"I'll try tapping against the shoring," Miss Pickerell said, picking up a rock from the ground. "I'll tap with this."

Miss Pickerell tapped systematically. Once, twice, three times—four times. Almost immediately, a trickle of earth began to sift down, and quickly broadened into a stream that poured and then surged toward her and Mr. Esticott.

"Oh!" Miss Pickerell gasped, not certain whether to jump back or to crouch down. "They must have heard the tapping. They know where we are now."

"I see something coming through!" Mr. Esticott cried out.

A dark, round object poked out of the earth above their heads. Slowly, the object thrust out farther and farther.

Miss Pickerell kept the dimmed flashlight fixed in that direction and peered anxiously. "Forevermore!" she blurted out in astonishment.

"What is it?" Mr. Esticott asked. "What is it?"

"It's a drainpipe," said Miss Pickerell, feeling very awed and trying hard to keep her voice steady. "The rescuers are pushing it through to make contact with us."

When the pipe stopped moving, Miss Pickerell approached it. She stood on tiptoe, her eye just reaching the level of the hollow end. She took time only to wipe off the right lens of her eyeglasses, then squinted cautiously up the length of the pipe. "I see daylight!" she shouted.

"Hooray!" yelled Mr. Esticott. "May I look, too?"

Miss Pickerell stepped away.

Mr. Esticott, cupping his hands around the end of the pipe and craning his neck as far as it would go, stared hard. "I see a little circle of daylight at the other end!" he announced. "And I think I see someone moving around up there!"

"We'll have to let them know that they have reached us," said Miss Pickerell. "We must attend to that at once."

Attend to means *take care of* or *see to*.

Miss Pickerell knew immediately what she had to do. She pursed her lips up as if she were about to whistle, pressed them hard against the hollow end of the drainpipe, and, making her voice as loud as she could, called out, "YOO HOO! YOO HOO!"

The muffled answer came back instantly, "Can you hear us?"

"Yes!" Miss Pickerell shouted.

"Are you all right?" the voice, which Miss Pickerell was beginning to distinguish as Professor Tuttle's, asked.

"We're both fine," Miss Pickerell answered.

"Good," the answer came. "We're digging down to you. We're coming straight through about a yard to the left of this pipe. Stay as far away from there as possible. It may be dangerous. Do you understand?"

"Yes," Miss Pickerell said, impressed by the urgency in Professor Tuttle's voice.

"One last thing," the professor called. "We have to shore up the top of this pit as we keep digging. It may take us a while. Don't be frightened."

"I won't," Miss Pickerell said. "Thank you, Professor."

She sighed with relief and turned to Mr. Esticott. "I guess our troubles are over now," she said.

At that precise moment, the flashlight went dead. Miss Pickerell could not see even an inch in front of her.

"This is the last straw," Mr. Esticott burst out.

"That may be," Miss Pickerell agreed, "but I don't intend to sit here in the dark until we're rescued." She reached for the pipe again and shouted up to the diggers, "Light, we need light!"

Mr. Esticott cleared his throat. "Do you think that will help?" he asked.

"I wouldn't have done it otherwise," Miss Pickerell replied in very definite tones.

"What did you say?" Mr. Esticott asked.

Miss Pickerell was not surprised that he hadn't heard her. Something was loudly clanking its way down the drainpipe. It came to a halt at the very end of the pipe. It was a flashlight and it was lit.

"Why, it's Euphus' new silver flash!" Miss Pickerell exclaimed. "I bought it for him myself on his last birthday. He must have gotten my message."

"Look," Mr. Esticott said, showing her how the flashlight was tied on to a piece of wool. It was the green knitting wool that she had given to Mr. Humwhistel when he was attaching labels to the finds.

"Of course," Miss Pickerell replied. "That's the way Euphus lowered the flash through the pipe. If he'd just thrown it down, it would have fallen right out at the end and broken to bits."

"You have a very smart nephew," Mr. Esticott said admiringly.

"All seven of my nephews and nieces are smart," Miss Pickerell replied proudly. "Each in a different way."

Now that they had some light, Miss Pickerell and Mr. Esticott felt considerably more cheerful. They felt even better when the first whiffs of fresh air began to drift down into the trench. Miss Pickerell stopped to draw in long, deep breaths. Mr. Esticott did the same.

"It shouldn't be long now," he said happily.

"I don't imagine it should," Miss Pickerell agreed.

They had nothing to do now but wait. Miss Pickerell thought about Professor Tuttle's old, old rock from far, far away, and about the strange cup-shaped room. And suddenly something fell into place in her mind. "Mr. Esticott," she said, "I've been thinking. Houses are like children. They resemble their parents."

"I beg your pardon?" Mr. Esticott said, looking quite bewildered.

Miss Pickerell tried hard to explain. To her, it all seemed so clear. "What I'm trying to tell you, Mr. Esticott," she said, "is that this rock in my pocket closely resembles a rock that Professor Tuttle showed me when I met him the other day. But his rock came from another continent, and was centuries old." She stopped suddenly, as the idea came to her. "Could it be," she said a few second later, "that the descendants of the people who fashioned Professor Tuttle's rock once lived in Square Toe County?"

Mr. Esticott stared, open-mouthed.

"Yes," Miss Pickerell continued, hardly able to contain her excitement. "That's why we see the same workmanship. Square Toe County may have a past we never even dreamed existed. We may learn who . . ."

But Mr. Esticott was no longer listening to her. He was looking up at the top of the pit. A noisy downflow of earth had suddenly opened up a large hole, revealing first a shovel, then a hand, and, at last, Mr. Rugby's round, shining face, peering down at them and smiling broadly.

See pages T180–T182 in the front of the book for suggested postreading strategies.

Questions

1. In this story, who got into deep, serious trouble? What was that trouble?

2. What three things did Miss Pickerell do to make the trouble seem less serious?

3. What was Miss Pickerell's greatest discovery? Why was the discovery important?

4. Complete these sentences by using three of these words from the story: **ladle, chamber, hearth, shoring.**
   a. Boards to keep dirt from caving in are called _____.
   b. A closed-up room is a _____.
   c. The floor of a fireplace is a _____.

Activity   Write a News Report

Sam Scoop, news reporter, wrote three headlines about Miss Pickerell's adventure. Readers said that Sam's headlines were puzzling and untrue. Fix the headlines. Make them truthful and important. Then write the first paragraph to put under one of the headlines. Include the following parts in your paragraph:

1. WHO was there;
2. WHAT happened;
3. WHEN it happened;
4. WHERE it happened;
5. HOW or WHY it happened.

Old Joe Clarke

A traditional folk song

See pages T183–T184 in the front of this book for a suggested teaching plan for this selection.

Round and round, Old Joe Clarke,
Round and round, I say,
Round and round, Old Joe Clarke,
I don't have long to stay.

Old Joe Clarke he had a house,
Sixteen stories high,
Every story in that house
Was full of chicken pie.

I went down to Old Joe Clarke's
And found him eating supper;
I stubbed my toe on the table leg
And stuck my nose in the butter.

I went down to Old Joe Clarke's
But Old Joe wasn't in;
I sat right down on the red-hot stove
And got right up again.

Illustrated by Marie-Louise Gay

BOOKSHELF

Reading Level Average

The Big Cheese by Eve Bunting. Macmillan, 1977.
This is a funny story about two very different
sisters whose lives are suddenly changed by a
big wheel of cheese.

Reading Level Average

Miss Pickerell Goes to Mars by Ellen MacGregor.
McGraw-Hill, 1951. No matter where she goes,
Miss Pickerell does surprising things.

Reading Level Average

**A Person from Britain Whose Head Was in the
Shape of a Mitten & Other Limericks** by
N. M. Bodecker. Atheneum, 1980. Some of
these ridiculous nonsense verses and limericks
are sure to make you laugh.

Reading Level Average

Wingman by Manus Pinkwater. Dodd, Mead, 1975.
Donald Chen read comic books all day until
he met a Super Hero he called Wingman.

Reading Level Average

Getting Something on Maggie Marmelstein by
Marjorie Weinman Sharmat. Harper & Row,
1971. Thad wants to get something on
Maggie. If he doesn't, she is going to ruin his
reputation at school.

Reading Level Challenging

Where the Sidewalk Ends by Shel Silverstein.
Harper & Row, 1974. All kinds of characters,
feelings, and events fill these poems that are
especially fun, and funny, to read aloud.

6 To Live with Animals

See pages T185–T186 in the front of this book for a suggested teaching plan.

355

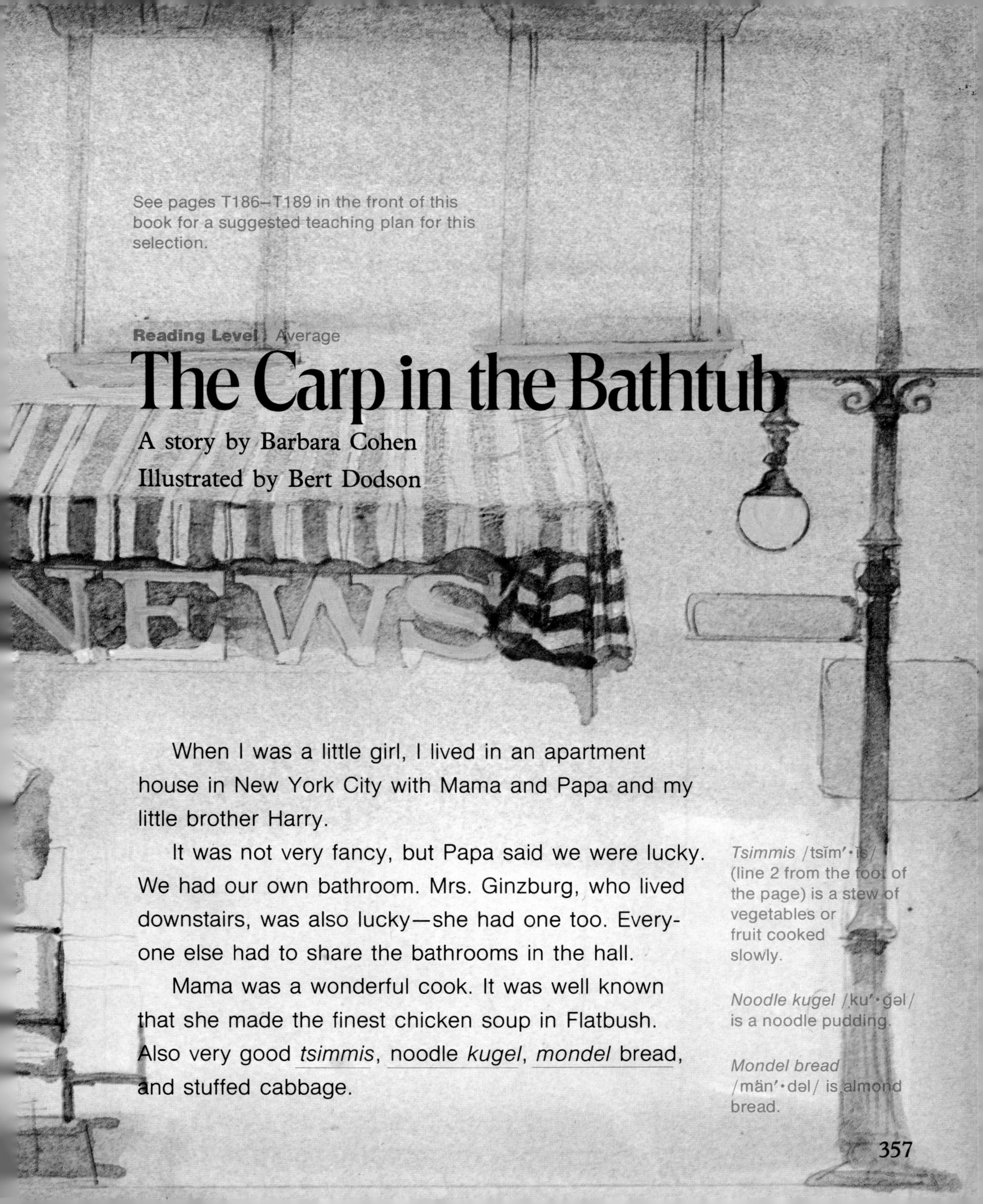

See pages T186—T189 in the front of this book for a suggested teaching plan for this selection.

Reading Level Average

The Carp in the Bathtub

A story by Barbara Cohen

Illustrated by Bert Dodson

When I was a little girl, I lived in an apartment house in New York City with Mama and Papa and my little brother Harry.

It was not very fancy, but Papa said we were lucky. We had our own bathroom. Mrs. Ginzburg, who lived downstairs, was also lucky—she had one too. Everyone else had to share the bathrooms in the hall.

Mama was a wonderful cook. It was well known that she made the finest chicken soup in Flatbush. Also very good *tsimmis*, noodle *kugel*, *mondel* bread, and stuffed cabbage.

Tsimmis /tsĭm′·ĭs/ (line 2 from the foot of the page) is a stew of vegetables or fruit cooked slowly.

Noodle kugel /ku′·gəl/ is a noodle pudding.

Mondel bread /män′·dəl/ is almond bread.

357

Pronounced /rosh hə-shä′·nə/ (line 2).

Pronounced /pä′·säкн′/.

Malke /mal′·kə/; Moishe /môy′·shĕh/.

Pronounced /tīt′·əl·boum/.

The Seder /sā′·dər/ (line 6) is the meal served on the first two nights of Passover.

But best of all was Mama's *gefilte* fish. Twice a year she made *gefilte* fish—in the fall for Rosh Hashanah, the Jewish New Year, and in the spring for Pesach, the festival of Passover. Aunt Malke and Uncle Moishe, cousin Zipporah, and Papa's friend Mr. Teitelbaum always came to our house for the Seder on the first night of Passover. They said that Mama's *gefilte* fish was not merely the best in Flatbush, nor the best in Brooklyn, but actually the best *gefilte* fish in all of New York City.

Harry and I loved the Seder because we got to stay up until midnight. It took that long to say all the prayers, read the Passover story out of a book called the Haggadah, sing all the songs, and eat all the food. But I will tell you a secret. I was nine years old at the time I am telling you about, and I had never put a single piece of my mother's *gefilte* fish into my mouth.

Pronounced /hə-gä′·də/.

Mama made her *gefilte* fish out of carp. For a day or two before Passover, carp was hard to find in the stores. All the ladies in the neighborhood had been buying it for their own *gefilte* fish. Mama liked to buy *her* carp at least a week before Passover to make sure she got the nicest, fattest, shiniest one. But Mama knew that a dead fish sitting in the icebox for a week would not be very good when the time came to make it into *gefilte* fish.

So Mama bought her fish live and carried it home in a pail of water. All the way home it flopped and flipped because it was too big for the bucket. It would have died if Mama had left it in there.

As soon as she got home she would call, "Leah, run the water in the tub."

And I would put the rubber stopper in the drain and run some cold water into the bathtub. Then Mama would dump the carp out of the pail and into the tub.

The carp loved it there. He was always a big fish, but the tub was about four times as long as he was, and there was plenty of room for him to swim around.

Harry and I loved the carp. As long as he was there we didn't have to take baths.

But the day always came when Mama marched into the bathroom carrying a big metal strainer and removed the stopper from the tub. The carp always seemed to know what was coming. He swam away from her as fast as he could, splashing the water all over her apron with his strong, flat tail. But he didn't have a chance. Before all the water was even out of the tub, Mama had caught him in her strainer. The way he was flopping around, he would have been on the floor before Mama got out the bathroom door, so she dumped him right into her bucket and carried him to the kitchen.

We knew what she did with him when she got there, although we would never look.

Mama once told us that her Mama had not thrown away the skin of the carp. She had removed it so carefully from the carp that after the fish was cooked, she could put it back in the skin and bring it to the table. That's why the fish is called *gefilte*, Mama said, which means "stuffed." At least, Harry and I were spared that!

You can see why we managed never to eat *gefilte* fish on Rosh Hashanah or Passover. Could *you* eat a friend?

The year I was nine was the worst of all. Most people think that all fish are pretty much the same, but this is definitely not true. Some carp are much more lovable than others, and that Passover we had an unusually playful and intelligent carp in our bathtub.

This carp was larger than the others too. We were having extra company that year. Mrs. Ginzburg from downstairs and her daughter Elvira were coming up. Mr. Ginzburg had died six months before, and Mrs. Ginzburg just didn't have the heart to fuss and prepare for Passover.

This particular carp was also shinier than the others. His eyes were brighter and he seemed much livelier and friendlier. It got so that whenever Harry or I went into the bathroom, he'd swim right over to the end of the tub as if he knew we were going to feed him. There was something about his mouth that made him seem to be smiling at us after he had eaten a bread crust or the lettuce we had given him.

In those days people like us, who lived in apartments in Flatbush, did not have pets. Harry and I would have loved owning a dog, a cat, or a bird, but Mama and Papa had never thought of such a thing, and it never occurred to us to ask. I'll tell you one thing, though. After that carp had been in our bathtub for nearly a week, we knew he was not just any old carp. He was our pet. In memory of Mr. Ginzburg, we called him Joe.

Explain that the children named the fish after Mr. Ginzburg, whose first name was Joe.

Two days before Passover, when I came home from school, Mama said, "You look after Harry, Leah. I have to go shopping, and I'll never get anything done if I have him trailing after me."

As soon as Mama was gone I looked at Harry, and Harry looked at me.

"We have to save Joe," I told him.

"We'll never have another chance," Harry agreed. "But what'll we do?"

"Mrs. Ginzburg has a bathtub," I reminded him.

Harry nodded. He saw what I meant right away.

I went to the kitchen, got the bucket, and carried it to the bathroom. Harry had already let all the water out of the tub. He helped lift Joe into the bucket. It was not easy for us because Joe must have weighed fifteen pounds, but we finally managed. We could add only a little water to the pail because it was already almost too heavy for us.

With both of us holding onto the handle and banging the bucket against every step, we lugged it downstairs to Mrs. Ginzburg's door. Then we rang her bell.

Lugged means carried.

362

363

"Why, Leah, Harry!" Mrs. Ginzburg said in surprise.
"I'm very glad to see you. Won't you come in? Why
are you carrying that bucket?" Mrs. Ginzburg was a
very nice lady. She was always kind to us, even when
she couldn't understand what we were doing.

We carried our bucket into Mrs. Ginzburg's front
room. "May I ask what you have there?" she said
politely.

"It's Joe," said Harry.

"Joe!" Mrs. Ginzburg closed her eyes and put her
hand over her heart.

"We named him for Mr. Ginzburg," I explained
quickly. "He smiles like Mr. Ginzburg."

"Oh . . . " Mrs. Ginzburg tried to smile too. Just then Joe twitched, his tail flashed over the top of the bucket, and a few drops of water dripped onto the oriental rug. Mrs. Ginzburg glanced into the pail. "My goodness," she said. "He looks like a fish to me."

"He is a fish," I said. "He's the best fish in the world, and Mama can't kill him for Passover. She just can't. Please let him stay in your bathtub. Please. Just for a little while. Until I can figure out where to keep him for good."

"But Leah," Mrs. Ginzburg said, "I can't do that. Your Mama is my dear friend."

"If you don't let us put Joe in your bathtub soon," Harry pleaded, "he'll be dead. He's almost dead now."

Mrs. Ginzburg and I peered into the bucket. Harry was right. Joe didn't look too good. His scales weren't shiny bright any more, and he had stopped thrashing around. There was not enough water in the bucket for him.

"All right," said Mrs. Ginzburg. "But just for now." She ran some water into her tub, and we dumped our carp in. He no sooner felt all that clear cold water around him than he perked right up and started swimming. I took a few morsels of chopped meat I had stored away in my dress pocket and gave them to him. He smiled at me, just like always.

"This fish can't stay here," Mrs. Ginzburg warned. "I'm afraid I can't help hide him from your mother and father."

"What shall we do?" Harry asked me, blinking his eyes hard to keep back the tears.

"We'll go find Papa," I told him. "Papa doesn't cook, so maybe he'll understand. We'll have to find him before Mama gets home."

Papa was a cutter in a garment factory in Manhattan. He came home every night on the subway. Harry and I went down to the corner and waited by the stairs that led up from the station. After a while, we saw a

A *subway* is an underground train.

big crowd of people who had just gotten off the train come up the stairs. Papa was with them. He was holding onto the rail and climbing slowly, with his head down.

"Papa, Papa," we called.

He looked up and saw us. He straightened his shoulders, smiled, and ran quickly up the few remaining steps. "You came to meet me," he said. "That's very nice."

We started home together. I was holding one of Papa's hands, and Harry was holding the other. "Papa," I asked, "do you like *gefilte* fish?"

"Why, yes," he said, "of course I like *gefilte* fish. Your mother makes the best *gefilte* fish in all of Flatbush—in all of New York City. Everyone knows that."

"But would you like to eat *gefilte* fish," Harry asked, "if the fish was a friend of yours?"

Papa stood absolutely still right in the middle of the sidewalk. "Harry," he said, "Harry, what have you done to Mama's fish?"

"Leah did it too," Harry said.

Papa turned to me. Putting his hands on my shoulders, he looked right into my eyes. Papa's brown eyes were not large, but they were very bright. Most of the time his eyes smiled at us, but when he was angry or upset, like now, they could cut us like knives. "Leah," he said, "what did you do to Mama's fish?"

"Please, Papa," I said, "don't let Mama kill our fish. His name is Joe. We love him, and we want to keep him for a pet."

"Where is he now?" Papa asked.

I looked down at my hands and began to pick my fingernail. I didn't want to tell Papa where Joe was. But he put his hand on my chin and forced my face up.

"Where's the fish now?" he asked again. His voice was gentle but those eyes were cutting me up.

"In Mrs. Ginzburg's bathtub," I mumbled.

Papa started walking again, faster now. We trailed along behind him, not holding his hands any more. He didn't say anything for awhile. But when we got to our

front <u>stoop</u>, he stopped to talk to us. "We are going to Mrs. Ginzburg's apartment and we are getting that fish," he said. "It's your mother's fish and it cost her a lot of money. She had to save a little out of what I give her each week just so she could buy such a big fish and make an extra nice Passover holiday for all of us." When we got to Mrs. Ginzburg's, Papa said to her, "We've come to take the fish home. I'm sorry for the trouble."

The front steps of an apartment building are called its *stoop*.

"Oh, he was no trouble," Mrs. Ginzburg said.

"Well, he would have been, as soon as you wanted to take a bath," Papa said.

We didn't say anything.

Mrs. Ginzburg let the water out of the tub. Papa didn't need a strainer to catch Joe. He just used his hands and the bucket.

It was much easier going back upstairs than it had been coming down. Papa carried the bucket. I ran the water, and without any ceremony Papa poured Joe in. He flitted through the water so gaily you'd think he was happy to be home. Foolish Joe.

"Carp are for eating," Papa said, "just like chicken.
You always eat two helpings of chicken."

"We never met the chicken," I said.

Papa shook his head. "That's not the point, Leah.
We don't kill more creatures than we need, and we
don't kill them for fun, but we eat what must be eaten.
It would break Mama's heart if she realized you children
didn't like to eat her *gefilte* fish. We won't tell her
about any of this. Mrs. Ginzburg won't tell her either."

So nobody told Mama about how we had stolen her
carp. Luckily, I was at school when she made Joe into
gefilte fish. When I got home, I asked Harry how he
could have stood watching her catch Joe with her
strainer and carry him off into the kitchen.

See pages T188–T189 in the front of this book for suggested postreading strategies.

"I didn't watch," Harry said. "When I saw her go for that strainer, I went right down to Mrs. Ginzburg's. But even there I could smell fish cooking."

Although Mama opened all the windows that afternoon, and no one else seemed to notice anything, Harry and I thought we smelled fish cooking for days.

We cried ourselves to sleep that night, and the next night too. Then we made ourselves stop crying. After that, we felt as if we were years older than Mama and Papa.

Tri-color (line 16) means *three-colored*.

One night about a week after Passover, we were sitting in the kitchen helping Mama shell peas when Papa came home. As he walked through the door, we noticed that he was carrying something orange and black and white and furry in his arms. It was a beautiful big tri-color cat.

"They had too many cats hanging around the loft," Papa said. "This one seemed so friendly and pretty that I brought her home."

Mama seemed surprised, but she let the cat stay. She was a clean cat. We called her Joe. Mama couldn't understand that.

I'm old now—a grandmother, as a matter of fact. My daughters buy *gefilte* fish in jars at the supermarket. They think their Uncle Harry and I don't eat it because it isn't as good as the kind our mother made. We don't tell them that we never ate Mama's either.

Questions

1. What did Leah and Harry like about the carp?

2. How did Papa know that Leah and Harry had tried to protect Joe?

3. Should Papa have helped the children protect the carp? Why or why not?

4. After Leah and Harry cried about the carp, Leah said, "We felt as if we were years older than Mama and Papa." What did she mean?

5. This story is about a carp, but it ends with a cat! Why is the cat in the story?

6. If you got into trouble, do you think that Leah and Harry would try to help you? Tell why or why not.

7. The story told you that *gefilte* means
   a. fish   b. stuffed   c. holiday

Activity   Make a Character Chart

Finish this chart to show what each character wanted and what each one did to get it.

Character	What Character Wanted	What Character Did
Leah & Harry		
Mama		
Papa		
Mrs. Ginzburg		

Buying a Puppy

A poem by Leslie Norris

See pages T189–T191 in the front of this book for a suggested teaching plan for this selection.

"Bring an old towel," said Pa,
"And a scrap of meat from the <u>pantry</u>.
We're going out in the car, you and I,
Into the country."

A *pantry* is a small room attached to a kitchen where food and dishes are kept.

I did as he said, although
I couldn't see why he wanted
A scrap of meat and an old towel.
Into the sun we pointed

Our Ford, over the green hills.
Pa sang. Larks bubbled in the sky.
I took with me all my cards—
It was my seventh birthday.

We turned down a happy lane,
Half sunlight, half shadow,
And saw at the end a white house
In a yellow meadow.

Mrs. Garner lived there. She was tall.
She gave me a glass of milk
And showed me her black spaniel.
"Her name is Silk,"

374

Mrs. Garner said. "She's got
Three puppies, two black, one golden.
Come and see them." Oh,
To have one, one of my own!

"You can choose one," said Pa.
I looked at him. He wasn't joking.
I could scarcely say thank you,
I was almost choking.

It was the golden one. He slept
On my knee in the old towel
All the way home. He was tiny,
But didn't whimper or howl,

Not once. That was a year ago,
And now I'm eight.
When I get home from school
He'll be waiting behind the gate,

Listening, listening hard,
Head raised, eyes warm and kind;
He came to me as a gift
And grew into a friend.

Illustrated by Bert Dodson

Wol to the Rescue

From the story *Owls in the Family* by Farley Mowat
Illustrated by Jenny Rutherford

*Wol, who was found when he was very young, is
an owl who doesn't know he is an owl. Wol prefers
walking to flying, enjoys riding on the handlebars of a
bicycle, and loves playing tricks on the dog. Weeps, a
smaller owl, was rescued from some boys who were tor-
menting him, and raised with Wol as his companion.
Both are very tame pets and love to go along on outings.*

See pages T191—T193 in the front of this book for a suggested teaching plan for this selection.

Toward the middle of July Bruce and I got permission from our parents to spend a night in the cave. We took Wol and Weeps with us, and of course we had both dogs, Rex and Mutt.

In the afternoon we went for a hike over the prairie, looking for birds. Mutt, who was running ahead of us, flushed a prairie chicken off her nest. There were ten eggs in the nest and they were just hatching out.

We sat down beside the nest and watched. In an hour's time seven of the little chickens had hatched before our eyes. It was pretty exciting to see, and Wol seemed just as curious about it as we were. Then all of a sudden three of the newly hatched little birds slipped out of the nest and scuttled straight for Wol. Before he could move they were underneath him, crowding against his big feet, and *peep-peeping* happily. I guess they thought he was their mother, because they hadn't seen their real mother yet.

Scuttled means *ran hastily; scurried.*

377

Wol was so surprised he didn't know what to do. He kept lifting up one foot and then the other to shake off the little ones. When the other four babies joined the first three, Wol began to get nervous. But finally he seemed to <u>resign</u> himself to being a mother, and he fluffed his feathers out and lowered himself very gently to the ground.

Wol resigned himself, or stopped resisting.

Bruce and I nearly died laughing. The sight of the baby prairie chickens popping their heads out through Wol's feathers, and that great big beak of his snapping <u>anxiously</u> in the air right over their heads, was the silliest thing I've ever seen. I guess Wol knew it was silly, too, but he couldn't figure how to get out of the mess he was in. He kept looking at me as if he were saying, "For Heaven's sake, DO something!"

Anxiously means worriedly.

I don't know how long he would have stayed there, but we began to worry that the real mother might not find her chicks, so I finally lifted him up and put him on my shoulder, and we went back to the cave for supper.

We'd had a good laugh at Wol, but he had the laugh on us before the day was done.

After we had eaten we decided to go down to the riverbank and wait for the sun to set. A pair of coyotes lived on the opposite bank of the river, and every evening just at sunset one of them would climb a little hill and sit there howling. It was a scary sound, but we liked it because it made us feel that this was the olden times, and the prairie belonged to us, to the buffaloes and the Indians, and to the prairie wolves.

Wol was sitting in the Hanging Tree, and Rex and Mutt had gone off somewhere on a hunting trip of their own. It was growing dusk when we heard a lot of crashing in the trees behind us. We turned around just as two big kids came into sight. They were two of the toughest kids in Saskatoon. If they hadn't come on us so suddenly, we would have been running before they ever saw us. But now it was too late to run—they would have caught us before we could go ten feet. The only thing we could do was sit where we were and hope they would leave us alone.

Pronounced /săs·kə·tōon′/.

What a hope *that* was! They came right over and
one of them reached down and grabbed Bruce and
started to twist his arm behind his back.

"Listen, you little rats," he said, "we heard you
got a cave someplace down here. You're too young to
own a cave, so we're taking over. Show us where it
is, or I'll twist your arm right off!"

The other big kid made a grab for me, but I
slipped past him and was just starting to run when he
stuck his foot out and tripped me. Then he sat
on me.

"Say, Joe," he said to his pal, "I got an idea. Either these kids tell us where the cave is, or we tie 'em to Ole Hanging Tree and leave 'em there all night with the ghost."

Just then the coyote across the river gave a howl. All four of us jumped a little, what with the talk of ghosts—but Joe said: "That ain't nothing. Just a coyote howling. You going to tell us, kid? Or do we tie you to the tree?"

Bruce and I knew they were only trying to scare us, but we were scared all right. I was just opening my mouth to tell them where the cave was when Wol took a hand in things.

He had been sitting on the big limb of the Hanging Tree and, since it was almost dark by then, he looked like a white blob up there. I don't think he'd been paying much attention to what was happening on the ground below him, but when that coyote howled he must have thought it was some kind of a challenge. He opened his beak and gave the Owl Hunting Scream.

Did you ever hear a horned owl scream? Usually they do it at night to scare any mice or rabbits that happen to be hiding near into jumping or running. Then the owl swoops down and grabs them. If you've ever heard an owl scream you'll know it's just about the most scary sound in all the world.

When Wol cut loose it made even my skin creep, and I knew what it was; but the two big kids didn't know.

Their heads jerked up, and they saw the ghostly white shape that was Wol up there in the Hanging Tree. And then they were off and running. They went right through the poplar woods like a couple of charging buffaloes, and we could still hear them breaking bush when they were half a mile away. My guess is they ran all the way to Saskatoon.

This expression means that the boys were still running through the bushes.

When they were out of hearing Bruce stood up and began rubbing his arm. Then he looked at Wol.

"Boy!" he said "You sure scared those two rough-necks silly! But did you have to scare *me* right out of my skin too?"

"Hoo-HOO-hoo-hoo-hoo-HOO!" Wol chuckled as he floated down out of the tree and lit upon my shoulder.

Wol *lit*, or *landed*, on the boy's shoulder.

See pages T192–T193 in the front of this book for suggested postreading strategies.

Questions

1. How do you think Wol got his name?

2. The chicks thought that Wol was a
   a. prairie chicken   b. horned owl   c. ghost
   2. Literal/Details   a. (page 377)

3. The two big kids thought that Wol was a
   a. prairie chicken b. horned owl   c. ghost
   3. Interpretive/Details (Inferred)   c. (page 383)

4. The story showed that Wol could be *funny* or *frightening.* How else do you think he could act? Tell how he would show his behavior.

5. If you were Wol, would you trust the two boys? Tell why or why not.

6. If you became the owner of an unusual pet, how would you help the pet learn to trust you?

7. Find the words the author used instead of the underlined words.   **7.**Literal/Details   a. creep
   a. It made my skin <u>tighten</u>. (page 381)
   b. Mutt <u>scared</u> a prairie chicken off her nest. (page 377)   **b.** flushed
   c. The tough kids went through the poplar woods <u>fast</u>. (page 382)   **c.** like a couple of charging buffaloes

Activity   Write a News Story

Write a news story for the *Saskatoon News* to report on Wol's heroic rescue of the two boys. Tell who was there, what happened, and why Wol is a hero. Give a headline, or title, to your story.

1. Critical/Analysis Possible responses: It came from mixing up the sound that the owl made; it came from scrambling the letters of the word *owl*.
4. Critical/Synthesis Before they answer this question, urge the students to think of Wol's relationship with his master and an owl's habits. Remind them to relate what Wol's actions might be.
5. Critical/Evaluation Possible responses: yes, because they were gentle and friendly; no, because humans are strange and sometimes harmful to owls.
6. Critical/Application Possible responses: Move slowly and nonthreateningly; speak softly and gently; give food and shelter.

See pages T193–T195 in the front of this book for a suggested teaching plan for this selection.

CONNECTIONS

How Animals Protect Themselves

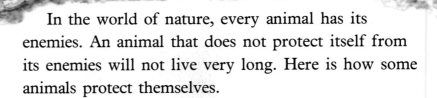

In the world of nature, every animal has its enemies. An animal that does not protect itself from its enemies will not live very long. Here is how some animals protect themselves.

Armor, Quills, and Spines

Nature has given some animals a thick coat of armor for protection. The *armadillo* is not a fighter. It does not need to be. Small plates of bone cover its body. When danger is near, the armadillo rolls itself into an armor-plated ball. Even the sharp teeth of a bobcat cannot bite through the armadillo's armor.

The *turtle* is built like an armored truck. When the turtle is scared, it pulls its head, tail, and legs into its hard shell. The common box turtle even has a shell that it closes tightly after its head, tail, and legs are safe inside.

Illustrated by Jeremy Guitar

Once a fox or weasel attacks a *porcupine*, the attacker will never try it again! When scared, the porcupine lifts its 30,000 or so quills. Each quill ends in a barb, like a fishhook. The porcupine strikes at its attacker with its quill-covered tail. It drives many quills into its attacker's face and paws. The quills keep working their way into the flesh of the enemy. If the quills pierce an important body part, the animal may die.

This *sea urchin* depends on long spines for protection. The spines of some sea urchins are poisonous.

Animals in Disguise

The *zebra* and *giraffe* have striking markings. Yet their coloring and markings make them almost invisible to their enemies. The zebra's stripes match the striped pattern of sunlight and shadows in the tall grasses where it feeds. The orange and brown marks on the giraffe's coat resemble patches of sunshine and shadows, like those in the leaves they eat.

In the Arctic, many animals have white coats that make it hard to see them against their snowy setting.

Some arctic foxes and hares change color with the seasons. In the summer their coats look like the gray-brown earth. In the fall the brown hairs are replaced by white ones.

The *chameleon* is also known for changing color to look like its background. The giant chameleon can change from bright yellow to blue to green in about a minute!

Animals That Flee

Many animals defend themselves by simply being fast on their feet. When danger is near, they run. As they run, they zigzag back and forth. This zigzagging helps to confuse their enemies. The table on the next page gives the top speeds of some animals that run from danger.

Animal	Top Speed
Pronghorn antelope	60 mph
Horse	47.5 mph
Jack rabbit	45 mph
White-tailed deer	40 mph
Giraffe	32 mph

Other Animal Weapons

See pages T194–T195 in the front of this book for suggested postreading strategies.

The *skunk* has a strange weapon, but it is a most powerful one! If an enemy comes near, the skunk beats its front feet on the ground. If the attacker comes even closer, then the skunk turns around and fires its famous smell. The enemy quickly learns a lesson it will not forget!

Even a coyote is afraid to attack the *badger*. With its sharp teeth and long claws, the badger is a fierce fighter. The honey badger of Africa fears no animal. It will attack even large snakes.

Some animals' teeth can be deadly weapons. Wolves' teeth are sharp and pointed. They fit together so closely, they can cut like the blade of a knife.

Nature has given some animals horns or antlers to use as weapons. These animals use their horns or antlers to keep enemies from getting close. Some also use their horns or antlers to push or throw enemies out of the way.

In the animal kingdom, each animal has its enemies. Each animal also has ways to keep itself safe. In the battle for survival, each animal uses whatever weapons it has for staying alive.

Questions

1. What are the main kinds of defenses animals have against their enemies?

2. Study this picture of a hedgehog. How do you think a hedgehog defends itself against its enemies? What part of the selection might help you?

Activities

1. **Make a List**

   List animals that nature protects in each of these ways:
   - a. with a shell
   - b. with coloring that matches its background
   - c. with long legs and a body built for speed
   - d. with sharp teeth or claws

2. **Keep a Nature Journal**

   Keep a nature journal about what you have seen in the natural world around you. Try to keep your journal for a week or longer. Study birds, insects, and small animals. See if you can find out and note how they protect themselves from danger.

See pages T195—T198 in the front of this book for a suggested teaching plan for this selection.

The Black Fox

From the story *The Midnight Fox* by Betsy Byars
Illustrated by Ron Himler

When Tom's parents leave on a two-month trip to Europe, he reluctantly goes to stay on his Aunt Millie's farm. Used to the city, Tom would rather stay there to work on his models and to be with his friend Petie Burkis.

The first three days on the farm were the longest, slowest days of my life. It seemed to me in those days that nothing was moving at all, not air, not time. Even the bees, the biggest fattest bees that I had ever seen, just seemed to hang in the air. The problem, or one of them, was that I was not an enormously <u>adaptable</u> person and I did not fit into new situations well.

I did a lot of just standing around those first days. I would be standing in the kitchen and Aunt Millie would turn around, stirring something, and bump into me and say, "Oh, my goodness! You gave me a scare. I didn't even hear you come in. When *did* you come in?"

"Just a minute ago."

"Well, I didn't hear you. You were so *quiet*."

When Tom says he is not an *adaptable* person, he means that he finds it difficult to change himself to fit new conditions or surroundings.

Or Uncle Fred would come out of the barn wiping his hands on a rag and there I'd be, just standing, and he'd say, "Well, boy, how's it going?"

"Fine, Uncle Fred."

"Good! Good! Don't get in any mischief now."

"I won't."

I spent a lot of time at the pond and walking down the road and back. I spent about an hour one afternoon hitting the end of an old rope swing that was hanging from a tree in the front yard. I made my two models, and then I took some spare plastic strips and rigged up a harness, so that the horse was pulling the car, and Aunt Millie got very excited over this bit of real nothing and said it was the cleverest thing she had ever seen.

I wrote a long letter to Petie. I went down to the stream and made boats of twigs and leaves and watched them float out of sight. I looked through about a hundred farm magazines. I weeded Aunt Millie's flowers while she stood over me saying, "Not that, not *that*, that's a <u>zinnia</u>. Get the <u>chickweed</u>—see? Right here." And she would snatch it up for me. I had none of the difficult chores that I had expected, because the farm was so well run that everything was already planned without me. In all my life I have never spent longer, more miserable days, and I had to keep saying, "I'm fine, just fine," because people were asking me how I was all the time.

A *zinnia* is a flower, but a *chickweed* is a weed.

The one highlight of my day was to go down to the mailbox for the mail. This was the only thing I did all day that was of any use. Then, too, the honking of the mail truck would give me the feeling that there was a letter of great importance waiting for me in the box. I could hardly hurry down the road fast enough. Anyone watching me from behind would probably have seen only a cloud of dust, my feet would pound so fast. So far, the only mail I had received was a post card from my mom with a picture of the Statue of Liberty on it telling me how excited and happy she was.

This Thursday morning when I went to the mailbox there was a letter to me from Petie Burkis and I was never so glad to see anything in my life. I ripped it open and completely destroyed the envelope I was in such a hurry. And I thought that when I was a hundred years old, sitting in a chair with a rug over my knees, and my mail was brought in on a silver tray, I would snatch it up and rip it open just like this. I could hardly get it unfolded—Petie folds his letters up small—I was so excited.

Dear Tom,

There is nothing much happening here. I went to the playground Saturday after you left, and you know that steep bank by the swings? Well, I fell all the way down that. Here's the story—

BOY FALLS DOWN BANK WHILE GIRL
ONLOOKERS CHEER

Today Petie Burkis fell down the bank at Harley Playground. It is reported that some ill-mannered girls at the park for a picnic cheered and laughed at the sight of the young, demolished boy. The brave youngster left the park unaided.

Not much else happened. Do you get Chiller Theater? There was a real good movie on Saturday night about mushroom men.

Write me a letter,
Petie Burkis

I went in and gave the rest of the mail to Aunt Millie, who said, "Well, let's see what the government's sending us today," and then I got my box of stationery and went outside.

There was a very nice place over the hill by the creek. There were trees so big I couldn't get my arms around them, and soft grass and rocks to sit on. They were planning to let the cows into this field later on, and then it wouldn't be as nice, but now it was the best place on the farm. . . .

Anyway, I sat down and wrote Petie a letter.

396

Dear Petie,

    I do not know whether we get Chiller Theater or not. Since there is no TV set here, it is very difficult to know what we could get if we had one.

    My farm chores are feeding the pigs, feeding the chickens, weeding the flowers, getting the mail, things like that. I have a lot of time to myself and I am planning a movie about a planet that <u>collides</u> with Earth, and this planet and Earth become fused together, and the people of Earth are terrified of the planet, because it is very weird-looking and they have heard these terrible moanlike cries coming from the depths of it. That's all so far.

Collides means crashes.

Write me a letter,

Tom

    I had just finished writing this letter and was waiting for a minute to see if I could think of anything to add when I looked up and saw the black fox.

I did not believe it for a minute. It was like my eyes were playing a trick or something, because I was just sort of staring across this field, thinking about my letter, and then in the distance, where the grass was very green, I saw a fox leaping over the crest of the field. The grass moved and the fox sprang toward the movement, and then, seeing that it was just the wind that had caused the grass to move, she ran straight for the grove of trees where I was sitting.

It was so great that I wanted it to start over again, like you can turn movie film back and see yourself repeat some fine thing you have done, and I wanted to see the fox leaping over the grass again. In all my life I have never been so excited.

I did not move at all, but I could hear the paper in my hand shaking, and my heart seemed to have moved up in my body and got stuck in my throat.

The fox came straight toward the grove of trees.
She wasn't afraid, and I knew she had not seen me
against the tree. I stayed absolutely still even though I
felt like jumping up and screaming, "Aunt Millie! Uncle
Fred! Come see this. It's a fox, a *fox*!"

Her steps as she crossed the field were lighter and
quicker than a cat's. As she came closer I could see
that her black fur was tipped with white. It was as if it
were midnight and the moon were shining on her fur,
frosting it. The wind parted her fur as it changed
directions. Suddenly she stopped. She was ten feet
away now, and with the changing of the wind she had
got my scent. She looked right at me.

I did not move for a moment and neither did she. Her
head was <u>cocked</u> to one side, her tail curled up, her
front left foot was raised. In all my life I never saw anything like that fox standing there with her pale golden eyes
on me and this great black fur being blown by the wind.

Her head was *cocked*,
or tilted, to one side.

Suddenly her nose quivered. It was such a slight movement I almost didn't see it, and then her mouth opened and I could see the pink tip of her tongue. She turned. She was still not afraid, but with a bound that was lighter than the wind—it was as if she was being blown away over the field—she was gone.

Still I didn't move. I couldn't. I couldn't believe that I had really seen the fox.

I had seen foxes before in zoos, but I was always in such a great hurry to get on to the good stuff that I was saying stupid things like, "I want to see the go-rilllllllas," and not once had I ever really looked at a fox. Still, I could never remember seeing a black fox, not even in a zoo.

The word *gorillas* is written this way because Tom was whining to his parents to hurry up.

Also, there was a great deal of difference between seeing an animal in the zoo in front of painted fake rocks and trees and seeing one natural and free in the woods. It was like seeing a kite on the floor and then, later, seeing one up in the sky where it was supposed to be, pulling at the wind.

I started to pick up my pencil and write as quickly as I could, "P.S. Today I saw a black fox." But I didn't. This was the most exciting thing that had happened to me, and "P.S. Today I saw a black fox" made it nothing. "So what else is happening?" Petie Burkis would probably write back. I folded my letter, put it in an envelope, and sat there.

I thought about this old newspaper that my dad had had in his desk drawer for years. It was orange and the headline was just one word, very big, the letters about twelve inches high. WAR! And I mean it was <u>awesome</u> to see that word like that, because you knew it was a word that was going to change your whole life, the whole world even. And every time I would see that newspaper, even though I wasn't even born when it was printed, I couldn't say anything for a minute or two.

Well, this was the way I felt right then about the black fox. I thought about a newspaper with just one word for a headline, very big, very black letters, twelve inches high. FOX! And even that did not show how awesome it had really been to me. . . .

The days and weeks passed quickly, long warm days in which I walked through the woods looking for the black fox.

The next time I saw her was in the late afternoon at the <u>ravine</u>.

This was my favorite place in the forest. The sides of the ravine were heavy dark boulders with mosses and ferns growing between the rocks, and at the bottom were trunks of old dead trees. The tree trunks were like statues in some old jungle temple, idols that had fallen and broken and would soon be lost in the creeping foliage. There was only an occasional patch of sunlight.

When a sight is *awesome*, it may inspire mixed feelings of wonder and fear.

401

At the top of the ravine was a flat ledge that stuck out over the rocks, and I was lying there on my stomach this particular afternoon. The rock was warm because the sun had been on it since noon, and I was half asleep when suddenly I saw something move below me. It was the black fox. There was a certain lightness, a quickness that I could not miss.

She came over the rocks as easily as a cat. Her tail was very high and full, like a sail that was bearing her forward. Her fur was black as coal, and when she was in the shadows all I could see was the white tip of her tail.

As I watched, she moved with great ease over one of the fallen trees, ran up the other side of the ravine, and disappeared into the underbrush.

I stayed exactly where I was. My head was resting on my arms, and everything was so still I could hear the ticking of my watch. I wanted to sit up. I am sort of a bony person and after I have been lying on something hard for a long time, I get very uncomfortable. This afternoon, however, I did not move; I had the feeling that the fox was going to come back through the ravine and I did not want to miss seeing her.

While I was waiting I watched an ant run across the ledge with an insect wing. He was running so fast with the wing that he would make a little breeze and the wing would fly out of his grasp. Then he would go back and get the wing and start running again.

Then I watched some birds on the other side of the ravine circling over the rocks, catching insects as they skimmed the air. It was a beautiful sight, and I thought as I watched them, *That* is what man had in mind when he first said, "I want to fly." And I thought about some old genius working up in a remote mountain valley actually making a little flying machine that he could strap on his back like a knapsack, and this old man would come down to a big air base and he would go out on the flight line and announce to everyone, "Folks, I have invented a flying machine." There would be a silence and then everyone would start laughing as if they would never stop, and finally the Captain would pause long enough to explain to the old man that flying machines had *already* been invented, that right over there—that big silver thing with the huge wings, *that* was a flying machine, and over there, those enormous bullet-shaped things, *those* were flying machines. "Well," the old man would say, shaking his head sadly, "I won't waste no more of your time. I'll just head on home," and he would press a button on his knapsack, and silently, easy as a bird, he would lift off the ground, and skimming the air, fly toward the hills. For a moment everyone would be too stunned to move, and then the General would cry, "Come back, come back," and everyone at the air base would run beneath the flying old man crying, "Wait, wait, come back, come back!" because that was the way every one of those men really wanted to fly, free and easy

and silent as a bird. But the old man, who was a little hard of hearing, would not hear their cries and would fly off into the distance and never be seen again.

Right after I stopped thinking about this, the black fox came back. She came down the rocks the same way she had gone up, her white-tipped tail as light as a plume, and I remembered a black knight I saw once in the movies who was so tall and fine and brave you could see his black plume racing ahead of all the other knights when there was a battle.

A plume *is a long feather.*

She had something in her mouth that looked like a frog—it probably was, for the creek was low now and you could always find a frog if you wanted one. She trotted on, apparently concerned only with getting the frog home, and yet I had the feeling that she was missing nothing. She passed across the ravine in a zigzag line and started up the other side.

405

I did not move, and yet all at once she looked up at me. She froze for a moment, her bright eyes looking at me with curiosity rather than fear, and she cocked her head to one side, listening.

I stayed perfectly still—I was getting good at this—and we looked at each other. Then she turned away and bounded up the side of the ravine, turning at the top and disappearing into the underbrush. I felt that somewhere in the shelter of the trees she had paused to see if I was going to follow. Perhaps she wanted me to follow so she could lead me back into the forest, but I stayed where I was. After a while, I got up and went back to the farm.

The next time I saw the fox, it was a marvelous accident. These don't happen very often in real life, but they do happen, and that's what this was. Like the time Petie and I were walking down the alley behind his house and there, on top of this lady's garbage, we saw a mayonnaise jar full of marbles—not just cat's-eye marbles but all different kinds, kinds I had never seen before. Petie and I turned them all out on the grass and first Petie chose one and then I chose one until they were all gone. And both of us right now, today, have every single one of those marbles.

This was an even better accident. For the past two weeks I had been practically tearing the woods apart looking for the den of the black fox. I had poked under rocks and logs and stuck sticks in rotted trees, and it was a wonder that some animal had not come storming out and just bitten my hand off.

I had found a hornet's nest like a huge gray shield
in a tree. I had found a bird's nest, low in a bush, with
five pale-blue eggs and no mother to hatch them. I had
found seven places where chipmunks lived. I had
found a brown owl who never moved from one certain
limb of one certain tree. I had heard a tree, split by
lightning years ago, suddenly topple and crash to the
ground, and I ran and got there in time to see a
disgruntled possum run down the broken tree and into
the woods. But I did not find the place where the black
fox lived.

Now, on this day, I did not go into the woods at all.
I had gone up the creek where there was an old
chimney, all that was left of somebody's cabin. I had
asked Aunt Millie about it, but all she could remember
was that some people named Bowden had worked on
the farm a long time ago and had lived here. I poked
around the old chimney for a while because I was
hoping I would find something that had belonged to
the Bowdens, and then I gave that up and walked
around the bend.

Crayfish look like small lobsters and live in fresh water.

I sat on a rock, perfectly still, for a long time and looked down into the creek. There were crayfish in the water—I could see them, sometimes partly hidden beneath a covering of sand, or I could see the tips of their claws at the edge of a rock. There were fish in the water so small I could almost see through them. They stayed right together, these fish, and they moved together too.

After a while I looked across the creek and I saw a hollow where there was a small clearing. There was an outcropping of rocks behind the clearing and an old log slanted against the rocks. Soft grass sloped down to the creek bank.

I don't know how long I sat there—I usually forgot about my watch when I was in the woods—but it was a long time. I was just sitting, not expecting anything or waiting for anything. And the black fox came through the bushes.

She set a small bird she was carrying on the ground and gave a small yapping bark, and at once, out of a hole beneath the rocks came a baby fox.

He did not look like his mother at all. He was tiny and woolly and he had a stubby nose. He tumbled out of the hole and fell on the bird as if he had not eaten in a month. I have never seen a fiercer fight in my life than the one that baby fox gave that dead bird. He shook it, pulled it, dragged it this way and that, all the while growling and looking about to see if anyone or anything was after his prize.

The black fox sat watching with an expression of
great satisfaction. Mothers in a park sometimes watch
their young children with this same fond, pleased
expression. Her eyes were golden and very bright as
she watched the tiny fox fall over the bird, rise, and
shake it.

In his <u>frenzy</u> he dropped the bird, picked up an older dried bird wing in its place, and ran around the clearing. Then, realizing his mistake, he returned and began to shake the bird with even greater fierceness. After a bit he made another mistake, dropping the bird by his mother's tail, and then trying to run off with that.

In the midst of all this, there was a noise. It was on the other side of the clearing, but the black fox froze. She made a faint sound, and at once the baby fox, still carrying his bird, disappeared into the den.

The black fox moved back into the underbrush and waited. I could not see her but I knew she was waiting to lead the danger, if there was any, away from her baby. After a while I heard her bark from the woods, and I got up quietly and moved back down the creek. I did not want the black fox to see me and know that I had discovered her den. My cousin Hazeline had told me that foxes will pick up their young like cats and take them away if they think someone has discovered their den. . . .

I decided I would never come back here to bother her. I knew I would be tempted, because already I wanted to see that baby fox play with his bird some more, but I would not do it. If I was to see the black fox again, it would be in the woods, or in the pasture, or in the ravine, but I was not going to come to the den ever again. I did not know that an awful thing was going to happen which would cause me to break this resolution. . . .

Explain that the promise Tom made to himself was his *resolution*.

410

Questions

1. The author uses three headlines in this story. The last one is FOX! What are the other two? Why does the author use these headlines?

2. At the start of the story, Tom is lonesome and bored. How does the black fox help him?

3. At the end, Tom says that "an awful thing was going to happen." What do you think the "awful thing" will be? How might the "awful thing" cause Tom to break his promise not to see the black fox again?

4. Tom said, "I was not an enormously adaptable person." Which sentence tells what *not adaptable* means? **4. Literal/Definitions** b. (page 393)
   a. "I have never spent longer, more miserable days."
   b. "I did not fit into new situations well."
   c. "I stayed absolutely still even though I felt like jumping up. . . ."

Activity Write an Exciting Letter

Although Tom wanted to write his friend Petie a letter about the black fox, he knew that writing "Today I saw a black fox" would not be enough. Write an exciting letter for Tom. Try to share with Petie what you (Tom) have seen.

Dear Petie,

Write soon,
Tom

frog

A poem by Valerie Worth

See pages T198–T199 in the front of this book for a suggested teaching plan for this selection.

The spotted frog
Sits quite still
On a wet stone;

He is green
With a luster
Of water on his skin;

His back is mossy
With spots, and green
Like moss on a stone;

His gold-circled eyes
Stare hard
Like bright metal rings;

When he leaps
He is like a stone
Thrown into the pond;

Water rings spread
After him, bright circles
Of green, circles of gold.

412

Illustrated by Christa Kieffer

Learn About

Similes and Metaphors by Myra Cohn Livingston

See pages T199–T200 in the front of this book for a suggested teaching plan for this selection.

Poets have exciting ways to help us see things differently and more clearly. For example, when one thing reminds them of another, poets may describe how these two things are alike by comparing them. These imaginative comparisons are called *similes* (SIM•uh•lees) and *metaphors* (MET•uh•fawrz). Poets use them to help us see something in a new way.

A simile is usually introduced by the words *like* or *as.* In her poem "frog," Valerie Worth uses three similes.

His back is mossy
With spots, and green
Like moss on a stone;

Ask the students to find the key word *like* in the poem.

His gold-circled eyes
Stare hard
Like bright metal rings;

When he leaps
He is like a stone
Thrown into the pond.

In the first simile, the poet compares the green of the frog's back to moss on a stone and says that

413

the moss and the frog's back are similar. In the next simile, the frog's eyes remind the poet of bright, metal rings. When the frog leaps, the poet says he is like a stone thrown into the pond.

Similes can be created about everything we know. In her poem "Some People," Rachel Field has two similes about thoughts.

> **Your thoughts begin to shrivel up**
> **Like leaves all brown and dried!**

Have your thoughts ever seemed like dried-up leaves? Perhaps, at times, they are

> **. . . as thick as fireflies**
> **All shiny in your mind.**

Poets also use metaphors to compare two different things. A poet usually introduces a metaphor with the word *is.* In his poem "Dreams," Langston Hughes uses metaphor to give us a vivid picture of what would happen if dreams should die. He says more than "life would be bad" or "things would be terrible." Instead, he paints a picture for us to see.

Life is a broken-winged bird
That cannot fly.
. . . .
Life is a barren field
Frozen with snow.

By using a metaphor, Langston Hughes gives us a new way of looking at life. So does poet Eve Merriam, who tells us how she feels about the day in her poem "Metaphor." How does the poet give us a new way of looking at the day in these first three lines from her poem?

Morning is
a new sheet of paper
for you to write on.

Now look at some things around you. Look at the shapes of clouds, people you know, buildings, windows, trees, rocks—even your own thoughts and dreams—and make your own similes and metaphors. You'll discover an exciting way of looking at and thinking about the world!

See page T200 in the front of this book for suggested postreading strategies.

BOOKSHELF

An Insect's Body by Joanna Cole. William Morrow, 1984. Have you ever wondered what a cricket really looks like? This book takes a close look at the common house cricket.

Hawk, I'm Your Brother by Byrd Baylor. Charles Scribner's Sons, 1976. Rudy Soto plans to steal a baby hawk from a nest, hoping the hawk will help him learn to fly.

Ground Squirrels by Colleen S. Bare. Dodd, Mead, 1980. The California ground squirrel and others have many different habits that this book will help you understand.

Nature's Champions: the Biggest, the Fastest, the Best by Alvin and Virginia Silverstein. Random House, 1980. For nature lovers, this book describes more than 25 plants and animals that are unusual in some way.

Misty of Chincoteague by Marguerite Henry. Rand McNally, 1947. Would you want a wild island-pony for your very own? Maureen and Paul hope that Misty will be theirs.

A Swinger of Birches: Poems of Robert Frost for Young People by Robert Frost. Stemmer House, 1982. Discover and feel the beauty of nature in poetry form.

Reading Level Average

Drawing from Nature by Jim Arnosky. Lothrop, Lee & Shepard, 1982. For anyone who wants to learn how to draw water, land, plants, and animals, this book will interest you. In it, you will see how to make the natural world come alive on your paper.

Reading Level Easy

Cross Fox by Jane Scott. Atheneum, 1980. When neighbors organize a hunt to kill the fox Jamie has been watching in the Pennsylvania countryside, he realizes he must do something to save its life.

Reading Level Average

A Frog's Body by Joanna Cole. William Morrow, 1980. Closeup pictures of a frog's body help to explain this interesting creature.

Reading Level Challenging

Orphans from the Sea by Jack Denton Scott. G. P. Putnam's, 1982. Sometimes birds need our help. This book tells about the people who work to rescue and heal orphaned or injured seabirds and other wild creatures.

Reading Level Challenging

Poisonous Snakes by George S. Fichter. Franklin Watts, 1982. Snakes have characteristics and behaviors all their own. Enter the world of these mysterious reptiles and learn about the different kinds of poisonous snakes.

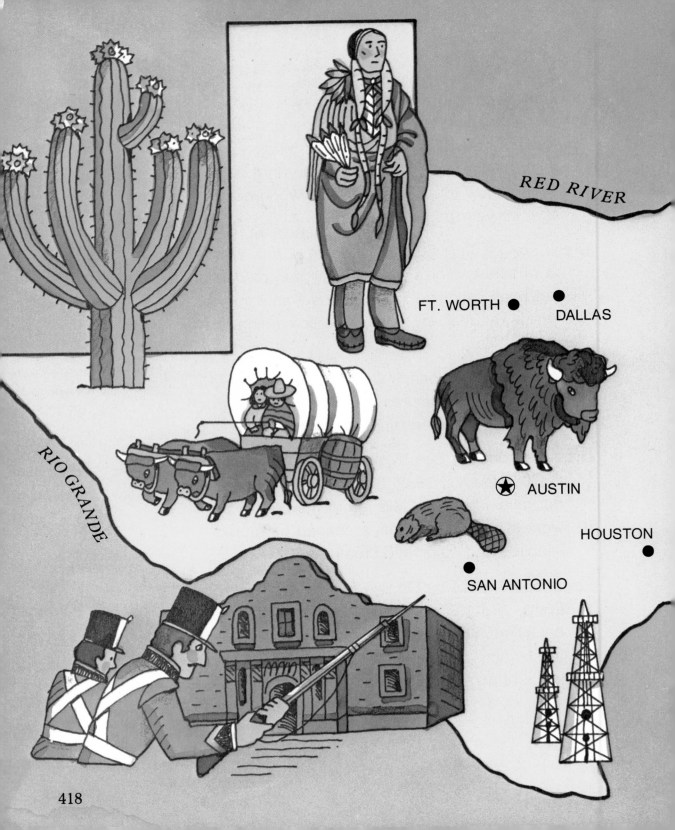

RED RIVER

RIO GRANDE

FT. WORTH

DALLAS

AUSTIN

HOUSTON

SAN ANTONIO

7 Tales of Texas

See pages T201–T202 in the front of this book for a suggested teaching plan.

See pages T202–T204 in the front of this book for a suggested teaching plan for this selection.

Indians of Early Texas

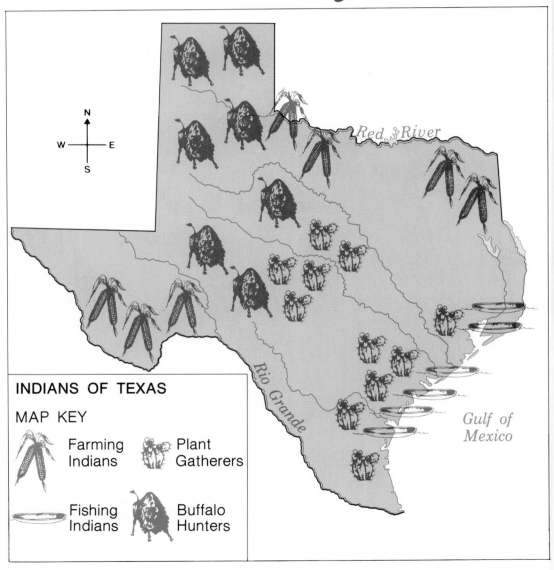

INDIANS OF TEXAS

MAP KEY

Farming Indians

Plant Gatherers

Fishing Indians

Buffalo Hunters

Red River

Rio Grande

Gulf of Mexico

The first Texans came from Asia. Experts believe they drifted through Alaska down to Texas about 12,000 years ago. Settlers from Europe later called these people Indians.

Ten Indian nations once lived in Texas. Each nation had its own rules, customs, and language. The ten nations can be divided into four groups. Some lived mainly by farming. Some lived mainly by fishing. Some gathered plants. Some hunted buffalo. The map shows where the different nations lived.

The **farming Indians** grew corn, beans, squash, and pumpkins. They hardly ever moved their villages, since they had to stay near their fields.

The **fishing Indians** ate oysters, turtles, fish, and roots. When they used up their food in one place, they moved to another. They traveled in canoes made from logs.

The **plant gatherers** lived on plants they found growing wild. They ate nuts, berries, wild beans, and prickly pear cactus. They too moved their villages when they had used up their food.

The **buffalo hunters** got nearly everything they needed from buffalo. They ate the meat. They made their tents and clothes out of buffalo hides. They even found uses for the bones and hooves. They lived on the move, following the buffalo.

Few Indians now live in Texas, but the Indians left their mark. The name *Texas* comes from a Caddo Indian word meaning "friend."

Comanche

Wichita

Caddo Indians greeted Spanish explorers with the word *Tayshas* or *Tejas*. The word *Tejas* was eventually used to designate the province and finally the state of Texas.

The Legend of
the Bluebonnet

**A Comanche legend retold and illustrated
by Tomie dePaola**

See pages T204–T207 in the front of this
book for a suggested teaching plan for this
selection.

"Great Spirits, the land is dying. Your People are dying, too," the long line of dancers sang.

"Tell us what we have done to anger you. End this drought. Save your People. Tell us what we must do so you will send the rain that will bring back life."

For three days, the dancers danced to the sound of the drums, and for three days, the People called Comanche watched and waited. And even though the hard winter was over, no healing rains came.

Drought and famine are hardest on the very young and the very old. Among the few children left was a small girl named She-Who-Is-Alone. She sat by herself watching the dancers. In her lap was a doll made from buckskin—a warrior doll. The eyes, nose and mouth were painted on with the juice of berries. It wore beaded leggings and a belt of polished bone. On its head were brilliant blue feathers from the bird who cries "Jay-jay-jay." She loved her doll very much.

"Soon," She-Who-Is-Alone said to her doll, "the shaman will go off alone to the top of the hill to listen for the words of the Great Spirits. Then, we will know what to do so that once more the rains will come and the Earth will be green and alive. The buffalo will be plentiful and the People will be rich again."

As she talked, she thought of the mother who
made the doll, of the father who brought the blue
feathers. She thought of the grandfather and the
grandmother she had never known. They were all
like shadows. It seemed long ago that they had died
from the famine. The People had named her and
cared for her. The warrior doll was the only thing
she had left from those distant days.

"The sun is setting," the runner called as he ran through the camp. "The shaman is returning."

The People gathered in a circle and the shaman spoke.

"I have heard the words of the Great Spirits," he said. "The People have become selfish. For years, they have taken from the Earth without giving anything back. The Great Spirits say the People must

sacrifice. We must make a burnt offering of the most valued possession among us. The ashes of this offering shall then be scattered to the four points of the Earth, the Home of the Winds. When this sacrifice is made, drought and famine will cease. Life will be restored to the Earth and to the People!"

The People sang a song of thanks to the Great Spirits for telling them what they must do.

"I'm sure it is not my new bow that the Great Spirits want," a warrior said.

"Or my special blanket," a woman added, as everyone went to their tipis to talk and think over what the Great Spirits had asked.

Everyone, that is, except She-Who-Is-Alone. She held her doll tightly to her heart.

"You," she said, looking at the doll. "You are my most valued possession. It is you the Great Spirits want." And she knew what she must do.

As the council fires died out and the tipi flaps began to close, the small girl returned to the tipi, where she slept, to wait.

The night outside was still except for the distant sound of the night bird with the red wings. Soon everyone in the tipi was asleep, except She-Who-Is-Alone. Under the ashes of the tipi fire one stick still glowed. She took it and quietly crept out into the night. She ran to the place on the hill where the Great Spirits had spoken to the shaman. Stars filled the sky, but there was no moon.

"O Great Spirits," She-Who-Is-Alone said, "here is my warrior doll. It is the only thing I have from my family who died in this famine. It is my most valued possession. Please accept it."

Then, gathering twigs, she started a fire with the glowing firestick. The small girl watched as the twigs began to catch and burn. She thought of her grandmother and grandfather, her mother and father and all the People—their suffering, their hunger. And

Tipi (paragraph 5) is the American Indian spelling of *tepee* and comes from *ti* meaning "to dwell" and *pi* meaning "used for."

before she could change her mind, she thrust the doll into the fire.

She watched until the flames died down and the ashes had grown cold. Then, scooping up a handful, She-Who-Is-Alone scattered the ashes to the Home of the Winds, the North and the East, the South and the West. And there she fell asleep until the first light of the morning sun woke her.

She looked out over the hill, and stretching out from all sides, where the ashes had fallen, the ground was covered with flowers—beautiful flowers, as blue as the feathers in the hair of the doll, as blue as the feathers of the bird who cries "Jay-jay-jay."

When the People came out of their tipis, they

could scarcely believe their eyes. They gathered on the hill with She-Who-Is-Alone to look at the miraculous sight. There was no doubt about it, the flowers were a sign of forgiveness from the Great Spirits.

And as the People sang and danced their thanks to the Great Spirits, a warm rain began to fall and the land began to live again. From that day on, the

little girl was known by another name—"One-Who-Dearly-Loved-Her-People."

And every spring, the Great Spirits remember the sacrifice of a little girl and fill the hills and valleys of the land, now called Texas, with the beautiful blue flowers.

Even to this very day.

See pages T206–T207 in the front of this book for suggested postreading strategies.

Questions

1. In the story, She-Who-Is-Alone says to her doll, "You are my most valued possession." Why was the doll so important to She-Who-Is-Alone? Give three reasons for your answer.

2. Why was rain so important to the People?

3. Which word best describes She-Who-Is-Alone? Give at least one reason for your answer.
   a. lonely   c. unselfish   e. bold
   b. kind   d. shy   f. unhappy

4. Match each word with its meaning.

   drought   a. enough for everyone
   famine   b. a long time without rain
   plentiful   c. a long time without food
   a sacrifice   d. something belonging to someone
   possession   e. the giving up of something loved

Activity   Write a Story

Choose one of the Texas wildflowers from the list below. Make up and write a story about it. First think of the characters who will be in your story. They could be people or animals from Texas history. Then think of a problem faced by one or more of the characters. The way the problem is solved should lead to the existence of the flower.

goldenrod   Mexican hat   Indian blanket

buttercup   Indian paintbrush

See pages T207–T209 in the front of this book for a suggested teaching plan for this selection.

CONNECTIONS

Texas Wildlife

Texas has grasslands, forests, and mountains. It has swamps and hot, dry plains. Animals and plants of many different kinds live in these very different places.

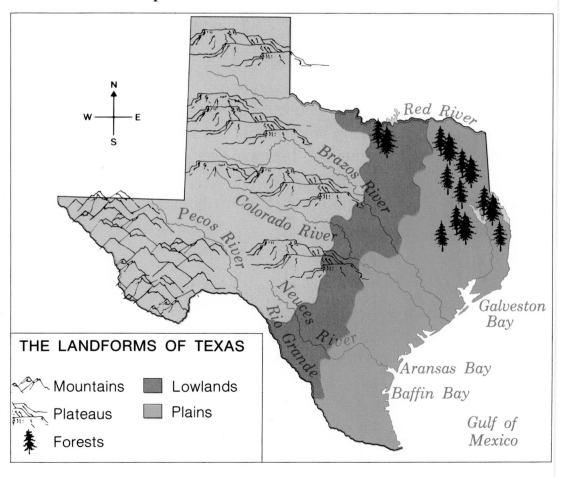

N
W — E
S

Red River

Brazos River

Pecos River

Colorado River

Neuces River

Rio Grande

Galveston Bay

Aransas Bay

Baffin Bay

Gulf of Mexico

THE LANDFORMS OF TEXAS

Mountains — Lowlands
Plateaus — Plains
Forests

434

Illustrated by Keith Freeman

bluebonnets

Texas Plants

In spring, some fields in central Texas look as if they are covered with a blue carpet. The color comes from millions of wildflowers called **bluebonnets**—the state flower.

Another Texas plant, the **mesquite** (mes·KEET), is not so pretty. It is a thorny bush that can live on very little water. Mesquite grows well in much of hot, dry western Texas. In dry areas, the mesquite is a small bush. The more rain it gets, the taller it grows. In wetter parts of Texas, a mesquite can grow to be a 60-foot-tall tree!

barrel cactus

mesquite

prickly pear cactus

teddy bear cactus

435

Cactus plants also grow well in western Texas. There are many different kinds of cactuses. The prickly pear cactus has provided food for the Indians.

Texas Animals

Dry western Texas is also a home for many kinds of snakes. **Diamondback rattlesnakes** can grow as long as nine feet. These snakes shed their skin several times a year. Each time, a little of the old skin is left on the snake's tail. These pieces of old skin make up the snake's rattle. When a rattler shakes its tail, the sound is a warning to its enemy.

The **roadrunner** is a Texas bird that sometimes eats small rattlers. This bird dances near the rattler. The snake strikes again and again, missing each time. When the poison in the rattlesnake's fangs is gone, the roadrunner moves in for a meal.

The bird was named roadrunner because it jogs along for miles. Roadrunners can fly, but they are fast runners. They can run at speeds up to 20 miles an hour.

roadrunner   rattlesnake

white-tailed deer

Deer live in almost every part of Texas. The **white-tailed deer** are the most common. The white tails of these animals go up like flags at any sign of danger. This warns other deer to be careful.

Texas also has many **coyotes** (ky·OH·teez). Most of them live on the west Texas plains. Coyotes eat almost anything. They eat birds, fish, insects, mice, and berries—and that is just for a start.

One small Texas animal a coyote cannot easily turn into a meal is the **armadillo.** Armadillos are covered with "armor"—very tough, thick skin. By day they sleep underground. At night they look for insects to eat.

armadillo

coyote

javelinas

The **javelina** (jav·uh·LEE·nuh) is another Texas animal. Javelinas are wild pigs with razor-sharp tusks. They eat roots and cactus plants.

bison

A few thousand **bison** still live in Texas. (Most people call them buffalo, but that is not their correct name.) Long ago millions of bison roamed the Great Plains. Today there are fewer than thirty thousand. Most of the bison in Texas live on ranches.

golden eagle

Bighorn sheep

mountain lion

antelope

bear

Protecting Texas Wildlife

Many parts of Texas have been set aside as state or national parks. These parks give plants and wildlife safe places to live and grow. The biggest park is called **Big Bend National Park.** The mountains of Big Bend are the home of the golden eagle and the mountain lion. Bighorn sheep, bears, and antelopes live there, too.

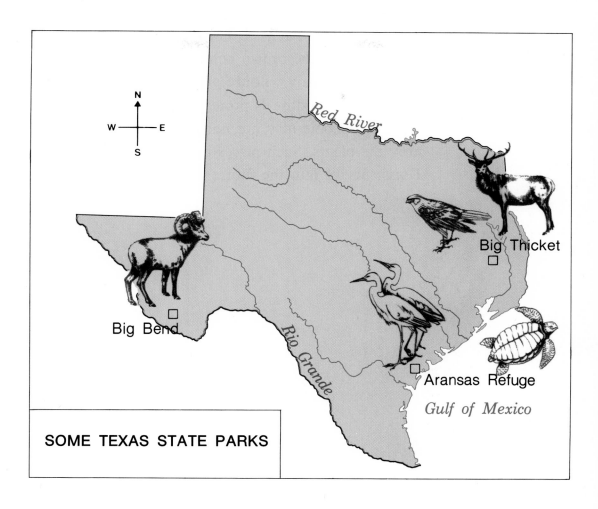

SOME TEXAS STATE PARKS

The **Big Thicket** is a special area in east Texas on the Louisiana border. In its 3½ million acres of swamps and dense forests, you may find more than 1,000 kinds of plants and 300 kinds of birds. Tiny orchids and insect-eating pitcher plants bloom in the swamps. In the forests, wolves and red-tailed hawks hunt for food.

See pages T208–T209 in the front of this book for suggested postreading strategies.

Rare whooping cranes nest in the **Aransas National Wildlife Refuge.** Fewer than 100 "whoopers" are left in the world. Many other rare animals can also be found at Aransas. They include five kinds of sea turtles and the brown pelican.

Texas has many wildlife *preserves* (prih·ZURVZ), places where wildlife is protected by law. In these preserves, people may not hunt the animals or destroy the plants. Such places help the wildlife of Texas survive into the future.

whooping crane

brown pelican

sea turtle

Questions

1. How are mesquite and cactus alike? How are they different?

2. How do the white-tailed deer, the armadillo, and the roadrunner protect themselves from enemies?

3. What are three Texas animals that either are rare or are in danger of dying out?

4. What is a wildlife preserve? What are some animals or plants you will find in a wildlife preserve?

5. Which word correctly completes each of the sentences below?
   a. The (rattlesnake, bison, roadrunner) is a dangerous reptile.
   b. The coyote eats almost everything except (birds, armadillos, fish).

1. Interpretive/Details They both grow in hot, dry western Texas. The mesquite is a bush with leaves; cactus plants do not have leaves.

2. Interpretive/Conclusion Both the deer and the roadrunner run from their enemies. The armadillo uses its armor to shield itself from its enemies.

3. Literal/Details whooping crane, brown pelican, sea turtle

4. Literal/Details a place where wildlife is protected by law; whooping crane, brown pelican, sea turtle

5. Literal/Detail a. rattlesnakes (page 436); b. armadillo (page 437)

Activity   Plan and Write a Report

Choose a Texas animal or plant that interests you. Find out the following facts about it: the place where it is found, what it looks like, a few interesting facts about it, if it is a rare or common creature. Then write or give a report on the plant or animal you have chosen. Try to find or draw pictures to illustrate your report.

CONNECTIONS

THE SPANIARDS IN TEXAS

See pages T209–T210 in the front of this book for a suggested teaching plan for this selection.

Indians were the only people in Texas until the 1500s. The first visitors were hardy explorers from Spain such as Alonzo de Piñeda (ah·LON·soh deh pee·NYAY·da). In 1519, Piñeda stopped at the mouth of the Rio Grande. There, he planted the flag of Spain on the land that was Texas and Mexico. For the next 300 years, Spaniards controlled and settled the land that they called New Spain.

Cabeza de Vaca (kah·BAY·sah deh bah·kah) was another Spanish explorer. In 1528, his ship washed up on Galveston Island. He spent seven years with the American Indians there. Then he walked to Mexico City, a journey that took him through much of southern Texas.

Early Spanish explorers had heard tales that somewhere in Texas were cities made of gold. Spain sent an army captain, Francisco de Coronado (fran·SIS·koh deh koh·roh·NAH·doh), to find the cities. Coronado failed, but many Spaniards still flocked to Texas looking for gold. They never found what they were looking for.

Spanish priests came, too. The priests built *missions*—churches surrounded by small villages. They hoped Indians would settle in the villages and become Christians.

In 1685, the first settlers from France came to Texas. Soon many French people were trying to settle Texas. Spain sent troops to drive the French from Texas. The French later settled in Louisiana, and Texas stayed under Spanish control.

In 1821, Spanish colonists in New Spain broke away from Spain. They set up the new nation of Mexico. Texas was part of this new nation. It was ruled by the government in Mexico City.

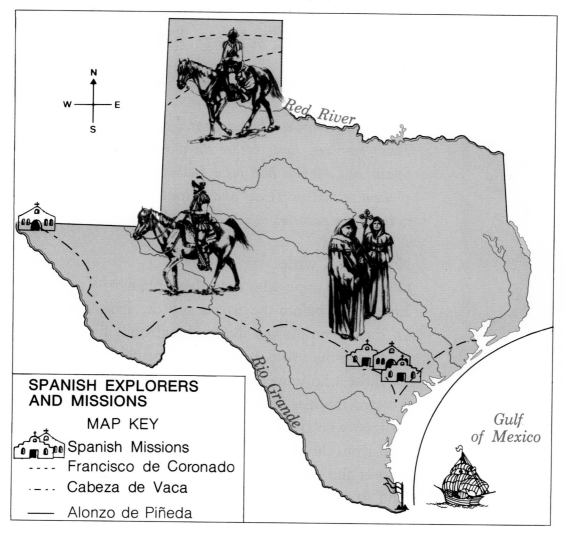

SPANISH EXPLORERS AND MISSIONS

MAP KEY

Spanish Missions

- - - - Francisco de Coronado

·- -· Cabeza de Vaca

—— Alonzo de Piñeda

From **The Other Pioneers**

From a poem by Roberto Félix Salazar

People from the United States were not the first
Texas pioneers. Long before their time, colonists from
Spain and Mexico had been pushing into Texas. Many
of them settled in Texas and helped it grow. They, too,
were Texas pioneers.

Now I must write
Of those of mine who rode these plains
Long years before the Saxon and the Irish came.
Of those who plowed the land and built the towns
And gave the towns soft-woven Spanish names.
Of those who moved across the Rio Grande
Toward the hiss of Texas snake and Indian yell.
Of men who from the earth made thick-walled homes
And from the earth raised churches to their God.
And of the wives who bore them sons
And smiled with knowing joy.

See pages T210–T211 in the front of this book for a suggested teaching plan for this selection.

Illustrated by Floyd Cooper

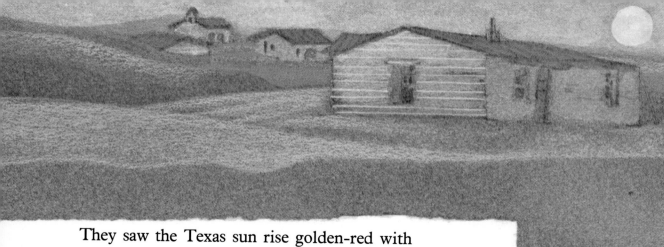

They saw the Texas sun rise golden-red with
    promised wealth
And saw the Texas sun sink golden yet, with
    wealth unspent.
"Here," they said. "Here to live and here to love."
"Here is the land for our sons and the sons of our
    sons."
And they sang the songs of ancient Spain
And they made new songs to fit new needs.
They cleared the brush and planted the corn
And saw green stalks turn black from lack of rain.

And the years moved on.
Those who were first placed in graves
Beside the broad mesquite and the tall nopal.
Gentle mothers left their graces and their arts
And stalwart fathers pride and manly strength.
Salinas, de la Garza, Sánchez, García,
Uribe, González, Martínez, de León:
Such were the names of the fathers.
Salinas, de la Garza, Sánchez, García,
Uribe, González, Martínez, de León:
Such are the names of the sons.

Nopal (no·pal') (line 3 below) is a type of cactus.

Salinas . . . de Leon (sah·LEE·nahs, day lah GAHR·sah, SAHN·ches, gahr· SEE·ah, o·REE·bay, gohn·SAHL·es, mahr·TEEN·es, day lay·OHN)

Stalwart (line 5 above) means strong in body and spirit; not likely to give up easily.

Texas Family Tree

See pages T211–T212 in the front of this book for a suggested teaching plan for this selection.

JUAN SEGUIN

Juan Seguin organized Hispanic Texans to fight against Santa Anna in the battles to be free from Mexican rule. He was among the few Texans to fight at both the Alamo and San Jacinto. After the war he was elected to the Texas government, and later became mayor of San Antonio.

Some Texans were jealous of Seguin, however, and spread rumors that he was a traitor. They forced him to flee for his life to Mexico. There the Mexican government put him in jail until he agreed to join the Mexican army. Meanwhile, the new Texas government sold Seguin's lands.

Seguin died in 1890, a man without a country. Years later the stories about him were proved false. His body was returned to the Texas town of Seguin, named in his honor. He was reburied as a Texas hero.

DOÑA MARIA CALVILLO

Doña Maria Calvillo (dohn·nyah mah·REE·ah kahl·BEE·yoh) was an expert at riding horses and roping cattle. She owned a large ranch in early Texas. On her ranch, she had cattle, sheep, and goats.

About 20 families lived on her land. Some of the families worked as ranch hands. Others worked as carpenters, blacksmiths, and tailors. Doña Maria also built a sugar mill and a *granary*, or

building for storing grain, on her land.

She was friendly with the Indians in her area, and in the winter gave them food. Born in 1765, Doña Maria Calvillo lived nearly 100 years.

LORENZO DE ZAVALA

Lorenzo de Zavala (loh·REN·soh deh sah·BAH·lah) was among the signers of the Texas Declaration of Independence. Before coming to Texas he had served as governor of a Mexican *province*, or state, and as the Mexican Ambassador to France.

De Zavala designed the first flag of the Texas republic. It was blue with one gold star in the middle. Around the star was the word TEXAS. De Zavala also served as the first vice-president of the new Republic of Texas.

FATHER FRANCISCO HIDALGO

Father Francisco Hidalgo (frahn·SIS·koh ee·DAHL·goh) was among the first Spanish priests to work among the Texas Indians. At the time, the Spanish government had little interest in setting up missions in Texas. Father Hidalgo asked for help from the French settlers in Louisiana. Some French people came to the Rio Grande Valley in answer to his call. When Spain saw that the French were beginning to settle in Texas, the Spanish government decided to work harder to settle in Texas. In 1716, the Spanish government helped Father Hidalgo reopen the first mission in Texas.

FATHER MIGUEL HIDALGO

Father Miguel Hidalgo (mee·GEHL ee·DAHL·goh) started the Mexican Revolution. In the early 1800s, he noticed how badly Spanish rulers treated the people of Mexico. So he tried to organize Indians and Spaniards who had been born in America to fight against Spain. Father Hidalgo's army won many battles but was finally overcome. Father Hidalgo was then taken and shot. Other leaders, however, continued the revolution Father Hidalgo had started.

WILLIAM GOYENS

William Goyens (wil·yuhm goh·ehnz), the son of a freed slave, moved to Texas in 1820. He

earned a fortune as a blacksmith making wagons and guns, two of the most important items needed by Texas pioneers. Goyens spoke several Indian languages. After Texas freed itself from Mexico, he became an Indian agent for the new government. He helped the government work with the Indians living in Texas.

PADRE NICOLAS BALLI

One of the first Spaniards to settle in Texas was the sea-going priest Padre Nicolas Balli (pah·dreh nee·coh·LAHS bah·yee). According to one story, King Charles of Spain offered Padre Balli all the Texas land he could drag a cowhide around in three days. Padre Balli sent food and fresh horses on ahead. Then, dragging a cowhide, he rode swiftly, changing horses from time to time. In this way he claimed several million acres of Texas. Padre Island, near Brownsville, is named after Padre Balli because he started a ranch there.

The Alamo: Texans Fight for Freedom

In 1836, a man named Antonio López de Santa Anna (ahn·TOH·nee·oh LOH·pehs deh sahn·tuh ahn·nuh) was the dictator of Mexico when Mexico ruled what is now called Texas. Santa Anna took away certain rights that had been promised to Texas. This made Texans very angry. Several times, they attacked and captured Mexican soldiers in Texas. In one attack, they captured the city of San Antonio, which was under Mexican rule.

Santa Anna decided to punish the Texans. He gathered a large army in Mexico and headed north. His path into Texas lay through San Antonio. There, a small band of Texans decided to block his way.

The Texans turned an old mission called the **Alamo** into a fort. Santa Anna and his army of 5,000 soldiers circled the fort. Inside the fort were

See pages T213–T214 in the front of this book for a suggested teaching plan for this selection.

451

less than 190 fighting men and about 15 women and children. The Texans held the fort for 13 days. During that time, Texas leaders met at a town named Washington-on-the-Brazos. They declared Texas a free country.

On March 6, Santa Anna's forces broke into the Alamo. They killed all the men inside. In doing so they may have lost the war. Santa Anna's cruelty made other Texans fight even harder against him. Other Texans remembered the brave men killed by Santa Anna. "Remember the Alamo!" became the Texas battle cry. Six weeks later, Texans attacked Santa Anna's army at San Jacinto (sahn hah•SEEN• toh). Shouting "Remember the Alamo!", they defeated the Mexican army in 18 minutes.

The fight for Texas independence would not have been possible without the help of very brave men and women. Many gave their lives. Some lived, but always remembered the battle. Whatever their role, all these men and women had a common bond—to be free from Mexico. Here are some of those brave men and women.

Stephen Austin   In 1821, Stephen Austin led the first settlers from the United States to Texas. He got permission to do so from the Mexican government. After Austin's group came to Texas, so did many other people from the United States. By 1830, they outnumbered Spaniards in Texas ten to one. Later, when Texas fought to free itself from Mexico, Austin got help from the United States.

Sam Houston Sam Houston was a lawyer. He moved to Texas from Tennessee. In 1836, Texas leaders said Texas was a free country. They raised an army to defend themselves against Mexico. The Texas leaders put Sam Houston in charge of the army. Later that year, Houston's army beat the Mexican forces at San Jacinto. Texas became a free country. Sam Houston was made its first president.

William Travis William Travis was one of the leaders in the war for Texan independence. He led the army of Texans at the Alamo. The Mexican army attacked the Alamo after Texas declared its freedom. Travis and his men fought the huge Mexican army in a battle that lasted 13 days. When Travis and all his men were killed, the Mexicans overran the fort.

Susanna Dickenson Susanna Dickenson was one of the few women at the Alamo, and an eyewitness to the battle. Mrs. Dickenson's husband was one of the soldiers who had decided to stay and fight at the Alamo. Mrs. Dickenson and her small child decided to stay, too. During the 13-day battle, Mrs. Dickenson helped to care for the wounded soldiers. When Santa Anna and his army finally took over the Alamo, he let Mrs. Dickenson and her child leave.

The battle at the Alamo was real. None of the Americans who fought was left alive. But Texans remembered the Alamo and told its story over and over again.

Colonel Travis Draws the Line

From the novel *The Boy in the Alamo* by Margaret Cousins
Illustrated by Bradley Clark

Reading Level   Average

One retelling of the famous battle is seen through the eyes of twelve-year-old Billy Campbell. Billy had followed his older brother Buck to the Alamo. Buck had come to help the small group of Americans and Texans fight the Mexican Army. Here, in Billy's words, is what might have happened at the Alamo when Colonel Travis called for volunteers.

See pages T215–T217 in the front of this book for a suggested teaching plan for this selection.

The next night we were surprised by pistol shots from one of our sentries. This was followed by a great pounding on the main gate, and into the fort trotted thirty-two men on horseback. They were led by Lieutenant George C. Kimball and guided by Lieutenant Smith. They were volunteers from the town of Gonzales, where Dr. Sutherland and Lieutenant Smith had taken the news of the siege. The recruits had inched their way through the Mexican lines around the Alamo without the loss of a man. (But our own sentry, who didn't recognize them as Texan soldiers, had shot one volunteer in the foot!)

Everybody cheered as they trotted in. We roasted the last beef in the plaza and ate supper. One of the

Mexican volunteers got out his guitar and played "La Paloma" and "La Golandrina." Colonel Travis welcomed Lieutenant Kimball and his men. They knew better than we did how much in danger all our lives were. The recruits manned our positions and relieved men who had been there for five days.

The next morning, March 2nd, at eleven o'clock in the morning, our lookout announced the approach of a solitary horseman, with a Mexican cavalry patrol

right behind, peppering him with bullets. The main gate was swung open, and Colonel James Bonham galloped in. As we slammed the gates shut, the Mexicans fell back and disappeared.

As soon as Colonel Bonham got his breath back he made his report to Colonel Travis. He had ridden many weary miles in five days and had made two sneaks through the enemy's lines.

"There will be no help from Goliad," he said. "Fannin has refused."

Colonel Travis shook his head.

"He says he cannot risk the whole Texas Army," Colonel Bonham said.

"The Texas Convention meets today at Washington-on-the-Brazos," Colonel Bonham continued. "If we can hold on—"

"We must hold on," said Colonel Travis. "But it may take weeks!"

"I was warned that it was suicide to come back into the fort," Bonham said.

"That may be true," Travis said. "You should have listened—"

"Ah, Buck," Colonel Bonham said. "How could I leave you in this hole? We will stand or fall together!"

They had gone to school together and had been friends for many years.

Colonel Travis' face was a study. It lighted up with new determination.

"How can we lose with such men as you on our side?" he asked. "Thank you, Jim. That was a good ride."

Colonel Bonham was the last man who came into the Alamo.

On that day, in Washington-on-the-Brazos, the Independence of Texas was declared and a new republic founded. But we had no way of knowing that. We knew only that the Mexican Army was closing in on us.

The next day we had heavy bombardment from all
sides and the lookouts reported that the Mexicans
were setting up their guns nearer and nearer our
walls. Colonel Travis went from one station to the
next encouraging the men. His face was gray.

That night he summoned the whole garrison to
the chapel, except for the sentries. Even me.

"Men of the Alamo," he said, "I have studied
Colonel Bonham's reports, and I have counted our
supplies and ammunition. I have studied our posi-

tions. I feel that I must tell you that I think there is no chance that help will arrive in time to save us. General Santa Anna will launch himself on us within days—maybe hours. When the final assault comes— and it may come at any hour now—it will mean death to all of us here. Our fate is sealed. For myself, I will stay to the end and die fighting."

Colonel Travis paused. He withdrew his sword from its scabbard, and with it he drew a long line on the dirt floor of the chapel. Then he stepped across it.

A *scabbard* (line 9) is a sword case attached to the belt.

"For those who wish to save themselves, there is still time. You may go if you wish. You will not be prevented. But those of you who wish to die fighting for the cause of liberty, step across to my side of this line!"

Quiet fell over the garrison as we stared at Colonel Travis. Then two or three men in the rear jumped over the line, and others began to shuffle across. Colonel Crockett and the Tennessee Volunteers crossed in a body. I crossed with them, hardly understanding what it all meant.

Colonel Bowie had been brought to the meeting on a stretcher. He was as weak as a kitten, and his face was as pale as his shirt, but the fever seemed to have gone down that day. He threshed restlessly around on his cot and then fell back. He lay there a second and then turned his face toward Travis.

"Boys," he said in a whisper, "I can't make it by myself, but I'd be much obliged if some of you would give me a hand."

Buck and I leaped to the foot of his cot, and two more Volunteers grabbed the other end, and we lifted Colonel Bowie over the line.

As soon as this was done there was a rush of feet, and everybody crossed over except one man.

He was a paid soldier, named Louis Rose, nick-named Moses, who fought for a salary. He was a Frenchman who had fought in Napoleon's Army. He was not a Texian.

"I fight to live, not to die," he shouted in broken English and walked out of the chapel. Nobody moved. He ran into the plaza, shinnied up over the wall and dropped down to the other side, where he made his escape. Nobody stopped him. Nobody missed him. The Alamo was not a place to fight for money.

We carried Colonel Bowie back to his room, in the front of the chapel. "The die is cast," he said. "Victory or death."

Buck and I walked back to the earthworks together. "If we don't get a chance to talk any more," Buck said. "I want to tell you this. You are a man—not a boy."

Earthworks is a barrier made of piled-up dirt.

461

"Oh, Buck," I said, and I felt like crying. "I only wanted to be like you."

"You're a better man than I am," Buck said. "For a minute there, I wanted to cut and run."

"Me, too," I said. "But we didn't!"

"No, we didn't," Buck said. "I guess that's the way Papa felt about the Comanche. You can't always be sensible. Some things are more important."

I wanted to tell my brother how much I thought of him, but I didn't know how.

"It was not Sarah Ellen Payne I was in love with," Buck said. "It was Texas."

That night Colonel Travis wrote his last letter. It was addressed to the Convention in Washington-on-the-Brazos. I don't think he had much hope that it would bring help, but he had to try. I made two copies of it for him.

"I look to the colonies alone for aid," he wrote. "Unless it arrives soon, I will have to fight the enemy on his own terms. I will, however, do the best I can . . . and although we may be sacrificed . . . the victory will cost the enemy so dear that it will be worse for him than defeat. I hope your honorable body will hasten reinforcements. . . . Our supply of ammunition is limited. . . . God and Texas. Victory or death."

When the writing was finished, Colonel Travis summoned Lieutenant Smith and gave him the paper.

See pages T216–T217 in the front of this book for suggested postreading strategies.

Under the cover of darkness Lieutenant Smith rode his horse out of the main gate for the last time. He was the last soldier to leave the Alamo alive.

Questions

1. Who was the last Texas soldier to *enter* the Alamo before the battle? Who was the last to *leave*?

2. The day that Colonel Bonham entered the Alamo, an important event in Texas history took place. What was it?

3. If somebody said, "The battle of the Alamo was a great defeat for Texas," would you agree? Why or why not?

4. Replace the underlined words with words from the story that have the same meaning.
   a. The <u>new soldiers</u> had inched their way into the fort. (page 455)
   b. A <u>single</u> horseman was approaching. (page 455)

Activity   Write a Cast of Characters

If you were planning to make the story "Colonel Travis Draws the Line" into a play, you would need to make a list of all the characters. Write a *cast of characters* for the play. Divide the characters into two groups. The *main characters* will play the most important parts. The *supporting characters* will play the less important roles. For each main character, write a short description of what the person looks like, and what he is wearing.

1. Literal/Details
Colonel Bonham; Lieutenant Smith
2. Literal/Details
The Independence of Texas was declared. (page 457)
3. Critical/Evaluation Possible responses; no, because it led to the freedom of Texas from Mexico; yes, because so many people lost their lives.
4. Literal/Definitions a. recruits; b. solitary

CONNECTIONS

See pages T217–T219 in the front of this book for a suggested teaching plan for this selection.

Texas Cowboys

Oh, I am a Texas cowboy, just off the Texas plains,
My trade is cinching saddles and pulling the bridle reins.
It's I can throw the lasso with the greatest of ease
And mount my bronco pony and ride him where I please.
—from "The Texas Cowboy," an old cowboy song

The Cowboys in History

The Texas cowboys have become well-known characters in American life. We know them well, from their tall hats to their high-heeled boots. We know that they love their horses, rope cattle, and ride the range, where they can be free. We know a lot about the Texas cowboys because we have sung songs, read stories, and told tales about them for more than a hundred years.

Yet Texas cowboys are not just characters from stories and songs. They were men who really lived long ago in Texas. The real cowboys were ranch workers. They were men who *drove,* or herded, and cared for longhorn cattle on the Texas plains. From about 1865 until about 1890, the Texas cowboys were an important part of the Old West. They are still a big part of its history.

Illustrated by Jim Pearson

That history begins around 1865. The Civil War had just ended. Texas soldiers were coming home from the war. The soldiers needed jobs, and Texas ranchers were hiring. The ranchers wanted men to help them handle the wild longhorn cattle that roamed throughout Texas. Many soldiers took those ranch-hand jobs. They became the first cowboys.

Cowboy Clothes

"I see by your outfit that you are a cowboy."
These are words from an old cowboy song. The
words happen to be true. Cowboys had to work outdoors in every kind of weather. They worked in dust
storms and snow storms, in rain and blistering heat.
For this outdoor work, cowboys needed certain kinds
of clothes. Their working outfits set the cowboys
apart from all other working men.

Because cowboy work was rough, they wore shirts
and pants made of tough cloth. Over their pants,

they wore leather coverings called *chaps.* The tough leather protected them as they rode through brush and thorns. High-topped boots protected their ankles from thorns and snakes. The high heels on the boots kept their feet in their saddle stirrups.

Every piece of clothing had a special use. The bandanas around the cowboys' necks could be pulled over their mouths when the air was dusty. Their big cowboy hats protected them from both sun and rain. Cowboy hats could also be used as pillows and water pails.

Cowboys used pistols, but mainly for noise. Pistols were useful in a cattle *stampede,* when the cattle became frightened and ran in all directions. A pistol shot could turn aside a charging longhorn and save the cowboy's life.

Cowboys owned very little, but most cowboys owned their own saddle and a rope for catching cattle. Some cowboys also owned a horse, but most horses belonged to the rancher. No cowboy could do his work without a good horse to ride.

The Roundups

The cowboys' work with the cattle was seasonal. The wild longhorn cattle needed little tending during much of the year. Few ranches had fences in those days, so the cattle wandered freely over the Texas range.

Then twice a year, in the spring and fall, the cowboys had to *round up,* or gather, the cattle.

Roundups lasted for several weeks. It was then that the cowboys rode miles and miles every day. They rode over trackless land, looking for cattle.

Each roundup had a different purpose. In the spring, cowboys rounded up cattle in order to brand them. A *brand* was a mark burned into a cow's hide. Each rancher had a different brand. A cow's brand identified its owner.

Most of the cattle branded each spring were calves, born just that year. A calf, or *dogie,* belonged to the same ranch that owned its mother. Sometimes,

cowboys also found *mavericks*—grown cows that no one had ever branded. Mavericks belonged to anyone who could catch and brand them. After the spring branding, all the cattle were released to graze for the summer and get fat.

In the fall, cowboys from each ranch rounded up the cattle again. This time they looked for branded cattle that were ready for market. They rounded up these cattle in order to drive them to the nearest railroad. From there, trains would carry the cattle to meat markets in the northern cities.

The Cattle Drives

Railroad towns were hundreds of miles from Texas ranches. Moving cattle to a railroad, therefore, took two or three months. On these cattle drives, 20 to 30 cowboys had to control thousands of wild cattle in a herd stretching two or three miles long. The cattle raised choking dust clouds, and their hooves rumbled on the prairie like the sound of distant thunder. The cowboys rode along the edges of the herd, keeping it together and moving.

Besides the cowboys, three other men were necessary to the cattle drive. The *trail boss* was the man in

charge of the drive. He gave orders and settled disputes, or disagreements. On the trail, his word was law. The *wrangler* was the person who took care of the extra horses. Fifteen or twenty extra horses were always brought along on a cattle drive. Wranglers were usually young men just learning to be cowboys.

The *cook* drove a wagon that carried food and all other needed supplies. Many times, the cowboys would keep their belongings in the cook's wagon, too.

During these cattle drives, the cowboys spent long, hard days on horseback. Every day they crossed miles of land and saw no other people. They heard little but the cattle's thundering hooves on the plains.

At night, the drive stopped and silence fell. Yet
even quiet times were times to fear, for silence made
the cattle restless. A herd of restless cattle could
stampede, or set off on a wild charge. Any sudden
sound—a rattlesnake rustling, thunder clapping, even
a twig snapping—could start a stampede. A few
cowboys had to stay awake each night and sing to
the cows to keep them calm. The next morning, the
drive would begin again.

The Cowboys in Story

Books and movies can make the cowboy age seem very long, but it only lasted about 30 years. By 1890, railroad tracks ran to many parts of Texas. Ranchers no longer needed to make long cattle drives to railroads hundreds of miles away. Many ranchers had built fences around their land, so they no longer needed to brand their cattle. As the cowboys' jobs disappeared, so did the cowboys.

By then, however, cowboys had caught the imagination of many Americans. People admired cowboys for the hardships they endured, the dangers they faced, and the rootless freedom of their lives. Stories were written and movies were made about cowboy heroes. These heroes were men of few words. They were men who never went looking for trouble but never ran from it. They lived by a code of honor. Real cowboys had passed into history, but the storybook cowboy had just been born.

Well come along, boys, and listen to my tale,
I'll tell you of my troubles on the old Chisholm trail.

Come a ti yi yippy, yippy yay, yippy yay,
Come a ti yi yippy yippy yay.

See pages T218–T219 in the front of this book for suggested postreading strategies.

—from "The Old Chisholm Trail"

Questions

1. Suppose you were a trail boss hiring workers for a cattle drive. What three jobs would you need to fill? What are some questions you might ask the men who applied?

2. How did railroads and fences each help bring the cowboy age to an end?

3. Would you have enjoyed working as a cowboy? Why or why not? Which parts would you have enjoyed the most? the least?

4. In each row of words below, which word does not fit with the others? Explain why it is out of place.
   a. spurs   stampede   chaps   bandana   boots
   b. maverick   saddle   dogie   brand   cattle
   c. plains   range   land   railroad   ranch

Activity   Draw a Map

Draw a map of an imaginary ranch. Show streams, gullies, hills, and other land forms on the ranch. Show what you would build on the land if you were the ranch owner. Mark at least five places on the map where you would look for cattle if you were a cowboy on a roundup. Make a key explaining what your map shows.

The Old Chisholm Trail

An old cowboy song

See pages T220–T221 in the front of this book for a suggested teaching plan for this selection.

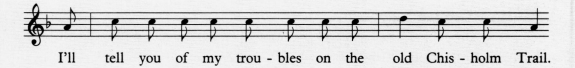

1. Well, come a-long, boys, and lis-ten to my tale;

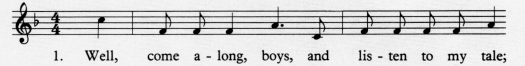

I'll tell you of my trou-bles on the old Chis-holm Trail.

Chorus

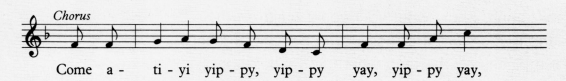

Come a- ti - yi yip-py, yip-py yay, yip-py yay,

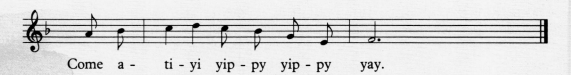

Come a- ti - yi yip-py yip-py yay.

476   Illustrated by Robert Masheris

2. With a ten-dollar horse and a forty-dollar saddle,
   I started in herding these Texas cattle.
   (*Chorus*)

3. I started up the trail October twenty-third;
   I started up the trail with the Lone Star herd.
   (*Chorus*)

4. I jumped in the saddle and grabbed hold of the horn,
   The best <u>cowpuncher</u> that ever was born.
   (*Chorus*)

A cowpuncher refers to an ordinary, working cowboy.

5. My foot in the stirrup, my seat in the saddle,
   The best cowpuncher that ever rode a-straddle.
   (*Chorus*)

6. I'm on my horse, and I'm going on the run,
   The quickest-shooting cowboy that ever pulled a gun.
   (*Chorus*)

From SPINDLETOP

A story by Sibyl Hancock   **Reading Level** Average
Illustrated by Lyle Miller

See pages T221–T224 in the front of this book for a suggested teaching plan for this selection.

In 1901, an event happened that changed Texas history. Oil was discovered on Spindletop hill near the town of Beaumont. Until then, people thought that oil could be found only on the eastern coast of the United States.

Jimmy and his family lived in Beaumont. Jimmy's father worked at Spindletop. This is Jimmy's story of what happened on Spindletop hill on January 10, 1901.

"I'll see you later, Mama," Jimmy said. "Papa and I are going now."

Mama hurried from the kitchen. She wiped flour from her hands onto her apron. She bent to pick baby Robert up off the floor.

"Both of you be careful today," Mama said.

"We will," Papa said. "Who knows? Maybe today we will strike oil."

Jimmy had heard Papa say those same words every day for more than three months. That was how long they had been in the little Texas town of Beaumont.

Today was January 10, 1901. It was Mama's birthday. When the day's work was done, Papa and he would go into town. They would pick up a locket they had ordered for Mama.

"What are you thinking about?" Papa asked. "You're so quiet."

Jimmy climbed into the wagon beside Papa. "I was thinking of Mama's locket," Jimmy said.

Papa nodded and flapped the reins. The horses started off toward a small hill named Spindletop. There wasn't enough money this year to buy Mama a new stove for her kitchen. Papa had taken all their savings and bought land near Spindletop. Papa and four other men were drilling for oil on the Spindletop land owned by Captain A. F. Lucas. Papa felt sure oil would be found there soon.

"Ouch!" Jimmy cried. He swatted a fat mosquito on his neck. "Whoever heard of mosquitoes in January!" Jimmy said.

Papa laughed. "You can find just about anything in Texas," he said.

As the wagon rounded a bend in the road, the top of Spindletop hill came into view. Jimmy could see the tall derrick that stood over the well.

"I wonder what it's like to strike oil?" Jimmy asked.

"Maybe we'll find out," Papa said. Papa stopped the wagon at the top of the hill. "I picked up the new drill bit," Papa called to the men at the derrick. "Good," Curt called back. "We will really need it."

Jimmy liked Curt. He liked the other men, too, but Curt was special. Curt wasn't as tall as Papa, but he was very strong. Curt had a wide grin, and he liked to tease Jimmy.

A drill bit is the part of a drill that fits on the end of the machine and does the actual cutting.

480

Jimmy followed Papa up the steps to the derrick floor. Curt reached over and rumpled Jimmy's hair with his big hand.

"Let's go to work," Papa said.

Jimmy handed Papa tools. The sharp new drill bit was put onto the end of the pipe that had been drilling far into the ground.

"So far we can't break through that last layer of rock," Curt said.

Jimmy stared at the drill pipe. His heart sank. If they couldn't drill through the rock, then they would never find any oil.

Papa started the machinery, and the clattering, grinding noise began.

"The drill is 700 feet down into the ground," Papa said.

Suddenly mud began boiling up past the drill. Then the drill pipe began rising. It went higher and higher and started going through the top of the derrick.

"Run!" Papa yelled.

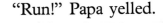

Jimmy scrambled off the derrick floor and ran as hard as he could toward the wagon.

"Look!" Curt shouted.

The drill pipe was still coming out of the well. It began to break into pieces and fall to the ground. The last piece of pipe was followed by rocks and a deafening roar of gas.

"What was that all about?" Curt exclaimed.

"Let's go see," Papa said. "Bring your shovel, Jimmy."

The floor of the derrick was covered with mud. And there was no sign of oil.

"What a mess," Jimmy said.

"Watch out!" Papa shouted.

A great chunk of mud flew out of the well with an explosion like a cannon. A cloud of blue gas followed. Jimmy threw down his shovel and ran. The other men were close behind him.

Once again the noise stopped. Slowly the men walked toward the well. Jimmy climbed back onto the derrick floor. He was a little scared, but he wasn't going to let it show.

Papa stood over the well and looked down the hole. They could hear a bubbling sound deep in the earth. Then foamy oil began to pour out of the hole.

"Oil!" Jimmy cried. "It's oil!"

It was as if the well had a heart beating beneath the ground. The oil pushed upward, then settled back. And it kept pushing up a little higher with each great heartbeat.

All at once the oil spurted through the top of the derrick and kept climbing until it reached twice the height of the derrick.

"Ya-hoo!" Curt shouted.

Everyone slapped each other on the back. Oil! They had struck oil. Jimmy blinked as the black oil soaked his clothes and sprayed into his face. Never in all his life had he seen anything like this.

"How are we going to keep the oil from spraying?" Jimmy asked.

Curt had stopped smiling. He looked worried. "It's going to be hard," he said.

It wasn't long before Captain Lucas came bouncing over the rough road in his wagon.

"It . . . it is oil!" he shouted. Captain Lucas was so excited he could hardly speak. He shook Papa's hand. "Wonderful job," he said.

Papa grinned. Then he sent a man into town to get the parts they would need to try and cap the well to stop the spurting oil.

In an hour's time people from Beaumont began to come to Spindletop. They came in buggies and on horseback and on foot.

Papa had asked extra men from town to hold the crowd back.

"Don't let anyone smoke," Papa told them.

But it wasn't long before Jimmy saw a young man on a horse light a pipe and drop the match to the oily ground. Flames leaped up.

"Fire!" Jimmy yelled. "Fire!"

Papa and Curt and some of the other men came running. They pulled off their coats and pounded the flames. When their coats burned, they used their shirts. Jimmy took off his coat and beat the flames.

The people who had gathered fled back to Beaumont. Oil spray had drifted in the breeze. Sulphur gas was in the air. People had to hold their noses because of the bad smell. Houses painted white were soon streaked with orange and black stains.

At last the men put the fire out. Jimmy had burned his thumb a little, but he was glad he had helped.

"Now you must go home," Papa told him. "Wash up and eat. Then bring us food and some clean clothes. Bring some slicker suits, too."

"But what about capping the well?" Jimmy asked.

Just then a huge rock flew from the well into the air with a great roar of gas.

"We can't cap the well until it stops throwing out rocks," Papa said. "We'll have to wait."

The men took turns staying at the well. Jimmy always took his turn with Papa. They watched as the oil kept shooting 160 feet into the air. Jimmy's face was always covered with oil. Everything smelled and tasted and felt like oil, even when he went home to rest.

One day passed. Then two. Then five. And finally ten days had passed.

Jimmy helped the men throw up dirt walls far around the well. The walls held back the oil that was pouring over the ground. First the oil fell in pools. And the pools turned into lakes of oil.

"Today we'll cap the well," Papa said. "There haven't been any more rocks thrown from the well since yesterday." Papa put on some special glasses to protect his eyes. "I'll cap the well," he said.

"No," Curt said. "I'm the only man who doesn't have a wife and family. I'll cap the well."

Papa thought for a moment. "All right," he said, "but I'll stand close by you."

Curt put on some special glasses like Papa's. Jimmy felt a cold knot of fear inside him. Jimmy knew that Curt was in danger as he began to fit pipes over the well. And Papa was standing so close to the well that he was in danger, too. The well could explode very easily.

Clouds of gas drifted past Curt's face. He stepped back to get fresh air. Then he was over the well again. Jimmy moved closer. He had to help if he could.

Curt worked at fitting pipes together for hours. Papa worked hard, too. He handed lumber and even some railroad track railing to Curt.

What Curt was putting together would one day be called a *christmas tree* by oil workers. That was because of the way it looked with all of its branches of pipes. The christmas tree helped cut down the great force that was blowing the oil high in the sky.

"Ready!" Curt yelled at last.

Papa helped lower a big valve over the pipe. The great hissing roar stopped, and there was silence. The well was capped.

The men who helped look for oil took many risks. They used new methods and equipment that were unknown and untried. Every day, the men at Spindletop worked in danger of losing their lives. But they felt it was worth it. The "black gold" known as oil could turn Texas from a farming state to an important industrial and manufacturing state.

See pages T223–T224 in the front of this book for suggested postreading strategies.

Questions

1. **Literal/Details** Possible responses: spurting oil—they capped the well; fire—keep people from striking matches
2. **Interpretive/Judgment** Possible response: They would have sold their land and moved on, because there would be no work or money for them in Beaumont.
3. **Literal/Details** and **Interpretive/Judgment** Possible responses: you would need a, b, c, and e because they are tools that are necessary once oil is struck. If you do not have them, the oil would just spurt into the air and pool on the ground.

1. The story shows that finding oil can be dangerous. What were two of the dangerous problems that Papa and Curt faced when they struck oil? How did they solve each problem?

2. What might have happened to Jimmy's family if oil had *not* been found? Why do you think so?

3. Which four things would you need to start an oil drilling business? Why would you need them?

   a. drill
   b. derrick
   c. christmas tree
   d. locket
   e. valve
   f. wagon

Activity **Write a Friendly Letter**

Imagine that you are living in Beaumont in 1902. One year ago, oil was discovered at Spindletop. Write a letter to a friend in another city, describing how the oil strike has changed your life. Think of ways in which the discovery of oil might have affected your family. Try to imagine how it might have changed your town. Remember that before oil was discovered Beaumont was a small, quiet city. Your letter should tell how you feel about the changes.

About SIBYL HANCOCK

Sibyl Hancock, a native Texan, began a writing career during her last years in college. At first, she wrote about experiences she had as a child. "I used to write stories about my pets, my family, and even about comic book characters." As she grew older, she would take parts of books she read and rewrite them according to how she wanted the characters to act. All this time, however, she had no idea that she wanted to become an author. Writing just seemed to come naturally for her.

Sibyl Hancock attributes her success to a number of things. "Living in Texas, I am lucky to be able to draw upon a heritage of cowboys riding the range, of booming oil wells, and of the experiences in riding out hurricanes." This, along with all the reading she did growing up, and the influence she had from her parents, gave her a good background for her writing.

More Books by Sibyl Hancock

Mario's Mystery Machine   (G. P. Putnam's, 1972)
Esteban & the Ghost   (Dial Press, 1983)

CONNECTIONS

See pages T225–T226 in the front of this book for a suggested teaching plan for this selection.

Texas Today

Texas is a big state with many faces. In some ways it is leading the nation into the future. At the same time, the past is very much alive in Texas today.

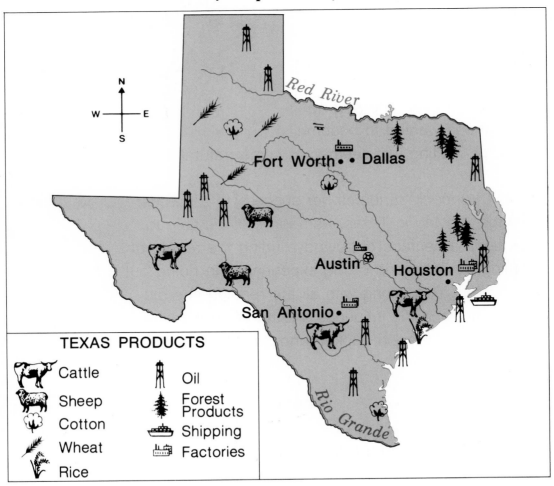

TEXAS PRODUCTS

- Cattle
- Sheep
- Cotton
- Wheat
- Rice
- Oil
- Forest Products
- Shipping
- Factories

Ranching

Texas raises more cattle than any other state—about 15 million head of cattle a year. Cowboys, therefore, are not just part of Texas history. Many Texans still work as cowboys.

Today, however, cowboys not only ride horses. They also drive around the range in pickup trucks. Sometimes they use helicopters to find their cattle. The cattle they find are no longer half-wild longhorns, but short-horned breeds such as Herefords.

Many Texas ranches have no cattle at all. They are sheep and goat ranches. These animals are now just as important to Texas as cattle. Texas produces the most wool of any state in the United States.

Farming

Texas is also a leading farm state. It has more than 185,000 farms, more farmed space than any other state. The first settlers from the United States started cotton farms in Texas. Cotton is still a leading crop. It is grown in many parts of the state. Rice is grown in the southern lowlands. Wheat is grown on the central and western plains.

To water all these farms Texans have built dams across rivers. They have made or enlarged more than 1,000 lakes in their state. The Dennison Dam across the Red River, for example, has made Lake Texoma. This lake stretches across 225 square miles of Texas and into Oklahoma.

Industry

Texas today has about one-third of all the known oil in the country. Texans pump more than a billion barrels of oil out of the ground every year.

Finding oil and gas has brought huge changes to Texas. Factories have been built to *refine,* or purify, the oil. Cities have grown up around the factories. The growth of cities has led to the building of more factories.

Today, Texas factories refine oil. Many factories also produce chemicals. Texas factory workers can food, pack meat, and build airplanes, spacecraft, and computers.

1. San Antonio
2. Austin
3. Dallas
4. Houston
5. Fort Worth

Important Cities

Only 50 years ago, most Texans lived in the country. Eight out of every ten Texans now live in a city or town.

Houston is the biggest city in Texas and one of the largest cities in the United States. More than 2,000,000 people live there. People in Houston work at many different kinds of jobs. Some work in oil refineries. Some work in chemical plants. Some work in Houston's busy port. There, oil and other products are loaded onto ships.

Another important business in Houston is medicine. About 26,000 people work in the Texas Medical Center. Each year, more than 1,500,000 people come there to be helped. Scientists at the Texas Medical Center are looking for a way to cure cancer.

Dallas is the second largest city in Texas. Most of the people in Dallas work in offices instead of factories. Many work for banks and insurance companies. Dallas has several important industries, too. One of these industries is the manufacturing of computers.

The city of **Fort Worth** started as a cattle town. Today, its stock yards and meat packing plants still provide many jobs in Fort Worth. Many people also work for oil refineries and for the aircraft industry, which builds most of America's helicopters. Fort Worth is also known for its fine museums.

Dallas and Fort Worth lie within 25 miles of each other. The two cities have spread out until their edges have almost met. They are like one big city with two downtowns.

San Antonio is the oldest city in Texas. Because it was started by settlers from Spain, it still has a Spanish flavor. Many people there speak Spanish. Many of the streets have Spanish names. The Alamo, carefully rebuilt, stands in downtown San Antonio.

Austin is the state capital. The Colorado River runs through the city. The river banks are lined with parks. These parks are the work of Lady Bird Johnson, the wife of Lyndon B. Johnson, who was the 36th president of the United States.

Future of Texas

Texas is a busy, growing state. People are streaming to its cities from all parts of the United States. New jobs are opening up every day. In the last hundred years, Texas has gone through great changes. If Texas continues to grow as it is doing, the next hundred years may be a time of even greater growth.

See pages T225–T226 in the front of this book for suggested postreading strategies.

Questions

1. Complete this sentence: Texas produces more _____, _____, and _____ than any other state.

2. How has oil changed the cities in Texas?

3. What is one important fact about each city?

   Houston   Dallas   San Antonio

   Fort Worth   Austin

4. Why are the following statements untrue? Give a reason for each one.
   a. Texas factories produce more Herefords than any other state.
   b. Many workers in Houston refine cotton.
   c. Texas farmers use machines to harvest chemical plants.

Activity   Write Questions for an Interview

Prepare a list of questions to ask someone who has lived in your area for at least ten years. Your questions should include how particular things have changed in the last ten years: new buildings, number of people, work.

When you interview the person, be sure that you take notes on the answers. Then write two paragraphs about your conversation. In the first, describe the person you interviewed. In the second, give a summary of what the person said about changes in your area.

BOOKSHELF

Reading Level Easy

Pecos Bill Catches a Hidebehind by Watts Blassingame. Garrard, 1977. Two tall-tale heroes from Texas, Pecos Bill and Sluefoot Sue, donate another present to the zoo when they realize the hidebehind they have lassoed is very shy.

Reading Level Challenging

Old Yeller by Fred Gipson. Harper & Row, 1956. Fourteen-year-old Travis is left in charge of his family's Texas home back in the 1860s, and he has lots of trouble at first with a big yellow dog.

Reading Level Challenging

How Did We Find Out About Oil? by Isaac Asimov. Walker, 1980. This book describes how oil is formed underground, what it is made of, and how we explore it, bring it up, and prepare it for our many uses.

Reading Level Challenging

Red Power on the Rio Grande by Franklin Folsom. Follett, 1973. This book discusses the American Indian Revolution of 1680 when the Indians fought for their freedom from Mexico.

Reading Level Average

The Black Mustanger by Richard Wormser. William Morrow, 1971. The Riker family has been hit with hard times and moves to Texas. When Mr. Riker breaks his leg, his son Dan must provide for his family. Dan goes to work for Will Mesteño, an expert at finding and rounding up wild mustangs.

LITERARY TERMS

CHARACTERS   *The people (or animals) in a story, poem, or play.* Sometimes authors are concerned mainly with bringing their story characters to life. How the characters think, feel, act, and change are more important than the story's main action, or *plot.* For example, in "Spunky Ramona," author Beverly Cleary gives us much information about Ramona Quimby. We learn what Ramona thinks and feels and how she acts. The story is *about Ramona,* not just about the events in Ramona's life. Other stories, such as "The Case of the Missing Roller Skates," are built mainly around the plot.

CHARACTERIZATION   *The ways in which writers present and develop characters to make the characters seem real.* Here are several ways in which writers develop their characters:

1. *By describing how the character looks* ("Her delicate face glowed like a peach beginning to ripen in the summer sun. And her dark eyes sparkled in the dancing firelight.").

2. *By showing the character's words and actions* ("Pa did not whistle about his work as usual, and after a while he said, 'And what we'll do in a wild country without a good watchdog I don't know.'").

3. *By telling the character's thoughts and feelings* ("I do not want anyone to sit with me, but he is sitting with me now. I am afraid I will spill and he will see me.").

4. *By telling what others think of the character* ("Mama was a wonderful cook.").

5. *By stating something about the character* ("After all, Wilbur was a very young pig—not much more than a baby, really.").

DIALOGUE   *Conversation between or among characters.* Dialogue is used in almost all forms of literature to move the *plot,* or main action, forward and to tell the reader something about the characters. In the story "The Case of the Missing Roller Skates," author Donald J. Sobol uses dialogue to show how Encyclopedia Brown solved the case:

"We just want to be sure you weren't in Dr. Vivian Wilson's

office this morning. That's all," said Sally.

"Well, I wasn't. I had a sprained wrist, not a toothache. So why should I go near his office?" demanded Billy.

These few lines of dialogue give the reader enough information to guess the solution of the case.

Dialogue is especially important in plays, where conversation is the main way to tell the story and to show each character's personality. In the play *Paddington Goes to the Hospital,* Paddington and a doctor named Sir Archibald discuss Mr. Curry, a patient at the hospital:

> Sir Archibald: Are you a friend of his?
> Paddington: Well, I'm not really a friend. He lives next door and I've brought him some food.
> Sir Archibald: Food! That's the last thing he needs. It will only make him stay longer. That man's entirely without scruples.

Through this conversation, the reader learns that Sir Archibald is upset because he feels that Mr. Curry is taking advantage of the hospital.

See also **Play.**

FABLE *A brief story that teaches a lesson.* Many fables state the lesson, or *moral,* at the end of the story. The characters in fables are often animals that speak and act like people. The best-known fables were written long ago in Greece by a man named Aesop. "The Lion and the Mouse" is one of Aesop's fables.

FANTASY *A fiction story with fanciful characters and plots.* A fantasy may take place in a world much like the one you know. Yet in the "real world" presented in a fantasy story, ordinary people and animals do impossible things. In the fantasy story *Charlotte's Web,* for example, an ordinary farm contains a pig that can talk and a spider that can write.

Often, however, fantasies take place in imaginary kingdoms or worlds that are quite different from the real world. Author C. S. Lewis has created the fantasy Kingdom of

Narnia in his series of seven books called *The Chronicles of Narnia.* It is a world filled with unusual creatures and magical events.

The different kinds of fantasy offer us the chance to wonder *"What if. . . ?" What if* you could be three inches tall, or ride a magic carpet, or travel through time?

See also **Fiction.**

FICTION *A story invented by the writer.* A work of fiction may be *based* on real events, but it always includes made-up (fictional) characters and experiences. A work of fiction may be brief, like a fable, a folk tale, or a short story, or it may be a book-length story called a **novel.**

FOLK TALE *A fiction story made up long ago and handed down in written or spoken form.* Many folk tales have no known authors. Though folk tales come from different parts of the world, many characters, plots, and ideas in them are similar. *Fairy tales* like the story "Cinderella" are a kind of folk tale.

LIMERICK *A humorous five-line poem written in three long and two short lines and containing a certain pattern of rhythm and rhyme.* In a limerick, lines 1, 2, and 5 always have the same rhythm and ending rhyme. Lines 3 and 4 have the same rhythm and ending rhyme, too. The poet Edward Lear has written many well-known limericks, including "There Was an Old Man with a Beard" on page 300.

METAPHOR *A way of comparing how two different things are alike.* A metaphor *suggests* a comparison by saying that one thing *is* another: "This car **is** a lemon" or "The sun **was** a bright, new penny." Writers use metaphors to help us picture things in new ways.

See also **Simile.**

NONFICTION *A true (factual) story; any writing that describes things as they actually happened, or that presents information or opinions about something.* One type of nonfiction is the written history of a person's life. When a person writes his or her own life story, it is called an **autobiography.** When someone else writes a person's life story, it is called a **biography.** Other common forms of nonfiction include news reports, travel stories, personal journals and diaries, and articles on science or history.

PLAY   *A story that is acted out, usually on a stage, by actors.* In its written form, a play begins with a **cast of characters,** or a list of the people, or sometimes animals, in the play. A play has a *plot,* or action, just like a story. However, a play is meant to be acted out. The characters in a play tell the story through their words, or **dialogue.**

During a play the actors follow **stage directions**, which tell them *how* to act and speak. Stage directions may also describe the **setting,** where the action takes place. Stage directions are usually not read aloud when a play is acted out.

See also **Dialogue.**

PLOT   *The action in a story.* When you tell *what happens* in a story, you are talking about the plot. For instance, in the story "The Escape," by E. B. White, the plot tells how Wilbur, a young pig, escapes from his pen to see the world but is lured back with a bucket of slops.

The plot is also the writer's overall *plan* of the action—how, when, and why things happen. The writer uses this plan to arrange the action in an interesting and reasonable order. Each happening becomes a link in a chain of events that makes sense and holds the reader's attention.

The most important part of plot is **conflict,** a character's struggle with opposing forces. Sometimes a character struggles with nature (as in Laura Ingalls Wilder's story "Crossing the Creek"). Sometimes a character struggles with another character (as in Eleanor Estes's "The Ghost in the Attic"). At other times the conflict is within the character's own mind. In the story "The Escape" by E. B. White, for example, Wilbur the pig struggles to decide whether he should give up his freedom in return for food.

SETTING   *When and where a story takes place.* If you say, "Today at school Susan won a race," you have given the setting (when and where) before describing the action. Authors can choose any time or place as a setting for a story. In the story "Crossing the Creek," author Laura Ingalls Wilder gives us a clear picture of how the prairie looked to the Ingalls family at sunset:

No road, not even the faintest trace of wheels or of a rider's passing, could be seen anywhere. That prairie looked as if no human eye had ever seen it before. Only the tall wild grass covered the endless empty land and a great empty sky arched over it. Far away the sun's edge touched the rim of the earth.

The writer does not always give us the setting so directly. Sometimes we figure it out as the story goes along. Most stories include several different types of information about where and when the story takes place. For instance, at the beginning of the story "An Eskimo Birthday," by Tom D. Robinson, the action begins in a schoolroom during a snowstorm. As the story continues, we find out that the school is part of a modern Eskimo village in Alaska.

SIMILE *A way of comparing how two different things are alike.* Writers use similes to surprise us or to make us look at our world in a new way. Similes are different from metaphors because they use the words *like* or *as*. In the story "Sound of Sunshine, Sound of Rain," author Florence Parry Heide describes two voices using similes to compare them: "My mother's voice is **as** warm and soft **as** a pillow. My sister's voice is little and sharp and high, **like** needles flying in the air."

See also **Metaphor**.

GLOSSARY

This glossary gives the meanings of unfamiliar words used in the text of this book. The meanings given here define words only the way they are used in the book. You can find other meanings for these words in a dictionary.

The correct pronunciation of each glossary word is given in the special spelling after that word. The sounds used in these spellings are explained in the following Pronunciation Key. Each symbol, or letter, stands for a sound, a sound you can recognize in the words following it. In addition to these sounds, each glossary pronunciation includes marks to show the kind of force, or stress, with which certain syllables are pronounced. A heavy mark, ′, shows that the syllable it follows is given the strongest, or primary, stress, as in **sis•ter** (sis′•ter). A lighter mark, ′, shows that the syllable it follows is given a secondary, or lighter, stress, as in **tax•i•cab** (tak′•sē•kab′).

Several abbreviations are used in the glossary: *v.,* verb; *n.,* noun; *adj.,* adjective; *pl.,* plural.

Pronunciation Key

a	add, map	m	move, seem	u	up, done
ā	ace, rate	n	nice, tin	û(r)	urn, term
â(r)	care, air	ng	ring, song	yōō	use, few
ä	palm, father	o	odd, hot	v	vain, eve
b	bat, rub	ō	open, so	w	win, away
ch	check, catch	ô	order, jaw	y	yet, yearn
d	dog, rod	oi	oil, boy	z	zest, muse
e	end, pet	ou	out, now	zh	vision, pleasure
ē	even, tree	ōō	pool, food	ə	the schwa,
f	fit, half	ŏŏ	took, full		an unstressed
g	go, log	p	pit, stop		vowel representing
h	hope, hate	r	run, poor		the sound spelled
i	it, give	s	see, pass		a in above
ī	ice, write	sh	sure, rush		e in sicken
j	joy, ledge	t	talk, sit		i in possible
k	cool, take	th	thin, both		o in melon
l	look, rule	th	this, bathe		u in circus

504

ac·cu·mu·lat·ing (ə·kyōō′·myōō·lāt′·ing) *adj.* Piling up; collecting.

al·fal·fa (al·fal′·fə) *n.* A cloverlike plant used for cattle feed.

am·mu·ni·tion (am′·yə·nish′·ən) *n.* Bullets, gunpowder, cannonballs.

ap·pe·tiz·ing (ap′·ə·tī′·zing) *adj.* Appealing in appearance or smell.

arc (ärk) *n.* Something that forms an arch or a curve.

ar·ro·gance (ar′·ə·gəns) *n.* Too proud; too convinced of one's own importance.

as·sault (ə·sôlt′) *n.* A violent attack.

a·strad·dle (ə·strad′·əl) *adv.* With one leg on each side.

awe·some (ô′·səm) *adj.* Inspiring feelings of wonder and fear.

bab·ble (bab′·əl) *v.* To make meaningless sounds.

ba·leen (bə·lēn′) *n.* The easily bent material that hangs from the upper jaw of whalebone whales and that strains the tiny sea animals on which they feed.

barge (bärj) *n.* A flat-bottomed boat used for carrying cargo.

bar·ren (bar′·ən) *adj.* Without growth; empty; lacking crops or trees or other plants.

bed·lam (bed′·ləm) *n.* A place or condition of noise or confusion.

bes·ti·ar·y (bes′·chē·er′·ē) *n.* A book of fables about the habits of actual and mythical animals.

blanch (blanch) *v.* To turn pale.

blub·ber (blub′·ər) *v.* To weep loudly.

blunt (blənt) *adj.* Having a tip or point that is not sharp.

blus·ter·ing (bləs′·tər·ing) *adj.* Speaking in a noisy, boastful, or bullying manner.

bolt (bōlt) *n.* A roll of cloth.

bom·bard·ment (bom·bärd′·mənt) *n.* An attack with guns and cannonballs.

brin·dled (brin′·dəld) *adj.* Having dark-colored streaks on a light gray or brownish background.

ca·nal (kə·nal′) *n.* A waterway dug across land, and connecting already existing bodies of water.

cap·tiv·i·ty (kap·tiv′·ə·tē) *n.* The state of being held prisoner.

ca·reen·ing (kə·rēn′·ing) *adj.* Lurching; moving rapidly in an uncontrolled way.

ca·reer (kə·rir′) *n.* Work one chooses and trains for.

car·i·bou (kar′·ə·bōō) *n.* A large North American deer closely related to reindeer.

cat·tle (kat′·əl) *n.* A word for cows.

cham·ber (chām′·bər) *n.* A cave or an enclosed space.

col·lapse (kə·laps′) *v.* To cave or fall in completely.

col·league (kol′·ēg) *n.* A member of the same profession.

Co·man·che (kə·man′·chē) *n.* A group of American Indians living in Wyoming and Nebraska south into New Mexico and northwestern Texas.

com·mo·tion (kə·mō′·shən) *n.* Noisy confusion or disturbance.

con·sci·en·tious (kon′·shē·en′·shəs) *adj.* Being careful to do things correctly and to be good.

con·tra·dict (kon′·trə·dikt′) *v.* To deny (a statement).

con·ven·tion (kən·ven′·chən) *n.* A group of people meeting for a single purpose, such as to organize a government and to select candidates for office.

cor·ri·dor (kôr′·ə·dər) *n.* A hallway.

cow·punch·er (kow′·pən′·chər) *n.* Cowboy.

crock·ery (krok′·rē) *n.* Pottery made of clay.

cun·ning (kun′·ing) *n.* Slyness or cleverness in getting something.

cur·sive (kûr′·siv) *n.* Handwriting in which the strokes of the letters are joined in each word.

daze (dāz) *v.* To confuse.

de·fi·ant (di·fī′·ənt) *adj.* Boldly refusing to obey.

de·mol·ished (di·mol′·isht) *adj.* Torn down completely; ruined.

der·rick (der′·ik) *n.* A tower built over the opening of an oil well, used to support drilling equipment and to lift and lower pipe.

di·ag·no·sis (dī′·əg·nō′·sis) *n.* A conclusion reached as to the nature of an illness or disease.

dig (dig) *n.* An archeological excavation or its site.

dis·in·te·grate (dis·in′·tə·grāt′) *v.* To break down into small parts.

dis·loy·al (dis·loi′·əl) *adj.* Breaking faith; not supporting another.

dis·solve (di·zolv′) *v.* To disappear.

dron·ing (drōn′·ing) *adj.* Making a continuous humming or buzzing sound with little variation.

drought (drout) *n.* A long period of time without rain.

ei·der·down (ī′·dər·doun′) *n.* Fine, soft duck feathers that are often used to fill comforters or quilts.

e·merge (i·mərg′) *v.* To come up into view.

em·ploy·ee (im·ploi′·ē) *n.* A person hired by another.

ex·treme·ly (ik·strēm′·lē) *adv.* Very.

fam·ine (fam′·ən) *n.* A great shortage of food.

fan·ta·sy (fan′·tə·sē) *n.* A fiction story with fanciful characters and plots.

fash·ion (fash′·ən) *v.* To carve, mold, or give shape to.

fast (fast) *adj.* Tightly.

fear·some (fir′·səm) *adj.* Scary.

feath·er bed (feth′·ər bed) *n.* A comforter stuffed with feathers.

fine (fīn) *adj.* Clear; sunny; used in speaking about the weather.

flint (flint) *n.* A stone that is shaped into sharp tools and arrowheads.

flush (fləsh) *v.* To drive or frighten (game birds) from cover.

folk·lore (fōk'·lôr') *n.* The stories, traditions, and superstitions of a group of people.

folk·lor·ist (fōk'·lôr'·əst) *n.* A person who studies the traditional beliefs, stories, and customs of a people or culture.

ford (fôrd) *n.* A shallow place in a stream or a river that can be crossed on foot, on horseback, or in a vehicle.

frank·in·cense (frangk'·in·sens) *n.* A gum or resin from various Arabian and African trees, and often burned as incense for its sweet, spicy smell.

fren·zy (fren'·zē) *n.* A fit of wild or violent excitement or activity.

gap·ing (gāp'·ing) *adj.* Wide open.

gar·ri·son (gar'·ə·sən) *n.* Troops stationed at a military post or fort.

gasp (gasp) *v.* To draw in one's breath quickly in surprise.

ge·fil·te fish (gə·fil'·tə fish) *n.* Oval fish cakes or balls made from a white fish such as carp.

ge·ni·i (jē'·nē·ī') *n. pl.* In Arabian stories, supernatural beings with magical powers who can take human or animal form.

glow·er (glou'·ər) *v.* To glare; to look or stare at angrily.

gnaw (nô) *v.* To chew.

grope (grōp) *v.* To feel about in the dark in search; to look for something in the dark.

hearth (härth) *n.* The fireside.

hud·dle (həd'·əl) *v.* To crouch; to bend close to the ground.

hys·ter·ics (his·ter'·iks) *n., pl.* Sudden uncontrolled laughter.

im·mi·grant (im'·i·grənt) *n.* A person who leaves a native country to live in another country.

im·pact (im'·pakt) *n.* A striking of one body against another.

in·tact (in·takt') *adj.* Untouched; with no part missing.

in·vest (in·vest') *v.* To spend money in order to earn more.

jeer·ing (jir'·ing) *adj.* Insulting; teasing in a mean way.

keg (keg) *n.* A small barrel.

ki·mo·no (kə·mō'·nə) *n.* A loose robe with short, wide sleeves and a sash, traditional to Japan.

lead (lēd) *n.* A clue.

lieu·ten·ant (lōō·ten'·ənt) *n.* An officer in the army ranked below a colonel.

lit (lit) *v., past of light.* Came down from the air and settled.

lug (ləg) *v.* To drag or move heavily.

lurch (lûrch) *v.* To sway or tip to one side suddenly.

lure (lōōr) *v.* To tempt or entice, especially into danger.

lus·ter (lus'·tər) *n.* Brightness.

lynx (lingks) *n.* A wildcat with long legs and a short tail, common in northern North America; also called a *bobcat.*

maid·en (mād'·ən) *n.* A young unmarried woman.

mal·let (mal′·ət) *n.* A hammer with a large head.

ma·nure (mə·no͝or′) *n.* Waste material from barns and barnyards used to improve the soil.

mes·quite (məs·kēt′) *n.* A spiny shrub in the southwestern U.S. and Mexico that has long roots to reach underground water.

mid·dlings (mid′·lings) *n.* A mixture of coarsely ground wheat and bran used for animal feed.

mi·rac·u·lous (mə·rak′·yə·ləs) *adj.* Marvelous; similar to a miracle.

mis·er·a·ble (miz′·ər·ə·bəl) *adj.* Very unhappy.

mourn·er (môr′·nər) *n.* A person who expresses sorrow for someone who is dead.

mourn·ing (môr′·ning) *adj.* Making a low, continuous sound that seems to express sorrow or grief.

muk·luk (mək′·lək′) *n.* A soft Eskimo boot made of sealskin or reindeer skin.

mus·tang (məs′·tang′) *n.* A small wild horse that is commonly found on the southwestern plains.

myrrh (mûr) *n.* A fragrant gum resin used in incense and perfume.

nav·i·gate (nav′·ə·gāt′) *v.* To steer or guide a boat or ship.

nudge (nəj) *v.* To get someone's attention by a push of the elbow.

om·i·nous (om′·ə·nəs) *adj.* Threatening; being an evil omen.

out·crop·ping (out′·krop′·ing) *n.* The coming out, at or above the ground, of a mineral.

out·skirts (out′·skûrtz′) *n., pl.* The edges of a city.

pan·try (pan′·trē) *n.* A small room off the kitchen where food or kitchen supplies are stored.

par·ka (pär′·kə) *n.* A fur or cloth jacket or coat with a hood.

Pass·over (pas′·ō·vər) *n.* A Jewish holiday celebrating the ancient Hebrews' freedom from slavery in Egypt.

pea·sant (pez′·ənt) *n.* A poor farmer.

pe·cu·liar (pi·kyo͞ol′·yər) *adj.* Strange; odd.

peer (pir) *n.* A person of one's own age group.

per·sist (pər·sist′) *v.* To go on stubbornly even though opposed.

pit·i·ful (pit′·i·fəl) *adj.* Worthy of pity or sympathy.

plume (plo͞om) *n.* A large showy feather.

pot (pot) *n.* Jar.

prai·rie (prâr′·ē) *n.* A large area of level or rolling grassy land, mostly the plains of the central U.S.

pro·ces·sion (prə·sesh′·ən) *n.* A long line of people moving in a slow, orderly manner.

punc·tu·al (pənk′·cho͞o·wəl) *adj.* Being on time; prompt.

range (rānj) *n.* Open land where cattle can roam.

rash (rash) *adj.* Acting without thought.

ra·vine (rə·vēn') *n.* A long, deep hollow in the earth usually formed by the action of a stream.

re·ac·tion (rē·ak'·shən) *n.* The act of answering quickly with little thought.

re·cess (rē'·ses) *n.* A hidden or secret place.

re·cruit (re·krōōt') *n.* A newly drafted member of an armed force.

re·fined (re·fīnd') *adj.* Free from anything coarse.

re·in·force·ment (rē'·in·fôrs'·mənt) *n.* A new member sent to help troops already in action.

re·lapse (rē'·laps) *n.* A falling back into an illness after improving.

re·luc·tant·ly (ri·lək'·tənt·lē) *adv.* Unwillingly; holding back.

re·proach (ri·prōch') *n.* Blame.

re·sem·ble (ri·zem'·bəl) *v.* To look like or be similar to.

res·o·lu·tion (rez'·ə·lōō'·shən) *n.* A promise to oneself.

roam (rōm) *v.* To wander.

rough·neck (ruf'·nek') *n.* A rough, rude, or disorderly person.

ruff (ruf) *n.* A high, full collar, in this case, made of fur.

run·ning gear (rən'·ing gir) *n.* The working parts of a wagon that help the wagon move.

runt (rənt) *n.* The smallest pig in a litter.

sac·ri·fice (sak'·rə·fīs) *v.* To make an offering of something precious.

sal·a·ry (sal'·ə·rē) *n.* Money paid for services.

salt·y (sôl'·tē) *adj.* Having to do with the sea.

scorn (skôrn) *n.* A feeling of disgust.

scrunch (skrənch) *v.* To squeeze together into a small bundle.

scru·ple (skrōō'·pəl) *n.* A misgiving or objection about something that one thinks is wrong.

scut·tle (skut'·əl) *v.* To run or move quickly, especially from danger.

Se·der (sā'·dər) *n.* The meal served on the first two nights of Passover, a Jewish holiday.

sen·try (sen'·trē) *n.* A soldier standing guard at a gate.

sha·man (shäm'·ən) *n.* A person believed to have special powers who performs sacred ceremonies for a people.

shor·ing (shōr'·ing) *n.* A group or system of supporting boards used to uphold something.

shriv·el up (shriv'·əl up) *v.* To wrinkle and dry up.

shut·tle (shut'·əl) *n.* A device used in weaving to carry a thread from side to side between the threads that run lengthwise.

sieve (siv) *n.* A utensil made of wire mesh or metal with many small holes, used for straining.

slops (slops) *n., pl.* Leftover food fed to animals.

snare (snâr) *n.* A kind of trap for small animals.

snow ma·chine (snō mə·shēn′) *n.* A machine that travels over snow; also called a *snowmobile.*

sod (sod) *n.* Ground covered with grass.

sol·i·tude (sol′·ə·tōōd′) *n.* The condition of being alone.

sooth·ing (sōōth′·ing) *adj.* Calming.

sou·ve·nir (sōō′·və·nir′) *n.* Something that is kept as a reminder of a place, a person, or an occasion.

spec·ta·cles (spek′·tə·kəlz) *n., pl.* A pair of eyeglasses.

spunk (spungk) *n. informal* Courage; spirit.

stoop (stōōp) *n.* A small porch, platform, or set of steps at the entrance of a house or building.

sub·side (səb·sīd′) *v.* To become less or quiet.

suf·fo·cat·ing (səf′·ə·kāt′·ing) *adj.* Making uncomfortable by not allowing one to breathe.

su·i·cide (sōō′·ə·sīd′) *n.* The act of losing one's life by one's own choice.

sur·geon (sûr′·jən) *n.* A doctor who can operate on people.

sus·pect (səs′·pekt) *n.* A person who is thought to be guilty of a wrongdoing.

taw·ny (tô′·nē) *n.* Brownish orange.

thatched (thacht) *adj.* Covered with straw, especially on the roof of a house.

thrash (thrash) *v.* To swing, roll, or move around wildly and rapidly.

thrum (thrum) *n.* The ends of thread left on a loom after the cloth has been cut off. *v.* To pluck on, as a guitar; to strum.

ti·pi, also **tepee** (tē′·pē) *n.* An American Indian tent made from animal skins and shaped like an upside-down cone.

toi·let wa·ter (toi′·lət wô′·tər) *n.* A light-scented liquid, like perfume.

tri·col·or (trī′·kəl′·ər) *adj.* Having three colors.

troll (trōl) *n.* In folk tales, a troublesome creature, either dwarf or giant, who lives in caves, in hills, or under bridges.

trudge (truj) *v.* To walk wearily or with great effort.

valve (valv) *n.* A mechanical device that opens and shuts to start or stop the flow of a liquid or gas.

vault·like (vôlt′·līk′) *adj.* Built with arches or curves.

vol·un·teer (vol′·ən·tir′) *n.* A person who freely chooses to join the armed forces.

weft (weft) *n.* In weaving, the threads carried by the shuttle from side to side across the fixed threads in a loom.

whisk (hwisk) *v.* To move quickly and lightly.

wol·ver·ine (wōōl′·və·rēn′) *n.* A meat-eating animal of the weasel family.

Words and Word Parts: PREFIXES

A **prefix** is a word part added to the beginning of a word. The word to which the prefix is added is the **root word**. The meaning of a root word is changed when a prefix is added. Knowing the meaning of a prefix can often help you define a word.

prefix + root = new word
un + kind = **un**kind (meaning ''not kind'')

The prefixes below are often added to words. Look at the meaning of each prefix. Notice how it changes the meaning of each root word.

un-

un often means ''not	**un** also means ''to do the opposite of''
un + able = **un**able	**un** + buckle = **un**buckle
unable means ''not able	**un**buckle means ''to undo the buckle''

Words from the Selection

unhappy p. 29	unlikely p. 18	unfastened p. 97
unload p. 64	unexpected p. 280	unharnessed p. 152
unpack p. 65	unlatched p. 90	unearthed p. 333

Which word above means ''not likely to happen''? *unlikely*
What is the meaning of unearthed? *to dig up from the earth*

re-

re often means ''back''	**re** also means ''again''
re + gain = **re**gain	**re** + do = **re**do
regain means ''to gain back''	**re**do means ''to do again''

Words from the Selection

repay p. 198	reactions p. 310	reconsider p. 228
returned p. 22	relapse p. 304	

Which word above means ''to get sick again''? *relapse*

Words and Word Parts: SUFFIXES

A **suffix** is a word part added to the end of a **root word**. The meaning of a root word is changed when the suffix is added. Knowing the meaning of a suffix can often help you define the meaning of a word.

root + **suffix** = new word
breath + **less** = breathless (meaning "out of breath")

The suffixes below are often added to words. Look at the meaning of each suffix. Notice how it changes the meaning of each root word.

-ly	**-able, -ible**
-**ly** means "in the manner of" polite + **ly** = politely politely means "in a polite manner"	-**able** and -**ible** mean "can be done" or "inclined to" adapt + **able** = adapt**able** adapt**able** means "can adapt"

Words from the Selections

completely p. 52	dependable p. 281	comfortable p. 310
cautiously p. 99	urgently p. 308	suitable p. 323

-ness	**-ment**
-**ness** means "state" or "condition of" dark + **ness** = dark**ness** dark**ness** means "the condition of being dark"	-**ment** means "action" move + **ment** = move**ment** move**ment** means "the act of moving"

Words from the Selections

excitement p. 84	advertisement p. 23	lightness p. 404
payment p. 117	roughness p. 232	quickness p. 404

-ion, -tion, -sion, -ition, -ation

-**ion**, -**tion**, -**sion**, -**ition**, -**ation** all mean "process, act of, or state of"
celebration + **ion** = celebrat**ion**   Celebrat**ion** means "the act of celebrating"

Words from the Selections

multiplication p. 33	direction p. 54	confusion p. 320
suggestion p. 37	attention p. 66	permission p. 379

The final **e** of a root word is dropped when adding a suffix that begins with a vowel. For example, **love** + **able** = lovable.

Define each word below using the prefixes and suffixes to help you.

unfriendly   rearrangement   movable   unpleasantness   reaction

unfriendly—not friendly; rearrangement—the act of arranging again; movable—can be moved; unpleasantness—the condition of being not pleasant; reaction—an action in response to something